THE CURMUDGEON'S GUIDE

The Curmudgeon's Guide

Hope for Heathens, Laodiceans, and other Losers

Christopher J. Wilkins

Xulon Elite

Xulon Press
555 Winderley Pl, Suite 225
Maitland, FL 32751
407.339.4217
www.xulonpress.com

Paperback ISBN-13: 978-1-66285-967-0
Ebook ISBN-13: 978-1-66285-968-7

PREFACE

"Devotional drivel! No thanks." If that's how you feel, DON'T DARE read another page. If the Last Days' Museum, a Black Plague victim, getting busted in New Jersey, the Valley of Seahorses, or traveling the Trans-Siberian Railroad are beyond your pale of interest, go ahead, put it down. If you've got a smidge of curiosity, pay up, sit down, close your mouth, and take a look.

Let me tell you the *Whys* for another devotional. It's not about you, so don't get your hopes up. My sons are the culprits. I'm a storyteller, and on occasion they've piped up, "Hey, you never told us that one." Wouldn't you say that's an invitation? These aren't rare but are usually of the order: "Please don't sing," "Whatever you do, don't embarrass me," and "So, you're gonna buy that game for me, right?" This one seemed positive, hence these happenstances, exploits, and faux pas are recorded for posterity. Ironically, now they're completed, the boys are too involved in their own adventures to care about mine.

A secondary inspiration for this collection finds its wind from living in Asia for thirty years. Everyone is so infuriatingly polite it makes one want to paint wings on frogs or fit chickens with dentures, anything to distract one from the strictures of etiquette. Added to this is the sentimental tone of many devotionals. Let's remember, now and again, God kicks butt. So, I tell it straight as often as I come in the side door. Half the time I get to pick on someone under the pretext of ministry. It's not bad work if you can get it. Anyway, that's three reasons for this collection; maybe one of them is good for something. Now, get ready to have your act put together—knowing you, you'll never do so by yourself.

Sincerely, in your face,

The Curmudgeon

APOLOGY

Apologies have gone the way of the Sonnet and the Oldsmobile. Nobody knows what they are, let alone likes them. This one comes in three parts: a confession, a disclaimer, and a revelation of the author's purpose. Don't worry, it's not as painful as it sounds.

The Confession is not for an abrupt manner, but a failing memory. I may be wrong about some things, only a few, and I may have fudged on some details—sorry about that. As for the Disclaimer, this is incumbent upon me by virtue of having an Irish Grandmother whose favorite maxim was: "Christopher, don't ye ruin a good story by tellin' the truth." I agree with Grandma. Hyperbole is both the storyteller's friend, and an art form. I have, however, swum against the tides of license, exaggeration, and prevarication to present you with an unembellished version of the events recorded. By comparison, Hercules' Twelve Labors were a picnic replete with bug repellent and wi-fi.

Finally, an apology can be the platform for divulging authorial intent. On this stage, there are three curtains, each revealing a treasure if not a stick in the eye. Curtain #1 opens to unveil a large mallet to crush your illogical fallacies. Curtain #2 discloses the most genteel of the three exhibitions, a picture frame of silver, highlighted by apples of gold (Proverbs 25:11). Therein are kind words to: "provoke you to love and good works" (Hebrews 10:24). The last jalousie opens to a mist—a pungent mist. Mist is not clear, it is subtle, and in this case, is negative. Dad is its inspiration. He used to say: "Fix your collar, Creep!" Over the years, it transcended into a metaphor that applied to exhortation, encouragement, sarcasm, and even a loving endearment with a quirky twist. Whichever form it assumed it was designed to get you in step.

These three veils are all drawn open by the somewhat coarse ribbon of Proverbs 27:6, "Blessed are the wounds of a friend."

I've never been big on Apologies, but that proverb is a disclaimer with a punch! You probably won't like it at first, being on the receiving side. Take heart, it is an acquired taste. I like it, and for that I have no apology.

HOW IT WORKS

As the Pennsylvania Dutch say: "Too soon old, too late smart!" I think this applies to most of us. It's from this viewpoint that I pursue a path that may be a wee bit intrusive, but hey, we're almost friends. After each day's adventure or tale, there is an assortment of wisdom, commands, encouragements and warnings. These come in two categories: Grace Lover, and Curmudgeon. I've saved the judgment verses for the latter. Don't blame me, I was not there when the Almighty instituted the principal of sowing and reaping. In The Lion the Witch and the Wardrobe, Aslan, the Lion, declares that He cannot go against the Deep Magic. Jesus says something similar in John's Gospel, verse 3:17: "the Son wasn't sent to condemn the world, but to save it." Notwithstanding, people are condemned because: "light is come into the world and men love darkness" 3:19.

I should stop here, but being neither wise nor subtle, there's no sense in foisting pretenses. If you're a Curmudgeon, it's time to smarten up and switch teams. At any rate, I hope to throw you some food for thought, though you'll probably moan about the bread and water, and as Scrooge said: "...you'll no doubt think yourself horribly used."

So, get your lamps trimmed, and get started on your journey. As you reflect along the way, you'll, hopefully, meet the Lamplighter. Let no one else light your lamp. Many will bring an impure fire, a grand display of fireworks, or a momentary hocus pocus. You will know the True Lamplighter by His free offer, and by the fire He bears—it is the true light. It will leave your eyes smarting, be contrary to expectations, and find disfavor with the majority. It will, however, send away the shadows that have kept you bound by misconceptions and blatant deceptions. A proud heart will not recognize it. I'd say Happy Trails, but this is not a walk in the park. "Thy Word is a light unto my path" (Psalms 119:105), would be a better word for parting. So, go! Go on, git.

Dedicated To:

Jiji, 1942-2019

The Wilkins and Shiraishi families, 2009.

INTRODUCTION

Being that our relationship will be strained, what with the exhortations, rebukes, et al., it may be helpful to put a face to your inquisitor. So, let's meet the family!

Santa Chris, and helpers, Yuko, Corey, and Caleb, Tokorozawa, 2016.

1. SASQUATCHING

Belvedere, N.J., May '70.

Warning: Lofty language.

It was a competition to catch us. The honor went to the Highway Patrol, the state and local police coming in 2nd and 3rd place. We can blame our progenitors and mentors of youth culture for the entire episode. Our perspective was a mix of Aristotelian Logic and the new Aquarian Age and its Sirens (Pharmacopoeia, Aphrodite, and Acid Rock). It was a volatile admixture. A sabbatical from education included a visit to my classmate's girlfriend. On the way, a promontory bid us ascend for a season of contemplation and a repast of ambrosia, i.e., Ballantine Ale. The idea arose to search for Sasquatch. To not frighten the creature, we divested ourselves of cultural accouterments, i.e., tie-dyed jeans, mail carrier's cap, etc. Peers called it streaking. Law Enforcement had a less Aquarian term—indecent exposure. Joe G. and I had an apt lawyer, and went to jail for just a few days. At court, the charges were dropped.

In retrospect, folks thought it improbable Sasquatch would reside in New Jersey bordering the State Turnpike. Hindsight is100%. We missed our finals and dropped out of college. Friend, this true, albeit fanciful depiction, isn't really about Sasquatch. Solomon says there is a time and a season for everything under the sun (Eccl. 3:1). Fun is ok, but we almost ran a bus off the road, and mortified our accuser. There is a time to wake up, to cut with the Matrix, to shake off the mantle of whatever keeps us from what we are supposed to do, or be. Or we can keep playing and wait for the authorities to arrive. I'm not saying put on your clothes and put your head on straight. Let's put on His clothes. He'll straighten out the rest. God has a real life for us if we'll leave Olympus, the gods that mock us, and the ambrosia. Folks say: "Clothes make the man." He has a set of threads that'll make you what you're meant to be. Your fitting awaits!

Grace Lover: But as many of you as have been baptized into Christ, have put on Christ (Gal. 3:27).

> And I said unto him, Sir, thou knowest. And he said to me, These are they which came out of great tribulation, and have washed their robes, and made them white in the blood of the Lamb (Rev. 7:14).

2. TROLLEY FOLLY

Moscow, Russia, 1993.

She kept screaming! I hadn't eaten that day. I was saving what little money I had to call Dad and give him my flight information. First, I prayed to find the Moscow International Airport. I found the domestic airport and went in search of the other. The Moscow Police sent me back to the domestic airport. I grumbled aloud. I remember the exact tenor of the grousing: "Lord, I know you will help me, but you always wait until the last minute." Just then, there was a shrill scream behind me. Not satisfied with the results, the screamer continued. I turned about to see a woman behind the nearby trolley. She put her hands to her face to scream again. From the opposite curb, a man waved his arms, and ran through traffic toward the trolley, caring nothing for his own safety. The screams continued. I couldn't see what was amiss. The trolley operator clicked the electric motor once, but stopped due to all the commotion. The running man quickly reached the trolley. I could see there was a space on the far side of the wheels where someone had crawled onto the tracks. I suspect it was a suicide attempt. With either coaxing or pulling, he extricated the man from certain death. It was an event of seconds after which I turned and said: "Sure Lord, but it's a lovely day, is it not?"

When Death draws near, perspectives change. Realizing that we can have life after this life, can really give us pause, if not to cause us to say: "Sure Lord tis a lovely day, is it not!"

P.S. At the domestic airport, there was a bus to the international one!

Grace Lover: LORD, make me to know mine end, and the measure of my days, what it is: that I may know how frail I am. [5] Behold, thou hast made my days as an handbreadth; and mine age is as nothing before thee: verily every man at his best state is altogether vanity. Selah. [6] Surely every man walketh in a vain shew: surely they are disquieted in vain: he heapeth up riches, and knoweth not who shall gather them. [7] And now, Lord, what wait I for? my hope is in thee (Ps. 39:4-7).

Curmudgeon: Verily, verily, I say unto you, He that heareth my word, and believeth on him that sent me, hath everlasting **life**, and shall not come into condemnation; but is passed from **death** unto **life** (John 5:24).

3. IN THE VALLEY OF THE SEAHORSES

What is the number one but the concept of a value of oneness? We have a symbol for the value, the number one. It's in our mind. We can write the number one. If we erase the symbol, does the concept end? Do we then start with two-ness? No, oneness remains. Was there oneness before we thought of it? The Seahorse, that is, the concept of the Seahorse, would say "Yes." So, where did it start?

In 1979, Benoit Mandelbrot stated: the set of all num-bers (C) for the sequence Zn remains small according to the formula Zn2+C=Zn+1. Later, computers enabled Benoit to chart the formula. There is an iterating aspect, i.e., the output of the last operation becomes the input of the next operation. Operations are infinite and unique. With that knowledge, one can lay hold of *Geek* status. What had looked like a simple formula divulged a universe of unseen patterns.

My inability to create a picture of this Mandelbrot Set rivals the Devil's incapacity to define *Holy*. Check it out online. Mandelbrot called his discovery Fractal Geometry. It's a trip into the infinity of the infinitesimal. One section is called the Valley of Seahorses, another is the Parade of Elephants. Staring into these unfolding operations is, like Johannes Kepler said, "...thinking the thoughts of God after Him."

We can attribute the Set to unthinking, natural causes, and say the universe operates according to mathematics, but some things in mathematics have no relation to the natural world. We have a limited number of dimensions in the physical universe, but in math, there are no limits. Looking deeper, numbers are universal, invariant and conceptual. These characteristics resemble God, who is omnipresent, unchanging, and Spirit. So, another option would be to gasp at the Set's infinite beauty and ponder the extraordinary mind of God. Someone termed it: "the thumbprint of God." Before deciding, take a look, then a swirl on a Seahorse in a sea of infinite space. It's awesome. Enjoy the thoughts of God. Bon voyage!

Grace Lover and Curmudgeon: The secret things belong unto the Lord our God: but those things which are revealed belong unto us and to our children for ever, that we may do all the words of this law (Deut. 29:29).

4. HOTEL CLERK

...for man looketh on the outward appearance, but the Lord looketh on the heart (I Sam. 16:7).

Moscow, Russia, '93.

Who could resist a stopover in lovely downtown Ulan Baatar? I'll spare you—it's Mongolia. I spent a week and attempted to get back on the train. The Office required an extra ticket, and a later train. As a result, I arrived late in Moscow, but in time for my reservation to be rescinded and my money forfeited. The Hotel Clerk had a face that could freeze the Basilisk. I'd lost my first ticket purchase and now my hotel room! None of this really bothered me, however. I was single, enjoying an adventure, and rich—well, richer than I'd ever been. But that was not all that happened at the front desk. Having lost my money and room, I pulled a piece of paper out of my pack. I did not speak Russian but with gestures, signed to the Clerk that I wanted to give it to him. He said something like: "*Hito etah?*" I answered: "*Kristos.*" He further inquired: "Eeh?" I returned: "*Kristos, Yesus Kristos,*" pointing up. He looked blankly at the paper. He then returned his gaze to me. The gargoyle transformed in an instant, the result being a lightbulb like a strobe. The scowl, used so often to ward off duplicity or requests, melted into a smile that could swallow Chaos.

"*Spaseeeeba,*" he said, stretching the word beyond its natural limits, to receive the text ever so graciously, a missive from royalty or, considering the context, a high-profile comrade. Later that day I went to the Kremlin to meet my train-mates, but we missed each other. At the end of the Square was St. Basil's Church, that beautiful, multi-colored collection of cupolas. The outside was exquisite. Inside, were layers of dust that began forming just after the Revolution. A jumble of wooden beams lay helter-skelter on the floor. It was a dump! What a contrast it was to the Clerk. The one, pristine on the exterior but a shell of beauty, a repository of cobwebs and brokenness. The other, a cold exterior with a heart that, when warmed, could lighten a room or another's heart. How often we who see with human eyes are fooled.

Grace Lover: For now we see through a glass, darkly; but then face to face: now I know in part; but then shall I know even as also I am known (I Cor. 13:12).

Curmudgeon: Thou hypocrite, first cast out the beam out of thine own eye; and then shalt thou see clearly to cast out the mote out of thy brother's eye (Matt. 5:5).

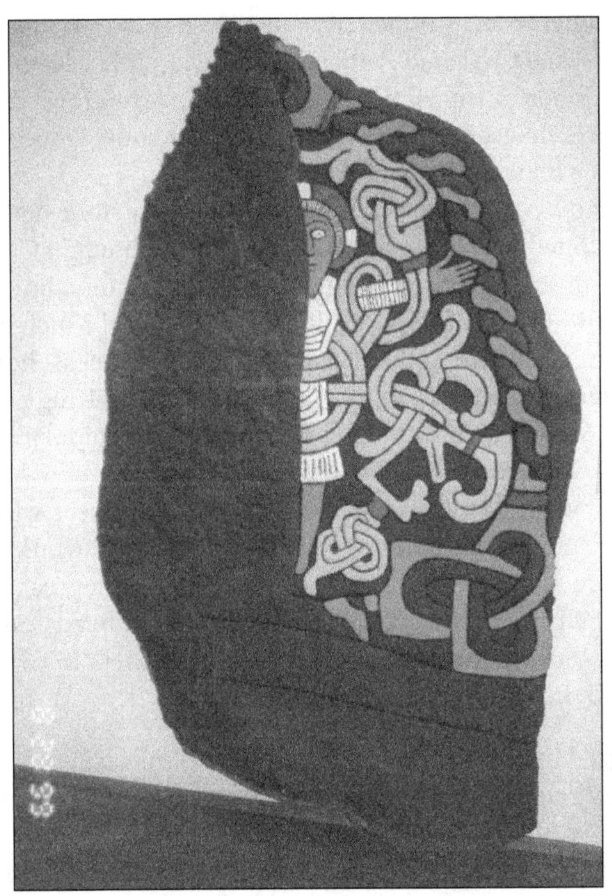

This is a Jelling Stone. This one is called Denmark's Baptismal Certificate.

5. RUNE STONE

Copenhagen, Denmark, 1999.

Forgive me, but when I was little, I wasn't big on nursery rhymes. I did read them later, in Japanese, to study the language. While traveling for a linguistics conference, I stopped in at Denmark and took a boat trip to see the home of Hans Christian Andersen, and the Little Mermaid. The trip ended at the door of the National Museum. I was in for a surprise. The Viking ship was magnificent, but what enthralled me was a stone—but not just a stone—a message.

In the year 965, King Harold Bluetooth erected a stone declaring it was he who had united the Danes and Norway, and had brought Christianity to the people. I'm sure the good King had some help from above and below, but he availed himself of opportunity. What a legacy! Much of our life is in the Realm Intangible. Influence, love, acts of kindness, how does one register these? We leave that to the Judge, but the Old King's word strikes a deep note. We can't know the denouement of our sojourn here, but we can enrich it. Don't you agree?

In the movie *It's a Wonderful Life*, James Stewart sees what would've happened to a town had he not lived there. *Dreadful* would describe it. He did live, and lives were affected for good. He had a great legacy. How are we doing? I hope to leave behind more than a headstone. I'd like a Runestone legacy that introduces my tribe and others to Christ. Way to go, Bluetooth. Runes Rock!

Grace Lover:-I have fought a good fight, I have finished my course; I have kept the faith: [8] Henceforth there is laid up for me a crown of righteousness, which the Lord, the righteous judge, shall give me at that day: and not to me only, but unto all them also that love his appearing (II Tim. 4:7-8).

Curmudgeon: Ye stiffnecked and uncircumcised in heart and ears, ye do always resist the Holy Ghost: as your fathers did, so do ye (Acts 7:51).

6. DEUS EX MACHINA

Last Days, Earth.

Newspapers use the Second Coming Font for Earth's news. Pundits attribute the end to human induced pollution, not God's hand. Earth's waters are poisoned (Rev. 8:11), and natural disasters occur (Rev. 16:1-12), but people still queue up for tax free recycle bags.

I first heard today's title in Creative Writing class. A student's story ending had no inference in the plot. The title is Latin; the English translation is–*cheating!* Ok, it means *god from a machine*. Half a millennium B.C., Greek playwrights would lower a god from a crane at play's end, to explain an unresolved plot. God works through His people, but occasionally a deus ex machina occurs. Know any? The institution of both Testaments? The Plagues of Egypt were rather over the top. The Resurrection and Ascension were also orchestrated outside our frame of reference.

Let's flip things. The Last Days of Revelation will be the *Deus ex machina* to set the bar—God appearing from out-side our world. Secular prophets have naturalistic examples, i.e., nothing creating everything and an exploding sun ending life. For some, aliens would be another player. Part of their problem with the Last Days is their view of the First Days. Contrary to Genesis, they have Death before sin, and Adam and Eve not present in the beginning (Mark 10:6).

The distance of stars has been used to discredit the Bible's position. Creationists have countered the speed of light may not be a constant. One bandage for the Big Bang Theory's anomalies is *Inflation*, which hypothesizes the Universe had plural explosions many times the speed of light today. This explains the number of elements we have, and the Cosmic Microwave Distribution. Inflation Theory suggests there's an infinite number of universes; universes in which the South won the Civil War and universes where the Civil War wasn't fought because the Colonies lost the Revolution. There are even universes without a Snickers Bar! One day, God will overturn our outlandish designs. The Lord stretched out the Heavens, and He will roll up the sky like a scroll. It is called the Day of the Lord (Joel 2:31), the Lord's return (I Thes.4), the Great Day of God Almighty (Rev. 16:14), the End of All Things (I Pet. 4:7) etc. Signs of the Lord's return will be ignored as folks line up for recycle bags, concerned with garbage, not sin. Sadly, the light of Creation will dawn on them too late. Please be ready.

7. MELON MAN

> I have set before thee an open a door, and no man can shut it (Rev. 3:8).

Shanghai, China '91.

The-trip from Shimonoseki, Japan, to Shanghai, was supposed to take two days. The first part of the journey was great; the second wasn't; a storm came in. I got seasick and just lay on the common section tatami mat (woven bamboo) trying to endure. Because of the typhoon, we arrived twelve hours late, at midnight. I was delighted. There was no one to check our bags! I had a pack full of contraband—Gospel tracts and Bibles in 3 languages. I stayed at a hostel with a dozen Japanese, and set off in the morning with a fellow named Masahiro, my pack itching to spill its contents. My first opportunity for *holy havoc* did not have long to wait. The fruit stand was a stack of watermelons on the road, and a vendor. He was doing a robust business but my focus was on giving him a Bible, not the simplest of tasks when the sum total of one's Chinese vocabulary was: *impossible, how much*, and *I'm American*, which are: *meo, dwo shou chien*, and *Meguo*. While leaning in his direction, I heard: "Excuse me, is that an English Bible?" I turned around to see 3 Chinese university students. Did they help me give Melon Man the Word of Truth? I don't recall. What did unfold were more visits to China to see one lady, Katherine, letters to the same, and mail by that newfangled fad—the internet. Later, I gave her a Bible handbook to explain between the lines or glyphs (pictographs).

I thought I'd not make it with my tracts past the opening gate, but having endured the storm, I found an open door. The doors that followed weren't the ones I expected. The closed doors directed me to some other opportunity. In the end, the tracts and Bibles were gone, and I came home with an empty pack—not counting the souvenirs and blessings.

Grace Lover: Fear thou not for I am with thee: be not dismayed; for I am thy God: I will strengthen thee; yea, I will help thee, yea, I will uphold thee with the right hand of my righteousness (Isa. 41:10).

Curmudgeon: Why do the heathen rage, and the people imagine a vain thing? [2] The kings of the earth set themselves, and the rulers take counsel together, against the LORD, and against his anointed, saying, [3] Let us break their bands asunder, and cast away their cords from us (Ps. 2:1-3).

8. THEY WISHED FOR THE DAY

Ostia, Italy, 89 A.D.

"Thank you for waiting, Maximus. He will see you now."

"We are indebted to your kindness, Olympas."

"To Him be the glory," the hostess said, waving off praise. "I beseech thee, keep him not long. The Kingdom's claim is close."

A curtain diffused light for aged eyes. Respect and appreciation preceded the group into the Centurion's stoic chamber.

"Julius," the hostess, spouse, and sister in the Lord, sweetly whispered, "you have visitors."

"Where's my short sword? I'll make quick work of them," he said. Whatever state their breathing was in, it all stopped at that moment. The Centurion lifted himself up, displaying a form that still spoke of the strength that had led men by the hundred.

"Oh, I speak in jest," he said, smiling; everyone's breathing resumed.

"Julius," Olympas remonstrated gently.

"I've been serious all my life. Is it not time to laugh?" he asked, though he needed no approbation. Seeing they waited upon him, he continued,

"Well, how may I serve you?"

In the hour that followed, the Centurion told nothing of his numerous Empire adventures, but limited his account to his first Kingdom episode. It's been kept through the ages in Acts 27, albeit two-hundred years later, Emperor Diocletian would try to have it put to the flame. Though they revered the Centurion, the pith of their pilgrimage was to hear about the Church's first persecutor, later to be the Paul, the Apostle to the Gentiles.

"I have seen Doctor Luke's account," Maximus said. "The Apostle seemed driven and courageous on one hand, and on the other, sometimes stern."

"I didn't hear it from him," Julius responded, "but he had much opposition, and suffered much. He was possessed of great strength, but not of himself. He did share with me his being encouraged by the word he received personally from the Lord, or, as in the events that involved me, by an angel sent from the Lord. He had the contradictions we all experience, but chose to honor God despite the peril."

Olympas' nod suggested further revelations would come on the Last Day.

"If I may impose, Sir," Maximus beseeched, "would you have a word?"

Without contemplation or pause, he spoke as he would to address his troop: "In times of distress, you would do better to hope in the Lord than to wish for the day." That said, prayer and farewells followed.

Though he no longer wished for the light of day, a new morning, just months later, ushered him into a light no mortal eye can behold. The Empire bestowed honors on his corpse, while Saints, and one shipmate in particular, welcomed him into the presence of the Captain of their souls.

Grace Lover: And Crispus, the chief ruler of the synagogue, believed on the Lord with all his house; and many of the Corinthians hearing believed, and were baptized. [9] Then spake the Lord to Paul in the night by a vision, Be not afraid, but speak, and hold not thy peace:[10] For I am with thee, and no man shall set on thee to hurt thee: for I have much people in this city (Acts 18:8-10).

> For there stood by me this night the angel of God, whose I am, and whom I serve, [24] Saying, Fear not, Paul; thou must be brought before Caesar: and, lo, God hath given thee all them that sail with thee. [25] Wherefore, sirs, be of good cheer: for I believe God, that it shall be even as it was told me. [26] Howbeit we must be cast upon a certain island. [27] But when the fourteenth night was come, as we were driven up and down in Adria, about midnight the shipmen deemed that they drew near to some country; [28] And sounded, and found it twenty fathoms: and when they had gone a little further, they sounded again, and found it fifteen fathoms. [29] Then fearing lest we should have fallen upon rocks, they cast four anchors out of the stern, and wished for the day (Acts 27:23-29).

> But I certify you, brethren, that the gospel which was preached of me is not after man. [12] For I neither received it of man, neither was I taught it, but by the revelation of Jesus Christ (Gal. 1:11-12).

9. THE GOLDEN LAMP

Osaka, Japan, '96.

I suspect the story doesn't live up to the title. A glazier, Michael, lived in the Mission House at the Osaka Christian Girls College. He installed treasures there: a soap dish, a light fixture, etc. His craft made a house a home. Proverbs 30:28 says: "the spider takes hold with her hands and is found in king's palaces." For me, it calls to mind Lady Macbeth. Some Rabbis say it means using our gifts helps improve our station. This leads us to my roommate. Our sole encounter was at an old lamp, a missionary supporter's offering. A gold border encircled its base. It was the setting of a drama. A jumping-spider faced the lamp, gazing into the gold sheen. He caught sight of his reflection. Set in front of his image, he turned to the right to check his opponent. Thereafter, he turned to the left to check again, and then faced himself squarely. He then leaned back and sprung. His power was superior to his distance, and he bounced off his opponent—talk about jousting with windmills. Then, espying the same enemy, he repeated the workout. I watched this show ten times. I never had guests so entertaining. At last, I went to fence my own windmills, but I always wonder who won.

Saul was courageous in the wrong battle. He fought the Church. When he took the quarrel to Damascus, God knocked him down, struck him blind, and said: "Saul, why do you persecute me? You kick against the goads," Acts 9:4,5. Paul, like us, fought against his own interest. Don't get rid of the Golden Lamp, change the spider. The Lord let Saul think about things and then sent His servant to heal him. He gave Saul a new name and eyes. He'll do the same for you.

Grace Lover: And the servant of the Lord must not strive; but be gentle unto all men, apt to teach, patient, [25] In meekness instructing those that oppose themselves (II Tim. 2:24-25).

Curmudgeon: For that which I do I allow not: for what I would, that do I not; but what I hate, that do I ... [25] I thank God through Jesus Christ our Lord. So then with the mind I myself serve the law of God; but with the flesh the law of sin (Ro. 7:18,25).

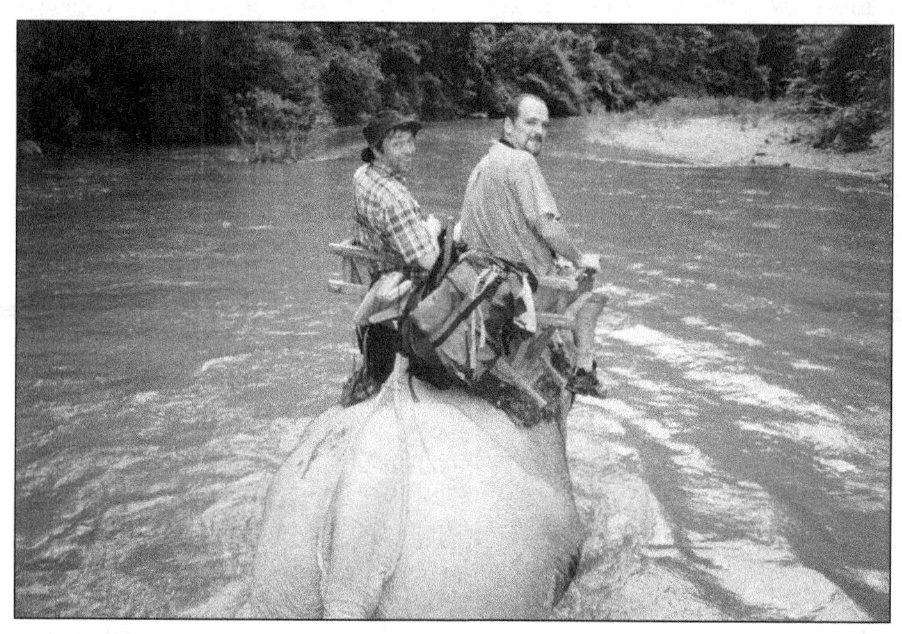

A three-day tour, 1998

10. UNCOVERED

If you are a person of faith, it is likely someone will approach you with this biased query: "Oh, come on, you don't believe in miracles, do you?" It is, as Falstaff said of another subject: "…a question to be asked," (*Henry IV* Part I, Act II, Scene IV). I suppose defining *miracle* would be a good place to get started. As this is a book for losers, not eggheads, let's dispense with dictionaries and stick to some good ole storytelling. I've heard the Jews have a saying that a coincidence is an anonymous miracle. In 1998, I left Japan, my destinations being Thailand, Laos, and last, Cambodia, to meet the mission team there. I was unable, however, to get any addresses before leaving. To start, I went to Thailand and took a three-day elephant tour. On the first day, just before boarding our elephants, I jumped in the river to cool-off. When I came out of the water, I realized something was missing—my camera lens cap. I knew it was gone for good. The water was moving too fast to retrieve it, even if I'd had time to search. We boarded our elephants and had a glorious trip. The Englishman with me asked: "Can elephants smell fear?" Not the valiant type myself. I was delighted to meet an even bigger wimp.

Our last day arrived. I was concerned about finding the Cambodian team. I stood on our meter-wide bamboo raft, waiting. It didn't have a deep draft, and I felt water on my toes. I looked and found something between my feet—my lens cap. I realized if the Lord could find a lens cap, He could help me find the Cambodian Team. Some miracles have two parts; Jesus prayed twice for a blind man when the first prayer left the patient seeing men like trees walking (Mark 8:24). I went to Laos and received my first e-mail address. I wrote to my mission, received the Cambodian contact information, and later met what would become my future mission team. Looking for something? Are you lost? Hang in there, your miracle may be as close as your feet!

Grace Lover: Whither shall I go from thy spirit? Or whither shall I flee from thy presence? [8] If I ascend up into heaven, thou art there: if I make my bed in hell, behold, thou art there. (Ps. 139:7-8).

11. THE GOSPEL BLIMP

It lit up the sky!

Its lightbulbs blinking in complex patterns, the Gospel Blimp hovered over suburbia, beaming salvation scriptures as it dropped love-notes from God on windshields, rockers, or picnic tables. Thousands would flock to the church, whose address and QR code. were on the back of the message. And to think it all started here in Pleasantville!

The evangelism committee met Wednesday nights. One member opted out to go bowling, but then things got exciting. The lightbulbs' magnitude kept old and young awake. City hall received complaints. Tracts were a litter problem. In one case, flyers with titles such as *Avoid the Flames, A Flood is Coming, The Heavens Unleashed*, and *Shower of Blessings*, were prophetic, clogging a hillside pool's filtration system, causing an electrical fire, incinerated toys, a flood, trashed heirlooms, and an irate community. The campaign's final Sunday had ushers trying to quiet visitors seeking redress, while the pastor offered an apology. Class Action Suit was on many minds. There was a plus—a baptism. The evangelism committee member who'd absented himself to go bowling, befriended a teammate, who discovered his search of years was not a 187 average, but finding a friend, and the living God.

Joseph Bayly's *The Gospel Blimp*, directed by Irwin Yeaworth Jr., '67, may impart wisdom for those moved by zeal in the absence of prudence. Thanks, Joseph, for a great story.

Grace Lover: And God said to Solomon, Because this was in thine heart, and thou hast not asked riches, wealth, or honour, nor the life of thine enemies, neither yet hast asked long life; but hast asked wisdom and knowledge for thyself, that thou mayest judge my people, over whom I have made thee king: [12] Wisdom and knowledge is granted unto thee; and I will give thee riches, and wealth, and honour, such as none of the kings have had that have been before thee, neither shall there any after thee have the like (II Chron. 1:11, 12).

Curmudgeon: The fruit of the righteous is a tree of life; and he that winneth souls is wise.[31] Behold, the righteous shall be recompensed in the earth: much more the wicked and the sinner (Prov. 11:30-31).

12. CLUTCH MOMENT

Long Island, N.Y.,'69.

"Did you steal the hitch?" he snarled.

"No," I said, dumbfounded, as he stormed off in a cloud of stench, chomping his cigar stub. Another question followed.

"Can you drive a standard shift?"

"Yes," I said, not caring to embellish further, given it was a lie.

That was my first day at Ogel's Florist. It had a big panel truck, and I was to deliver flowers to funeral parlors. I liked to drive, but couldn't drive standard shifts! To compound this negative scenario, it was winter. I drove in second gear to get the truck moving and up to a reasonable speed. The van had a vengeful spirit. I can't blame her; I'd been chewing up her gears for weeks. One bleak day, atop a hill, she decided to stall. She had no brakes when the engine wasn't running. So, I started rolling down the hill toward an intersection—unpowered, no brakes. Did I mention this wasn't forward motion? Yes, it was backwards! The lilies were ok, but the carnations were hysterical! It was a commercial vehicle—no windows! I couldn't see what death awaited me! I tried slowing down by rubbing up against the curb. With such a dramatic buildup, I should remember the outcome. Other than living through it, not totaling the van, taking a year off my life, and hating my boss for giving me the job, I don't recall. I'm rather sure I navigated the intersection. Then, that nasty van decided to start.

It was good I left the job. I was on the Dean's List, his Probation List. Other positives are I've made peace with standard shift vehicles, and I have an even greater appreciation for crysenthamoms. I can even spell them, given a few chances. In addition, I have an example for my boys about the fruit of a froward tongue. You also can use it, if you like. I thought up some titles: *Wilkins Wild Ride, The Backward Van, The Vengeful Vehicle, or Touring the East Coast in Second Gear: A Handbook for Liars.* You can add I went through a red-light backwards. I hesitated to say so, hoping to err on the side of Truth—for a change.

Curmudgeon: Ye are of your father the devil, and the lusts of your father ye will do. He was a murderer from the beginning, and abode not in the truth, because there is no truth in him. When he speaketh a lie, he speaketh of his own: for he is a liar, and the father of it (John 8:44).

13. ISAIAH AND THE BEAR CLAW

"I hate getting God for a tip," Jane groused, eyeing a tract. David, contrariwise, would take God for his blessing. God helped him defeat a lion and a bear! He didn't care about the King's daughter, or tax-cuts; his concern was God's reputation. Except for you heathens, unschooled, and unchurched, most of us recall this tale. But who can recount the Tale of Isaiah and the Bear Claw? C'est moi!

San Francisco, '77, non-union, Kosher-style, Stage Deli, Geary Street. Annie was playing, 900 locals had died in Jonestown, Guyana, victims of Jim Jones and Poison Cool-Ade, and Harvey Milk, the first openly gay mayor, was assassinated. My life was quieter. I had the exalted position of busboy. I liked the crew. We had the Irish-American, Jane. The owner, Max, had a Japanese wife. Manuel, an illegal alien, washed dishes. The server, Lulu, embodied all that name intimates. Michael was a switch-hitter, and Tanaka, my roommate, was an ethnic Chinese from Laos, who took a Japanese name. Our cooks were Mike and Bill. One had a boyfriend, the other had cirrhosis. Joel and his dad were our Jewish bakers. I went bowling with them all, and having the lowest score, paid the bill! It was there I first played Pong. It wasn't all lanes and arcades, however. Other adventures were dinner at Mike's, and visiting Bill in the hospital. There was the BASEMENT, too. There, Joel's dad reigned over a dominion of bear claws, sticky buns, and a powdered host innumerable. A formidable despot, not to be truffled with, even dust, dare not enter uninvited.

"Hey, those Bear Claws go up, and don't bang them on the stairs!" was his opening greeting. Days later, he changed the lyrics if not the tune: "What are you looking at? Just take it upstairs!" In the months following, as I posed no threat, we even chatted. I enjoyed talks with Joel. My contribution was "the more sure word of prophecy" (II Pet. 1:19). We talked about the Torah, Psalms, and Prophets regarding Messiah. His dad started calling me *Preacher* besides, *Hey You!* Though with a little melted butter, those bear claws were great, they were a distant second to Isaiah's Suffering Servant (Isa. 52, 53).

Curmudgeon: All we like sheep have gone astray; we have turned every one to his own way; and the LORD hath laid on him the iniquity of us all (Isa. 53:6).

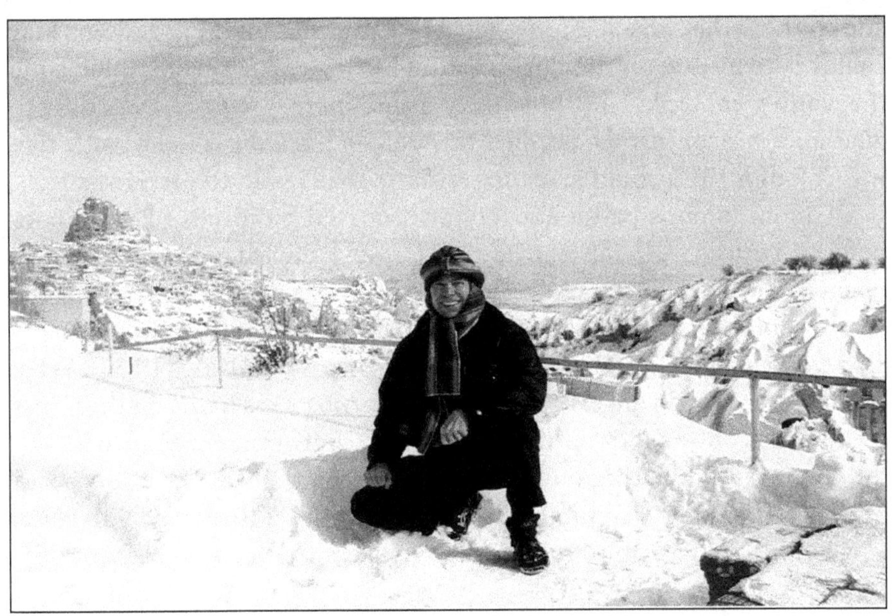

The Anatolian Plateau, scene of the battle that wasn't!

14. THE FAMOUS BATTLE NEVER FOUGHT

It is May 28th, 585 B.C.

The setting is the Halys River on the Anatolian plateau, Turkey. The cast is tens of thousands of Median and Lydian soldiers. Thousands have died in previous filming and the battle is set in array, again. The name players are the Sun, Moon, Lydian King Alyattes, Median King Cyaxeres, and Thales of the Ionian Philosophers. Herodotus provides the script. The war has been going on for 6 years. Thales informs the leaders the gods are not happy, and to show their displeasure, they'll blot out the sun on the 28th of May. Thales puts his life on the line, trusting his logic. At the appointed time, the world went dark. Hostilities ceased, and there was a royal wedding to guarantee peace…da, da, da, da! The Battle of the Eclipse—the battle that wasn't fought! You could give the credit to Thales, and to the Sun!

A more famous battle not fought occurred hundreds of years later. Before Thales lived, Isaiah described it: "Like a lamb led to the slaughter, he openeth not his mouth…" Angels, ten-thousand, were ready to destroy the enemy—maybe the planet (Matt. 26:53). The Angel of the Lord, working alone, wiped out King Sennacherib's Assyrian army (II Kings 19:35). What could ten-thousand angels do? But Jesus' purpose was to die on the Cross. He had the power to stop the Crucifixion, but went through with it—for you. Are you betting on stars or logic? Stop the war. Take His peace offer. Jesus fought to not fight back. How's your battle going? Surrender is victory! Do that and have peace, forgiveness, and eternal life. Give the credit to the Son.

Grace Lover: Yet it pleased the Lord to bruise him; he hath put him to grief: when thou shalt make his soul an offering for sin, he shall see his seed, he shall prolong his days, and the pleasure of the Lord shall prosper in his hand (Isa. 53:10).

Curmudgeon: He is despised and rejected of men; a man of sorrows, and acquainted with grief: and we hid as it were our faces from him; he was despised, and we esteemed him not. [4]Surely he hath borne our griefs, and carried our sorrows: yet we did esteem him stricken, smitten of God, and afflicted (Isa. 53:3-4).

15. KAKU DASU

Kaku dasu, in English, is *the opening paragraph.* Tax offices have inspired passionate thoughts through the centuries, but this one is positive. To redeem the time, I read standing in line. The man behind me asked if I read a Bible. We discovered we were brothers in the Faith. I gave him a tract; he gave me origami. Later I studied Japanese and found our opening phrase.

Here are some examples: "It is a truth universally acknowledged, that a single man in possession of a good fortune, must be in want of a wife," *Pride and Prejudice* by Jane Austen

"All children except one, grow up," *Peter Pan* by J. M. Barrie

"It was the best of times, it was the worst of times…" *A Tale of Two Cities* by Charles Dickens

"In a hole in the ground lived a Hobbit." *The Hobbit* by J. R. R. Tolkien.

Now let's look at a few great kaku-dasu from the Bible: "In the beginning, God created the heaven and the Earth" (Gen. 1:1).

What Christians call *Leviticus* – is *Vaickra* in the Hebrew Torah. It means: *And the Lord called.* The first line of the Book of Numbers, *Sefer vayadabar* means: *The Book of: And He spoke.*

In a rare occurrence, a Chinese woman matriculated at Asbury seminary in the '90's. China, a Communist state, did not offer many visas for religious studies. At Emigration, they asked: "What's the opening of *The Song of Solomon*?" Blushing, she responded—"The song of songs, which is Solomon's. [2] Let him kiss me with the kisses of his mouth: for thy love is better than wine." Impressed, the interviewer granted her visa. She later graduated.

Let's look at some entries of New Testament kaku dasu: "In the beginning was the Word, and the Word was with God, and the Word was God" (John. 1:1). Luke addressed Acts to *Theophilus*, which means *Friend of God.* He opened with: "The former treatise have I made, O Theophilus, of all that Jesus began both to do and teach" (Acts 1:1).

So, grab a beverage, and crack open The Book and a new start. You don't know today's phrase? He does. Take His word for it. *Vayadabar!*

16. THE HORONITE HERALD

Journalist: Tobiah of the Ammonite Annals

In the 20th year of the Inestimable lord of the World, Artaxerxes.

The people rejoice in their High Emperor. They are, however, perplexed. The old order, put down by the mighty and righteous hand of his forbears, raises its head again. Nehemiah, who through deceits was appointed governor, is strengthening his hold by building a wall. He has slaves to lead the work and subjugates poor Jews to build his own kingdom. "I will not come," he has said to each cordial invitation of Sanballat, the Horonite leader, to address a town meeting. When we send a contingent to meet him, his people carry weapons and threaten us. They are deplorable, irredeemable. Reports of disagreement we bring his way, he terms, "Disingenuous news." He uses provisions of the Emperor, for his own household. He does not release the receipts or tax records. Furthermore, he will not allow any but those he views as true Jews to work on the project. His discrimination knows no bounds. He would break up families, saying international marriages are not to be honored. He would not allow the non-Jews to enter. He cites conspiracies among what he calls "The Slough." Undisclosed sources have testified he said: "We Jews will build the wall and make the Gentiles pay for it!" He says he is right, and the right will make Jerusalem great again. We who are left must resist the collusion we know to have transpired. We must resist his appointments and programs. We must create issues with which to bring him down. We must proclaim the news of his tyranny even before it begins, so that those of us who are left, will rule.

More news at 11 from couriers provided by Meshullam's Donkey Rentals. Remember: Rent a pair from Messhy and get a discount every fifth Tuesday of the month. Offer not available in Samaria and where restrictions apply. Papyrus for the Herald provided by Shaphat's Reed and Write, your super stationery supply. Open on Shabbat!

Sound familiar? Half-truths, conspiracy theories, hyperbole, agendas, the end justifying the means, etc. This retro-account is a take-off on the Books of Nehemiah, Ezra, II Kings, II Chronicles, and… your news program. It's a good time to both speak the truth in love (Ephesians 4:15) and have a just balance (Prov. 16:11). Still think the Bible is irrelevant?

Trafalgar Square. I stand alone—
the result of not bathing for a week.

17. THE GEOLOGICAL TABLE

Moscow, Russia, 1993.

All I had was a few dollars in coins. I called my father and said: "Dad, listen, no money, arrive Kennedy, 12:39 P.M., flight BOA 2194. Send limo. Love u." Out of necessity, I had fasted at least a day, maybe two. I wanted to fly Aeroflot, the Russian carrier, but they only took Master Card; British Air took VISA but charged double. Hard times make for hard choices.

Comedians of the 60's had a rite of passage to stardom, a theme I've entitled: *Airplane Food Rant.* On late-night T.V. you'd hear about abusive broccoli, or the revenge of the rigatoni! I, however, inhaled the meal and ate the napkin, too. Arriving in London, my hotel had a glass elevator with brass bannisters. Outside were three turreted chimneys of Dicken's lore. As I lay in the tub, the dirt and dust of five days on the Trans-Siberian railroad turned the tub-water brown, forming sedimentary layers all about me. It was like an expensive terrarium. My situation had witnessed quite a change. On the morrow I'd tour London, buy trinkets (a cup enumerating Great Britain's kings and queens), and later, arrive in New York for a trip by limousine—thanks for listening, Dad.

The deprivations I've suffered have been self-inflicted. Finances change. Full or empty, our hearts can be full. We're "co-heirs with Christ" (Romans 8:16-17). That means? Jesus will share his inheritance with us. I can only speculate what that is, but does it not make finances and airport hassles insignificant by comparison?

Grace Lover: But you shall remember Yahweh your God, for it is he who gives you power to get wealth; that he may establish his covenant which he swore to your fathers, as at this day. (Deuteronomy. 8:18).

> Not that I speak in respect of want: for I have learned in whatsoever state I am, therewith to be content (Phil. 4:11).

Curmudgeon: For the love of money is the root of all evil: which while some coveted after, they have erred from the faith, and pierced themselves through with many sorrows (I Tim. 6:10).

18. LONDON FOG

We've all seen those black, traditional cabs that serve the London streets. That's why we watch movies. They help paint the romanticized views we love, in this case, old London. Wouldn't it be nice to ride one of those cabs, boasting an umbrella and the perfect accessory, a bowler? In 1998, I started a new job in Kyushu. The package had a stipend for conferences on education. I went to London, on summer break, for a symposium of linguistics. It sounds highbrow, but the foci all intersected on one point: empowering foreign English-speakers to say, "Huh?" or "Eh?" instead of "I beg your pardon?" or "Sorry?"

Before smart phones, we had maps. I'd gained some proficiency with them, and used one to locate the meeting. I had a little difficulty and thought to inquire of a local. The strategy was wise, my choice, a barrister of the barstool, was not. The personification of the London Fog, he floated towards me, unable to navigate the sidewalk let alone directions. Notwithstanding, he insisted my location bordered the other side of the moon. I hailed a cab only to hear: "Well, that's it there." My reply was: "That's ok, it's my first time in a London cab." I left him my entire note, feeling enriched. It was a beautiful cab.

We all have dreams. The Lord says He will give us the desires of our heart (Ps. 37:4). C. S. Lewis said God cannot give happiness and peace apart from Himself, because it doesn't exist (pg. 50, *Mere Christianity*). He engineers or coaxes events, so some of our dreams come true. For me, the Lord used a man who could barely stand up. For the Jews, He used King Cyrus the Persian, a Gentile, for Elijah, ravens (I Kings 17:4). The unexpected circumstance or person may be His preferred tool of choice. So, take your umbrella, and if you're feeling dreamy, grab your bowler.

Grace Lover: And Jethro, Moses' father in law, came with his sons and his wife unto Moses into the wilderness, where he encamped at the mount of God:[19] Hearken now unto my voice, I will give thee counsel, and God shall be with thee: Be thou for the people to God-ward, that thou mayest bring the causes unto God: [21] Moreover thou shalt provide out of all the people able men, such as fear God, men of truth, hating covetousness; and place such over them, to be rulers of thousands, and rulers of hundreds, rulers of fifties, and rulers of tens (Ex. 18:5,19, 21).

19. KINTSUGI: A THING OF CRACKS

I couldn't believe it. She bit me on the nose! Our house has a beautiful wooden floor that enjoys a southern exposure. For hours of the day, the sun pours in, and the wooden floor's golden varnish conspires with golden ray in some wondrous alchemy to produce a home. Added to this will be the golden mane of our loving mutt. On that day, however, her golden fleece came close to becoming a rug. Careful to avoid staining the carpet, I went to a mirror for a damage report. I can't explain my concern for the rug, a threadbare patchwork—a little color would've improved it. Nonetheless, the scar left me looking rugged, a laurel without a knife fight. Brokenness has beauty. Recently, I bought an old, used book in Japan. The seller, to remove any blemish, had torn out the dedication page. Sadly, the character and history of the book were gone.

To unveil the truth about Kintsugi, we should note that it is what it is *cracked up to be*. Kintsugi is a melding of two words, *gold* and *join*. It describes an art form begun in the fifteenth century by the Japanese Shogun, Ashikage Yoshimasa. When a treasured piece of chinaware broke, he sent it to China for repair. It was returned later with staples, ugly ones. As a result, gold was mixed with lacquer to celebrate brokenness, to restore instead of destroy.

We can think we're for the trash bin, or we can celebrate our precious scars. Have you heard of Joni? She is a mouth-painter and paraplegic. Her accident is the reason for her intimacy with the Lord. She said:

"I had to trust God for my next breath. I wouldn't trade places with anyone."

Hear the words of Job, a voice of another age: And he took him a potsherd to scrape himself withal; and he sat down among the ashes. [9] Then said his wife unto him, Dost thou still retain thine integrity? curse God, and die. [10] But he said unto her, Thou speakest as one of the foolish women speaketh. What? shall we receive good at the hand of God, and shall we not receive evil? In all this did not Job sin with his lips (Job 2:8-10).

We met Sremom in Cambodia, in 2002, selling postcards. Her face was mutilated by acid thrown by thieves. Today she has the Lord's joy, and her own shop.

YOU are precious in His sight. No other opinion matters. He'll fill our cracks with gold.

20. THE KGB: SIGNS AND WONDERS

I shared the room with two French women and a Frenchman. I had the upper bunk. They had brought their bikes and traveled through Mongolia by grit and gears. I opened sardines every lunchtime. With that exception, we enjoyed each other's company during the five days it took from Ulan Baatar to Moscow. We had many a rousing chorus of *La Mer*. Other times saw me with my favorite jailbird, O' Henry, studying Cyrillic, or devouring the *Lonely Planet Guide.*

Upon arrival, I stopped at a dilapidated Russian Orthodox Church. My spirit rose with the incense. Priest and laity echoed a liturgy reminiscent of High Masses I'd attended as a boy. I wondered what price they paid to continue their addiction to the opiate of the masses.

From there, I took a walk. From my map, I learned there were Inner and Outer Ring roads. I knew I was near the Outer Ring, so when I found signs at each corner with the same lettering, I assumed I had my reference point. As I continued down the way for some time, however, the landscape and map did not concur. I soon approached the unique architecture of the KGB skyscraper. I guess you have to go up when information gets piled higher and deeper. Alas, I took out my dictionary, now that I could read Cyrillic, and checked out my road-sign. It gave me a chuckle as my finger landed on it… S T O P. I sighed as I checked the map. I should have known there would be a stop sign at the end of each street, my mistake, but I never would have known I'd erred had I not seen the KGB building—there's a message in that. Signs and wonders, think about it. If we even notice them, we get them mixed up. Watch your step!

Grace Lover: For there shall arise false Christs, and false prophets, and shall shew great signs and wonders; insomuch that, if it were possible, they shall deceive the very elect. [26] Wherefore if they shall say unto you, Behold, he is in the desert; go not forth: behold, he is in the secret chambers; believe it not. [27] For as the lightning cometh out of the east, and shineth even unto the west; so shall also the coming of the Son of man be (Matt. 24:24, 26-27).

Curmudgeon: -And then shall that Wicked be revealed, whom the Lord shalt consume with the spirit of his mouth, and shall destroy with the brightness of his coming: Even him, whose coming is after the working of Satan with all power and signs and lying wonders (II Thess. 2:8,9).

A card I received from Blong, 1974.

21. LDM: THE BOTTLE OF REMEMBRANCE

Eliakim looked at the Last Days' Museum brochure, then ignored it, licked his finger, and stuck it in the air.

"Why lick your finger? There's no wind in a building!" Thy Venn said.

"I'm sure the Hall of the Tearless is this way," Sau Fan said.

"But we wanted to see The Bottle of Remembrance," Eliakim explained.

An Angel Curator, hearing the conversation, asked: "Which Bottle did you want to see?"

"There's more than one?" Fung Chil asked.

"Yes," Hiro erupted, "one is in Psalms 56:8. the other is alluded to in ..."

"Don't tell us all," Thy Venn requested, "let's discover it when we get there."

"Go through there," the Curator said, "even the Town of Bethlehem...."

"Wow, the original Bethlehem!" Blong exclaimed.

"Well, no, the original was consumed by fire on the Last Day."

"Thank you," Fung Chil said. On arrival, Thy Venn noted: "It's small to hold so many tears."

"Well..." Hiro observed, raising his brochure...

"Wait," Fung Chil requested, "That's because it's a miracle bottle."

"Look at this," Blong said, "there is a sole tear kept aside."

"I know," Hiro said, using his brochure. "It's Earth's last tear shed before the Lord's return. A Kikuyu woman, beaten by brigands. Her tear never reached the ground. It filled both this bottle and the Cup of His Wrath. simultaneously. The Lord returned in the twinkling of an eye.

The group visited her, sharing tales of pilgrimage. Fung Chil summarized their joint feeling:

"Of all the attributes God could have, He is compassionate." They all praised Him.

Hiro folded up his ubiquitous flyer, and said: "You don't need a brochure to know that."

Grace Lover: Thou tellest my wanderings: put thou my tears into thy bottle: are they not in thy book (Ps. 56:8)?

22. THE WEATHERWOMEN'S FORECAST: STORMS AHEAD

Kealakekua, 1975.

"We have to stop meeting like this," I joked. Our meetings were clandestine, being we lived on the slope of a dormant volcano. They were FBI agents so *secretive* was ok. They never stayed, leaving with my wife for questioning. The *wheres* and *whats* I don't know. She'd been in the Weatherwomen. They made bombs, and except for one fellow who blew himself up, knew how to use them. They made Antifa or the Proud Boys look like a sewing circle.

In *Mary Poppins,* Sir Reginald Owen played Admiral Boom. One day he warned Bert: "A word of advice, young man; storm signals are up at #17. Bit of heavy weather brewing there." Mr. Banks, didn't hear the warning. In my marriage, the first forecast of a coming storm was our honeymoon when my bride revealed she no longer believed the Bible. Couldn't that have happened earlier? Then church attendance stopped. At the library, she borrowed New Age books. I pleaded, but she was adamant. Minutes later, her forehead beading with sweat, she fainted. I thought it would help if we left Hawaii. Two years later, she went to visit her sister in San Francisco. Then, she called to say she was not returning. I went to San Francisco, but she wanted a divorce. I couldn't stop her downward spiral. I fasted, prayed, and still wore my wedding ring years later. A relative told me people were talking. The word *pathetic* wasn't mentioned but was inferred. I hung on to God. Others just added chaos. When she became pregnant in Africa, I let her loose. Even as His servants, not every trial turns out like our hopes. In retrospect, I now have a wonderful wife and two boys who fill my life with love.

Grace Lover: And the Lord, he it is that doth go before thee; he will be with thee, he will not fail thee, neither forsake thee: fear not, neither be dismayed (Deut. 31:8).

In your patience possess ye your souls (Luke 21:19).

Curmudgeon: What? shall we receive good at the hand of God, and shall we not receive evil? In all this did not Job sin with his lips (Job 2:10).

23. NEITHER: THE NEVER STARTING JOURNEY

What follows is a good ride if you take it slow from the onset. You may need to step into a circle of abstraction, or don a Conundrum Cap, or spit into the air, and turn about twice before a fairy counteth thrice. Whatever your method, I hope it prepares you for the trip ahead.

A compilation of substantiating errors equals Neith. "I ain't a Neither," is deplorable grammar, but if altered to: "I'm not a Neither," not an English faculty eyebrow would wrinkle. The statement, however, is a matter of Astronomy, not English. Still lost? Neithology and Neithisms new to you? I can't boast, I'm a recent initiate. You see, there were those who held to the existence of Neith, Venus' moon. Early telescopes, heavenly bodies and phenomena such as asteroids, planets, reflections, and a smidge of lunacy, conspired to make the theorem plausible. Respected men ascribed to it. Giovanni Cassini, in 1672, viewed an object close to Venus. Upon a second sighting, years later, he declared Venus had a moon. Other astronomers confirmed his claim, among them, James Short, Andreas Mayer, Joseph Louis Lagrange, and Christian Horrebow. In 1777, J. H. Lambert proposed Neith had an orbit of eleven days. A century later, Jean-Charles Houzeau, said the moon was a planet with an orbit of two-hundred and eighty-three days, and was in conjunction with Venus every one-thousand and eighty days. The data fit. One outstanding problem remained. Neith, despite human machinations, did not, and, to this day, does not, exist. It is altogether possible it will never exist! Nevertheless, I will neither say I am not, or am, a Neither. Neither, that is, not one or the other, reconciles my intellectual integrity and penchant for fantasy. Others, whose feet are more firmly planted on Terra Firma, or Venus Firma, than mine, can confidently nix Neith, because the theory has gone the way of the once planet, Pluto, even more so. Pluto owes its fate to human classifications. Neith's legend owes itself to imagination. So, you can safely say: "I'm not a Neither." You could even say: "I ain't a Neither," if you feel rowdy.

Your head may be orbiting an imaginary moon or a real headache about now—I apologize, but I have a point. People align themselves with those of similar causes. Luther, for instance, said he was a Hussite. He risked a heated response in that Huss had been burned at the stake. President Kennedy, it has been said, when giving his famous Berlin speech, instead of claiming he was a Berliner, declared: "I am a donut!" It may have been a matter of pronunciation, not politics or culinary preference. I suspect regional differences were an ingredient in the claim, but that position may just be circular reasoning with a big hole in it.

My original book title involved Venus. Once the Curmudgeon booted her out of the universe, I should've nixed all things Venusian. But, having put much energy into being clever, I was reluctant to exile her. Since truth has come full orbit, let's carry on as if we're normal people. Grab this idea, it's the soundest reasoning so far. You've heard the phrase: *Beyond here be there dragons*, well, I think we've passed the Dragon Fields. Things should be less challenging from here.

Let's consider what this tale offers us. Obviously, it would suggest we be not haphazard in our book selections. Another take away would be that experts, at times, confirm each other's errors. Extrapolations upon extrapolations get one so distant from the foundation upon which one once stood that the entire structure is in jeopardy of a sudden, sobering, loss of integrity—a crash.

Below is my Bible's frontispiece. If you've been Neithing, why not enjoy this solid ground?

Grace Lover: The voice said, Cry. And he said, What shall I cry? All flesh is grass, and all the goodliness thereof is as the flower of the field:[7] The grass withereth, the flower fadeth: because the spirit of the Lord bloweth upon it: surely the people is grass.[8] The grass withereth, the flower fadeth: but the word of our God shall stand for ever (Isa. 40:6-8).

> O Timothy, keep that which is committed to thy trust, avoiding profane and vain babblings, and oppositions of science falsely so called[21] Which some professing have erred concerning the faith. Grace be with thee. Amen (I Tim. 6:20-21).

Curmudgeon: Where is the wise? where is the scribe? where is the disputer of this world? hath not God made foolish the wisdom of this world? [25] Because the foolishness of God is wiser than men; and the weakness of God is stronger than men (I Cor. 1:20,25).

^ *Kragh, Helge (2008). "The Moon that Was not: The Saga of Venus' Spurious Satellite". Birkhäuser. ISBN 978-3-7643-8908-6.*

24. BRANDED

Belvedere, N.J., '70.

Chuck Connors was an L.A. Dodger. He wasn't great, but made the Majors. Later, he starred in The Rifleman, and Branded, in which, as a Cavalry Officer, he was wrongly convicted of cowardice.

Let's talk Honor. It was 1970. I was incarcerated during college finals. It was a time of flowing locks, bell-bottom jeans, riots, and the Vietnam War. My landlord, a Marine, was dishonorably discharged. Though he didn't depart with his honor, he did leave with a military jacket, which he gave me. A dandy, good-looking but useless, I wore it to a bar with Joe G. while visiting his girlfriend in N.J. I was not a strutting-peacock. It would have been presumptuous at one hundred and twenty-six pounds. Rather, I floated into the bar, with my Postman's cap and tied-died jeans, looking my revolutionary best. That, and fifty-cents, would have gotten me a cup of coffee, but I didn't put caffeine in my body; other drugs were welcome. After a beer, a Marine came over. He strutted unintentionally.

"I had friends who didn't come back from Nam. I'll be outside waiting for you. You don't deserve this," he said, sliding me out of the jacket. My teeth were grateful I offered no resistance. The bartender said I could crawl out the backdoor, appropriate being I assumed laurels for which I'd sacrificed nothing.

"Isn't it sad war has twisted him?" one of us observed. And another, "Why do we have wars?" HONOR wasn't mentioned. It wouldn't have found a chair at the table had it stayed in the company of the uninitiated. Later, I was a draft-dodger. Now I thank those who served.

What's the most infamous Branded story? The King of Glory was dishonorably discharged by secular and religious leaders. Isaiah, gives an 8th century B.C exclusive. It's confirmed by Matthew, Mark, Luke, John, and non-believers, Josephus, Pliny, Tacitus, and others. We're all Branded. We've not been honorable, but we can be reinstated in a place of HONOR. First, do what's honorable; dump your pride. A plea of guilty will get you pardoned. You're standing in the Celestial Court. How do you plead?

Curmudgeon: But he was wounded for our transgressions, he was bruised for our iniquities: the chastisement of our peace was upon him; and with his stripes we are healed (Isa. 53:5).

25. BUNGALOW BAR

W. Babylon, N.Y., '57.

The lyrics of a 50's song were: "There were bells on the hill, but I never heard them ringing til there was you!" Contrariwise, kids of the '50's loved the bell! The ice cream truckdriver pulled a bell-rope. When I was eleven, Mister Softee came to town. I avoided him. His ice cream was soft, and his bell was phony. It sounded like an enemy sub's sonar ping. Good Humor was the stuff for me. Grandpa Clark laughed when I asked for a two-stix, a double stick popsicle with two flavors. Everyone knew the Good Humor folks were clever. My big brother did too; he sold Good Humor from a cart the summer of '61.

One day Uncle Norman visited. Norman means from the North, like Norsemen, but my uncle was a Hungarian Jew. I knew what a Hungarian was, I liked geography. But a Jew? We didn't have many at Our Lady of Perpetual Help School. I heard he invented the Peter Pan collar. I liked him, but he said: "Let's get a Bungalow Bar." He wanted to be friends–but Bungalow Bar? They had ice cream trucks with a bungalow style roof. The *bar* was the ice cream. Mom said wait for after supper. I don't know if I ever tasted Bungalow Bar. And now, they're extinct. The founder, a Greek, immigrated before WWII. Its end was Chapter 11, bankruptcy. Rumors had the Underworld involved. When you lose, people say anything. Look at this kids' song:

Bungalow Bar tastes like tar. The more you eat, the sicker you are!

I never stooped to defamation, nor did I eat Bungalow Bar. We all have a negative chorus about someone that rings its bell in our thoughts. And there's always one friend that loves to hear an evil report. We only heard the bells of Bungalow Bar and Good Humor in the summer, but our negative bells go off anytime. Another ditty of yore, was: "Sticks and stones can break my bones but words can never hurt me." Really? Words affect reputations, families, and self-image. If Bungalow Bar were around today, I'd give them a chance. I'd want them to do the same for me.

Grace Lover: Let no corrupt communication proceed out of your mouth, but that which is good to the use of edifying, that it may minister grace unto the hearers (Eph. 4:29).

26. 33 A.D., BETHEL: FUN WITH THE RABBI

"Knock, knock!!!"

"Who is it?"

"Hi Matityahu, It's Mary, shalom aleichem."

"Yes, neighbor, aleichem shalom. What can I do for you?"

"We're having a gathering tonight. Rabbi Jesus is here. Can you come?"

"Oh, so nice, we appreciate it. However, my wife's brother is with us. So, I think not this time."

"Oh, your brother-in-law is welcome, too. You are all welcome!"

"You are too kind, Mary. Thank you, but I think he is tired from his travels. Maybe next time."

"Okay, Matityahu, peace on your house."

Later, at the home of Lazarus, Martha, and Mary:

"Mary, I need to plan the meal. How many are coming?" Martha asked.

"I think it will just be the Rabbi, his disciples, and us."

"What? Everyone's afraid of the Sadducees?" Martha quipped.

Not much later, Jesus and his disciples arrived. After feet were washed, it was time to chat. Following this, the disciple left to visit others, leaving Jesus with the family of Lazarus. Martha enters bearing a platter of freshly baked barley bread. Of course, she offers it to Jesus first.

"You bring the Rabbi this cheap bread, Martha? Don't we have wheat?"

"If Little Sister hadn't spent a year's wages on that alabaster jar, we'd have wheat and other things, too," Martha complained. "Maybe a servant to help with the cooking and washing and… but who am I to complain? I have a roof, and a meal, and health."

"And a tongue," Lazarus whispered.

"Maybe Mary will use it for a good purpose," Jesus suggested.

"There, see," Lazarus said, glad to be supported.

"So, money grows on vines?" Martha said, beaning her brother with a roll.

"You should have respect for your older brother," Lazarus remonstrated.

"I do," Martha confided, "just not as much as before."

"What?" Lazarus asked, surprised, "and why not?"

"You're not as old as before—you lost four days," she explained, making Jesus laugh.

Lazarus took this opportunity to throw the roll back at her, but missed. Jesus dove to catch it.

"Not eating? Good," Martha said, "you've gotten fat since you died!" Jesus grinned widely.

"Rabbi," Lazarus asked, "next time I die, please, don't bring me back to this house of women!"

At this point, Mary, who'd been listening, came in with a tray of cups Martha had prepared.

"Did you mean I shouldn't serve you this, older brother?" she asked.

Lazarus, aghast at this outcome, raised his hands in dismay, only to catch Martha's latest high-speed offering. He quickly returned the favor, this time knocking over a cup. Jesus held his head in his hands, possibly to groan, laugh, or protect himself.

"You're more fun now that you died," Martha threw in once more.

"But you still can't throw," Mary observed. As everyone reached for a roll, Jesus spoke up:

"Shall we ask a blessing for the meal before we have to eat it off the floor?" They prayed, but not until eyes, wet from laughter, were properly dabbed. Jesus was full of surprises. As the *Narnia Chronicles* declare, He's not a tame Lion. Sometimes we put him in a box. This adaptation would suggest we not try to close the lid too tightly.

Grace Lover: Then Jesus six days before the passover came to Bethany, where Lazarus was, which had been dead, whom he raised from the dead (John 12:1).

Curmudgeon: Then saith one of his disciples, Judas Iscariot, Simon's son, which should betray him, [5] Why was not this ointment sold for three hundred pence, and given to the poor? [6] This he said, not that he cared for the poor; but because he was a thief, and had the bag, and bare what was put therein (John12:4-6).

Shannon, Tony and I, September, 2021

27. SHOWDOWN AT JAKE'S BAR

N. Chili, N.Y., 2011.

Jake's Bar, nestled in the middle of a small shopping area, is near Roberts Wesleyan College. Toward the end of a home assignment, I thought I'd go in and strike up some friendships with the locals. I was to meet Barry S., a college official, for lunch, and thought to surprise him by dining at the neighborhood watering hole. The college, however, has stipulations about cowpokes straying far from the corral, so our venue changed. He paid, but Jake's went on hold for another two years.

Our next furlough was in winter. I was in my car wrapping a Dollar Store present for my friend, Jim, when a pickup bumped my trunk. The driver got out, saw no damage, and walked at an oblique angle into Jake's. I tapped my ash tray for its quarters and followed. The place was packed, and I couldn't find the guy who'd made an impression on my car. I stood there in my over-sized coat and dorky ski cap, looking…dorky. Jake came around the corner and, in a rare moment, I was at a loss for words. I shrugged and walked out. The next week, Jake's had three customers. I sat next to a truck driver at odds with the jukebox. BTW, a mere repetition of expletives doesn't make up for a lack of imagination. He also quarreled with the barmaid, whose name I'll not divulge, not should a hundred maighdeana (mermaids) grant my wishes. I ordered lunch, and we talked a little treason. My neighbor, E., when he wasn't jousting S., the lady of mention, continued to wrestle the juke box. My first impressions of Jake's were not positive. In furloughs since then, E. has bought me lunch, and shared aspects of his life I felt privileged to hear. Others, too, have shared their story. I learned when I get bumped, don't get bummed. Shrug it off. One impression continues unchanged; Jake's baked beans are to die for!

Grace Lover: Thou therefore endure hardness, as a good soldier of Jesus Christ (II Tim. 2:3).

Curmudgeon: And be not drunk with wine, wherein is excess; but be filled with the Spirit (Eph. 5:18).

28. THE GLASS HOUSE

Hilo, Hi., '74.

"I wanna go back to my little grass shack in Kealakekua, Hawaii, where the Humuhumunukunukuapuaa go swimming by," (*Little Grass Shack*, by Harrison, Cogswell, and Noble). Ever hear of the Humuhumu…? It's a fish, and the longest word in the world! You'll need to know that someday. Ever hear of the Shepherding Movement? The Fellowship of Christian Pilgrims, a commune, was part of it. We imitated the Early Church. We took mothers off welfare, and didn't use Food Stamps. Folks gave up insuring their cars to put more trust in God. Submission to elders was where we got a little off-balance. We all have feet of clay, or pumice in our case. In Hilo, fifteen of us rented the mansion of a former senator of the legislature. We shared resources, had daily devotions, and sexuality was in line with scripture—usually.

In the back of the premises, near a waterfall, was a greenhouse. Here I held my first revivals. I preached my first sermon to anthuriums, spider lilies, and mothers'-in-law tongues. The latter were the most receptive. Having tried the plant circuit, I moved to a larger venue—chapel. Everyone wanted to get saved, if we don't count the Heavenly Host. David, my audience of one, was a wonderful brother challenged with depression. He'd prayed the Sinner's Prayer before. The next year, I became the steward of a household. In devotions one morning, I threw in some alliteration: "the dead, the damned, and the dying." One of the two attenders objected to hot-dogging a holy office. Not all movement was forward. A few years earlier I'd stood outside the auditions for our school play, vacillating between a thespian debut or enjoying the safety of the audience. In the end, I walked away. Now I'm a street busker for the Lord. If you heard me croon, you'd think me exceptionally brave. It appears our doing the impossible brings the Lord great delight. What does He want to do with us today? What Spirit adventure? What thing foolish in the World's eyes? So, Pilgrim, let's circle up those flower pots, and…

Grace Lover and Curmudgeon: Wherefore take unto you the whole armour of God, that ye may be able to withstand in the evil day, and having done all, to stand (Eph. 6:13).

29. THE OREO COOKIE PRINCIPLE

Do your eyes glaze over at lists of multi-syllabic words? At a Coaching Seminar of One Mission Society, *affirmation* found itself in the discussion. While I translated the gobbledygook into colloquial vernacular, our instructor, Bob Warren, held up a cookie.

"Let me show you the Oreo Cookie Principle," he said. Call it transference, but I expected him to eat it. "This outside is affirmation," he said. "This white part is feedback, and the last part, also, is affirmation." Now he was speaking my language—*Oreoish*. I'm in my golden years, and a bit generous at the core of my being, so, when it comes to Oreos, I scrape out the center. Then I hide it so my son doesn't gobble down a wad of sugar and oil. On that day, my son being absent, Bob noted the ball of goop on my plate.

"You like affirmation, but not feedback," he said. He was spot on! Like Pooh, my ears seem to be stuffed when advice arrives. Bob said the key to unlocking potential in others is listening and asking probing, open questions that one can't answer with a "Yes" or "No." The coach lets people discover their own obstacles, goals and solutions. People are more likely to act on their own plan than a suggested scenario. Pouring wisdom and knowledge into another is mentoring. Coaching encourages self-discovery. It's a way of thinking. It starts with a question. What kind of coach are you? That's an open question. What did you think of it? Oh, there I go again. You see, it's catchy.

Grace Lover: When Jesus came into the coasts of Caesarea Philippi, he asked his disciples, saying, Whom do men say that I the Son of man am? [14] And they said, Some say that thou art John the Baptist: some, Elias; and others, Jeremias, or one of the prophets. [15] He saith unto them, But whom say ye that I am? [16] And Simon Peter answered and said, Thou art the Christ, the Son of the living God (Matt. 16:13-16).

Curmudgeon: And they sent out unto him their disciples with the Herodians, saying, Master, we know that thou art true, and teachest the way of God in truth, neither carest thou for any man: for thou regardest not the person of men. [17] Tell us therefore, What thinkest thou? Is it lawful to give tribute unto Caesar, or not (Matt. 22:16-17).

30. THE GLASS BOAT

Bradenton, Florida, 1960.

"You're kidding me, right? Glass can't float," I said.

My father assured me it could. Though usually very trusting, I remained somewhat skeptical regarding his claim. Grandpa was going with us, so even if we sank, I would die happy having him close. Hours later, speeding through the waters of a Florida lake, the ability of glass (fiber glass) to float was a forgotten topic. We were catching tons of fish. I can say tons, this is a fish story, ok! Yes, it was double figures for everyone-even me—at the age of ten.

We hadn't brought any lunch, and it took us a little longer to get back than expected. Suddenly, Dad remembered he had a slice of American cheese in his pocket. He pulled it out to unveil a warm slice of orange colored, processed cheese product. You would have thought it were aged Jarlsberg from the King's cellars the way we spoke of its texture and bouquet.

It was a glorious trip until we arrived home with the bucket of fish. I was enthusiastic about helping Grandpa, the Poseidon of the Floridian waters, prepare our fish dinner! But, at home, we dug a hole, my role being to dump our fish in it. Not even one would be de-scaled, not one destined for the frying pan. Why had we taken their lives if not to eat them? It was the first and only time I realized Grandpa's feet had not descended from Mt. Olympus. I, of course, made excuses to save his reputation in my own eyes. That was the first and only disappointment I remember about Grandpa.

Was David's offense with Bathsheba a disappointment to God? God's anger, love, even regret is logged in scripture. David's illegitimate son of an adulterous affair died, and David's family had no peace until the day he died. Our faux pas have consequences, but how is David remembered? He is the Sweet Psalmist. People disappoint, love restores. Are you disappointed with someone? Consider them a Sweet Psalmist. Then look in the mirror; that should heal you. You've been a disappointment too! Did I mention my grandpa was the best grandpa ever?

Grace Lover: Moreover if thy brother shall trespass against thee, go and tell him his fault between thee and him alone: if he shall hear thee, thou hast gained thy brother (Matt. 18:15).

Curmudgeon: But if ye do not forgive, neither will your Father which is in heaven forgive your trespasses (Mark 11:26).

31. KENJO SENSEI

Kusanagi, Japan, 1992.

Years ago, the Norwegian government was giving away money to encourage people to change their name. There were so many Johannsen families it was confusing. The most prevalent family name in Japan is Suzuki. Ok, you could research that, but do you know the family in Japan with the record for the most members? At one time, the honor belonged to a friend, Pastor Kenjo. He had either ten or eleven siblings. Since that time, another family has taken the record.

There was something even more distinguishing about Pastor Kenjo. I don't believe he went to seminary or was accepted by any denomination. The first time I met him was at the Kusanagi train station. He had a guitar, was singing, and sharing the word of God. He had a wondrous smile, a big heart, and a ten-gallon hat. Our meeting moved me. I sang along as best as I could, which was rather feeble, but it was too late. I'd been stirred. Soon I had my own guitar and was doing the same thing, though not with the same skill or fulness of heart.

One day, I received an invitation from Kenjo Sensei. He, I, and a banjo player who'd played at the Grand Ole Opry, participated in a Bluegrass Festival at a bar. It was awesome! We had six bands and fans in an area that would constitute the size of an American living room. The two men played guitar and banjo, and I reinforced the orchestra with a tambourine. They sang parts; I sang melody—easy peasy. Our song, *I'll Fly Away*, had most folks joining in—they knew the hymn in English! It was one of the best experiences of my life. Kenjo Sensei took it in stride. He did the same the day we had a T.V. interview—he was humble. But my favorite memory of him isn't sensational. I saw him early one morning pushing a cart, collecting roadside recyclables. He supported his family by collecting garbage. He distributed God's jewels, hither and thither, and gathered garbage for himself. No degree, no mega-church, just Jesus' love.

Grace Lover: Be ye followers of me, even as I also am of Christ (I Cor. 11:1).

32. SNOOKY, BUTCH, SKEETER, AND THE MOUSE

W.B., N.Y., '58.

Post War Camelot, the era included "See the USA in your Chevrolet," the Yankee Dynasty, and Disneyland's Opening. The end of Prohibition ended Dutch Shultz' reign as a rumrunner, nevertheless, we still had crime fugitives. The Eel, was apprehended nearby. Neighborhoods had holdovers of earlier times. Nomenclature lacked nothing of those gangster days. We had the Bowen Gang, and Butch, Snooky, Skeeter, and The Mouse. What names! Was it parents punishing progeny? Did kids pick monikers in defiance? Or did the populace label them in retribution for the reign of terror imposed upon the fiefdom?

The Bowens had an underground outpost in the Scrub Pine we called—The Woods. The gang's name invoked fear. We'd heard they were 12 years old and 10 feet tall. Other names were of solo brigands. Butch stole my family's garbage pail cover, filled it with gas, and attempted to burn down The Woods. He also pilfered my Al Kaline Trap-Pocket, baseball mitt—a hangin' offense! Snooky, at 9 years of age, had the girth of a sequoia. Like the *Sauria* of old—the Earth shook under his tread. Assaulting us with a gun left us soaked! His dad confiscated it publicly, much to our fear of reprisal. Skeeter's dad was a Flying Tiger and awarded me a scarf from his silk parachute. Skeeter could've serviced his dad's airplane. He knew about pistons, carburetors, and infernal combustion, but his real genius was procuring contraband—cigarettes. Last, The Mouse was led at knife-point to take his gun, and help a drug dealer to recover some cash. Such was Camelot. So, what's in a name? The Bowens grew up without incident. Butch moved away. Snooky became a musician—cool. He was a Christian—not so cool, but I no longer feared him. Skeeter joined the Air Force, and I stowed away in his barracks. I lived at the Mouse's house after flunking college, a Food and Drugs for Work program. We all have our Butches and Snookeys. At those times, it's good to have The Name to call on.

Grace Lover: For whosoever shall call upon the name of the Lord shall be saved (Ro. 10:1).

33. THE SHOT HEARD ROUND THE GOURD

The Country Garden Market, Lewisburg, Pa., '77.

A 22 caliber, as guns go, is rather unimpressive. Then again, when it's pointing in your direction instead of a squirrel, attitudes may change. It was late summer and I don't know if we had gourds or not, it just sounds better than rutabagas. Then again, *The Rutabaga Rampage* has a certain wild freshness to it. Anyway, I was sweeping the floor near the front doors. The clerk had taken the money tray out of the register and carried it and the keys to lock up. It was 11 P.M. She stuck the key in the door and began to turn it when a masked figure appeared and pulled on the door. He demanded she open it. He pulled violently on the handle. Then there was a shot. The bullet passed through the glass and hit the floor. The girl screamed and ran toward the back of the store. I ran as well. My first thought was two individuals were involved. I wanted to get the back door secured quickly. To be honest, I screamed too; at least not as loud, and called the police.

A peaceful summer evening changed dramatically. Bodies, money, and rutabagas were still intact. What is a rutabaga? I think it's purple on the outside and white on the inside—kind of like me after attempting sports. Regardless, God knew all. We however… We don't know much, do we? Do we know of the world unseen and Heaven's time-tables? It gives some pause, but most of us go blindly on our way. Wake up, Neighbor. Open your eyes before you are resurrected with an unregenerate heart that will leave you naked and dumb in His presence. He wants better for you. Now His Spirit is restraining evil. He will not always do so. Come on home, Friend. Call on Him today.

Grace Lover: We then, as workers together with him, beseech you also that ye receive not the grace of God in vain. [2] (For he saith, I have heard thee in a time accepted, and in the day of salvation have I succoured thee: behold, now is the accepted time; behold, now is the day of salvation) II Cor. 6:1-2.

Curmudgeon: Wherefore he saith, Awake thou that sleepest, and arise from the dead, and Christ shall give thee light (Eph. 5:14).

34. 900 B.C.: The Gezer Grammar

"'Why am I writing this line upward?' You ask a good question, teacher. Can you guess why?"

"Shovav, your father will whip me if you do not surpass the others."

"You avoid the question. Is it because you do not know?"

"If I provide you with an answer, will you resume your study?"

"It is possible, is it not?"

"Since you are determined to have me beaten, I'll say, due to your artistic leaning."

"No, it is because we speak of the cycle of life, sowing, harvesting, and so forth. This horizontal line is life sprouting; Man reaching toward the heavens. It is doubly appropriate. yes?"

"I think you are clever beyond your years, and I shall be both beaten and unemployed."

"Fear not, I will bury this so it's never found, and make one to your liking. Am I a good boy?"

1902-1909

"The expedition of the Palestine Archaeology Foundation has, exceeded the expectations of its collaborators. The Calendar is a monumental find. Robert Macalister will not be forgotten."

"Who did it?" Macalister asked. "Who wrote it? A scribe? A scholar in the making?"

"Unanswerable but interesting, Robert," the chairman admitted.

"Yes, but a written record on frail limestone gives testimony to a life three thousand years ago—a real person. It's reminiscent of the biblical account of the "books being opened"?

"Perhaps, Robert, or maybe you spent too much time in the desert!"

Grace Lover: And I saw the dead, small and great, stand before God; and the books were opened: and another book was opened, which is the book of life: and the dead were judged out of those things which were written in the books, according to their works [15] And whosoever was not found written in the book of life was cast into the lake of fire (Rev. 20:12,15).

35. PAST-DUE PICNIC

Lewisburg, Pa., '77.

Summer picnics and tag football, great! I like tag football—I break easily. Pastor Paul's wife, Miriam, was genteel. The week after the picnic, we all chatted about the fun. I'd had a long touchdown pass. Doug Flutie had his Hail Mary pass; I had my Apostles' Creed launch. It took more prayer for my passes. Miriam said:

"Chris, that was a nice fruit salad you brought." She knew I was working at the local market. Bruised and past due items went into the dumpster. She didn't know I helped myself to the remnants.

"Oh, thanks. I got a lot from the dumpster," I noted. Marley's untethered, flapping jaw could not hold a candle to Miriam's inward reaction. Her gentility on auto-pilot, she responded,

"Oh," and grew quiet, probably to stifle her gag reflex. They say there is no such thing as a free lunch—well, there was once. Most of the time, we need to pay as we go. King David realized this. To stave off the plague the Lord had sent upon Israel because of the King's census, David went to Mt. Zion to sacrifice to the Lord. Araunah, offered to sell the land there to the King, and throw in the sacrifice for free. David's response was:

"How can I sacrifice to the Lord that which has cost me nothing?" II Sam. 24:24.The best gifts are difficult to give. It's not special if it's easy.

Grace Lover: But I will sacrifice unto thee with the voice of thanksgiving; I will pay that that I have vowed. Salvation is of the Lord. [10] And the Lord spake unto the fish, and it vomited out Jonah upon the dry land (Jonah 2:9-10).

Curmudgeon: And in process of time it came to pass, that Cain brought of the fruit of the ground an offering unto the LORD. [4] And Abel, he also brought of the firstlings of his flock and of the fat thereof. And the LORD had respect unto Abel and to his offering: [5] But unto Cain and to his offering he had not respect. And Cain was very wroth, and his countenance fell (Gen. 4:3-5).

36. THE LAVA TUBE

Kealakekua, Hawaii, 1975.

Forty times more viscous than water, the hot lava flowed down the hillside, cooling on the outside to create a crust left behind as the inner contents continued toward the sea. The result was a tube of rock to be discovered in 1975 by me. Probably others had noticed, too. When I stumbled along, the entrance was on an angle, and the opening filled with rock. The tube was on my land—well… Bishop Estates was designed as a refuge from developers, to give Native Hawaiians a place to live. It was on one of these that I found myself a squatter. I subleased the property, contrary to the stipulations of the lease. I was told I would have to vacate the property. Before leaving, there was one thing I wanted to do. You guessed it; I entered the tube. Lying down, I slid in, slowly. I brought in candles with me and lit them along the way. The first chamber was the size of a living room. One section of rock, the size of a large couch, had fallen from the ceiling. As I proceeded in, the tube got smaller. Fifty feet in, it had decreased in height and width of a meter. Having gone as far as I could, I followed my candles out. I left them and matches in the cave for future spelunkers. *The Late Great Planet Earth* was a recent phenomenon. I was of the opinion the End Times were upon us; I left one other thing for anyone forced to hide in the tube—a Bible. In my studies I color coded various topics, e.g., salvation, widows and the fatherless, healing, etc. It was an excellent study, but I had God figured out, compartmentalized. Nevertheless, the Word has a way of breaking down walls of any kind, mental, spiritual, or igneous.

Grace Lover: God is not a man, that he should lie; neither the son of man, that he should repent: hath he said, and shall he not do it? or hath he spoken, and shall he not make it good (Num. 23:19)?

> Wherewithal shall a young man cleanse his way? by taking heed thereto according to thy word. [105] Thy word is a lamp unto my feet, and a light unto my path (Ps. 119:9,105).

Curmudgeon: Then took Jeremiah another roll, and gave it to Baruch the scribe, the son of Neriah; who wrote therein from the mouth of Jeremiah all the words of the book which Jehoiakim king of Judah had burned in the fire: and there were added besides unto them many like words (Jer. 36:32).

37. OF PRINCES AND PAUPERS

Waikiki, 1974.

Johnny Mathis sang in the lounge, and Nissan was still Datsun. Mathis was smooth, Datsun tinny. The Sheraton is known for its beautiful exterior tile. I worked with Filipinos behind the mosaics. My boss wanted me to pledge to the United Way. He wanted a high percentage of participants. Some groups I didn't wish to support. One can designate money to certain groups, but I was new to faith, and a purist. I'd distanced myself from God in the past, and didn't want to let a molecule of space come between us. The boss shared he, too, was a Christian. He asked:

"On what page is John 3:16?" His question baffled me. "Page 157," he said, secure in his moral superiority.

"It depends on your translation," I said. That was that. My boss was reasonable, but that held no sway for me. Only eternal edicts had meaningfulness. I did things folks considered goofy, i.e., burn National Geographics teaching evolution, rebuke a dog in Jesus' Name, etc. When we're tykes, everything is an adventure. It was like that again, only in the Spirit. Folks thought I was a lau lau without the fish, but I was yoked to the Burden Bearer.

Eric Liddell wouldn't run his Olympic heat on Sunday. The Prince of Wales asked him to be reasonable. Eric had a choice: please the Prince or choose the King of Kings. He chose his King. Eric wasn't reasonable, he was spiritual. In China, he'd be martyred by folks who, in their view, were reasonable.

Listen to a Narnian perspective: "A Lion!" Susan said. "Is he safe?"

"Of course He isn't safe. But, he's good," Mrs. Beaver said.

"He's not a tame Lion," Mr. Beaver added. Being reasonable will, on many occasions, not please an untamed Lion. The Beavers agree. What do you think? Feel free to be unreasonable.

Grace Lover and Curmudgeon: Why do the heathen rage, and the people imagine a vain thing? [12] Kiss the Son, lest he be angry, and ye perish from the way, when his wrath is kindled but a little. Blessed are all they that put their trust in him (Ps. 2:1,12).

38. NEVER ASHAMED

California, '84.

Deputation at last! No, not law-enforcement. Missionaries use the word for enlisting prayer and financial supporters. Nowadays, *partnering* is in vogue. On my faith trek, I took my office, counseling center, and recreation room with me—the Trailways Bus. I rested on God's Word. even slept on it. My Bible had a padded cover. My M.O. was to go to a town, and call pastors from a phone booth. One day I took a roll of dimes and a folding chair, and sat by a library to make calls. The operator cut in once to say,

"That will be 5 cents additional, please."

"Really, how reasonable." I responded. She threw back at me:

"Yeah, talk is cheap!" I laughed, thanked her, and paid up. Then a police car drove up while I chatted with a pastor. I motioned to the Officer I'd be with him shortly. I showed him I hadn't torn out the phone book pages. After I explained, I was free to go.

My first *person of peace* (host) was a pastor's family. I stayed in their son's room. A poster on the wall inspired today's title. Pictured was a hybrid creature, a mix of dragon, unicorn, and a toadstool. Beneath it were the words: "Never Be Ashamed of What You Are: By the Way, What Are You?" We may dismiss it as a silly poster, but its message gripped me. Watch the crowd at any train station, sports stadium, or park, and you'll see all kinds of image boosting paraphernalia. People are trying to find, create, or re-make themselves. It calls to mind the question of Wonderland's Chair of Psychiatry, the Caterpillar: "Who are you?" Scripture says a follower of Christ is: a king (Rev. 1:5), a priest (Rev. 1:5), a servant (I Cor. 4:1), a child of God (Ro. 8:16), a soldier (II Tim. 3:20), an ambassador (II Cor. 5:20), redeemed (Col. 1:14), the salt of the Earth (Matt. 5:13), the light of the world (Matt. 5:14), a co-heir with Christ (Ro. 8:17), the Bride of Christ (II Cor. 11:2), and more. "Who are you?" We are a sinner or all the things mentioned. To be changed, admit you are a sinner. Who would you like to be? Tired of being ashamed?

39. 536 B.C.: THE TREASURES OF BABYLON

Ecbatana, Persia,

Dear Betrothed, Ardvi Banu,

My family is glad you adopted a name offering fealty to our deity! It will bring peace to the family, and cause the gods to allay chicanery toward us. It pleases me you aren't departing with other Jews to their wasteland home. Accompanying this letter is the earnest of your inheritance, nothing less than the gold of Ophir. What King Solomon couldn't procure I have ransomed for you, a testimony of our future wedding covenant. I await our union.

Barid, Satrap XVII

Six months later, after the funeral of Barid, in Ecbatana:

"Josiah, shalom aleichem."

"Aleichem shalom, Aradvi..., Avardi..." Josiah stumbled.

"Josiah, I am Rachel; I no longer play with blasphemy. I am a Jewess."

"I'm doubly glad. One, who can say that name? And two, you're back."

"Josiah, you always make me laugh."

"Make me sing; tell me you'll be in the caravan for Jerusalem."

"My father wouldn't survive a day of the journey. We will stay."

"When he sits with Abraham, come. The Temple work begins!"

"That is why I am here."

"I'm doubly downcast. You didn't come to see this old camel, Josiah?"

"Take this," Rachel said. It was so bright Josiah had to turn aside, but so beautiful he had to look. "It is my gift for the Temple."

"Oh, daughter of Abraham." he said, a tear reflecting the jewel.

"Lehitraot, Josiah."

"Some year in Jerusalem. Lehitraot, Rachel."

Grace Lover: Thus saith Cyrus king of Persia, The Lord God of heaven hath given me all the kingdoms of the earth; and he hath charged me to build him an house at Jerusalem, which is in Judah (Ezra 1:2).

The Wilkins home, 341 12th St., 1951-1969

40. THE ADDRESS BOOK

San Francisco, Ca., '79.

Caleb is moving into my office, and I'm down-sizing. I get Yuko's excuse of an office, a closet doing impersonations. Far be it from me to complain, but obviously, not very far. As we moved boxes, I found my address book of fifty years. The addresses are useless, except to use as clues. I was delighted my first entry was The American Bible Society—I'm so spiritual! Grandma Clark's address is there as is Bob C.'s, from the Bethpage Colonial Fife and Drum Corp (from which I was asked to leave in '69—details withheld). There are Pilgrims from the Hawaii commune (1972-75), the Andersons, Carcamos, Churchills, Brodies, Blatts, the Herricks, the Davis family, and more. To drop names, Mrs. Davis was a Miss Hawaii.

Each name has a tale. Brother Brodie, I, and several Pilgrims tried to capture a steer. We did well until his ten tons came my way, and the proverbial circle was broken. Al Herrick led our choir. Edgar Carcamo hunted wild goat, which I ate, and stayed awake all night. Mr. Davis did my janitorial service receipts. Richard and I ate lau-lau together, and Michael Anderson tempered my zeal with his wisdom. A surprise was finding Anatoly Dobrynin, the Russian Ambassador, and Senator Henry Jackson, listed. I wrote them about the persecution of Christian pastors and Jews, in Russia. Also included was a host, Furman Taisacan, from Guam. Many people have had input in our lives, some a blessing, some a challenge. God used them to shape us. We're told to pray for the household of faith and those that despitefully use us. Let's grab our address collection, whatever generation, paper or digital, and pray. Start at "A." If you're as popular as I am, this won't take long.

Grace Lover: But I say unto you, Love your enemies, bless them that curse you, do good to them that hate you, and pray for them which despitefully use you, and persecute you (Matt. 5:44).

> Rejoice evermore. [17] Pray without ceasing (I Thess. 5:16-17).

> I exhort therefore, that, first of all, supplications, prayers, intercessions, and giving of thanks, be made for all men (I Tim. 2:1).

41. NEW NUMISMATICS AND PHILATELY LATELY

San Francisco, Ca, '84.

Michael O'Shaughnessy's Mom came over from Ireland, and I traversed the USA on a Greyhound Bus. Returning from N.Y, I was short for cash, but decided to trust God, and go as far as the money took me. At the station, Dad gave me $20, which put me $2 over, but thin gleanings for meals. The services I'd scheduled canceled as I traveled west. I was happy to get a letter in Salt Lake, but discovered two fellow missionaries had died in an accident. Following that, I continued to San Francisco, arriving at Michael's church at announcement time:

"Brother Chris, welcome. Have you any news?" I told them to get bus-fare I'd asked a police officer if he'd buy some postage stamps.

"You have any of those stamps left?" Michael asked. He then had me stand by the door to have a stamp sale. Many missionary handshakes later, I had $200. I then had dinner with Michael, his wife, Doris, and his mom. It was hearty fare only improved by the conversation.

"Brother, would ye be so kind as to be passin' me the butter?" I asked.

"Nuthin' would be so plasin' to my heart as to do so," he said.

The conversation went on in like manner, when his mom piped up:

"I want you both to know they don't talk like that in Ireland."

What a trip! There was want, sorrow, provision, fellowship, and a wee bit of foolishness. I bet you thought stamp collecting was boring. Maybe, but walking with Jesus, or taking the bus, is a trip.

Grace Lover: Then he called his twelve disciples together, and gave them power and authority over all devils, and to cure diseases. [2]And he sent them to preach the kingdom of God, and to heal the sick. [3]And he said unto them, Take nothing for your journey, neither staves, nor scrip, neither bread, neither money; neither have two coats apiece. [6]And they departed, and went through the towns, preaching the gospel, and healing every where (Luke 9:1-3, 6).

42. THE HOLODECK

Space: Starship Enterprise NC-57; Osaka, Japan, '95.

Worf was walking the plank of a frigate, his destination—Tommy Jones Locker. I don't recall if he got wet, but suddenly the holodeck program froze, and everyone re-entered Stardate: #%^*@ and reality, or Star Trek's view of it. Fiction inside fiction—cool. What would you do with such a machine? I've tried this exercise in English classes in Japan. This leads to a spiritual question. Would you like to walk with Jesus? I love to imagine myself as one disciple in Jesus' band.

"Thaddeus, how is your mother?" Jesus asks, helping an old woman move a clay pot. And there's the time He cut a piece of discarded wineskin, to give Judas a belt for the money purse. Ok, let's not ad-lib scripture. But we can fill in the blanks. Take the Emmaus Road account. Who was the *other disciple*? This would be a great one to personalize., e.g., you and Cleopas walking to Emmaus when… What Old Testament scriptures did Jesus tell you? If you disciples ran back to Jerusalem, what was your time for the 11K run? Possibilities abound. What's your favorite story? Why not put on your Levitical robes, join the choir, go out before King Jehoshaphat, and sing praises to God while the enemies of Zion destroy themselves? Or eat at the house of Zacchaeus, or Simon the Leper? Can you smell the nard? Did you hear Lazarus' neighbor? Well, that's enough exercise for today, but do tell, where will you and the Lord go? It's great to personalize the Word, to own it, to ask the Lord to direct your steps as you go with Him that day, even today!

Grace Lover: Whither shall I go from thy spirit? or whither shall I flee from thy presence?

> 8 If I ascend up into heaven, thou art there: if I make my bed in hell, behold, thou art there. 9 If I take the wings of the morning, and dwell in the uttermost parts of the sea; 10 Even there shall thy hand lead me, and thy right hand shall hold me (Ps. 139:7-10).

I'm so blessed being with Jesus today, I couldn't think curmudgeonly. Blessedness does that.

43. SHOPPING CART SWEEPSTAKES

Claude Kirschner's T.V. Terry-toon Circus, 1957.

The colored curtains parted to show a large drumhead. Music at the Big Top blared, and then…then…the drumhead exploded as a puppet poked through inviting you to the Circus! First rate drama like that made it my all-time favorite show at seven years of age. Claude Kirschner was the Ringmaster, Warner Brothers had the cartoons. A contest awarded the clown, the name *Clownie*. Who would have guessed?

Almost as thrilling as Clownie were the Sweepstakes. I sent in a card, helping my mom with the entry letter and stamps. 1st, 2nd, and 3rd. place winners would have a trip to a toy store. The winners could pack as many shopping carts with toys as they were able in their allotted time. It was exciting to watch the kids scrambling, grabbing, and stuffing. Squealing with delight was the norm, but I remember one shy child who left with nothing. I can't say I felt sorry for her; she irritated me. I wanted to take her place. This memory, as it regards the girl, not my lack of charity, seems similar to our situation with God, don't you think? He lays out possibilities. Some of us take advantage of them, others go along blindly, unaware, or ignore them. It's sad, no, it's tragic. I know we all let His opportunities slip by, we just do it to different degrees. We are able not only to know God; we can join Him in great undertakings. Let's not waste our chances! Let's fill those baskets.

Grace Lover: And all these blessings shall come on thee, and overtake thee, if thou shalt hearken unto the voice of the Lord thy God (Deut. 28:2).

Curmudgeon: And Elisha said unto him, Take bow and arrows. And he took unto him bow and arrows. [18] And he said, Take the arrows. And he took them. And he said unto the king of Israel, Smite upon the ground. And he smote thrice, and stayed. [19] And the man of God was wroth with him, and said, Thou shouldest have smitten five or six times; then hadst thou smitten Syria till thou hadst consumed it: whereas now thou shalt smite Syria but thrice (II Kings 13:15,18-19).

44. SHOTGUN

N.Y., '71.

"The Good Lord watches over drunks and fools, Christopher."

Why Grandma Clark said this was beyond me until years later when I stared down the muzzle of a shotgun from the wrong end. I was with the band that night at a Long Island disco. The bearer of arms stuck it in the car window. It seems I'd voiced some unpleasantness to a member of his household. Ok, it was his daughter. I wasn't nasty until sweetness got me nowhere. Seeing the firearm, my attitude had a reversal. I apologized with ardor, and gun and Reaper retreated. I had more success with the father than the daughter. Later, band members distanced themselves from me, except one fellow who thought to set things straight by punching my face crooked. That was ok, I didn't need those guys. I could make mischief anywhere—and I did. "Man is born unto trouble as the sparks fly upward" Job 5:7. This doesn't mean since you're going to get burned go sit in a fire. In Acts 2, Peter laid it on the line to the Jews:

"You killed the Christ, the Holy One." The people asked the question:

"So, what shall we do?"

Peter told them to be baptized and ask for forgiveness. Thousands did. How about you? The Grim Reaper walked off that night, but we never know when he'll show up and expect us to have business finished. Don't wait to call on the Lord until a gun or scythe is poking through your window. Just a suggestion, Friend.

Grace Lover: In meekness instructing those that oppose themselves; if God peradventure will give them repentance to the acknowledging of the truth; [26] And that they may recover themselves out of the snare of the devil, who are taken captive by him at his will (II Tim. 2:25-26).

Curmudgeon: Thou fool, this night thy soul shall be required of thee: then whose shall those things be, which thou hast provided? [21] So is he that layeth up treasure for himself, and is not rich toward God (Luke 12:20-21).

45. THE ISLAND OF MISFIT TOYS

The Island of Misfit Toys is in the longest running Christmas Special, *Rudolph the Red Nose Reindeer.* The Toys are stranded on an island; nobody knows their plight, but Santa rescues them, finding homes for the Pink Fire Engine, the Spotted Elephant, the Charlie in a Box and all the Misfit Gang. There was joy that day on the IOMT.

The story has comparisons and contrasts to the Kingdom of God. Like the Chosen People and the Church, the Misfit Toys are different, in trouble, and have an unseen Advocate. To contrast them, the Toys are grateful regarding their deliverance; the Israelites grumble shortly after their Songs of Deliverance (Num. 14). In Psalm 106:7,8, we see the character of Yahweh and His People; the People fail repeatedly, Yahweh forgives repeatedly. The Toys are also analogous to the Gentiles. Though outcasts, God brought them into a relationship with Him. The Church has problems, too, e.g., Ananias and Saphira, and their real estate debacle (Acts 5). The Church will have scandals, heresy, and worldliness. Some Christians are embarrassed by the Church, but God is still doing business—family business. We all start as Satan's Misfits. Ready for recycling? It won't be a paint job or a re-stitched seam, it'll be a total remake. Why not invite the author of Christmas to your island? Why be a Misfit? You can be reclaimed.

Grace Lover: But God hath chosen the foolish things of the world to confound the wise; and God hath chosen the weak things of the world to confound the things which are mighty;[28] And base things of the world, and things which are despised, hath God chosen, yea, and things which are not, to bring to nought things that are: [29] That no flesh should glory in his presence (I Cor. 1:27-29).

Curmudgeon: Our fathers in Egypt did not understand Your wonders; They did not remember the multitude of Your mercies, But rebelled by the sea—the Red Sea. [8] Nevertheless He saved them for His name's sake, That He might make His mighty power known (Ps. 106:7-8).

46. 46

One is The Loneliest Number is a '60's song by Three Dog Night. Its theme represents many disciplines of our ethos. I thought Math could be an exception, but a line is an infinite collection of singular points. It may be a stretch to say they are lonely points, but even when the lines fall in pleasant places (Ps. 16:6), they dissemble into an archipelago of dots. In truth, any line is a lonely line. No #2 pencil makes a solid line of defense against isolation. i.e., there will always be a space somewhere, a lonely space, and in that lack of wholeness, there is chaos. You may be curious where this line of thought goes. Forty-six is not lonely. One reason would be its numberness. It isn't 1 or 2, it's more. Second, it's surrounded by a vast number, and no, I don't mean 45 and 47 (let the reader understand). Last, though there is no lastly with this representative of quantity, it is singular, though expansive, pervasive, and all-encompassing. Considering the gravitas of the topic, I've written rather frivolously. To be faithful to the topic, and the One behind all, we should realize any presentation will be inadequate. Suffer me one last digression. In Douglas Adams' *The Hitch-Hiker's Guide to the Universe*, a contingent of life-forms seeks an audience with God to inquire as to the answer to life. The answer they receive is 42! They then must wait several million years for the Question of the Universe, at which point, the average life-form would say: "Oh bother." Adams' book offered a farcical, satirical view of life—and everything. What is offered today is the consummation of meaning, of life, and everything. Adams had it wrong. The answer was 46, not 42. Not the thing itself, 46 is the number of times the idea is mentioned. In the Book of Revelation, a phrase or word, with that frequency, occurs. The book has 404 verses. This topic is involved in 10%. That phrase or theme is the *Throne of God*. Considering the upheaval revealed, it's reassuring the Throne of God, and He who sits upon it, in particular, retains His prominence in the affairs of the Universe. Would topsy-turvy, alone, or stressed, describe your life? Don't *go-it alone*. We can go boldly to the Throne of God, in a time of need, seeking mercy (Heb. 4:16)—no millions of years wait or royal run-around. He has an answer. He is your answer.

47. FATHER AND DAUGHTER: FIRST DANCE

"Hello again. You are my Father?"
"Yes, my little one, I am."
"I am happy you are here."
"Actually, I never leave you. I was with you before you were here."
"Where was that?"
"You were in my heart."
"Such things are beyond my pool. I like this place, Father."
"Oh, can you tell me why?"
"Before I couldn't move; now I have freedom. It is warm. Sound comes in low tones that make for nice thoughts."
"That brings me joy, my Dear."
"Oh, and my mother and I share things."
"Sharing is nice, isn't it?"
"I think so, too. It's also nice to talk with you. It…it feels right."
"It cheers me to hear you say so."
"That cold, hard thing is what?"
"That is coming to take you away from your mother."
"But I want to stay, Father."
"I know, and it is right that you should, but many others said 'No.'"
"Can you tell them to let me stay, Father?"
"They don't listen to me or hear you, my Dear."
"They don't want me, Father?"
"They are not worthy of you."
"I'm feeling strange."
"My Little One, you feel pain. I will take you home. It is peaceful there."
"I know you, Father, but before I go, can you tell me who am I?"
"You are: She Who Dances with Daddy."
"I really like that. Oh, it's starting to hurt."
"I know, Princess. Take my hand. We will dance as we go to my home."
"Thank you, Father, I'm coming. Goodbye Mother. I love you."

Grace Lover: Blessed be the God and Father of our Lord Jesus Christ, who hath blessed us with all spiritual blessings in heavenly places in Christ: [4]According as he hath chosen us in him before the foundation of the world, that we should be holy and without blame before him in love (Eph. 1:3-4).

48. TREE-HUGGERS

Lindenhurst, N.Y., '71.

"NO HOTPOTS, NO GIRLS" was old man Rendine's mantra. I had my girlfriend up once just to be free of a clear conscience. As for a hotpot, we used a heat-lamp to warm stuff, dumping the bulb into the pot. It's a wonder we didn't unleash some horrific contagion. We weren't total ruffians, however. My brother, John, had a 40's style phonograph. Our favorite LP record was Debussy's *Afternoon of a Faun*. The Moody Blues played back-up. We also had a curfew. Missing it, I once slept in the snow, awaking at 4:30 A.M, still alive. I warmed up at a gas station. Bless that attendant, Lord!

I frequented a bar that moonlighted as a brothel. I took years off the bartender's life when I declared myself a narc, and displayed my nephew Nathan's toy plastic badge. It was unconvincing to anyone who could see straight, but he couldn't. Well, I lived through that one, too. On my way home, I talked to the trees. A casual conversation progressed to touching and hugging. It wasn't kinky; I was just moved. What was I thinking? You've a right to know. You shelled out something for this book. Trees withstand the storms of life. They are long-lived and never complain. My bent was not as much ecology as idolatry.

In the *Narnia Chronicles*, Aslan warns the Talking Beasts about turning into Dumb Beasts. People who won't believe God's Word will subscribe to anything. A guy in Laguna Beach, Ca., wanted to align my stomach with the universe. One friend put prisms in her house to promote well-being. Satanists tried to groom me, but I still had enough sense to resist. So, what say we don't turn into Dumb Beasts? Want to hug a tree? Make it the Tree of Life. You need the Gardener's permission, but He turns no seeker away.

Grace Lover: In the midst of the street of it, and on either side of the river, was there the tree of life, which bare twelve manner of fruits, and yielded her fruit every month: and the leaves of the tree were for the healing of the nations (Rev. 22:2).

49. MRS. BUTLER

W. Babylon, N.Y., '59.

It was 4 hours if it was a minute. Ok, it was 20 minutes, but I was only 9, and it was cold outside. Occasionally, my brother and I were enlisted for the trek from 4th Ave. and 12th St. up to Straight Path and 11th. Street. My sibling, my senior by 6 years, and I, would head out for our destination, and upon arrival, be entrusted with an envelope. On this day, we took the Radio Flyer sled we had just received for Christmas from Uncle Ed and Aunt Christine. Dad had taken moving pictures with huge lamps. It was a winter, but after filming we had a dark tan. On arrival, Mrs. Butler offered hospitality. Everything was old. "Old" like *crafted*, and deserving the designation of *heirlooms*. We got older just being there, while Mrs. Butler retrieved dad's stencil. They were trustees of the Homewood Farms Civic Association. The publication, for a square mile, had zoning and voter info, and b-days. I wasn't a fan—I delivered it! Mrs. B, as was custom, returned with Milky Way bars. We gave thanks, stuck our prizes in an accessible pocket, and readied to do battle with the elements. I got the first sled ride. We could have counted telephone poles, but my brother had other ideas. On his turn, he said: "Up to that tree." Upon reaching the goal, it was moved to a more distant tree. What a contrast between this treatment and that of the angel who had received us, the champion of a community institution, now a memory for eternal ledgers. People pass away, trickery remains.

Japan, in addition to designating things as National Treasures, honors people as Living National Treasures, *Ningen Kokuho*. Scripture tells us to honor the ancient landmarks, parents, and the elderly. If we do, what riches we may discover—a home from a previous age, hospitality to warm frozen forms, a candy jar, wisdom, and…

Grace Lover: Thou shalt rise up before the hoary head, and honour the face of the old man, and fear thy God: I am the Lord (Lev. 19:32).

> Render therefore to all their dues: tribute to whom tribute is due; custom to whom custom; fear to whom fear; honour to whom honour (Ro. 13:7).

50. THE GRANDMA CLARK MYSTERIES:

THE GUMSHOE

Gum was verboten. It was a cause of tooth decay, a sign my generation lacked discipline, and was vulgar, like putting on make-up in public. It had links to Connumist sufertuge. That's when I was 9. When I'd come of age at 11, the world had changed. I was an Initiate to a new era. The price of admission to this secret world was an afternoon with Grandma. It was her name, more than a title. To say it wasn't a title would demean it, nevertheless, as with the name, Grandma was its sole designee, no usurper ever took to the field. As for my rite of passage, what changed? For Grandma, gum was a dentifrice, an adhesive, and the possessor of no little magic. Grandma was a gumshoe. Adventures with Grandma, a common thing only by their frequency, were affixed to this goo, like fragrance to lasagna, or frost to A&W root beer. But how did *Gumshoe* become synonymous with *detective*? Did said stuff accumulate on one's sole by pounding the pavement for clues? Regardless of that mystery, we were the obverse of the coin, the shoe on the other foot. We'd not venture forth without first gumming things up. On one occasion, Grandma's knees being more mischievous than usual, it fell to me to administer the Ointment of Mystery to her footwear, Wrigley's Spearmint, it holding the most propitious properties for our capers. Turgor in the extreme caused a gradual depletion of one's supply as sticky strands suffered loss with each step. The opposite, a composite of little vibrancy, would soon lose its ability to cloy to clues. Having made ourselves attractive, we set out to pick up the pieces of our puzzle. After an hour chatting about the nice, young man she met on the train, and noting 11 times how *that* little house was just right to make *this* grandma cozy, young Christopher hoped the Magic Goo had witnessed a miracle. An iron-wrought bench sandwiched between a lamppost and a phone booth invited a needed bivouac.

"Christopher, dear, shall we see what we have today?" Grandma asked.

"Ok, but I should call my mother," I said. Frisking myself, I found a hole in my pocket. It wasn't large, but wide enough for hope to slip out.

"Shall we look, my dear?" she suggested with unflagging zeal. I took the proffered tissue, and set to extracting a clue from her shoe, when she exclaimed: "A double blessing. Probably because you went left at Forsythe. Aren't you clever!" Grandma called me clever if I could open a door or fold a napkin. I began to uncover our miracles, clues, and tickets to hours of endearing discourse, or practically speaking, filthy litter from an anonymous sidewalk. Part of the filthy litter, however, was filthy lucre.

"Oh look, my dear, a quarter. You can call your mother," she said. "Should we first discover our other shoe's offering?" she asked. Being practiced unveiling Grandma's verbal nuances, I could be a candidate for any world-class intelligence agency. Questions often tipped the balance with suggestions. I massaged the shoe, enticing it to surrender, like rubbing an alligator's belly. Alas, the footwear fell asleep. The prize was mine.

"It's a coupon." The pavement's make-over left it shredded. My stomach rumbled. Yes, I was for abrogating the prefix to our super-natural escapade. I wanted to eat! This wasn't helped as I espied The Donut Express. I moaned from a cloud of whipped cream atop an incline of glazed fruit.

"Christopher, dear, I have 84 cents. That, and our quarter, covers the bill, leaving *two cents* to throw in," she said. I hadn't heard about two cents. I was only an 11-year-old kind of clever. "If we find this place, we get a free donut with coffee. I'm sure they'd switch that for a cup of tea, don't you think, dear?" she asked, her 80-something years coming across more like 7.

"I think so, Grandma."

"That young man may know where it is," she added. Were beards like tree rings, he'd not be a day under 100.

"Christopher, dear, do you know the place?" I pointed across the street; Grandma's feet took to the air. "I'll enjoy the tea, and you, the donut. Is that acceptable?" I shook my head in agreement. Moments later, the waitress took the gooey coupon and let us have tea.

"Next time we'll have one sole gummed for fancy, and one un-gummed, for fact. We wouldn't want people to think we're total dreamers, would we?" she continued before I could respond. "All this and Heaven, too, Christopher, my dear," she said, sighing as she lifted herself up.

"Amen," I said, clasping her hand lest Elijah's chariot whisk her away. I don't remember our chat, but it was musical accompaniment to eating the best donut ever.

Maybe today's tale didn't present a deep mystery but alas, gave a sense of mystery. As we look at Isa. 11:6, Matt. 18:3, and 19:14, it appears adulthood has left behind some things helpful to a full, spiritual walk. If a little mystery can spice up a day, a chat, or a donut, what else could it do? Walking in the Spirit doesn't mean we have to lose a sense of magic or mystery.

51. MARDI GRAS

New Orleans, La., '71.

I awoke peering into the eyes of a 6' long cat, *felis hominis*. You probably smell a rat from the very nomenclature! Also, I've noticed most cats don't wear make-up. Yes, I was incarcerated, in the hoosegow—jail! My evening had been too spirited. In the paddy wagon, I railed on the arresting officers, a rare thing as I'd always been a happy drunk.

Two things happened in jail. Twenty-five of us waited in a cell. One fellow had no shirt, or much of a neck—it appeared he'd had an operation. Please forgive what follows, it's a little raw, but in my condition was quite compelling. He stood with his knees partially bent, like Christ on the cross. and slowly undid his pants. He then stretched his arms out. I mean no disrespect, but for me he was a Jesus figure. The scene evoked deep feelings in me. I was caught between laughing and crying. The cell group was also quiet. Someone, at last, broke the trance:

"Sit down, you pervert." Perhaps the metaphysical plain, though elevated, is not a wide place in such a setting. But God can meet us in the strangest ways and in unexpected circumstances.

The second thing was my Court-hearing. The arresting officers that I'd maligned had written my name as: "Chris T. Opher." The judge threw out the charges. It wasn't a mistake; the officers just wanted me off the street. I missed the Mardi Gras, but was reminded of Christ. I did meet some Christians, and except for the pretty one, ignored them. It would take a few more doses of pain and mercy for the Lord to get through to me. As I left the Courthouse, I jumped up and clicked my heals. I waited to do so, however, until I was right next to the exit!

Grace Lover: Or despisest thou the riches of his goodness and forbearance and longsuffering; not knowing that the goodness of God leadeth thee to repentance (Ro. 2:4).

Curmudgeon: For the grace of God that bringeth salvation hath appeared to all men,

> 12 Teaching us that , denying ungodliness and worldly lusts, we should live soberly, righteously, and godly, in this present world (Titus 2:11-12).

52. THE PILLOW

Bethpage, N.Y., '69.

Going steady with Debbie was rocky. I was in college; she was in high school. Why didn't her sister approve? The vending machine ring I gave Debbie was a generic high school style ring without even enough imagination to pose a fictitious school name. Its purchase was witnessed by friends, so my knowledge of gemstones would not go unnoticed or unpublicized. Cheap offerings can suggest shallow, self-serving interests; but not always. I really liked Debbie, and was crestfallen when she dump… um, pursued other interests.

Enter the pillow. Shortly after we got married, I presented Yuko with a fire-engine red pillow, bearing four letters: LOVE. Fire-engine red does not equate with tacky! It was presented with other gifts for Mother's Day, so the fact it was only a dollar purchase should not diminish the reputation of my ardor. This morning, I arose and drew the drapes. The pillow which has adorned our bed for 15 years, had fallen and was collecting dust, as if to say: "That's what happens when you neglect me." Dusting it off was difficult. The dust was small, and attracted to the pillow, or the pillow to it, and resisted removal. I took the symbol of our love and rubbed it on my pants, taking the dust on myself. Cleaning up our love meant getting dirty, taking effort, using wisdom. And so, devotion #52 comes gratis my unkemptness, and God's grace. We must put effort into getting our love in shape. This includes massaging, dusting, getting dirty, and placing it in the center of our attention.

Grace Lover: Though I speak with the tongues of men and of angels, but have not charity, I am become as sounding brass or a tinkling cymbal. [2]And though I have the gift of prophecy, and understand all mysteries, and all knowledge; and though I have all faith, so that I could remove mountains, and have not charity, I am nothing. [4] Charity suffereth long, and is kind; charity envieth not; charity vaunteth not itself, is not puffed up, [6] Rejoiceth not in iniquity, but rejoiceth in the truth; [7] Beareth all things, believeth all things, hopeth all things, endureth all things (I Cor. 13:2,4,6-7).

Curmudgeon: Nevertheless I have somewhat against thee, because thou hast left thy first love (Rev. 2:4).

53. NOBURO YAMAMOTO

Hilo, Hi, 1973.

The blue box was for Moana Loa Macadamia Nuts, the brown one was our competitor's. They were bigger, but we were growing. I had many jobs. As a flag-waver, fertilizer planes dropped pellets on my head as I marked the row of their cargo drop. I also rode flatbeds, tossing trees in holes the backhoe had drilled. I once found a wounded Io owl there. My boss, Yamamoto, Noboru, was a diligent, quiet, Nikkei (2nd generation Japanese-American). One day he told me his name was propitious because his surname and given name fit together. *Noboru*, means *ascend.* His family name, Yamamoto, meant *the origin of the mountain.* This chat was one encouragement to study Japanese. Yamamoto san made hybrids by splicing branches together. He'd cut the host's end in a "V," and the scion to fit the host. To finish, he'd use paraffin or tar. He was a craftsman. It was a pleasure working with him, even though planes dropped pellets on my head.

We have an artisan without peer, Yahweh. The fruit of His labor is… just look in the mirror. He still has some trimming to do, so don't get smug. Some pellets may come your way, but don't worry, He grafts us in nice and snug. Enjoy, and bear fruit! If you're not grafted in, what are you waiting for? You don't want to end up a dead branch, do you? There just isn't any life without Him.

Grace Lover: I am the true vine, and my Father is the husbandman. [2] Every branch in me that beareth not fruit he taketh away: and every branch that beareth fruit, he purgeth it, that it may bring forth more fruit (John 15:1,2).

> Above all, take the shield of faith, wherewith ye shall be able to quench all the fiery darts of the wicked.[17] And take the helmet of salvation and the sword of the Spirit, which is the Word of God (Eph. 6:16-17).

Curmudgeon: Therefore let all the house of Israel know assuredly, that God hath made the same Jesus, whom ye have crucified, both Lord and Christ (Acts 2:36).

Corey's homecoming attendants: Uncle Rob, Aunt Flo,
Big brother, Mom and Dad.

54. THE OFFERING

N. Chili, N.Y., 2007.

We'd made a trial run to the hospital so that we'd have no problems on the big day. On the night of the full moon, time and tide had done their perfect work. Nine hours later, we were celebrating Corey's birth; days later we brought him to the Mission House. Caleb, two years-and eight months old, waited in bib overalls, as Ambassador of Welcome. When the baby basinet and new family member cozied up in a chair, Caleb made his move to present him with two gifts, one on each side of the infant. What was the nature of these benefices? In each hand was a favorite of the bearer, from a land afar, a Japanese Tomicar. Corey was oblivious to the proceeding, but the parents were moved. It was a grand beginning to our foursome. Since then, relations have had some downturns. Last night one lad's water bottle went whizzing past me, its intended target, the launcher's sibling. Overall, the intent of that initial offering has continued to the present day.

As I sit in a food court with the target of that water bottle, many parents are here with their recent arrivals. It's a parade of joy, exhaustion, hope and anxiety. What variety of offerings and gifts have been exchanged? Hopefully, the most important one has not been overlooked. Corey was unaware of the offering made at his homecoming, but our Heavenly Father never overlooks our offerings. Even so, His concern is not with us making an offering, but receiving one.

Grace Lover: What shall I render unto the Lord for all his benefits toward me? [13] I will take the cup of salvation, and call upon the name of the Lord (Ps. 116:12-13).

Curmudgeon: How shall we escape, if we neglect so great salvation; which at the first began to be spoken by the Lord, and was confirmed unto us by them that heard him (Heb. 2:3).

55. REFORMED FEMINISM

Jeanne of Navarre was born in 1528, the daughter of King Henry II of Navarre, and the sister-in-law of King Francis I of France. She was a formidable force in politics and religion. She was also stubborn. When 12 years old, and commanded by King Francis to marry Duke William the Rich, she resisted and was tied-up for the ceremony. Later, the marriage was annulled. Jeanne's mother led her in the Reformed faith. In 1548, she married Antoine of the Bourbons, a nominal Protestant and unfaithful husband. In 1560, he led the Catholic army in France, and died. As sole ruler, Jeanne declared Navarre to be Protestant, and forced out Catholic clergy. Situated between France and Spain, she was pressed to return to Catholicism. A cardinal wrote to her:

"Your Majesty, you are being misled by evil men who want to plant a new religion in Navarre. If you go ahead with this, you will never succeed, your subjects will not stand for it, and your enemies will stop you. You do not have an ocean to protect you like Queen Elizabeth of England. Madame, don't let these (Huguenot) murderers, rebels and heretics ruin your conscience, your goals, and your grandeur. I implore you with tears to return to the true fold."

Jeanne was not slow to reply: "Your feeble arguments do not dent my tough skull. I am serving God, and He knows how to protect His cause. Our ministers preach nothing but obedience, patience, and humility. Keep your tears for yourself. I pray from the bottom of my heart that you may be brought back to the true fold and the true Shepherd."

In 1572, Jeanne went to Paris to arrange the wedding of her son, Henry II, to the daughter of Catherine de' Medici. It was a political marriage to bring peace to Catholics and Reformers, however. she died suddenly at 43. It's unknown if foul play was the cause. She'd been a woman of character trying to advance the Reformation and protect Huguenots. She resisted clerics, nobles, husbands, and armies. Pope Pius IV plotted to send her to the Inquisition. All was not intrigue and wars, however. She commissioned translations of the Bible into Basque and Bearnese, and opened a seminary at La Rochelle. Her son, Henry II, left the Reformed faith when he became King of France. Others wavered, she did not. She was a princess, a warrior, a peace-maker, and the handmaiden of the Lord. What a woman!

Grace Lover: And Mary said, Behold the handmaid of the Lord; be it unto me according to thy word. And the angel departed from her (Luke 1:38).

56. THE MAGIC RABBIT

W. Babylon, N.Y., '54.

I remember the Arfy Gaffy show, being too young to pronounce Arthur Godfrey. If I wanted Mom in the morning, she would be in the living room. One day, feeling peckish, I slid across the floor to the big T.V. with the small screen. I passed my bow and arrow, and then averted my eyes from the erased but still visible pencil marks on a fortress duplicated many times on the living room's wallpaper. Finally. I approached the Queen Mother. Playing his ukulele for my amusement was the Court Minstrel, Arfy Goffy.

"Mother, I'm hungry. Could you summon the Magic Rabbit?" I didn't actually say "summon," but it sounds courtly, don't you think?

"Of course, dear," she said. In moments, the Canopy Royale was erected. One churlish knave spoke of its resembling a coffee table with a sheet, and thereupon was banished without cookies. I entered the canopy to discover hot waffles and syrup. I expressed my royal pleasure. Weeks later, unable to finish my morning repast, I summoned the Magic Rabbit again. The Lavender Rabbit and the Brown Teddy Bear were both in attendance prior to their exile. They joined the feast only to discover the cold toast that had failed to please earlier. I was livid;

"That Magic Rabbit won't be summoned again!" I promised, departing the court, quaking subjects, and ukulele music. "Let them eat toast," I declared. Be wary of Magic Rabbits—they're tricky. They don't deliver on promises, but folks keep calling them back. It's better to eat breakfast when you're supposed to.

Grace Lover and Curmudgeon: If a son shall ask bread of any of you that is a father, will he give him a stone? [13] If ye then, being evil, know how to give good gifts unto your children: how much more shall your heavenly Father give the Holy Spirit to them that ask him? (Luke 19:11,13).

> And no marvel; for Satan himself is transformed into an angel of light (II Cor. 11:14).

57. HOTTENTOTS

Fort Lauderdale, Fl., '70.

I had the questions to rattle Jesus Freaks:

"How can a just God send African Hottentots or Japanese Buddhists to Hell if they haven't heard of Jesus?" Or, "What about the Jewish Targums?" I didn't know about the Targums, but they didn't either. My friend Rich and I ate with a Christian group at Thanksgiving, and stayed the next day to help clean up the left-overs. I dropped the Targums on Tom. His limp response was:

"I have no answer, but I know Jesus loves you."

"Ha," I thought, "more Jesus Freak pablum," but the answers are in scripture and culture. Paul tells us people know of the invisible God and His nature (Ro. 1). God has given us a conscience—a sin detector (Ro. 2), and sent the Holy Spirit to convict us of sin (Jn. 14). These are internal revelations. An objective witness, regardless of place or tribe, is Creation: "The heavens declare the glory of God" (Ps. 19).

The second portion of this one-two punch is culture. Parts of Genesis are widespread in oral tradition and written records, e.g., the *Enuma Elish* creation tale of Babylon, or clear Biblical truths imbedded in ideographs in China and Japan. Missionaries do not account for the global knowledge of Noah's Flood. There is an embarrassment of riches in evidence if…IF we are honest. Everyone knows Him, though many reject Him. In judging God, we indict ourselves. He's the Judge, not us, but He's merciful. So, what about the Hottentots? Their conscience will judge those who do not have the Law of God. The Law will judge those with the Law. Sadly, none of us follows either 100%. Jesus, however, paid the price for your acquittal. Will you take His offer? I suspect many a Hottentot would say: "Go for it!"

Grace Lover: Which shew the work of the law written in their hearts, their conscience also bearing witness, and their thoughts the mean while accusing or else excusing one another (Ro. 2:15).

Curmudgeon: For the invisible things of him from the creation of the world are clearly seen, being understood by the things that are made, even his eternal power and Godhead; so that they are without excuse (Ro. 1:20).

58. THE COIN

Crack! The sound sped through the courtyard. The targeted shale shattered; stone slivers burst into the air. The whip recoiled into the hand of its master. The speaker's voice exercised an even more impressive display. The whip commanded attention, the speaker, submission.

"Hear me slaves. Listen well. To your credit, you were skilled artisans in your native lands. That life is over. Now, you have the privilege of serving in Caesar's foundry. If you work hard, you will eat well. You will work hard or you will die. Crescens keeps the daily tallies; Aristobulus keeps the whip. If there's a problem, they send you to me. You won't like that. Now, go to work. Oh yes, the reward for pilfering is torture. Enjoy your stay. Hail Caesar!"

Years Later in Capernaum…

"Hey, Aged Mother, come back and pay your tax!"

"Must I pay? I go to the Synagogue to make an offering and pray."

"If you can fly, there is no tax. Otherwise, you must pay."

"Master Matthew, I have one of Caesar's coins, and two Temple coins for my trip to Jerusalem."

"It's not enough. Though I'm not required to do so, I'll let you pay with Temple coins." Her silence was worse than a complaint.

"Oh, you tire me. Take your two mites before I come to my senses."

"These will be my offering in Jerusalem. I will pray for you," she said.

Matthew grunted, watching her pass slowly through the gate. His thoughts were not so slow. He loathed these poor Jews, and hated the Romans, not, however, as much as he hated himself.

Sometime Later at Capernaum…

Jesus' troupe arrives at Capernaum. Tribute tax collectors find Peter.

"Does your master pay tribute?" they ask.

"Yes," Peter answers, as if it was an accomplished deed. Later, Jesus asks Peter:

"Of whom do the Kings of the Earth take tribute, their children or strangers?"

"Strangers?" Simon answers, wondering if this is one of the Master's trick questions.

"In that case, so we don't offend them, go to the sea, and throw in a line. There will be a coin in the mouth of the first fish you catch. Use that to pay for the both of us" (Matt. 17:24-27).

Jerusalem, not long thereafter…

Two High priests, current and former, walk to the Temple area. Ananias reproaches his son.

"Caiaphas, if you'd listened to me, things would not be like this."

"I have spies following him. He'll trip up one day, and then we'll send him to the Procurator," Caiaphas counters. They arrive to witness their hireling question Jesus.

"Master, we know dignitaries do not impress you, and you teach the truth regarding God. Can you tell us, is it lawful to pay tribute to Caesar or not?"

Jesus looks him in the eye. "Why do you tempt me?" he asks, and pauses. "Show me a coin." The inquisitor does so. "Whose image and inscription are on it?"

"Caesar's," the Hireling answers.

"Then render to Caesar what is his, and to God what is His." The Priests turn away.

Grace Lover: And there came a certain poor widow, and she threw in two mites, which make a farthing.[43] And he called unto him his disciples, and saith unto them, Verily I say unto you, That this poor widow hath cast more in, than all they which have cast into the treasury:[44] For all they did cast in of their abundance; but she of her want did cast in all that she had, even all her living (Mark 12:42-44).

> Give, and it shall be given unto you; good measure, pressed down, and shaken together, and running over, shall men give into your bosom. For with the same measure that ye mete withal it shall be measured to you again (Luke 6:38).

59. DAY 1

"Bummer, he's a Christian!" I murmured to my brother, John, and friend, Richie.

It was Painted Post, N.Y., '72. Chris invited us to his home with: "Praise the Lord." I could not believe it. This was the heavy dude who introduced me to LSD years earlier. Now he was a Freak! Things got better. He had beer from Canada that was 6% alcohol. He'd stopped smoking grass, but we had our own. That high point didn't last long because, for some reason I couldn't get stoned that week. Even worse, Chris and Paula, his wife, wanted to go to a Bible study almost every day. They were fanatics. I made a deal—I go with them, then we hit the bar. So, I'd get ticked off and then get tanked up. After a while I decided to leave, but, experienced hitch-hiker of 10,000 miles that I was, I could not get a ride out of town! So, I went back to Chris' house. My brother John gave his heart to the Lord at one meeting. I had always questioned his commitment to the Age of Aquarius. His desertion did not surprise me. The next day, All the nicey-niceness oozing amuck seduced Richie as well!

That night I couldn't sleep. The Word of God and people who lived it assailed my doubts. My refined logic was: God wants people to be happy. I know miserable Christians, so I shouldn't be a Christian. I wanted to talk with Chris, but it was midnight. My brother awoke to say: "I left my cane downstairs." I offered to get it and descended the stairs to discover Chris talking to his mom. My knees were shaking. I knew this was a divine appointment and said so, though not graciously: "I give up. Praise the Lord!" That was my Day One, but the prelude began before time (Eph. 1:4). Will you heed the Divine Appointment?

Grace Lover: And suddenly there was a great earthquake, so that the foundations of the prison were shaken: and immediately all the doors were opened, and every one's bands were loosed. [27] And the keeper of the prison awaking out of his sleep, and seeing the prison doors open, he drew out his sword, and would have killed himself, supposing that the prisoners had been fled. [28] But Paul cried with a loud voice, saying, Do thyself no harm: for we are all here. [29] Then he called for a light, and sprang in, and came trembling, and fell down before Paul and Silas, [30] And brought them out, and said, Sirs, what must I do to be saved? [31] And they said, Believe on the Lord Jesus Christ, and thou shalt be saved, and thy house. [33] And he took them the same hour of the night, and washed their stripes; and was baptized, he and all his, straightway (Acts 16:26-31,33).

60. THE BOOK OF KELLS

Golden Gate Park, San Francisco, '77.

Most folks don't get excited about Tuesdays. For me, it meant Golden Gate Park, Tea Garden, Japan Town, and the Cinema double feature. In the evening I'd see Kiyoshi Atsumi (Torasan), in the world's longest running comedy series. Mifune Toshiro, Kurosawa's Musashi, was in many samurai movies. The morning was for the Tea Garden—jasmine tea, almond cookies, Japanese study, and a devotion. One week, King Tut's exhibition came to town. Not as popular, the 8th century Book of Kells, the Gospel on vellum, also arrived. The colors and Irish depictions of interweaving knots and dragons were so vivid. Even more amazing was that the Word of God was intact after many centuries.

Later, I met a Dalek, from *Doctor Who*, at the British National Museum, and viewed the *Codex Sinaiticus*, a mid-4th century Bible, and the *Codex Alexandrinus*, an early 5th century Bible. The Dalek bid me travel time, these however, suggested I pause, as I had entered holy ground.

Last, after our presentation of The *Fourth Wiseman* in Japan, Adhi, a student's dad, mentioned religious education in Germany and suggested "The Bible has been changed." We talked about the Masoretes. They were scribes, who had their issues, but they also ascribed numeric value to letters. They destroyed pages with incorrect sums. Ahdi countered: "Translation changes meaning." He then discovered translators use a collection of ancient Greek manuscripts (Interlinear Greek New Testament). The Dead Sea Scrolls also made the roll, as did the fact they have no major differences from copies they predate by 900 years. I could see Ahdi squirm somewhat, so our topic segued to Christmas stollen. His misconceptions remained but with less confidence. It's difficult for the leopard to change his spots (Jer. 13:23). Changing hearts is the Holy Spirit's purview. If you want truth, you'll discover the Word of God to be accurate, reliable, relevant, and inspired. That's a colossal *if*. Some folks find Tuesdays, a park, and a pot of tea, accommodating to such searches of import.

Curmudgeon: For we have not followed cunningly devised fables, when we made known unto you the power and coming of our Lord Jesus Christ, but were eyewitnesses of his majesty (II Pet. 1:16).

61. DOCTOR WHO

Honeoye Falls, N.Y., '86.

"Those crazy Texans just shot the President!" he said.

It was November 22nd, 1963. I was sitting in the music department of the junior high school. My music teacher, Mr. Bard, made this comment while exiting a practice room. We were broken in America. Britain had lost a giant, also. C.S. Lewis died the same day. They at least had a consolation. A new era had begun. It was the debut of *Doctor Who*.

I was introduced to the Doctor in the 80s. My brother John and I would meet to watch the Doctor travel through time in his British phone booth, dubbed the Tardis, the inner dimensions of which exceeded the exterior measurements. I remember watching it for the first time. I was an English major, a late returnee to the Halls of Academia. I knew the parts of a story: Exposition, Rising Action, Climax, Falling Action and Resolution. There are various ways of describing the same concept. Another model labels some parts as the Problem, and the Inciting Incident. As I watched, it took forever to understand the Problem. I wasn't even sure, after forty minutes, what had to be reconciled. The Inciting Incident, if you distinguish it from the Problem, was also a question mark. I didn't know what stage I was in. I loved every second of this multi-quadrant Space chaos. We went here and there in both time and Space. I wasn't sure if the protagonist would resolve or further the mayhem; or if intention and practice were in opposition. Was he a genius or a buffoon? It was awesome. It was outrageous. It was…Life.

You haven't been in a time machine lately? Okay, but thanks to media we can change Time with the flick of a switch. And as for chaos—ask someone about the future of the planet, or the purpose of life. Or, here's a good one: is there an afterlife? How will they fix the problem cited, and who's the main character in the process of Resolution? Most folks don't know where they are in the story! Welcome to the Timeless Doctor Who Chaos Scenario! Not to fret, there's Resolution and Reconciliation. It's a well-known secret. It's an Inciting Incident that's gone unnoticed by most folks. It's the Problem upon which they've have not yet acted. Their story keeps going in circles because they don't take the next step—the Rising Action, or Embracing the Problem or Enjoining the Quest, however, one likes to label it. See below for the timeless cure to personal and cosmic chaos:

Grace Lover: Call unto me, and I will answer thee, and show thee great and mighty things, which thou knowest not (Jer. 33:3).

62. THE BRIDGE

Ft, Lauderdale, Fl., '70.

Bridges have a purpose, everybody knows that, but people think of them as having different purposes. Most folks use them to traverse large rivers or chasms. If you are homeless, they are excellent for shielding one from insensitive elements. In this tale, number me with the latter group, and color me insensitive. I was traveling with my friend Richie. Our money was low, but then, when wasn't it? Disney World had just opened. We stopped at a mission for a free meal and shelter; chapel attendance was mandatory. "What? That's brainwashing!" was my take on the offer. Richie was inclined to take them up on it, not me—I was principled. I was also hungry the rest of the night as we took shelter under a bridge that was there for that purpose. There was another problem with this view of public housing—the public decided to be there, in particular, one fellow who had TB. He coughed all night. He was interesting, too. He shared a little background of the life in Bridgeland:

"Alcoholics," he told us, "to stave off cravings, buy sterno when they can't buy liquor." As we were somewhat novices to the vagabond thing, this was an eye-opener, but not one we'd care to drink. What a night. Misplaced principles didn't keep me warm, and Mr. Sterno kept me awake. Sometimes winning is losing. We'd received a tract that had the Cross spanning the Chasm of Separation of Man and God, but we still preferred bridges for other reasons.

Curmudgeon: And the LORD said, My spirit shall not always strive with man, for that he also is flesh: yet his days shall be an hundred and twenty years (Gen. 6:3).

> For the wages of sin is death; but the gift of God is eternal life through Jesus Christ our Lord (Ro. 3:23).

Washington D.C. The March for Life Parade, January 1986.

63. SEMANTICS AND THE SUPREME COURT

Washington D.C., 1986.

In the 80's, I twice marched in the March for Life Parade, in Washington D.C, in January, the month of the Roe vs. Wade Supreme Court decision. They were no picnics; it was cold. The symbol of the movement was a little red rose. It's ironic that we, who were trying to save lives, were called anti-abortionists? We were more *pro* than *anti* anything. Let me show how pro we were. I boarded a bus at a Catholic Church. I'd paid to a fund for a ticket, thinking each pick-up area was the same group. I had it wrong, but the Catholic brethren took me in, fed me donuts, and were happy to have me walk in their midst. On the other team, four young people, with two placards, accosted us loudly as we passed. We ignored them or said a prayer. On that night's news, we heard of Pro-Choice advocates and Anti-Abortionists clashing. It sounded like a confrontation. It came off that our opposition held considerable sway—all four of them. Our numbers, contrariwise, received some depreciation from the media, so what we had that day was an alliance of misdirected youth, negative semantics, and purposeful deception.

I grew up on Fifties T.V. i.e., Cowboys and Indians (Native Americans). The bad guys were said to have a forked tongue—they were liars. Later, shows about lawyers were popular. I remember the swearing-in oath of witnesses: "Do you solemnly swear to tell the truth, the whole truth, and nothing but the truth, so help you God?" There were fewer grey zones back then. Whaddya say we go retro! Grandma Clark would say: "Christopher don't ruin a good story by telling the truth." It's a great axiom for storytelling but, with respect, Grandma, it's bad theology.

Curmudgeon: Thou shalt not bear false witness against thy neighbour (Ex. 20:16).

> A false balance is abomination to the Lord: but a just weight is his delight—11:1. Lying lips are abomination to the Lord: but they that deal truly are his delight (Prov. 11:1, 12:22).

64. ARE YOU MEPHIBOSHETH?

He was the grandson of King Saul who had sought to kill the shepherd of Bethlehem, the present king of the Twelve Tribes, King David. He knew the grandsons of former Kings were often sent to meet their forbears before the coronation's hors d'oeuvres turned lukewarm.

"Open in the name of the King." boomed a voice outside his door. By the strength of it, the possessor was one of the King's Mighty Men. It was a message meant for him, but heard by every neighbor. They would be wise to leave their doors shut; he would be insane to do so. He waved off his wife and grabbed his crutches. With shaking knees, he rose to meet his fate.

"Are you Mephibosheth, Bar Jonathan, grandson of King Saul?"

"I am Mephibosheth, a nothing living in Lo Debar, the Land of Nothing."

"Then you will not be missed," the Mighty Man remarked. The prisoner was then escorted to Zion. Upon arrival, a plank supported by four members of his escort was his modest palanquin.

"Does it take such a troop to convey one lame, dead man?" he wondered. People averted their gaze. Upon arrival, he was ushered before the King, who did not wait for a sign of fealty.

"Mephibosheth..." said the seated sovereign, rising.

"Behold thy servant," the lame and prostrate answered. The King then spoke the unexpected: "I will shew thee kindness for Jonathan's sake, restore thy land, and you shall eat at my table."

Mephibosheth bowed: "What is thy servant that thou should look upon such a dead dog? I know not what to say, my lord," Mephibosheth replied.

"Well, I'm as ravenous as a she-lion with a full brood, so offer thanks, and then let's eat!"

The King of the Universe, has the right to judge you, but He's sent you an escort, and an invitation to dine at His table, continually. Reverence Him, give thanks, and eat. Bon appétit!

Grace Lover: The angel of the Lord encampeth round about them that fear him, and delivereth them.[8] O taste and see that the Lord is good: blessed is the man that trusteth in him (Ps. 34:7-8).

65. THE FROG POND

Columbus, OH., Summer '72.

We entered Painted Post, N.Y. as Hippies. John sported a cane. I had bellbottoms mended with different color strips, a suit jacket, and a Postman's cap—a dandy if ever there was one. Richie, our friend, was almost bald. The rest of him was equally boring, but he had a good heart—always shared his drugs with me. We left days later, New Creations, adorned with the same raiment, plus a robe of righteousness. Richie elected to go through Canada, John and I, the U.S. Interstate routes. John read the Word while I hitched; the next time we would switch roles. Upon arrival at Hawaii, we'd made it to the Book of Job-indicative of our experiences. One ride was with a Lutheran pastor. He had an old pulpit Bible. As babes in Christ, we knew everything about God and let our host in on it. We spoke oft of the Holy Spirit, a topic of which he was curious. However, we imparted no further knowledge to him, regardless of our impassioned repetitions of "Yeah, it's the Holy Spirit, man!"

At a commune near Columbus, we attended seminars for a week, and for board, worked in the cornfield. They made candles to support the place. One day, during devotions, an Indian, Brother Jon, said: "Ask me anything from the Bible?" It seemed presumptuous to me. An elderly gentleman stood to utter heresy, but Jon, with chapter and verse, was on him like ducks on bread crust. Later, we had an exorcism to round things off. I felt like the pastor had when talking to us about the Holy Spirit. The group's faith challenged me to go deeper in this New Life. I submitted to baptism, this time choosing to do so. As the setting was a frog pond, I considered coming up spitting tadpoles, but chose, rather, to glorify the Lord. People may not make positive changes by themselves, but God does change people. We left shortly thereafter, continuing in fellowship and the reading of the Word (Acts 2).

Grace Lover: For the word of God is quick, and powerful, and sharper than any twoedged sword, piercing even to the dividing asunder of soul and spirit, and of the joints and marrow, and is a discerner of the thoughts and intents of the heart (Heb. 4:12).

66. THROTTLED

Illinois, '72.

We left the commune riding high and full of ourselves. The problem was the Lord wanted us full of Him. Fortunately, we got a ride to the West Coast! Two guys in 1950 International Harvesters were going west, and then to Alaska to homestead, build log cabins and fish for dinner—awesome. Freezing one's butt lends a few reservations, but no plan is perfect. We were grateful, but it seemed like we traveled forever. You know why those Harvesters lasted for decades? They set the throttle to 50 mph. We had a lot of idle time. We read the Word, but there wasn't much by way of putting it into action. Once, our friends pulled over and lit up a joint.

"The Lord wouldn't mind if I had a sniff," I said.

"Oh yes, He would!" John shot back. I then understood why the Lord sent them out by two. We went two-thirds of the way across the USA with them and never took a toke! So, we did act on the Word! We went through the Badlands at sunset, which was beautiful, but did not see Mt. Rushmore. At our speed, I could have run over there and caught up with them later! At California we met one fellow's mom. A hog had attacked her, but she fought it off. Our driver was from strong stock. As for us, that long trip weaned us of some bad habits. Figuratively, John and I were throttled. Slowing down and getting out of the flow was good for us. The Lord has His ways. I wonder about our hosts' trek. Marijuana does not grow well up north, but the Tree of Life can be found anywhere.

Grace Lover: There hath no temptation taken you but such as is common to man: but God is faithful, who will not suffer you to be tempted above that ye are able; but will with the temptation also make a way to escape, that ye may be able to bear it (I Cor. 10:13).

Curmudgeon: Submit yourselves therefore to God. Resist the devil, and he will flee from you (James 4:7).

67. PLEASANTVILLE

Pleasantville, Pa., 2013.

Camp! We not only went to camp, we were the speakers. In one dormitory was a picture of a little girl next to a tent. She was the mom of one man at camp that year; he was in his eighties. Camps have history. Nowadays folks have cabins. As for adventure, I'd just bought Caleb a bike. Behind the dining hall was a lake. I was remiss sharing with my son that the bike had almost no braking action—okay, zip. So, reaching the bottom of the hill, he got his shoes washed up to the hip. BTW, Caleb disputes this version.

One day while I was sharing the Word, Pastor Brett H. was in the back with another pastor. I expressed my disappointment to the crowd. Raised an Irish Catholic, I'd heard about wild Holiness People, but to date they seemed a wee staid. I then confessed, in my best Irish brogue, I felt a Hallelujah coming on. I apologized and said,

"Sure, but I can't help meself, I'm gunna run before the Lord with all me might. If'n ye want to join me, you're surely welcome." Just then I jumps up and begins running around the chapel praising the Lord. A bunch of crazies took up the challenge. I was tuckered out in no time but waved them on to keep going! On one lap, as I passed Brett, I became aware their topic was the Holy Spirit in the contemporary Church. As he pointed to the Holy Hobblers, I heard Brett say: "That's what the Holy Spirit is doing today!" Come on, are you going to tell me Jeremiah and his siege mound wasn't a little outside the box? How about Isaiah going around naked? The Holy Spirit came upon them (Acts 2:4, 11:15, 19:6). Shall we get wild for Him? Are you claustrophobic in that box? Let's get out. One, two, three, jump!

Grace Lover: And David danced before the Lord with all his might; and David was girded with a linen ephod. [15] So David and all the house of Israel brought up the ark of the Lord with shouting, and with the sound of the trumpet (II Sam. 6:14-15).

Curmudgeon: And the LORD said, Like as my servant Isaiah hath walked naked and barefoot three years for a sign and wonder upon Egypt and upon Ethiopia; [4] So shall the king of Assyria lead away the Egyptians prisoners, and the Ethiopians captives, young and old, naked and barefoot, even with their buttocks uncovered, to the shame of Egypt (Isa. 20:3-4).

68. OF PAIUTES AND PREJUDICE

Reno, Nevada, '84.

She was an enchanting Faerie. Rising and falling on her equine mount, we crossed the desert astride each other—when I could catch up. She was my host's daughter, and I was recruiting ministry supporters. So, I died to myself daily (I Corinthians 15:31). I've multiple horror tales of horses, but that day we enjoyed a slow gallop on the soft sand. As support wasn't coming in, I dug a sprinkler trench at one home. Another day, I met a weathered-looking crew at a job center. Some folks, like one unruly job prospector, nobody hired. As for me, a farmer needed a silo cleaned. The conveyer belt bogged down when the grain got wet. I didn't work solo; my partner was a Native American. He didn't talk much, neither did I, a phenomenon only witnessed when I attempt manual labor. He told me the noisy fellow was a Paiute, a tribe disliked because of their substance abuse. Handed shovels, the farmer told us to break every 15 minutes. We ignored him. It was strenuous work, and hot, but it smelled like hay, and I liked that. By noon, the belt was clean, so the farmer paid us extra. I walked home feeling no pain. I had gas, but not the usual kind. I slept for 14 hours.

Prejudice has many roots. Nature versus Nurture is a controversy of old. One of the first attacks against Mary, Jesus' mother, was by Celsus, a Roman philosopher. His discrimination stemmed from Mary's lowborn status. A god should be the scion of the upper class. For Celsus, ethnicity was not a disqualifier, rank was. Contrariwise, the Apostle Paul spoke of racism, gender, and rank. Underneath the pigment, we are the same.

Grace Lover: For ye are all the children of God by faith in Christ Jesus.
[27]For as many of you as have been baptized into Christ have put on Christ.
[28]There is neither Jew nor Greek, there is neither bond nor free, there is
neither male nor female: for ye are all one in Christ Jesus (Gal. 3:27-28).

Curmudgeon: And hath made of one blood all nations of men for to dwell on all the face of the earth, and hath determined the times before appointed, and the bounds of their habitation (Acts 17:26).

69. THE FLYING GAIJIN OF IWATE

Iwate, '90.

"Oh yes! Oh, no! You've done it this time, Wilkie. Ooh!"

Takagi Sensei invited me to go para-gliding. I was delighted, excited, and terrified. On the way, he clued me in that he was busy and he'd drop me off. What is terror notched up a step? It doesn't matter, my scale starts at craven. Inside, I watched a video to get prepped for my final fiasco. The tape trainer was a young woman. There comes a time you tire of fear, you don't care anymore. You spit in its face and say,

"Let's do this! Besides," I said (forgive me ladies), "if she can do this, so can I." I viewed the video, met the instructor in person, not the attractive one from the recording, and went up the ski hill with my parachute and burial shroud. Only the trainer, I, and the blaring speakers were there. I couldn't speak Japanese, so, though he had a megaphone instruction was inconsequential. At the summit, I got strapped in, my strings untangled, and signaled—READY. He said something, and I started running downhill. The chute lifted behind me and towered over my head. Soon, I was doing a Fred Flintstone with my feet running in place in the air. The wind was weak and didn't take me very high. I was above the low trees, and level with the top-branches of the taller trees, which kept biting my knees. Most were of the latter category. This kind of thing is a working principle with me. So, the trainer megaphoned:

"Kurisu san, migi, migi (go right)." I smiled outwardly, thinking: "Speak English, you moron!" a sentiment no doubt incited by oxygen deprivation. Anyway, I was busy treading branches. The flight took less time than the Wright Brothers' debut. I pulled a few strings and the chute slowly closed. I landed one pace from my trainer, and bowed, surprised I'd lived. Upon reflection, I learned, to a *higher* level, what God can help us do. As for my trainer, I'm sure his memory of that day regales his fellows—the Tale of the Flying Gaijin (Foreigner).

Grace Lover: Even the youths shall faint and be weary, and the young men shall utterly fall: [31]But they that wait upon the Lord shall renew their strength; they shall mount up with wings as eagles; they shall run, and not be weary; and they shall walk, and not faint (Isa. 40:30-31).

70. TWELVE VOLTS AND OTHER POWERS

Kalakaua Boulevard, Waikiki, Hawaii, '74.

I walked, but I was on automatic pilot. We passed the Ala Wai Canal. Don Ho sang there. Daniel, my commune roommate, put a car battery, guitar, etc., in our shopping cart. At last, we arrived at Kalakaua Boulevard. It was at least six lanes in total. We set up on the wide sidewalk. It was great in those days—no trouble with the police, but I was butterflies anyway. In the course of an hour, thousands of folks passed us. We prayed for strength. Daniel strummed; my knees did the percussion. What did I say? Only God remembers. It was a mix of radio preacher, my heart, and babble. Later, the hands that had hung low were lifted.

We continued shopping cart adventures, singing and passing out the Fellowship of Christian Pilgrims' newspaper, Acts 29, twice a week. Once, a small parade came toward us. As they drew closer, we could hear music and song. Their paraphernalia shone in the sun and waved in the breeze. Dressed in orange, they spun as they danced, and drums beat as they approached with banners and spears. They were the Hare Krishna. As it was too loud to sing, Daniel and I bowed in prayer. As we finished, they had disappeared. I just glimpsed one getting in a police van. It was the work of a minute. Maybe they needed a parade license. We had interesting times on the Boulevard. What began in weakness, continued, and grew in His strength—better than 12 volts!

Grace Lover: For the preaching of the cross is to them that perish foolishness; but unto us which are saved it is the power of God. [23] But we preach Christ crucified, unto the Jews a stumbling block, and unto the Greeks foolishness; [24] But unto them which are called, both Jews and Greeks, Christ the power of God, and the wisdom of God. [26] For ye see your calling, brethren, how that not many wise men after the flesh, not many mighty, not many noble, are called: [27] But God hath chosen the foolish things of the world to confound the wise; and God hath chosen the weak things of the world to confound the things which are mighty; [28] And base things of the world, and things which are despised, hath God chosen, yea, and things which are not, to bring to nought things that are (I Cor. 1:22-24, 26-28).

71. LAMENT OF THE LUKEWARM

Stephen Foster wrote great tunes and lyrics, "Camptown Races," "Old Black Joe," and more. Many songs were about the South, though he went there only once. A favorite, "Oh Susanna," is filled with non-sequiturs. I haven't the talent to describe what he does; I have, however, tried to imitate his style:

I've fled from grace to race toward death,
His mercy was so deep.
Cheering my team I'd lose my breath.
At church raised not a peep,

Oh, my goodness,
Oh, who will cry for me?
I'm headin' fer dat Perdition
I'm so blind, yet I can see.

The preacher came and talked of Him,
My nose it touched the sky.
God's love can wash away our sin,
I vowed I would not cry.

Oh! my goodness,
My Mama cries fer me?
Her son fled to the wilderness,
In darkness to be free.

My friend came by to wake me up,
And bid me join the fold.
Come to His table, come and sup,
I scorned him thrice fourfold.

Oh! my goodness,
What friend will cry for me?
I made my choice concupiscence,
I'll pay eternally.

He that is often reproved,
And hardeneth heart's way,
Shall suddenly be destroyed,
And without remedy.

Oh! my goodness,
I have spurned them all.
Mama, preacher, my friend and God,
I'm headin' fer a fall.

Oh! my good Lord,
Help me to turn around.
To bend the knee and cross the fiord,
Let your grace to me abound.

Hey Friend, don't lament. Repent!

Grace Lover: If we confess our sins, he is faithful and just to forgive us our sins, and to cleanse us from all unrighteousness (I John 1:9).

Curmudgeon: He, that being often reproved hardeneth his neck, shall suddenly be destroyed, and that without remedy (Proverbs 29:1)

72. BUSTED WITH PORN

Waikiki, Hi., 1974.

"WE'RE BUSTED!" Daniel said. I was supposed to be the lookout. I obviously wasn't good at it. Daniel summoned me with his index finger to follow. He, David, Jim, Ken, Short Nancy, Tall Nancy, Zipporah, Ron, and I were the crew of the Kapili St. House, of the Fellowship of Christian Pilgrims, part of the early 70s Shepherding Movement. Most of my adventures were with Daniel. These included handing out our Fellowship publication, Acts 29. On one occasion, I met George Foreman. He'd just come back from Japan with an Olympic Gold for boxing. I didn't know who he was until later. Two young 20-something men talked with him. As I came up, they finished, and I had George to myself. He had big, gentle hands, and took mine in his. I told him that the paper was about the love of God. His response, that he repeated several times, was:

"Yes Sir, I'm gonna read this upstairs. My Momma, she's a Christian. She's praying for me."

Daniel and I also witnessed to Ladies of the Evening, bars, and porn shops. The latter came in two varieties, soft and hard. Soft porn was at the pharmacy. The hard porn was at separate storefronts. The clerk at one looked like a bouncer. So, what was involved? Daniel and I would split up and slip tracts into the books and magazines. We had to be careful; there were mirrors. We adapted our strategy at the pharmacy. One of us would watch for salespersons, the other did the tracts. We had several successful runs at both establishments until... So, how'd we get busted? The manager knew something was up, but not what it was.

"What are you guys doing?" he demanded. Daniel opened a magazine, and removing its tract, handed it to him. The Manager looked at it and returned it.

"Don't do it again," he said, and walked away.

Grace Lover: A bundle of myrrh is my well-beloved unto me; he shall lie all night betwixt my breasts (Song 1:15).

> Galatians 5:19—Now the works of the flesh are manifest, which are these; Adultery, fornication, uncleanness, lasciviousness (Gal. 5:19).

Curmudgeon: A talebearer revealeth secrets: but he that is of a faithful spirit concealeth the matter (Proverbs 11:13).

Fung Chil, Taiwan, 1976.

73. LDM: HALL OF THE TEARLESS

This pavilion of the Last Days' Museum had an ambience that invited respect. We forbade Hiro to look at his brochure.

"Pigs don't cry," Fung Chil whispered, but Eliakim countered,

"No, they don't sweat."

"Crocodiles cry," Thy Venn said, "oh, that's the opposite of tearless."

"A dead crocodile won't cry," Sau Fan said, smiling.

"Who builds pavilions for dead things?" Hiro asked. The rooms had collections of instruments from past ages. Gradually, the Hall's theme became apparent. They were ready to exit before finishing. A kiosk bore a receptacle devoid of decoration but for a muted red light. The robed man with a nametag declaring him to be Jeremiah, told Hiro that the Bottle of His Indignation would be mixed with the Bowl of His Wrath.

"How many lives?" Fung Chil asked.

"So why show us all this?" Sau Fan further inquired.

"It contrasts that which is to be consumed and that which will remain."

"I don't know if I will come here again," Eliakim thought aloud.

"That is true," the Old Man said.

"Is that a prophecy?" Thy Venn asked.

"No, it is already known that the days of this museum are short."

"Why?" Blong asked.

"This can't enter His eternity." They all nodded and thanked him.

Grace Lover: For thou hast possessed my reins: thou hast covered me in my mother's womb. [14] I will praise thee; for I am fearfully and wonderfully made: marvelous are thy works; and that my soul knoweth right well (Ps. 139:13-14).

P.S. I've never met these youth. I painted bookmarks for them. I once plucked a pheasant's feathers in Pennsylvania for Sau Fan and Fung Chil. Please remember them all in your prayers.

74. A PIG'S EAR

Taiwan, '91.

In Taipei, I saw red sputum on the sidewalk. Later I met a lady with a box, selling gum. I took some red fruit sticks and held out my coins. Soon after, she returned for more coins. Those sticks caused the red sidewalk phenomenon. They were beetle-nut! It was the first time I bought drugs on the installment plan.

I then went to the Chinese Treasure Museum to see its scrolls, pottery, and boxes with secret drawers. Chiang Kai Shek brought the items during his retreat from Communist forces. He hoped to preserve a way of life. Later, on a train for Kaohsiung, I talked with an ethnic Taiwanese who wanted political recognition. He also hoped to pass on his culture. Deboarding, I met Wilma Kasten, four feet and some inches, with grey hair spun into a bun. We went to the Holy Light Seminary, and I met a classmate, Alan Kilgore, a fellow student of CinA. He and his Chinese wife were ministering, using what we'd learned from older workers. Wilma took me to the Aborigine area, where she'd labored. They had large modern homes. We ate a specialty at the Aborigine Church: fat, skin, and cartilage—pig's ear. It rivaled a Mongolian sandwich—a slab of liver and two slabs of fat. Wilma's walk with her Lord was clear; she didn't speak much; she didn't need to. We prayed together, and I received the address of her married niece, who followed her aunt's mission example. She serves in Mongolia. It was great to see one generation pass the baton. This principle is in the Torah. The reading of the blessings for following the Lord in covenant, and the curses for neglecting it, were to be continued every year (Deuteronomy 11). In Philippians 4:3, Paul speaks of Clement as a fellow-laborer, possibly the same Clement who became a Bishop of Rome. Clement also wrote to the Corinthians, and was martyred. It's crucial to pass on what we've received, though it can be challenging for both parties involved.

Grace Lover: And the things that thou hast heard of me among many witnesses, the same commit thou to faithful men, who shall be able to teach others also (II Tim. 2:2).

75. RETREAT OF THE TUXEDOES

NYC, '86.

An hour earlier, *Zer Gud* rebounded off the walls of Carnegie Hall. Had we really sung Beethoven's *Fidelio* with the Metropolitan Opera Company? Fifteen of the Roberts Wesleyan Chorale sat down in the Russian Tea Room. The movie *Tootsie*, starring Dustin Hoffman, was in part filmed there. We looked smart in tuxedoes and dresses. We'd been victorious in NYC, and were ready for anything, except... The waiters in their Cossack uniforms of silk, twirled to place a butter dish; then, with a flourish and a pirouette, delivered a bread basket. Once seated, we had the foresight to request a price list. Spaghetti, the cheapest item, was $25.00, or was it $50.00? I was faint, and can't remember. We weren't booked there, but performed perfectly. On the count of three, we rose, turned left, and exited, single file.

Something else stood out that week. A music major confided: "If I had no voice, I'd have nothing." We talked a little about identity being tied to talent. For me, I had none, so life was easier—I didn't aspire to greatness. I don't want to single-out musicians; any field would do, but I remember one overweight singer, who, after a successful diet, seemed to attract praise rather than send it to whom it belonged. The big lights made her heart smaller. I can't fault her; it happens to all of us. A lot of scripture comes to mind, which suggests my penchant for vanity. Let's reflect on this from a few directions, but not from a mirror.

Curmudgeon: And Miriam and Aaron spake against Moses because of the Ethiopian woman whom he had married: for he had married an Ethiopian woman. [2] And they said, Hath the LORD indeed spoken only by Moses? hath he not spoken also by us? And the LORD heard it. (Num. 12:1-2).

> Then spake Jesus to the multitude, and to his disciples, [2] Saying The scribes and the Pharisees sit in Moses' seat: [5] But all their works they do for to be seen of men: they make broad their phylacteries, and enlarge the borders of their garments, [6] And love the uppermost rooms at feasts, and the chief seats in the synagogues, [7] And greetings in the markets, and to be called of men, Rabbi, Rabbi (Matt. 23:1-2, 5-7).

> And he said unto them, Ye are they which justify yourselves before men; but God knoweth your hearts: for that which is highly esteemed among men is abomination in the sight of God (Luke 16:15).

76. SO FAR AWAY: A SONG OF GILBOA

They are dead, or distant of heart, or changed, and you're alone, missing what gave you peace, wholeness, and happiness. There's no going back. It hurts so much; breathing needs effort. Sleep gives rest, but the gnawing, gaping abyss resurges when you awake. To let go of the pain would betray the loveliness that was life together, so you clutch it to your breast. At other times, you throw it away, only to have emptiness replace it. Which is better? Thoughts turn grey; somber is the new joy. Like Job, you can loathe your birth, or you can blame God, yourself, or someone—anyone. Rancor, however, is a fleeting medication. You find some escape there, but it only minimizes what had been grand, sublime, and beautiful.

Carole King's *Tapestry* album featured *So Far Away*, a haunting song of lost love, a cry for more time together, and recognition that it just will not be. We all have a *So Far Away* song. In *The Muppet Christmas Carol*, after Tiny Tim dies, Kermit, (Bob Cratchit), addresses the family: "It's all right, children. Life is made up of meetings and partings. That is the way of it. I am sure that we will never forget Tiny Tim, or this first parting that there was among us." Not bad wisdom from a frog! But it still hurts—bad. The ultimate insult is: "Time is a healer." Can an impersonal tick of a clock lessen our loss? But to say time is not a tool in the Lord's blessing bag would not be wise. I've lost three loves, one to each of my decision, death, and divorce. The years have lessened the pain. Loss hurts. Before he was king, David lost Jonathan, his close friend: And David lamented with this lamentation over Saul and over Jonathan his son:[19] The beauty of Israel is slain upon thy high places: how are the mighty fallen! (II Sam. 1:17,19).

After fainting in my arms, I was told Yuko had cancer. For 2 days, it was as if I'd removed my shoes at the Burning Bush. The doctor misdiagnosed her, and I left the Presence for the hubbub of life. Ecclesiastes 4:12 speaks of a three-fold cord. Think of it as you, your missing love, and the Lord. It's a lanyard that gives strength. Slowly, loss becomes a trophy on the Shelf of Grace. Pain is not forever. Don't just hang in there, dear friend, hang onto Him. He's been there.

Lover: Turn thee unto me, and have mercy upon me; for I am desolate and afflicted (Ps. 25:16).

77. THE HEINZ MANUEVER

West Babylon, N.Y., 1964.

Dad served in France during WWII. He was a radioman in the Battle of the Bulge. Other boot-campers at Fort Dix used to call him *Happy*, but he was to surrender the moniker to a big surly fellow who declared: "Around here, they call me Happy!" That's the only war story he told. As a boy, my friends and I played war games. If you lost the draw, you were the Japanese. My neighbor, Mr. McGuire, fought the Japanese before the War started. He once gave me a silk scarf made from his parachute. One day, Mr. McGuire invited me to the family BBQ. He had a Willy's Woody, and a picture of the Flying Tigers. With him was General Chiang Kai Shek. It was obvious my host was a warrior, not just because of his flying exploits. After dinner, we enjoyed chess on an exotic board of teak and mahogany he'd brought back from India. As the game progressed, I had the advantage of pieces and strength. I could feel a win coming. Then the Tiger flew in with the Heinz Maneuver! Ketchup to King's Pawn 1, Check and Mate! Similarly, Evil thought it had a victory at the Crucifixion. Were they in for a surprise: Suffering Servant to Resurrection – WIN!!! He is Risen! He is Risen indeed!

Grace Lover: For I delivered unto you first of all that which I also received, how that Christ died for our sins according to the scriptures; [4]And that he was buried, and that he rose again the third day according to the scriptures: [5]And that he was seen of Cephas, then of the twelve: [6]After that, he was seen of above five hundred brethren at once; of whom the greater part remain unto this present, but some are fallen asleep. [7]After that, he was seen of James; then of all the apostles. [8]And last of all he was seen of me also, as of one born out of due time (I Cor. 15: 3-8).

Curmudgeon: And when they heard of the resurrection of the dead, some mocked: and others said, We will hear thee again of this matter (Acts 17:32).

78. KARMA

Mountains of Thailand, 1998.

This is not a typical Christian topic. That doesn't mean it's absent from scripture. Once, when Jesus and the Disciples arrived at Jerusalem, they encountered a man blind from birth. The Disciples asked: "Who sinned this man or his parents that he should be born blind?" Jesus answered: "Neither this man nor his parents but that the glory of God may be manifest" (John 9:3). The disciples, not Jesus, held to a concept of Karma. This is suggested in Luke 13, as well.

A dozen of us joined the Elephant Tour. Our first night we arrived at a Karin village. Someone commented the Karin would belong to whichever faith group offered the best deal. Nonetheless, I was impressed, that on Sunday, the Karin sold no wares. After dinner, a large moth flew into the kitchen. A Thai said it was poisonous. It was a bright red. I tried to drop some wax on it to encourage it to leave, but missed. Another took up the torch, and hot wax ignited the moth's wings. The flame slowly enveloped the moth. Its poison turned its body into a wick.

Karma resembles truth, but leaves an individual expiating their own sin through generations. God's holiness requires punishment for sin. Jesus took the penalty, so you don't have to. Sin consumes; it will burn us, Friend. Let's not play with fire. Let's not end up there, either.

Grace Lover: But now the righteousness of God without the law is manifested, being witnessed by the law and the prophets; [22] Even the righteousness of God which is by faith of Jesus Christ unto all and upon all them that believe: for there is no difference: [23] For all have sinned, and come short of the glory of God; [24] Being justified freely by his grace through the redemption that is in Christ Jesus (Ro. 3: 21-24).

Curmudgeon: Can one go upon hot coals, and his feet not be burned (Prov. 6:28).

79. HALLOWEEN

Lindenhurst, N.Y., 1969.

"Joe, stop! The light is red!" I shouted.

"You're wearing red sunglasses, you idiot!" Joe reminded me. Lindenhurst was our target. I was bedecked in a sheet. As I had shoulder length hair, my impersonation of Jesus would be complete by taking with me a fish shaped comb and arrogance. The fish was for doing miracles, i.e., feeding the multitudes. When I hit the sidewalks, however, I focused on judgment.

"You're saved!" I proclaimed, pointing at a pretty lass. "You're damned," I told an older gentleman. It was late for common folk, and I discovered another voice of authority on the shores of Galilee. A keeper of the peace, the modern counterpart of a Roman Centurion, inquired as to our intentions.

"I'm out saving the world!" I humbly informed him. I mocked the greatest drama of history, but my attitude waned before this sincere servant of the people. He shared Christ with me, but not explicitly enough for me to jeopardize his position. I searched for a flaw in his character, but came up wanting. I liked him. He informed us it was time to hang up our nets. We parted amicably, once more escaping jail. My fish comb performed no miracles but had witnessed one.

Grace Lover: And Ananias went his way, and entered into the house; and putting his hands on him said, Brother Saul, the Lord, even Jesus, that appeared unto thee in the way as thou camest, hath sent me, that thou mightest receive thy sight, and be filled with the Holy Ghost [20] And straightway he preached Christ in the synagogues, that he is the Son of God. [21] But all that heard him were amazed, and said; Is not this he that destroyed them which called on this name in Jerusalem, and came hither for that intent, that he might bring them bound unto the chief priests? [22]But Saul increased the more in strength, and confounded the Jews which dwelt at Damascus, proving that this is very Christ (Acts 9:17, 20-22).

Curmudgeon: A soft answer turneth away wrath: but grievous words stir up anger (Prov. 15:1).

Masahiro, Edward, and James are on the left in the front row.
Doris and Winnie are on the ends of the back row.

80. MASAHIRO

Shanghai, '91.

Our ship arrived at 12 A.M. I stayed at a hostel. In the morning, Masahiro and I set out. The first evening, we attended a Chinese Opera. Masa procured a Pekin Duck for his backpack. In Beijing, we took a taxi in a route a crow flies, a one-eyed crow with a broken wing, and got overcharged. Our hotel smelled like cooking oil. The squat toilets had no doors. A man came by while I was so engaged and struck up a conversation. Another first for Wilkins. My mention of "Meguo" informed him I was American, and he shuffled off in his slippers. Having provided some sights for the locals, we went touring. Beijing had the largest McDonalds in the world. It had platforms, like little islands in the air, and 30 registers. Whereas the Chinese discovered the hamburger, they had no clue as to the nature of a cue. We left with our order days later.

We went north, leaving the Han for the Hun. The Chinese were struggling, but creative. A truck driver baked potatoes on the engine block. Wheat was put on the road for cars to thrash and thresh. In Inner Mongolia, we toured with Hong Kong Chinese, stayed in a Yurt, did a skit, and wrestled our Mongolian hosts—Masa flew in the air, his red bandana flapping. At another site, foreigners paid double. Masa had a strategy, declaring: "I Mongol." He paid the single price, but had to do it twice!

Returning, we sat under the smokestacks. STINKY! Masa ended our journey with the traditional cutting of the Pekin Duck. We sat in the grime and soot, and ate the gristle with a pocket knife, the excess oil spilling, leaving our apparel with a bouquet to turn heads (and stomachs). The Duck disappointed. Things don't always turn out as we hope. I returned to China and other parts of Asia. Masa worked in Indonesia. Adventures are great, but let's not Duck the actual issue. Let's seek the things that are eternal!

Grace Lover: But lay up for yourselves treasures in heaven, where neither moth nor rust doth corrupt, and where thieves do not break through nor steal: [21] For where your treasure is, there will your heart be also (Matt. 6:20-21).

81. MOM'S THEOLOGY

West Babylon, N.Y., 1950-68.

Dad and Mom met at the Belvederes Theatrical Society. They loved musicals. At our home, Mom set the radio to WOR, for the Broadway Hits. On Sundays, that good Catholic would turn on the *Lutheran Hour*. I remember the intro: "The Lutheran Hour, bringing Christ to the nations." The speaker, Dr. Oswald Hoffmann, had a commanding voice and a command of scripture. One day Mom declared her THEOLOGICAL GEM #1:

"I don't care what anyone thinks. That man loves God."

When in Catholic school, I loved Jesus, and leaned toward legalism. Supposedly, following rules gained merit, or a clear conscience. I was raised a good Irish Catholic, so I speak not as one peekin' through a smudged window. We had a German family living next to us, the Eichengers. Mrs. E. hung her wash on Sunday. Enter Mom's THEOLOGICAL GEM #2:

"How can that woman say she is a Catholic and hang her wash out on Sunday?" Listen to Paul's take: "By faith are ye saved, through grace, and not of works, it is the gift of God, lest any man should boast" (Eph. 2:8,9). Mom was boasting she was more righteous than Mrs. E, because our clothesline carried no burdens on the Sabbath. Jesus called the Pharisees whitewashed sepulchers of dead men's dried bones (Matthew 23:27), even though they followed 612 rules! This is a great example of how good works fail to justify. How then do we please God? "You must be born again to enter the Kingdom of God" (John 3:3). Let me quote John again: These things have I written unto you that believe on the name of the Son of God; that ye may <u>know</u> that ye have eternal life, and that ye may believe on the name of the Son of God, (I Jn. 5:13). Is our confidence in a ritual, the Church, good works, or do we have the new birth? Mom had Lupus Erythematosus. It ended her earthly pilgrimage when she was a mere 48 years old. The last things she spoke to me was THEOLOGICAL GEM #3:

"Christopher, please bring my Bible with you tomorrow."

"Sure, Mom. See ya soon."

Grace Lover: And the Jews marvelled, saying, How knoweth this man letters, having never learned? [16] Jesus answered them, and said, My doctrine is not mine, but his that sent me. [17] If any man will do his will, he shall know of the doctrine, whether it be of God, or whether I speak of myself (John 7:15-17).

82. THE UNIVERSAL LANGUAGE

Osaka, Japan, '95.

Huang Di, the first Emperor of China, has something to say, but let's hear from you. What is the Universal Language? Music? Love? Was there ever a universal language and belief system? Would over a hundred cultures with a Flood account suggest commonality? Huang Di, in 2,400 B.C., became the first Emperor of the Middle Kingdom, China. Shang Ti was the Chinese name for the God of the Universe. The emperor devised the world's oldest writing system. It has roots in a belief system from earlier times, evident in the Chinese ideographs. I'll share a few. The ideograph for a *ship* is a combination of characters for *boat, people*, and the number *eight*. (Genesis 5). The one for *righteousness* is me, and a lamb (positioned above *me*). Righteousness comes through the sacrifice of a lamb (Gen. 4). Are these biblical allusions coincidental? Let me give a couple more. *Problem*, is a garden with a tree inside it (Genesis 3). Lastly: *God, one man*, and *garden*, equals *happiness* or *blessing*.

We could do this for hours—I have. Many negative adjectives will include the garden and the two trees of Eden. The truths of Genesis were known, 4,400 years ago, before the book was even written. That knowledge was only up to Chapter 11, because the later events had not yet happened. Many folks, especially Chinese, know about this. At one time, there was one language and culture in a young world. Why isn't it well known? The god of this world, Satan, blinds people's eyes (II Cor. 4:4); culturally popular beliefs and trends reinforce error; state-supported schools have agendas that suppress and misrepresent Truth. Don't be a dupe, there is evidence. https://www.youtube.com/watch?v=AczRnue7zeY

Grace Lover: God that made the world and all things therein, seeing that he is Lord of heaven and earth, dwelleth not in temples made with hands; [26] And hath made of one blood all nations of men for to dwell on all the face of the earth, and hath determined the times before appointed, and the bounds of their habitation (Acts 17:24, 26).

Curmudgeon: And the whole earth was of one language, and of one speech. [4] And they said, Go to, let us build us a city and a tower, whose top may reach unto heaven (Gen. 11:1,4).

83. LOUISIANA MAYBE

Louisiana, ‘71.

What’s a nice Jewish boy like you doing in a place like this? Maybe you aren’t familiar with this question, but I’m from New York. Regardless of origin, you can glean its meaning, i.e., don’t put yourself in harm’s way. Bless my parents, they tried to keep us safe from the world. We lived in the suburbs and I attended parochial school. I had such a safe upbringing that when I reached eighteen, I was ready to let life bite me. It may seem Louisiana and I are on bad terms. Let me state unequivocally: “Where would we be without Gumbo?” Ok, that’s a question, nevertheless, on the day I was hitch-hiking in Louisiana, a VW van pulled over. The driver was in biker regalia, including tattoos, bandana, chains, and expletives. His first love, a Harley, was getting fixed. We swung into a market so his girlfriend could shop, but she left with nothing, her shorts having failed the dress code. That they were the size of a postcard may have influenced the owner’s decision. This got our driver into a froth. He produced a handgun, waving it in the air. I’ve no training in Gesticulation, but his mannerisms suggested disdain squared. His intentions seemed less than conciliatory, although he invited them to come down the road and work things out. We then hit the road again. Coincidentally, the next exit seemed the best option to reach my destination, any destination, besides a premature grave. As they drove into the sunset, I wondered if they’d outlive the day. I was glad to escape. Contrariwise. when a plague hit Rome, and the ill were put in the streets, the Christians went there to help.

How are we in that regard? My wallet is a collection of apologetics. We’re told to: “…contend for the Gospel once delivered to the saints,” Jude 3. I carry tracts to share as opportunities arise or I make one. You’ve been an unbeliever. Someone left their *safe-place* to share the Good News. The night of my arrest at the Mardi Gras, I ignored Christians. At last, I heard! I’m grateful folks stepped out for me.

Grace Lover: Watch ye, stand fast in the faith, quit you like men, be strong (I Cor. 16:13).

> But sanctify the Lord God in your hearts: and be ready always to give an answer to every man that asketh you a reason of the hope that is in you with meekness and fear (I Pet. 3:15).

84. THE WORLD'S FAIR

New York World's Fair, 1964-5.

The World of Tomorrow! Wow, I wanted to see that pavilion. The Fair was AMAZING! I memorized the tune of the horns on the People Movers, met a polar explorer, coveted the Belgian waffles, and saw pavilions of the '39 Fair! I wasn't the only one enthralled. Kids were collecting ticket money from the fountains at night. It was just Mom, Dad, and me that day. My girlfriend couldn't get permission, and my brother, Rob, was floating on an ice island in the Arctic Ocean. Each of us picked a pavilion that interested us.

"Let's go to the Mormon Pavilion," Mom said. I didn't know The Fair had a bottom, but it dropped out just then! Father objected to the idea, but had a plan.

"Let's let Christopher decide. What should we do, son?" Why couldn't I decide between pineapple-vanilla or choco-crunch sundaes? I thought. Suddenly, I'm the Oracle at Delphi!

"We're Catholics, Mormons teach something else, so let's not go," I said. Discounting its lack of intellectual curiosity, Jude's appeal that we contend for the faith, or mom's feelings, it wasn't a bad answer. Mom shocked and disappointed me. Now I think of her as a noble Berean; she questioned things. Beware groups that discourage inquiry. We only had a couple more years with Mom, but she had her Bible when she entered the believers' Land of Tomorrow!

Grace Lover: Wherewithal shall a young man cleanse his way? by taking heed thereto according to thy word (Ps. 119:9).

> And the brethren immediately sent away Paul and Silas by night unto Berea: who coming thither went into the synagogue of the Jews. [11] These were more noble than those in Thessalonica, in that they received the word with all readiness of mind, and searched the scriptures daily, whether those things were so (I Peter 3:15).

Curmudgeon: But I certify you, brethren, that the gospel which was preached of me is not after man. [12] For I neither received it of man, neither was I taught it, but by the revelation of Jesus Christ (Gal. 1:11-12).

85. THE GREATS: PART I, A.D. 871-899

Most folks don't think of the 9th century as great. The latest rage was VIKINGS, and you can take that literally. Thomas Paine of the Revolutionary War Period, penned: "These are the times that try men's souls." Trying times strengthen some. It was so for Alfred and Charles. Alfred was a Saxon, a Germanic tribe that had come to what is now England, several hundred years earlier, as new settlers, or invaders, depending on the version. By the 9th century, Britons and Saxons were playing nice. Then another invasion occurred. These folks didn't play by the rules. Theodore, and his thirty monks at Crowland Abbey, had heard of the invaders' arrival, but as monasteries didn't stockpile weapons, the monks thought themselves safe. They, and many others, died the first day the Danes arrived. Having enjoyed years of relative peace, the Saxons were not a match for the Norsemen. With the death of Alfred's father and elder brother, Alfred acceded to the throne of Wessex in 871.

Over the next several years, he lost most campaigns. Despairing, he retired to Wessex to pray, prostrating himself on the chapel floor, to sing Psalms. Then, a besieged castle routed its attackers, and requested the King rally the surrounding villages. Alfred did so and defeated the Vikings. Ironically, the survivors took sanctuary in an un-provisioned castle. Two weeks later they surrendered, hoping for better than they had meted out, a quick death without torture. But Alfred offered the Viking leader peace and an area to settle. Guthrum, scarcely believing his good fortune, inquired why the King made such a gesture. Alfred's response was: "I serve the Prince of Peace." Guthrum not only agreed, but spoke with Alfred regarding the Christian God. The Saxon sponsored the Viking in baptism, thereafter becoming friends and brothers. Alfred helped his son in the faith deal with other Viking leaders. He also appointed judges, encouraged education, restored London, and strengthened the Church. Of all the British monarchs of the land, he is the sole bearer of the assignation, GREAT.

Grace Lover and Curmudgeon: Except the Lord build the house, they labour in vain that build it: (Ps. 127:1).

Give us help from trouble: for vain is the help of man (Ps. 60:11).

86. NOVEMBER TOMATO

Shakespeare's *Tempest* is a story of reconciliation. It was the last of his plays and closes his career with a positive word. Great things can happen later in life. It is more common than we think. The Kaufmann Index says the most entrepreneurial time of life is the 55-64 age group. For you adventure fans, Defoe wrote his first fiction, *Robinson Crusoe*, at 59, and two more in his sixties. Next to the Bible, it is the most translated book.

Though not as exciting as Robinson finding footprints on his island, I took a walk in my garden today. It's rather barren, being we are in November. Pulling some weeds in passing revealed a speck of color, an undersized tomato. The flavor scale rated it a 6 of 10, but I appreciated its rarity. In the late seasons of our lives, we can still produce wonderful things. With my tomato, it was a humble offering, but you may be a *Crusoe* that opens eyes to new vistas.

How is the garden? Barren? Are you God's November Tomato? There is still time for a harvest, a breakthrough. Moses, at 120, was strong and his eyes were not dim (Deut. 34:7). Old men shall dream dreams (Joel 2:28). I married two weeks short of 52. I'm now 72 with two boys in high school. Maybe I am a December Chrysanthemum!

Grey Lover: And there was one Anna, a prophetess, the daughter of Phanuel, of the tribe of Aser: she was of a great age, and had lived with an husband seven years from her virginity;[37] And she was a widow of about fourscore and four years, which departed not from the temple, but served God with fastings and prayers night and day.[38] And she coming in that instant gave thanks likewise unto the Lord, and spake of him to all them that looked for redemption in Jerusalem (Luke 2:36-38).

(http://sites.kauffman.org/pdf/KIEA_041408.pdf.).

87. THE GREATS: PART II, A.D. 748 -814

With Alfred the Great providing such frolic, let's revisit the 9th century. Can anything good come from a Carolingian? It sounds pestilential. The founder of the clan, however, Charles Martel, the Hammer, delivered Europe from the Moors at Tours. Ok, I won't jeopardize our friendship with dates. His son, Pepin, saved the Pope from the Lombards, meriting him a Broadway play. And his grandson, Charles, is called the Great. But wait, what do you think of a man of four wives, one of them thirteen, who forced subdued rivals to convert to Christianity, and who gained an empire by warfare? Not a candidate for "Man of the Year?" Charlemagne was such a man. What are we to think? World-views change. *Noblesse oblige*, and the divine right of kings are ideas of earlier times. Removed by centuries, it's easy for us to be objective, but fish don't know the world isn't under water, and worms think dirt is all. Now, terms like gender affirming care for minors and assisted death join the social arena, so don't judge the past too harshly; another generation will follow you! In Charlemagne's defense, he funded foreign Christians in peril. He fought Europe's oppressors, protected the Papacy, and was concerned for the spiritual welfare of non-believers. He sent criers to town squares to proclaim the Word and encourage piety. He financed peasant education and codified laws. It is said that on his deathbed, his last words imitated our Lord: "Father into thy hand I commend my spirit." Are we convinced? Don't be. Everyone has feet of clay.

When a lawyer called Jesus, "Good Master," Jesus responded: "Why do you call me good? there is none good but God" (Matt. 19:17). Many *Greats* will be revealed on the Last Day; the nurse, the maintenance man, the fallen soldier, even a couple we've called Great, but considering God's glory, they'll go unnoticed. Charles the Great signed his documents: "Charles, by the grace of God, King of the Franks." That is all any of us can say of our accomplishments; they are by *the grace of God.*

Curmudgeon: So likewise ye, when ye shall have done all those things which are commanded you, say, We are unprofitable servants: we have done that which was our duty to do (Luke 17:10).

88. MR. AND MRS. FRANKLIN

N. Chili, N.Y. '17. 6 A.M.

Men's Prayer Breakfast, Mary the waitress presiding: "Ok, Dave, I know you like eggs with your pepper; I'll get your shaker after I take Dave #2's order. You guys like prophets, right, I bet #2 gets the gruel with no salt. Uugh, I papered my walls with that stuff once—really did the trick!" Mary seemed divinely appointed to get us revving a few RPMs above catatonic. If she forgot anyone's name, she'd say, "Dave," that would suffice for five of us. I've been going to the breakfasts on home assignment for over twenty years. Some guys have graduated and have pleasures more engaging than the breakfast special.

On one furlough, an elderly Black couple with brochures, stood across the street on Tuesdays. I greeted them. They were the Franklins. I met another couple down the road on Thursday. Both couples devoted themselves to the cause. I always compliment the Jehovah's Witnesses on their diligence. All this provoked me to go to the Kingdom Hall on Tuesday night. I took my Bible, prayed, and went, expecting a dozen people and a chance to share. Over a 100 folks were there. The men and children were all in suits. We saw a video about witnessing, and another about not joining the military. There was a Bible study, and a song—very dry. The moderator said they had over 1,000 years of service represented. Even the lowest level Witness must do 10 hours of witnessing a week. When I'd entered, the couple I'd met on Thursday welcomed me. As I left, Mr. Franklin held the door for me. The organization has a dark side, too. They must work for salvation. Blood transfusions are forbidden. Reading material from other groups is taboo. They promote their literature above Scripture and criticize the private interpretation of God's Word. Let's reach out to these nice folks whom Jesus loves.

Grace Lover: If any man will do his will, he shall know of the doctrine, whether it be of God, or whether I speak of myself (John 7:17).

> Knowing that of the Lord ye shall receive the reward of the inheritance: for ye serve the Lord Christ (Col. 3:24).

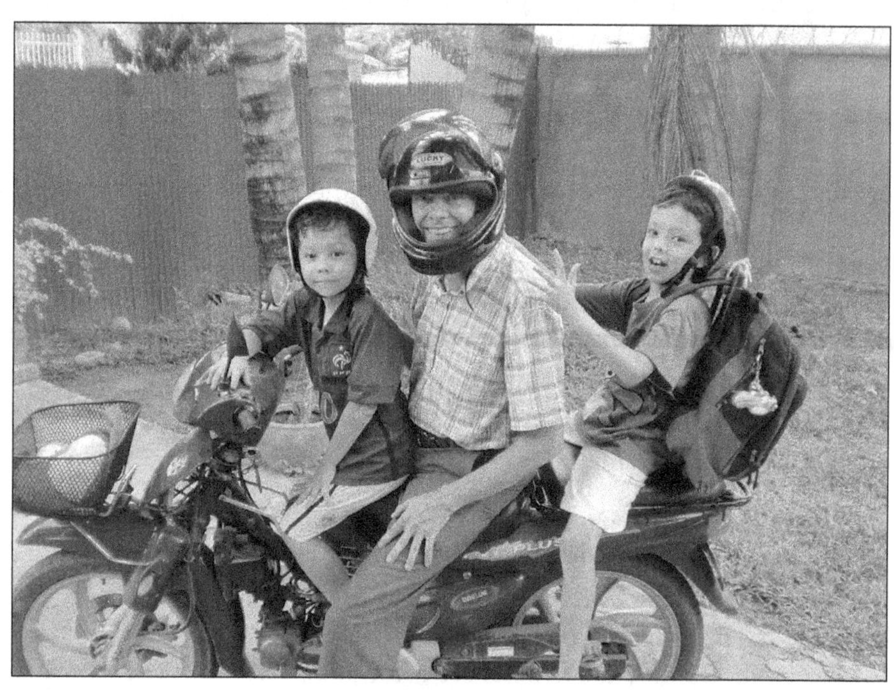

Destination Hope School, Cambodia, 2013!

89. MOTO

I bought my first motorcycle for $400.00, when I was sixty-three. I'd had a 50-cc scooter in Japan, but the motorcycle was a 100 cc Korean Daelim. I loved loading the boys on it and driving to school. It was just one kilometer, and so crowded we couldn't speed. Life was at risk of riding a motorcycle in Cambodia, however. We lost several students from our fellowship to accidents. When I was in the countryside, a lady in front of me got upended by a dog. I stopped at the clinic to pray, and found her, thank God, not badly injured. In Cambodia, water, accidents, English, twelve-volt batteries, and smart phones are topics of everyday life. One day I rode to Prek Thei village, the site of our first Cambodian church. I stopped at our first childcare center, the House of Love. We had two others also, the Houses of Joy and Peace. We named them after the Fruit of the Spirit (Galatians 5). We stopped at three, not wanting a House of Long-suffering! On the day mentioned, I saw Pastor Lum. We co-pastored the Phnom Penh church. The engine of his new motorcycle wasn't turning over. I prayed for the bike and left. The students there later asked Lum why I'd asked God to break the pastor's motorcycle. I had asked the Lord to *chap* (stop) instead of *choup* (help) it. I apologized, and he smiled, a formula repeated frequently. I got used to making cultural blunders. It comes with the territory. Two churches in different countries requested I not share the Word in their language. Sometimes we make the cut, sometimes not; stay humble, keep chuggin', and hold no grudges.

Grace Lover: But the Lord said unto Samuel, Look not on his countenance, or on the height of his stature; because I have refused him: for the Lord seeth not as man seeth; for man looketh on the outward appearance, but the Lord looketh on the heart (I Sam. 16:7).

Curmudgeon: Or despisest thou the riches of his goodness and forbearance and longsuffering; not knowing that the goodness of God leadeth thee to repentance (Ro. 2;4).

90. THE WAITRESS STATION

Clearwater, Fl., '83.

Pepsi kept me going from N. Carolina to Florida. I got in late, but Grandma Clark waited up. Without caffeine, I soon slept. Senior citizen co-ops are fun. The fire truck came often because Mrs. L. left her toast in too long. Billows of carbonized cinders proselytized other toasters. The bouquet helped detect the culprit. Mrs. Cowart preferred rye toast, Mrs. Levison, bagels. By far, their most fun was watching the young men in their fire gear. We also peered out of Grandma's seven splendiferous 13th floor windows, heckled the Meals on Wheels, taped her life story, and watched 60 Minutes with Mrs. Gillespie. We went out for dinner once, nothing high-brow. I was a missionary, after all. As we left, Grandma, her cane aloft, queried: "Christopher, dear, what is that?" Having credentials in that field, I said: "It's a waitress station." She sallied forth with a flair, declaring:

"We must get one in our next restaurant." One fellow, witnessing the affair, roared, but we executed decorum. She didn't have two nickels, but was happy and humorous. Checks for two dollars to a St. Francis charity were all about the house. She was always positive. I never saw Grandma have a bad day, never, even though she had rebellious knees. Regardless, we enjoyed our walks. Her storytelling was unique, though her themes, traditional:

"Oh Christopher, dear, that's a splendid little house," she would chime. Grandma loved to think of cozy little places. I'd seen one of her basement apartments that didn't have enough space in which to change one's mind. A less than adroit attempt was rewarded with yet another burn from the water heater. The men in her life were another popular theme: "Oh, Christopher dear, I met the nicest young man on the train today." I told her I appreciated her staying true to the Lord, even though her spouse had left her. "Well, Christopher, no one asked me to marry," she answered. She didn't complain, she didn't blame, she always encouraged—wisely. As a youth, my fingers often found my nose. Grandma's response: "Are you sure you wouldn't like a tissue, dear?" Grandma, what a treasure!

Grace Lover: The Lord hath done great things for us; whereof we are glad (Ps. 126:3).

91. GUM

Moscow, '93.

I missed my rendezvous! The French folks with whom I'd traveled across Asia were to meet me at the Kremlin. Lenin was there, so all was not lost. Though I'd regaled them in song (*La Mer*), and offered to share my sardines, it was time to move on—next adventure! It would be the GUM Building. GUM is an acronym for *government shopping place*. The Moscow arcade of glass, in 1993, was 100 years old, and 794 feet long. It was impressive. The architects were Pomerantsev and Shukhov.

The USSR had ended. I bought a Matryoshka Doll of Russian leaders: Yeltsin, Gorbachev, and Brezhnev. My travel, however, was not tourism. I carried Russian tracts for the short term, and was headed to Asbury Seminary. I'd served in Japan as a volunteer. It was distant from home, and I could monitor my commitment. Eventually, I yearned for discipleship. A hundred years earlier, Pomerantsev and Sukhov erected the GUM building, their legacy. Reaching middle age, I thought about what I would leave behind for future generations and His glory. I'd been in counter-culture movements; it was time to jump in with both feet, to throw myself into the Lord's hands. Looking back, the more I've allowed myself to be *under construction*, the more useful I've been in construction. As for legacies, the Lord has promised fruit. I'll never get my name on a glass arcade, but that's ok, I'll take the fruit.

Grace Lover: A good name [is] better than precious ointment; and the day of death than the day of one's birth (Eccles. 7:1).

> And are built upon the foundation of the apostles and prophets, Jesus Christ himself being the chief corner stone; [21] In whom all the building fitly framed together groweth unto an holy temple in the Lord (Eph. 2:20-21).

Curmudgeon: Having your conversation honest among the Gentiles: that, whereas they speak against you as evildoers, they may by [your] good works, which they shall behold, glorify God in the day of visitation (I Pet. 2:12).

92. RADIO FLYER

W. Babylon, N.Y., '56, '64.

Mother was sophisticated. That I call her *mother* is telling. Raised by nuns, she stayed with her mom on weekends. Consequently, the Christmas red Radio Flyer was not a wagon, with the high-gliding "a" of the New York accent. It was a waagon, a pronunciation accomplished only by raising of one's nose in the air. Hoity-toity for some folks, I was up to the task. At school in January, '56, everyone talked Christmas. My announcement: "I got a waagon," caused confusion. Even after explaining the machine's dimensions, utility, turn radius, etc., it was a bridge too far for the masses. Disheartened, I caved to the common: "It's a wagon."

As a garage decoration, the wagon served us well, but failed me in the summer of '63. Dad and Rob were in the pool. As for the instigation of hostilities, it was THEM! Someone splashed inappropriately. Infuriated at this lack of propriety, I stormed off to make war plans. My offensive campaign involved a large box, rain coat, broom handle, bucket, and the glorious red waagon! Tank assembled, attired in protective gear, I sallied forth backward, necessitated by my need to steer with a protected front. Pushing the broom handle, I progressed toward the enemy. There were no minefields but plentiful crabgrass! Oh, the derision hurled against my crusade. The villainy to which my person was subjected. Resolute, I continued forward, albeit backward. The enemy also had plans. Impropriety not being sufficient erratum, they added captivity. Nearing the pool, I departed the safety of my armored vehicle, cardboard though it was, and approached, said bucket in hand. I withstood their water offensive, safe in my protective gear. They, however, made a coordinated assault, rushed me, pulling me into the pool, gear and all. Oh, the humiliation! The laughter abated days later.

Grace Lover: Honour thy father and thy mother: that thy days may be long upon the land which the Lord thy God giveth thee (Ex. 20:12).

I thank my God upon every remembrance of you (Phil. 1:3).

Curmudgeon: And he said unto them, Full well ye reject the commandment of God, that ye may keep your own tradition (Mark 7:9).

93. CAMBYSES

Sixth Century B.C.

The Court was large, replete with a plentitude of columns, and as many echoes, for wherever one went, they were no further away than a spoken word. Though aided by the vast plain of flat stone, the echoes did not reign with any authority, as a myriad of fountains muffled or confounded their voice. There was one challenger to the muted music that day—the Prince.

Thank you for seeing me, Father, King of the Four Winds," said the young man of ten years, his squeaky voice addressing the sovereign of the Persian Empire. The little fellow, though he had a vellum tucked under one arm, looked winded, as if he'd been wrestling, not researching.

"I believe it is Four Worlds," the King corrected. A smile endeavored to usurp the King's stern countenance, but the coup found insufficient inspiration to overthrow the Royal Demeanor.

"A thousand pardons," the lad squeaked.

"One is sufficient. Who taught you such a phrase?" And why are so many necessary? Have you that many grievances laid against you? Is that the reason for the redness of your face? Are you outrunning, for the moment, a throng of accusers?"

The lad needed no time to tally the questions and respond: "My tutor, social etiquette in the presence of royalty, no, no, no." This time, the Royal Demeanor was put to flight by the Royal Scion's sentience. He burst out in laughter so loud, the heir took a step back.

"What manner of extortion, pardon, or bequest brings you to Court?"

"History," the son returned.

"What history?" the King inquired.

"Jewish history," the Prince proffered.

"Jewish?" the King mused, mentally scanning a plethora of parchments. "What be the nature of this history?"

"Prophecy, my King."

"I tire of questions. Tell me what you will."

"While with the sons of lords, the matter of your surpassing majesty arose. Two of them had the audacity to suggest their fathers matched your excellence. I was prone to beat them."

"You were going to beat them…" the King began.

"Your Majesty tires not of questions?" the son asked. His cheek gained his Father's acquiescence.

"I was about to beat them, but was interrupted by a Jewish slave. Being a perceptive fellow, he was of the mind I might unleash uncertain consequences, and spoke thus: 'Far be it from the Prince to prove that which is beyond question, seeing the glorious name of the Great King of all Persia and its 124 satraps, is established by the Most-High God, to deliver the Jewish people from bondage.' I therewith demanded of him the cause for such assertions upon the pain of the beatings I'd intended for others. He thereupon informed me, O King, thou art spoken of, by name, in the writings of the Seers of these foolish Jews."

Frivolity left the King, ego, curiosity, and a cohort of companions driving it from the field.

"What is the name of this slave?" the King required.

"Asaph, my Lord," the Prince rejoined respectfully, noting the tone in the voice of the King of the Four Winds, was gathering strength prior to unleashing a gale of significant force.

"Have him in my presence in one space of the sundial, and we'll consider your benefice together. After that, and I will devise something less favorable. Am I understood, Prince?"

"Yes, Ruler of Persia and..." the Lad declared. He'd come to boast but left, having changed the world.

Grace Lover: For thus saith the Lord, That after seventy years be accomplished at Babylon I will visit you, and perform my good word toward you, in causing you to return to this place (Jeremiah 29:10).

> Thus saith the Lord to his anointed, to Cyrus, whose right hand I have holden, to subdue nations before him; and I will loose the loins of kings, to open before him the two leaved gates; and the gates shall not be shut; [4]For Jacob my servant's sake, and Israel mine elect, I have even called thee by thy name: I have surnamed thee, though thou hast not known me (Isa. 45:1,4).

The Blackham girls, Emily, Louise, Mary and their mother. Circa 1915.

94. PLOP

Clearwater, Fl., '83:

CAUTION:
Offensive Content.

Grandma Clark and I taped her life's highlights, but the Grand Prize was—*60 Minutes* news and commentary. Back then, even the media, distinguished between the two. At 5:15 we went to Mrs. Gillespie's. The weekly ritual was initiated with a glass of port to insure getting the finer details. With today's editorializing, it's doubtful a liter would be equal to the task. One port led to two. I remember pleasant banter interspersed with a modicum of giggles. Later, at the apartment, I suggested we tape something fictional. With the recorder and participants lubricated, we had *Grandma's Weather Analysis*, but "Yes, we had some weather today," merited no awards. Back in the 70's the Huntley-Brinkley Report was popular. One reporter was in Washington D.C., the other in N.Y. At the closing, Chet said: "Goodnight, David," and David returned: "Goodnight, Chet." So, we imitated them. I'd say: "Goodnight, David," and Grandma said: "Goodnight...," here she'd pause, and finally respond... "Plop." She forgot his name, I reminded her, and we tried again: "Goodnight David..."

"Goodnight...Plop," Grandma repeated, giggling. I roared and tried again.

"Goodnight, David." I led in.

"Goodnight...what the heck was his name?" she asked. We laughed 'til we cried. Except for the bed, the *plopping* was over. Being 90, the family wanted Grandma to plop elsewhere, to give up her 7 windows overlooking the bay. Not given to wisdom, I told her to do as she wanted. Later, she asked me to take her to Corazon de Jesus nursing home. The usual six month wait ended in a month.

"I can go to Mass every day," she said, cheerily, a custom once ended by old knees. Some folks didn't approve of Grandma's port, but she knew her real Port, and has set sail on the HMS Faith. I can hear her saying: "All this and Heaven, too, Christopher."

"Amen, Grandma, Amen."

Curmudgeon: Judge not, that ye be not judged (Matt. 7:1).

95. KOJIKI: ACCOUNT OF ANCIENT THINGS

Zippangu, 7th Century.

Not seeing the forest for the trees? The oldest book in Japan, the Kojiki, was written by Ono, Yasumuro, in 711-712, at the bequest of the Empress Genmei. One god in this account is Ame No Naka Nushi: *God at the Center of the Universe*. He is called the first god in the Heavenly Plain, one of three linked creators. He hides his presence, he's a hitorigami, a god by himself. One sees parallels in this account to the Old Testament, Yahweh. The *Hidden God* is, with variation, in many cultures. The truth is, He is not hidden as much as He is ignored. The Lord has left a God-print throughout the centuries, though His pointers are often missed. Asians think Christianity has a Western God, but the Bible tells a different story. Paul, in the Letter to the Romans (1:19,20, 2:15), says God put in each of us a knowledge of the Godhead, and a conscience. There's no tabula rasa. Yet another witness is the Heavens declaring the glory of God in every language (Ps. 19:1-6). We already discussed two historical proofs, i.e., the Universal Language, the truths of Genesis clearly seen in the ancient Chinese ideographs, and Flood stories in over one hundred cultures around the globe. In more recent times there is the witness of the Incarnation, and the Church. We're not standing in the shadow of Charlie Brown's scraggly Christmas tree. We're in the Forest of God's revelation. My Friend, open your eyes! Behold the Truth!

Curmudgeon: Then Paul stood in the midst of Mars' hill, and said, Ye men of Athens, I perceive that in all things ye are too superstitious. [23] For as I passed by, and beheld your devotions, I found an altar with this inscription, To THE UNKNOWN GOD. Whom therefore ye ignorantly worship, him declare I unto you. [24] God that made the world and all things therein, seeing that he is Lord of heaven and earth, dwelleth not in temples made with hands; [28] For in him we live, and move, and have our being; as certain also of your own poets have said, For we are also his offspring. [30] And the times of this ignorance God winked at; but now commandeth all men every where to repent (Acts 17:22-24,28,30).

Curmudgeon: For the invisible things of him from the creation of the world are clearly seen, being understood by the things that are made, even his eternal power and Godhead; so that they are without excuse (Ro. 1:20).

96. MOUSETRAP REVELATION

This devotion is a 3-for-1 deal. Hamlet calls his play the *Mousetrap*, hoping it will snare the King of "murder most foul," *Hamlet*, Act I, Scene V. A second revelation also involves murder, Agatha Christie's *The Mousetrap*. Sorry, no telling *who dunnit*. Our last revelation puts to rest a bad idea. An average mousetrap has 6 pieces. It's inoperable without them all. Which brings us to Darwin. As a teen, I read the *Voyage of the Beagle*. Dad got the Harvard Classics. It's ironic, Charles had a copy of Mendel's pea genetics, but it escaped perusal. Evolution had no basis on genes. Scientists thought cytoplasm was like Jello, an amorphous glob of goo. Now we have electron microscopes. My huge point is the miniscule cousin of the Paramecium. It has a flagellum that rotates clockwise 10^4 times, which is then reversed. This appendage enables the creature to move at high speeds relative to its size. A machine of organic components, 40 in all, including gears, and a photon generator that propels the gear mechanism, moves the flagellum, Remove one piece and you disable the machine. Comparing the mousetrap to this single cell's complexity leaves the former looking like the invention of limited minds, and the latter, the work of a creative genius. The concept of something being inoperable, if one piece is missing, is called *Irreducible Complexity*. How did this single cell evolve something needing 40 parts? A listless flagellum waiting for parts a few million generations later, is like having an anchor. The creature wouldn't survive, let alone pass its' incomplete gene collection to the next generation. Evolutionist friends have offered an idea, i.e., components of the incomplete mobility machine could be utilized for other purposes. This proposal leaves the cell motionless in a pool of mobile attackers. The Creationists have the better science. Credible explanations, from scientists, are at Creation Research or Answers in Genesis. Are we talking mousetraps? There's a conspiracy to entrap you, to set you adrift in life's sea without a working flagellum, or faith. Be wary!

Curmudgeon: And no marvel; for Satan himself is transformed into an angel of light (II Cor. 11:14).

97. RADIO FLYER: THE SEQUEL

N. Chili, N.Y., and Cambodia, 2007-10.

This Radio Flyer is a seat with handlebars and tires. The sum of its measure fills two feet, but its impact far outdistances that. It is at times generous of spirit and at others, *exacting*. Its proverbial stork was a Goodwill store or a surprise parcel on the porch. Early on, Caleb, the Great Explorer, rode it on the Roberts Wesleyan campus. One day, he parked at the Shewan Fine Arts Center to plant sandals and socks in a puddle, an occurrence insufficient to deter further acts of bravery. He prevailed to the farthest point on campus, where if one went further, he'd be returning or fall off the Earth, the latter being what I told him. All was well, except the return. Campus circumnavigation always became a discarded pursuit, and the Adventurer's arms would go up in surrender to nap time. Not surprisingly, the Flyer refused to help, and baby and vehicle were carried, one under each arm, the girth of these being not up to the magnitude of the task. That was the Flyer's *exacting* dimension.

We must travel to Cambodia for the *generous* aspect. There, it met its nemesis—Big Wheel, causing Corey much happiness, and the oft construction of a race track lounge. The figure eight, utilized the furniture. I walked; the boys rode. The race was chaos, fun, and a pinch of villainy. The intersection was a rite of passage called the *near-miss*! One day, Caleb, stroking madly, darted in and out of opponents, the personification of Washington Irving's Ichabod Crane, who, when mounting a steed, took on the appearance of his "cognomen," the crane. The only difference for Caleb being the crane was fitted with more flesh. Suddenly, he slipped off, hit the floor, and was up again. He looked back to say: "Don't touch my butt." His six octaves above high C., and English Vulgate, made me laugh. What had been exacting, with a little imagination, became a harbinger of memories. Circumstances and people can change—or be changed.

Grace Lover: And Zacchaeus stood, and said unto the Lord: Behold, Lord, the half of my goods I give to the poor; and if I have taken any thing from any man by false accusation, I restore him fourfold. [9] And Jesus said unto him, This day is salvation come to this house, forsomuch as he also is a son of Abraham. [10] For the Son of man is come to seek and to save that which was lost (Luke 19:8-10).

98. TONY

Long Island, N.Y., 1970.

Dropping out of college had its perks: freedom, drugs, and bad friends. The minimum wage tilted the scale the other way a smidge. I worked at factories: pool chemicals, metalworks (making parachute parts), and garments. The latter is where I met him. He was small, old, and Italian. He sucked up to the bosses, too. I did my work; it wasn't a bad job. The lady manager wasn't difficult, but I wasn't about to sacrifice my self-esteem for $2.25 an hour. Nobody owned me. One day, the Boss, Mike, was coming in. Oh, my goodness, the Boss is coming. Let's get excited and really earn that living wage! You may detect a note of humbug. At any rate, I'd done my work, and it was my break time. I sat down with a cold drink.

"What are you doing? The Boss, Mike, is coming!" Tony said. My vituperative spirit rejoiced at a chance to defend the downtrodden masses:

"Labor law says I get a break after two hours, and I'm taking it."

I stayed there while the Boss came and walked past me. Tony said nothing. I felt vindicated having showed him the back door, so to speak. At lunch, it rained buckets. I ran to the car to eat. The windows fogged. There was a tap on the window. I looked up. I could hardly see—it was him, Tony. I let him in. He didn't look threatening, because he wasn't. He was quite wet.

"Hey bud, what was that all about?" he asked me. I made the same complaint, happy to do so. "Hey, nobody is taking your stuff. We just wanted to show the Boss that we do a good job." It wouldn't win a Pulitzer, but his genuineness of heart won me.

"Okay," I said, a little sheepishly. He wished me an enjoyable lunch and went back into the rain. What a guy. I wish I knew more of his story. It was a fuller volume than my thin, coarse pamphlet.

Grace Lover: Reprove not a scorner, lest he hate thee: rebuke a wise man, and he will love thee—9:8. A soft answer turneth away wrath: but grievous words stir up anger—15:1. A word fitly spoken is like apples of gold in pictures of silver (Prov. 9:8, 15:1, 25:11).

Curmudgeon: Faithful are the wounds of a friend; but the kisses of an enemy are deceitful (Prov. 27:6).

99. THE TEVYEN PRINCIPLE

Phnom Penh, Cambodia, 2013.

"Rabbi, is there a prayer even for the Czar?" The Rabbi had just extolled the efficacy of prayer, but did not the Czar persecute the Jews? The crowd drew quiet. You could hear a goat bleating a mile off. "Yes," he affirmed, "May God bless and keep the Czar…far away from us!"

Church councils, though prayerful, have made mistakes. Doctrines interconnect; a clarification of one necessitates adjustments on another. The Rabbi did some juggling. Can you juggle? Try these two objects. "All that the Father gives me will come to me" (John. 6:37), and "…who would have all men to be saved and come to a knowledge of the truth" (I Tim. 2:4). Who chooses? Some folks narrow this to Calvinism and Arminianism, but forget Tevye, of *Fiddler on the Roof.* Asked to judge the truthfulness of a petitioner's position, he responded: "This is true." The position posed by the adversary was also awarded a "Yes, this is true." Confused by this, another asked: "How can this be true and this also be true?" Tevye's response: "Yes, this also is true!"

Still juggling? God chooses us-yes! We choose God-yes! Both true? Call it the Tevyen Doctrine. It won't fly in most churches, but no council got it 100% right. The Bible speaks of the mysteries of godliness, iniquity, of the ages, and others. We seek, but don't cross completely to the shores of revelation. Hidden in the Tevyen Doctrine is an addendum called humility. It doesn't aspire to things too high (Ps. 131:1). Is everything rational in the wisdom of God? A Biblical scholar once said his positions allowed him to maintain intellectual integrity. Sounds good, but explain floating axe heads or God walking on water. Hamlet comments: "There are more things in heaven and earth, Horatio, then are dreamt of in your philosophy." *Hamlet* Act 1, scene 5. Regarding doctrines, I default to Tevye. To do otherwise may suggest an agenda, not an anointing. This is true. But, it's good to be adamant about what we believe. This also is true!

Grace Lover: To whom God would make known what is the riches of the glory of this mystery among the Gentiles; which is Christ in you, the hope of glory (Col. 1:27).

Uncle Giim and Caleb, at Heeks Forest, 2010.

100. JAMES THE LESSER

The Lord sends some people into our lives to encourage, exhort, and instruct. James came to insult. It's not your everyday gift, but by application, trial and error, and imagination, he has become the penultimate pestilence—pest for short. BTW, his moniker is self-inflicted. Kidding aside, we like *straight talk*, no facades. Feigned piety is met with: "This is me you're talking to."

Our first encounter was Thanksgiving, 1986, delivering turkeys from Pearce church to an inner-city church. I've joined his catering affairs, eaten at his table, and received his hospitality. I helped him plant a field of pines which, when I went on a mission, he let die! In addition, he helps finance our labors overseas, and I still get to insult him! Not a bad deal. We enjoy some things in common; critiquing our betters, musicals, Homer Simpson, and our own custom, *hot n' cold*—nurturing two drinks. We differ, too. Jim is a business entrepreneur in catering, antiques, estate sales, and donuts! I, on the other hand, have an aversion to overexertion, my physiology being challenged from an early age by weather and gravity. Jim is also given to a measure of hypocrisy. His favorite adage is: "No good deed will go unpunished," yet he helps everyone. Jim manages the church kitchen. During home assignment. I go there, after any major lifting is finished, have a cup of tea, and watch him work. You may detect some flaws in the relationship described, but Jim is like a paper streamer from shore. He connects me to home. How much more are we connected to Heaven, where the Lord is preparing our place? (John. 14:2-3).

Grace Lover: And hath raised us up together, and made us sit together in heavenly places in Christ Jesus (Eph. 2:6).

> By faith Abraham, when he was called to go out into a place which he should after receive for an inheritance, obeyed; and he went out, not knowing whither he went. [10] For he looked for a city which hath foundations, whose builder and maker is God (Heb. 11:8,10).

Curmudgeon: But Jesus said unto him, "Judas, betrayest thou the Son of Man with a kiss (Luke 22:48).

101. STIFFED

San Francisco, Ca., '79.

"Aaaaaargh," he shouted, shaking all over. I considered rebuking him in Jesus' name, like in the Book of Acts, but faith retreated as volume increased, and I pushed a chair between us. Having had the last shout, he left.

"He's harmless, just a little twisted," said Max, the owner, and the deli went back to its version of normal. I was only there six months, but I wore out a pair of shoes busing tables at The Stage, Kosher Style Deli. It was an amazing place. One day, a Hasidic Jew came in and spent over a hundred dollars on lox. That was like three months of car insurance! On another day, I found $20 decorating the floor and gave it to Max.

"Stick it in your pocket," he said, so I did. He then had second thoughts and asked:

"Are you gonna declare that on your taxes?"

"Yes," I answered.

"Then give it here," he joked. I liked Max and all the crew, but that was tested. One morning I sat with my Bible reading a Deprecatory Psalm, thinking about she who'd stiffed me the night before. Her name was Marcy. I was ready to lay a load on her, not praise, mind you. Finally, she arrived.

"Is that a Bible you're reading?" she asked.

"Yes," I answered.

"I'm a Christian, too," she said. I told her that was great and meant it. How ironic, the person I'd chosen to confront, out of a collage of unbelievers, was the only other believer of the crew.

"Someone stole my tips," she said. "That's why I stiffed you. But now I see it wasn't you."

"Oh, thanks," I said, as she placed some bills in my hand.

Grace Lover: But the fruit of the Spirit is love, joy, peace, longsuffering, gentleness, goodness, faith, [23] Meekness, temperance: against such there is no law (Gal. 5:22-23).

Curmudgeon: Wherefore, my beloved brethren, let every man be swift to hear, slow to speak, slow to wrath: [20] For the wrath of man worketh not the righteousness of God (James 1:19-20).

102. BEETLEBAUM

W. Babylon, N.Y., '60.

Big brothers do amazing feats. On my tenth Christmas, mine said: "Mele Kalikimaka," the Hawaiian Christmas greeting. Only big brothers are that smart. He'd discovered some 78 RPM records—they were rare, going back to the 30s. He found Spike Jones and the Wacky Wackateers. Listening, one would think dad's generation was a bunch of great kids, as goofy as us! The *One Horned, One Eyed, Flying Purple People Eater*, was the music of my brother's generation, but Mom taught us the lyrics. Back to Spike, I remember one skit's opening: "Here is *Spike Jones and the Wacky Wackateers* on the island of Lulu, spelled backwards, Ul Ul." It got even better. There's a great parody of a horse race. The announcer listed the horses' order as they rounded various posts. One entry, Beetlebaum, was always at the bottom of the field. Somehow, at the close, Beetlebaum won! It was unforeseen, and an illustration of the End Times. The Lord will return when the World doesn't expect it; those accompanying Him will not be the expected winners.

Tempted to think negatively about someone, or yourself? Remember Beetlebaum! As *Humbug* was the standard of naysayers in days past, shall we let Beetlebaum be our present cry of affirmation? Beetlebaum—it has a ring to it, don't you think? Then again, the Word has better advice: Some trust in chariots, and some in horses: but we will remember the name of the LORD our God, (Psalm 20:7). Sorry, Beetlebaum, 2nd place this time.

Grace Lover: But God hath chosen the foolish things of the world to confound the wise; and God hath chosen the weak things of the world to confound the things which are mighty; [28] And base things of the world, and things which are despised, hath God chosen, yea, and things which are not, to bring to nought things that are: [29] That no flesh should glory in his presence. [31] That, according as it is written, He that glorieth, let him glory in the Lord (I Cor. 1:27-29, 31).

Curmudgeon: Lift not up your horn on high: speak not with a stiff neck. [6] For promotion cometh neither from the east, nor from the west, nor from the south. [7] But God is the judge: he putteth down one, and setteth up another (Ps. 75:5-7).

103. WINDOWS

Bethpage, N.Y., '69.

In 1969. humans walked on the moon, riots broke out in inner-cities, hippies protested the Vietnam War, and I, I broke up with Peggy. It was a romance of star-crossed lovers. I was Irish, she was Italian. I was nineteen, she was fourteen. I was a hippie, her father was a pig, er, an officer of the Law. Everyone knows by whom the break-up was initiated! We had a good relationship. My feelings were honorable, most of the time, and she possessed a maturity enhanced by her alto voice. I was melancholic and could cry over a poem, a change in weather, a butterfly's broken wing. A popular song, *These Eyes*, became my mantra—crying over lost love. I was sad, but I lived to date again. Love was all about me, not others.

When serving with Christians in Action, in Long Beach, Ca., Amy Grant released *Father's Eyes*. Eyes that expressed God's love were its theme. The focus was on others.

One year, for my birthday, I received a DVD set. One episode epitomized "...deep calling unto deep" (Psalm 42:7). The adventure begins with Detective Monk on a sidewalk, chatting with his nurse. Suddenly, he yells: "STOP," and begins chasing a woman. His befuddled nurse runs after him. After a chase of minutes, the woman escapes. The nurse asks Monk: "Why did you do that?" His answer: "I don't know." Later, we learn Monk's deceased wife was an organ donor. Monk saw his wife's eyes on the woman passer-by. He ran after her for one more look into the eyes of love.

Eyes are something. Provers 30:17 tells us eyes are the window to the soul. Our eyes will have an exceptional experience in the future. We'll die and kneel before the Lord's Judgment Seat. When before Him, what will He see? What will you see? Will you want to behold the eyes of Him who said: "Father forgive them they know not what they do," or will you wish to escape the holiness of His gaze? Do you want to look into His eyes?

Grace Lover: But Noah found grace in the eyes of the Lord (Gen. 6:8).

Curmudgeon: For the eyes of the Lord run to and fro throughout the whole earth, to shew himself strong in the behalf of them whose heart is perfect toward him. Herein thou hast done foolishly: therefore from henceforth thou shalt have wars (II Chron. 16:9).

104. FAITH TREK

Long Beach, Ca., 1979.

We had some coins in our pockets, but we weren't allowed to use them for food. I don't remember being tempted. My partner was Ken H, which was great. He and I really got along. We were going on Faith Trek, our third semester highlight. Every Christians in Action student took part. Modeled after Luke Chapters 9 and 10, we shared the Good News door to door. The Lord opened up a house at which we could stay. A dear, middle-aged woman asked if we'd eaten. We weren't allowed to ask for food but could answer inquiries. She gave us some crackers and milk. We visited politicians' offices and were well received. Ken tried to buy flowers on the way home for his future fiancé. The peddler asked Ken to make an offer; he did.

"Would ya take a quarter?"

"A quarter?" the guy balked. He took it and gave Ken one flower. Yes, we'd had a trip of memories; the milk lady, her neighbors, politicians, and a peddler. We learned about faith, fasting, and the early disciples. We have so much, don't we. We seldom have our faith stretched. When we do, it's usually not voluntarily. Need a faith boost? Try a FAITH TREK!

Grace Lover: Every place that the sole of your foot shall tread upon, that have I given unto you, as I said unto Moses. [9] Have not I commanded thee? Be strong and of a good courage; be not afraid, neither be thou dismayed: for the Lord thy God is with thee whithersoever thou goest (Joshua 1:3, 9).

> Go your ways: behold, I send you forth as lambs among wolves. [4]
> Carry neither purse, nor scrip, nor shoes: and salute no man by
> the way. [5] And into whatsoever house ye enter, first say, Peace be
> to this house (Luke 10:3-5).

P.S. Ken and Sylvia got married. The last time I saw them they had three youngsters, all of whom are near forty, and older.

Happy Mongolian friends outside Lenin's Hall.

105. I GO TO PIECES

Ulan Baatar, Mongolia, 1993.

The girls pictured, giggled, and waved their hands incessantly. The twins in green focused on the girl in the middle. She was a deaf mute. The girls had their own sign language to exchange their ideas. Meeting them was a nice prelude to things to follow. I entered the Hall dedicated to the memory of Lenin, the man who called religion the "opiate of the masses." Inside were three-hundred Mongolian youth worshipping the Lord! That story calls to mind Italy in 1999. I visited Hadrian's Tomb. Inside, a painting depicted the Cross of Jesus. Lying in pieces before it was the statue of a Roman god. It was symbolic of Christianity's ascendancy over idolatry. What was happening in the Hall of Lenin that day in Mongolia was like that painting. Youth heard God's Word. Lenin was not only neglected, he was despised. The Kingdom of God will eventually overcome every evil and empire. He who tried to end religion in Russia has had his crypt removed from the Kremlin. See Daniel Ch. 2.

Eusebius wrote a history of the Church during the early 4th century. He records it elated believers to have a Christian Emperor. There'd be no more persecution. Standing in Lenin's Hall with Mongolians, I understood a measure of the peace earlier Christians felt so long ago.

Grace Lover: These things I have spoken unto you, that in me ye might have peace. In the world ye shall have tribulation: but be of good cheer; I have overcome the world (John 16:33).

Curmudgeon: When the Philistines took the ark of God, they brought it into the house of Dagon, and set it by Dagon. [4] And when they arose early on the morrow morning, behold, Dagon was fallen upon his face to the ground before the ark of the LORD; and the head of Dagon and both the palms of his hands were cut off upon the threshold; only the stump of Dagon was left to him (I Sam. 5:2, 4).

106. POOH CORNER

Kumamoto, Japan, '98.

"See that Pooh Bear in the window? That's my apartment. Please stop by," I said. They did. They were young, enthusiastic, and Mormon. One had the first name, Reuben, another, the last name, Lamb. Together they made a great sandwich! Seriously, I enjoyed our times together. I surprised Mr. Lamb, once, noting that Mormonism is materialistic. He asked what I meant, being that volunteers were eating bread crusts to save money. I shared that their view of the Holy Spirit as a physical being limits His office. Also, having planets and children in the next life limits God's plans. I also taught them Mormonism not addressed nowadays, i.e., the *Pearl of Great Price*. The hieroglyphs Joseph Smith translated, we now know, were a funeral oration, nothing to do with Abraham or Moses. Mr. Lamb was not sheepish about questions. I told him Joseph Smith said there were people on the moon, with Quaker style hats. "Really?" was his response. His elder said Smith was speaking figuratively.

"No, he wasn't," I responded. "He spoke to specifics!" There is a time for a feather duster, and a time for a hammer. I never gloated; these were precious souls. They invited me to lead worship at their convention. I thanked them, but declined. I then received permission to speak. Some leaders from Utah came. A third of the 75 workers were Japanese. The teaching that day was: Use Your Testimony-No One Can Deny It, i.e., you can't disprove the subjective. My turn came. I thanked them for the opportunity and opened to Jude 3:

"Beloved, when I gave all diligence to write unto you of the common salvation, it was needful for me to write unto you and exhort you that ye should earnestly contend for the faith which was once delivered unto the saints." We received our sacred writ long ago. More recently, Reuben married a Japanese girl, and Mr. Lamb went back west. I enjoyed our time together. Pooh Corner was a field. Let's break up our fallow ground (Hosea 12:10).

Curmudgeon: But though we, or an angel from heaven, preach any other gospel unto you than that which we have preached unto you, let him be accursed (Gal. 1:8).

107. THE STUMP: 1350 A.D.

Thirteen-year-old Lucinda returned from Mass with a song upon her lips. Opening the latch-less door of the one-room thatched hut, she discovered Uncle Ross stuffing his few things into a patched cloth bag.

"Dearest Uncle, do you depart on some journey?" she asked with surprise.

"I shall not hide it from you. I do indeed, and I hope you will be my companion."

"Whence go ye?"

"I know not with certainty, only that wherever it is, we must go there with haste."

The homily today was from Luke 14, about the King who made no great endeavor without counsel."

"Can you tell me on the way, precious, for time not only flies, in our respect, it kills?"

"Your dark speech does heap fear upon me, Uncle."

"As dark as can be, for I speak of the Black Death. I will tell you to allay more questioning. It has arrived in England, and we must flee this corrupted cauldron or be cooked."

"Where to, O Uncle? No place is safe, except it be in the hands of God."

"To put it in Bible speech for you, the Forest is our City of Refuge."

"But what of friends and neighbors? Would you leave the ancient Beatrice to fare on her own, she and her one goat? Or that poor fool, Will, who cannot even draw water without calamity visiting?"

"Maiden, you will talk us to the death."

"Uncle, surely the hand of our Good God will stretch forth to either help or comfort.

"Come to sense. It is the year 1350. You speak of the Church. The Popes have been in France, our enemy, for forty years. Put your hopes there if you are so brave, I go to the Forest."

"God keep ye," she offered, invoking a blessing. Before he could escape, she hugged him strongly, no easy task as he was of good girth. The door closed partially, never having an understanding of security or privacy. It was a poor hovel, with naught to steal. Besides, with many guests, an open door was best.

Too soon, the village became a dark place, Black, actually. Lucinda visited the ancient Beatrice, and buried the poor fool, Will, along with many others she comforted during their last Earthbound days. Between diggings, she walked on the village road, to rest body and spirit. In an act of a moment, she stepped aside. to pull some weeds and vines, revealing a loose stump.

"You," she said, smiling, "shall be my memorial. You shall not rest atop my ruins, but shall stand here in my stead. And when you are gone, it will matter little, as I was not born to great things." With this accomplished, she returned to the village. When the end came, they did not bury her body. No one remained for the task. She'd lovingly tucked them all into their graves, all except the ancient Beatrice. She died in the girl's arms, Lucinda shortly thereafter, the two serving as each other's death shroud. The scene, for a score of years, was undisturbed, until a party of travelers cut a path on the old village road.

"What say we sleep here this night?" the heartier of the fellows suggested.

"It be a dismal place, Ross, and a dark," the other responded.

"Fear not, Tomas, I will make a fire to frighten off the Sprites," Ross encouraged. Though the Plague was harsh, it left many posts vacated. Ross had left the Forest, found work, and then fortune.

"Aha," he said, extracting a weathered stump from the weeds. "This will warm you to your soul."

"You speak of the soul, that's a laugh. So, tell, what news from London?" Tomas cajoled.

"Well, there's a Pope in Rome, again," Ross replied.

"Saints alive," Tomas exclaimed.

"Don't offer your prayers yet. There's still a Pope in Avignon; now there are two Popes, a twofold blessing, eh Tomas," Ross snickered, availing himself of the stump's sufficient succour.

Grace Lover: And there shall come forth a rod out of the stem of Jesse, and a Branch shall grow out of his roots: [2] And the spirit of the Lord shall rest upon him, the spirit of wisdom and understanding, the spirit of counsel and might, the spirit of knowledge and of the fear of the Lord (Isa. 11:1-2).

Curmudgeon: And when they arose early on the morrow morning, behold, Dagon was fallen upon his face to the ground before the ark of the LORD; and the head of Dagon and both the palms of his hands were cut off upon the threshold; only the stump of Dagon was left to him (I Sam. 5:4).

> And whereas they commanded to leave the stump of the tree roots; thy kingdom shall be sure unto thee, after that thou shalt have known that the heavens do rule (Dan. 4:26).

108. COAST HIGHWAY #1

California, '70.

Tony's Pizza van got as far as Oklahoma, where it ran a stop sign and collided with the town preacher's car, totaling both vehicles. Tony was ok, like the dancers of Keats *Ode to a Grecian Urn*, they preserved in perpetual dance, he with a smile, and an eye on the pizza. We survived a crash, bar rednecks, a runaway van in the wrecking lot, and litigation. I also lost the tapes I'd stolen. Rich and I continued west, hitch-hiking. Once, we received hospitality from a free-spirited family, escorted there by the police, who checked our ID for warrants. In California, we took refuge in the forests. A girl, Maggie, was so taken with these Wisemen from The East. She landed a big kiss on my cheek. It was nice, but we were zephyrs streaming in cross currents. We met Frog, too, a big guy. We swapped stories and a joint over a campfire. On Hwy. #1 we got a lift and had some smoke laced with a horse tranquilizer. It set me on my head. It was the better part of preservation to leave the vehicle after he ran a red light. Visual distortion almost got me killed climbing down a precipice. I then ran through thorn patches on a hill and forgot my name.

We encountered lots of folks on that journey, people looking for a new experience, or reality, or a fantasy of their own making. Paul says believers are new creations (II Corinthians 5:17). Jesus calls it being *born again*, and *born of the Spirit*, (John 3:5,7). If that weren't controversial enough, He tells us He is, the way *the truth and the life*, (John14:6). Jesus gives us a new heart and models what to do with it. In every circumstance, Christ is the *what* and *who* you need, my Friend. Accept no substitutes, they're dangerous!

Grace Lover: This is the stone which was set at nought of you builders, which is become the head of the corner. [12] Neither is there salvation in any other: for there is none other name under heaven given among men, whereby we must be saved (Acts 4:11-12).

Curmudgeon: But the Pharisees said, He casteth out devils through the prince of the devils (Matt. 9:34).

DIMENSION

There's no number today.

Give a dimension a number and it goes crazy. Though there isn't a dimension God doesn't inhabit, I drifted off while we were talking today. My distraction started with a line and a question. Is there such a thing as one dimension? If you have one dimension, don't you really have two? Apart from my finances, nothing has length and no breadth. Is it the same for two? As dimension was bouncing off the angularities in my mind, or unfolding or whatever it is dimensions do, I thought of this as an apologetic. How is it we can construct abstractions that don't seem to exist in part, but in concert, do? There is no one dimension, only an abstraction. Hear this phone call: "Oh Honey, are you at Walmart? Good, could you pick me up a dimension of one? They're in the Abstraction Aisle. What's that, there's no Abstraction Aisle? Well, just think about it and there will be."

Much philosophy posits how we know what we know. It's good stuff, but sometimes I'd prefer a peanut butter and apricot sandwich. Back to apologetics, Soviet Cosmonauts said they had no sighting of God. I've never found the Abstraction Aisle, but I know there is such a thing as one dimension. I can't show it to you, but when added to other dimensions, it's recognizable. It is the same with God. He may be an abstraction to you, but when you add His grace, with faith, you see Him. Other evidences are more concrete, i.e., creation, fulfilled prophecy, changed lives, miracles and more, however, proof doesn't have to be objectively evidential. Do naturalists have evidence? No, they have theories. The burden of proof is on them. How is it they believe in a dimension of one, but no God? How about you?

Curmudgeon: Jesus said unto them, If ye were blind, ye should have no sin: but now ye say, We see; therefore your sin remaineth (John 9:41).

109. BUFFALO GAL

Zishoubana, China, '96.

I awoke that morning in my bus hammock, looking into the face of an elephant. It was a profile, so I knew it wasn't charging me. That was nice, but I was sick again! Why did my body and Asian vermin have such an attraction? I rented a bicycle when we got to town and went off; I didn't really know where. When I got there, I took the bike on a small boat. I mean a *small boat*—two feet wide, if it were an inch. I took pictures in a village and returned. The road was packed! Not a human was in sight, however, there were water buffalo, and they weren't going anywhere. I was sick, feverish, and I'd had my camera doused with water. Just a side note: Don't take pictures during a Water Festival. Anyway, I was beat. The water buffalo had their calves with them—to add to my paranoia. I imagined the mothers being protective, bordering on homicidal. Time to pray!

On the far side, a village girl made her way through the herd. They ignored her. Hallelujah! Deliverance! I pushed forward with my bicycle, hoping its slight frame could protect my slighter frame. Well, Buffalo Gal and I passed each other half-way. I offered a greeting and a prayer of thanksgiving and tarried not in the way. I made it back to the hotel, bedraggled but blessed, to discover someone had stolen my passport. My I.D. was gone, and I'd spend two-hundred dollars to fix a camera worth a hundred dollars, but I had all my vital organs, a delightful adventure, I'd persevered, and the Lord had provided. Not a bad day for a one-hundred and thirty-pound teacher of English.

Grace Lover: The Lord is my light and my salvation; whom shall I fear? the Lord is the strength of my life; of whom shall I be afraid? [3]Though an host should encamp against me, my heart shall not fear: though war should rise against me, in this will I be confident. [4]One thing have I desired of the Lord, that will I seek after; that I may dwell in the house of the Lord all the days of my life, to behold the beauty of the Lord, and to enquire in his temple (Ps. 27:1, 3-4).

> And call upon me in the day of trouble: I will deliver thee, and thou shalt glorify me (Psalm 50:15).

Curmudgeon: Ye lust, and have not: ye kill, and desire to have, and cannot obtain: ye fight and war, yet ye have not, because ye ask not (James 4:2).

P.S. Nuclear physicists believe some atomic particles are one-dimensional.

Maybe they found the Abstraction Aisle!

110. JEREMIAH AND THE TATTOOED LADIES

The K-Mart in Chili, N.Y. was always a barren wasteland, as difficult to find a clerk as it is to tread applesauce. I liked it. Before it closed, in 2017, I found a discounted treasure—Mario Monopoly! It's not a game of skill, so I have a chance to win! What followed was neat too! Two young ladies on line, chatted. They talked about a bar they frequented and their tattoos. Then what happened perked my ears up.

Girl #1: "Oh what's that?" one asked regarding the other's bracelet.

Girl #2: "Oh, that's my Jeremiah 29:11. My Mom gave it to me.

Girl #1: "What's it all about?"

Girl #2: "Oh, it's about God having a plan for us, or something like that."

Person in line: "Excuse me, I couldn't help overhearing you. Years ago, I asked the Lord for a theme verse for each year. The first one I received was Jeremiah 29:11: "I know the plans I have for you, saith the Lord, plans for good and not for evil to give you a hope and an expected end."

Girl #1: "It's amazing you knew that!"

Cashier: "That will be $13.47, Ma'am,"

Person in Line: "God bless you, have a nice day."

Waiting on line doesn't have to be spent resisting the chocolates of destruction, or averting your eyes from tabloids. It could be an opportunity to share a blessing, a Word, a thank you.

Grace Lover: Let them now that fear the Lord say, that his mercy endureth for ever (Ps. 118:4).

Our lovely host family at Calle Doce.

111. CALLE DOCE

Sonora State, Mexico, 1979.

"No, that's wrong," I said.

Ken tried again: "'Juan 3:16, 'Porque de tal manera amo Dios el mundo que ha dado su...'"

Unbeknownst to him, I tied his shoelaces together as he studied our evangelism tract. Our leader, Bobby Mendoza, then introduced the pastor with whom we'd be working. Ken stood up, extended a hand, and almost ended up in the pastor's embrace, his footwear accomplishing that for which I conscripted it. Bobby was livid, later chastising us for disrespect. He was right, but come on, Jesus had a mixed bunch. Did they tease occasionally? I just followed tradition.

After this, we went on to the village, *Calle Doce*—Twelfth Street. I loved it, and not because I was raised on Twelfth Street in New York. We handed out invitations for a Jesus Only crusade. We didn't agree on doctrine, but they were evangelical. Folks invited us in, listened to our broken Spanish, and made coffee. They didn't have two beans to rub together, but shared. It was moving. The men were away in the mines during the week, returning on weekends. We had a good turnout for the crusade. One speaker on the podium fell asleep, woke up, and shouted, "Amen." I understood why he napped. The heat could melt a frappe in under a minute!

The family that hosted us for five days was great. Mornings, at 4 A.M., the father went to the market for steer heads. At home, he hacked off the fur with a hatchet, cracked open the skulls, and extracted the brains for tacos. With hot sauce and cilantro, they were quite good. When it came time to leave, we shared hugs and tears freely. I'd come home. It wasn't my Twelfth Street, but it challenged my heart and perspectives. I made international friendships. Theory became experience.

Grace Lover: Let us make a little chamber, I pray thee, on the wall; and let us set for him there a bed, and a table, and a stool, and a candlestick: and it shall be, when he cometh to us, that he shall turn in thither (II Kings 4:10).

112. 430 A.D.: AUGUSTINE'S WAR

"Noble Quirinius, it is good to see you."

"You embarrass me, Augustine; it is I who should first bring greetings. But I am not surprised, your piety is known to all."

"With such an opening, you leave me nothing to say except to offer refreshment. Let me challenge all you have claimed of me by saying you look tired.

"Yes, it is true, and there is a reason for such a state," Quirinius conceded.

"Vandals?"

"That would be part of the whole."

"That is a heavy enough burden for any soldier. There is another beside it?" Augustine asked.

Here Quirinius lowered his head, embarrassed a second time, only now his face changed color.

"A woman?" Augustine surmised.

"Well..."

"A sleeveless tunic bows a head no armour nor sword could hope to bend. Did God not make us an interesting collection of contradictions?"

"You mock, but you have not walked this path before."

"On the contrary, this is one war I fought for years."

"How did you..." Quirinius began.

"There is not time with a more pressing conflict near our gates, but let me say, it is a war I lost to a commander of great fortitude—a godly mother. I am glad to be the vanquished. Now I can follow what our beloved Christ called the Ephesians' 'first love.'"

"You speak of Christ as your conqueror?"

"Yes, my friend. Here, drink this and have a moment's rest. I have a deep well."

"Of that I was already aware," he said, receiving the cup. "Thank you. Let me ask you..."

"Quirinius, stand not upon ceremony with me, we are close, brothers in His sight."

"What do you think of the fight?" the soldier asked.

"I am troubled by it."

"Am I wrong to resist?"

"Circumstance presses us deeper into an understanding of His heart. Years ago, I opposed the struggle. Now, I lean another way. Though it is subject to the conscience of the man, I am of the thought it is conscionable to fight for community, to protect others. It is less supportable to do so for oneself. I'm beginning to think that to save others from evil is a just cause."

"What is confusing is that these Vandals name the name of Christ. They do not, however, hold to the divinity of the Lord or the Holy Spirit. In a sense, they are like Jews."

"Yes, Quirinius, but our Jewish friends often affirmed the truth of their Covenant. Our Vandal neighbors hold to a small part of theirs. Embrace me, Brother, I see a messenger coming for you. Grant me this chance to pray. Dear Father, lead us in truth, and help us live in peace with them that make peace. In the name of the Father, the Son, and the Holy Spirit. Amen."

Grace Lover: Therefore all things whatsoever ye would that men should do to you, do ye even so to them: for this is the law and the prophets (Matt. 7:12).

Curmudgeon: Let every soul be subject unto the higher powers. For there is no power but of God: the powers that be are ordained of God. [2]Whosoever therefore resisteth the power, resisteth the ordinance of God: and they that resist shall receive to themselves damnation. [3]For rulers are not a terror to good works, but to the evil. Wilt thou then not be afraid of the power? do that which is good, and thou shalt have praise of the same (Ro. 13:1-3).

113. PIOUS LYING

Hermosillo, Sonora State, Mexico, 1979.

"Your Mission, Mr. Wilkins, should you decide to accept it, is to detonate this disc in the square." I didn't get this message from Mission Impossible, but from our Mexico Mission Leader, Ted. I was soon walking down a winding street. I never got to the town square; kids came out of the cobblestones! I took out the disc, a paper-thin plastic sandwiched between two pieces of cardboard harboring a needle, creating a phonograph powered by Bic technology—a pen. On one side was the John Chapter 3, on the flip side, a testimony and sinner's prayer. I think many children believed that day. We gave them tracts and went house to house, witnessing.

Most families opened their door. We'd studied our tract in Spanish. Many people prayed with us and said they'd come to the Sunday service. We promised an escort. I had trouble entering the Mission door, being ten feet tall and having angel wings! We vied with each other to share our victories. Ted however, dismissed us with a: "Oh, that's nice." I couldn't believe his lack of enthusiasm. I didn't say so, but I did take his sorry condition to the Throne. Sunday came, and I went back to lead the flock to the pastures of God. I could hear people at the back of homes. It was as if a leper came to town. I returned to the Church, a small gathering of local converts who had come to the Lord with the help of the consistent witness and prayer of the missionaries.

"But they all said they would come…" I told Ted.

"Pious lying," he responded. "It would be rude to refuse."

Ted's attitude improved after that, and I had a lot to think about.

Curmudgeon: Let another man praise thee, and not thine own mouth; a stranger, and not thine own lips (Prov. 27:2).

> Who art thou that judgest another man's servant? to his own master he standeth or falleth. Yea, he shall be holden up: for God is able to make him stand. (Ro. 14:4).

114. SUPER HERO: LAVA MAN

In 435 B.C.

Empedocles was a Greek philosopher in Italy, a Corporeal Pluralist (not everything can be reduced to one material substance), a position his Ionian Greek (West Turkey), counterparts proposed. Also, there's no spirit, and the physical world is the combination of four elements. Heraclitus proposed that life derived from fire. Anaximenes, from air, and Thales, from water, all the conclusions of observation. Empedocles put them together and came up with the elemental chart. It would last for two-thousand years. Who can say anything that lasts for two-thousand years? Even God has trouble with that! I speak tongue in cheek. God's problem is He speaks to idiots who ignore Him.

Empedocles was smart, but vain. The latter was his end. Afraid a corpse would disprove his demi-god status, the Super Synthesist, became an alchemist, turning flesh into lava, with a big splash. Pushing sixty, he climbed Mt. Aetna to the cauldron and joined the magma. As for being a Pluralist, he believed something held the four elements together, the "Fifth Essence," or the "Quintessence." Paul asserts, in Roman 2, that God has put the knowledge of Him in our hearts. Behind the scenes are the soul, the conscience, and the spirit. The assertions of empiricists and logicians have had astute conclusions, but there is always another question posed. Those who follow Logic alone will lead a cold life with a cold end, or, in Empedocles' case, a hot one. The grave isn't the end. Acts 17:28 tells us: "In him we move and live and have our being." The best philosophy (love of wisdom) is to: "...fear God and to keep his commandments" (Eccles. 12:13) Have you discovered the Quintessence of Life? It's Him!

Grace Lover: In a moment, in the twinkling of an eye, at the last trump: for the trumpet shall sound, and the dead shall be raised incorruptible, and we shall be changed (I Cor. 15:52).

Curmudgeon: Pride goeth before destruction, and an haughty spirit before a fall (Prov. 16:18).

115. THE FAIRMONT

San Francisco, Ca., '78.

"Frankly Charlotte, I don't give a d..." Rhett said, leaving her to a decaying mansion and disappearing dreams. That scene is from the Civil War epic movie, *Gone With The Wind*. The staircase scenes were filmed at the Fairmont Hotel, San Francisco.

The year before moving to San Francisco, my wife left to visit her sister. After months of waiting for her return, I moved to California. We would get reconciled, or I'd join a mission. She worked at the Fairmont, so I applied there and got a job. We met one day, joined by her bridesmaid who was pregnant, unmarried, backslidden, and considering an abortion. I was not welcome.

The Fairmont had a split-shift. I went twice a day. Senior busboys collected tips and distributed according to their grasp of division. They were devotees of some new math. Things weren't always fair at the Fairmont. After my wife became adamant about our separation, the hotel was only a reminder of failed love. She was so close, but so far. I quit the job. It split my time and my heart. Then, the Simpsons, missionaries to Japan with Christians in Action, came to my church. The Mission Training course would start in two months. I was there.

The 5-Star Fairmont is grand, has history, and is death to me. We all have a Fairmont. I left for CinA and was involved in street ministry 3 times a week. We struggled together to see the Kingdom spread. The Fairmont's big, classy doors closed, but another door opened—His door.

Grace Lover: And the key of the house of David will I lay upon his shoulder; so he shall open, and none shall shut; and he shall shut, and none shall open (Isa. 22:22).

> For a great door and effectual is opened unto me, and there are many adversaries (I Cor. 16:9).

Curmudgeon: If thou doest well, shalt thou not be accepted? and if thou doest not well, sin lieth at the door. And unto thee shall be his desire, and thou shalt rule over him (Gen. 4:7).

On the train to Urumqi. The lad taught me Chinese chess.

116. CHINA CALLING

Lanzhou, China, 1995.

She signified her price, stretching four fingers across the flap of her bag!

We lived in Kampong Cham when Caleb was born. Once a month we went to see the team in Phnom Penh. We liked the Lanzhou Restaurant in the N.Y. Hotel. We'd get a three-course dinner, and tea, for five dollars, at The Lanzhou. I'd been to Lanzhou. When traveling there by train, I sat with a country doctor, a lady. She'd become a Christian during the Cultural Revolution. I had a fever and was happy to get some medicine. Her pretty daughter requested I take her to New York—the city, not the hotel. I graciously declined and stepped out of the window into the sunset. The train line sold too many tickets, so people sat in the aisle. I had to get out by the window. Many Chinese chain smoke, so I was glad to breathe again. I bought a melon for four yuan and had a hotel room in five minutes. Beat and dehydrated, I took out a pen, made a dozen perforations in my melon, pulled it apart and stuck my face in it. Oooh, that was good! I took the medicine and slept for fourteen hours. I awoke thinking I should get started, but couldn't remember what had to be done or where. The next day, I opened my curtains to expose a mosque! Big surprise. I was in the Semi-Autonomous Region of Mongolia. Mao Tse Dong had made concessions for semi self-rule, with certain groups, to gain support for the Revolution. I went to the mosque with my pack of Bibles and tracts in the Chinese, Mongolian, and Russian languages. The Imam was out, so I left the Bible with others. I then met two ladies from differing walks, a lady of the evening and a vendor of cold drinks. I gave the latter a tract; she gave me a drink. She'd take no money! I blessed her, climbed a dusty hill, and prayed to the Lord Most High, feeling very blessed, myself.

Grace Lover: How beautiful upon the mountains are the feet of him that bringeth good tidings, (Isa. 52:7).

> And whosoever shall give to drink unto one of these little ones a cup of cold water only in the name of a disciple, verily I say unto you, he shall in no wise lose his reward (Matt. 10:42).

117. PSA FLIGHT 182

While a student at Christians in Action, Long Beach, I went to San Francisco to visit friends, and got the idea to go to Mexico to see the team in Hermosillo, the Sonora state capital. Soon, I was enjoying the city's sights. I didn't know the team's location, and had to call CinA for the address. I had to call collect, as it's impossible to stuff so many pesos in a phone. The receptionist stated that they weren't allowed to receive collect calls. As I was an under-classman, she was intent, at first, to let me squirm. At last, I received the information needed.

My first shower there uncovered a small scorpion—the worst kind, but the team was warm, the weather hot, and I enjoyed *jugo naranja* (orange juice) at the juice stand. Too soon, it was time to leave. I remember reading The *Narnia Chronicles* on the various buses I rode through Mexico.

As for PSA Flight 182, I'd taken an airplane to San Diego to get me close to the Mexican border. I think I took Flight 182, but could be mistaken. I remember flying out of San Francisco; but Flight 182 was out of Sacramento. I did visit friends hither and thither, so that may explain it. At any rate, I gave the stewardesses Christian tracts as I disembarked. A few weeks later, I heard of the fatal crash of Flight 182, and thought it was the crew I'd met. Only the Lord and PSA records know for sure. I hope, before they left this Earth, they accepted His invitation to the Banquet Supper of the Lamb. Unbeknownst to us or to the person to whom we share, we are sometimes giving a last call. This is not a drill, Friends. We play a part in the Eternal Affairs Department. Let's not wait for Mayday to share the Good News. Let's be good stewards of the flight on which He puts us.

Grace Lover: So teach us to number our days, that we may apply our hearts unto wisdom (Ps. 90:12).

> (For he saith, I have heard thee in a time accepted, and in the day of salvation have I succoured thee: behold, now is the accepted time; behold, now is the day of salvation) II Cor. 6:2.

> Praying always with all prayer and supplication in the Spirit, and watching thereunto with all perseverance and supplication for all saints;[19]And for me, that utterance may be given unto me, that I may open my mouth boldly, to make known the mystery of the gospel (Eph. 6:18-19).

118. YOU KILLED HIM

Honolulu, Hawaii, 1974.

They pelted him with snowballs. He was on in years, standing outside their factory. His offense was proclaiming the love of God. The barrage was not without good fruit. In the secret of darkness, one came to see him. The visitor heard the Gospel.

"So, who killed Jesus?" the evangelist tested his guest.

"Those awful Romans," the man answered.

"Yes, they did, but who else?" the teacher asked. The guest was quiet. "It was you. You killed Him. It was your sin that put Jesus on the cross."

This moving scene is from the movie *Shiokari Toge* (Shiokari Pass), a true story by Miura, Ayako. It was not the most moving scene, however. Toward the end of the story, the protagonist, Nobuo, receives permission to marry. He's waited years for his fiancé to recover from TB. It's a time of celebration, but while riding a train in the Shiokari Pass of Hokkaido, his train car gets disconnected. The separated car begins to retrace its path, backwards, down the mountain, rapidly picking up speed. It will soon roll off the tracks, causing many deaths. Nobuo, who has been preaching about God's love, uses the only tool at his disposal to stop the train—his body. Jumping on the tracks, he stops the runaway car. I saw the film in a Honolulu theatre filled with a lot of old, weeping, second generation, Japanese-Americans, and one, young, weeping, Irish-American. I decided I must go to Japan. I also killed Him. I was indebted to His love. I didn't feel I could do as well as the film's lovers of God, but I wanted to go.

Today, at the dental clinic, I offered the technician a New Testament. "Today you polished my teeth," I said, "this book can polish your soul." Was it corny? I'm a foreigner; they expect me to be weird. It wasn't the pithy preaching of the evangelist, just me—following the Holy Spirit the best I knew. She took the Bible. Some folks take enormous risks for the Lord; others put their ego in jeopardy of a dose of rejection. We may not get it perfect, but we all can do something.

Grace Lover: Now also when I am old and grey-headed, O God, forsake me not; until I have shewed thy strength unto this generation, and thy power to everyone that is to come (Ps. 71:18).

119. SILENT-WITNESS

Kampong Cham, Cambodia, 2004.

Do you remember your child's first laugh? We bought a purplish mattress with a bear print for Caleb. We put it on the second-floor porch. One day, Caleb sat on it, next to my open Bible. A breeze blew, and the pages fluttered. Caleb thought it was the greatest thing since Winnie the Pooh mobiles, and laughed and laughed. Later, when we'd go on our nightly gecko searches, he added squeaking to laughter. While he was in the womb in Kyushu, Japan, I remained in Cambodia. During that time, I decorated to get ready for Yuko and the baby's return. I put up a mosquito net, lamp, urns, and a variety of flora on the porch. I painted Blue Star flowers, our wedding flower, in the kitchen. I painted a desert with a stream, and wrote a portion of Isaiah 42, our wedding verse, in Japanese, in the bedroom. Over the main entrance, I drew a vine and wrote John 3:16 in Khmer.

In two-thousand and six we moved. Ten years later, we transferred to Japan. Before going, we took a trip back to Kampong Cham to visit. We stopped by the old house and asked the renters, a water company, if we could look inside. It was a step back in time. I was sad to see the disrepair of what had been our home, but something else cheered me. Over the mantle was the vine and John 3:16, still sharing its message over ten years after I'd painted it. This episode, in Kampong Cham, was reminiscent of the woman with the alabaster box at Simon the Leper's home (Matt. 26). I was blessed to see my life had left a witness. It's okay if I don't know all, it's in the Record Book. We'll be surprised at what God has used in our lives for His glory.

Grace Lover: So shall my word be that goeth forth out of my mouth: it shall not return unto me void, but it shall accomplish that which I please, and it shall prosper in the thing whereto I sent it (Isa. 55:11).

> For in that she hath poured this ointment on my body, she did it for my burial.[13] Verily I say unto you, Wheresoever this gospel shall be preached in the whole world, there shall also this, that this woman hath done, be told for a memorial of her (Matt. 26:12,13).

Curmudgeon: And this is the writing that was written, MENE, MENE, TEKEL, UPHARSIN. [26] This is the interpretation of the thing: MENE; God hath numbered thy kingdom, and finished it.[27] TEKEL; Thou art weighed in the balances, and art found wanting (Dan. 5:25-27).

Squatter Village kids at Vacation Bible School, Kampong Cham, 2005

120. GARAGE EVANGELISM DAY

Kampong Cham, Cambodia, 2004—

Spiders, 3" across, were a popular item at road-stands. We posed with a sample in our mouth. Taste? I say, "Just like the sauce." We were excited! The Keo family invited us to start a church in Kampong Cham. We were going there, and Kompot, each twice a month. Later, we moved to Kampong Cham. The Margins took the Kompot work.

But we're putting the roteh (cart)before the seh (horse). The Margins got a truck from our Team Leader, Pol Guazon, and we inherited the Margin's Korean made Towner. It was the size of a bathtub and ran almost as fast. We piled in young volunteers and headed out. On the way, the Towner overheated, so we pulled into a garage. I called her *Nellybelle*, after the broken-down jeep in the *Roy Rodgers Show*. While the car was being teased, Pareak and I witnessed to the workers (it may have been Pareak's twin, Pheroam). After 20 minutes and a few dollars, we left. We were good for 20 minutes when the symptoms reappeared. We repeated the M.O.; go to a garage, give out tracts, a few dollars, lose time, and off again. It was like the repetitions in the Book of Judges, only more positive. By the time we arrived, we'd repeated the pattern 5 times—a day of God's appointments. Many students came for English and Bible classes. Within the year, we moved to town, had a church, school, development group, and a church plant closer to the Vietnam border. An *iffy* road-trip was not an accurate forecaster. Was the Towner built poorly or had it just reached its end? This reminds me of the question put to Jesus, of the man born blind. Was it because of his or his parent's sin? Jesus said it was neither, but that God could be glorified. It is the same for Towners.

Grace Lover: And when they had fasted and prayed, and laid their hands on them, they sent them away. [4] So they, being sent forth by the Holy Ghost, departed unto Seleucia; and from thence they sailed to Cyprus. [5] And when they were at Salamis, they preached the word of God in the synagogues of the Jews: and they had also John to their minister (Acts 13:3-5).

Curmudgeon: But Jonah rose up to flee unto Tarshish from the presence of the LORD (Jonah 1:3).

P.S. The photo on the next page is not a Towner, it's a triangle wing. I thought it would be useful for long distances in Mongolia. I wrote up a prospectus, but the Mission did not want to pioneer a new field, choosing to go where invited, instead.

On a wing and a prayer in neighboring Thailand.

121. WINESKINS

A Generation X youth walks into a church. He knows the majors about Christianity; Noah gave the Ten Commandments, and Jesus said don't judge anyone-cool! He looks at a wall sign; Attendance: 37, Offering: $119.13, Songs: Rescue the Perishing, The Church's One Foundation, Battle Hymn of the Republic. Evangelism Committee: Bowling Wednesday.

"Hello, may I help you?"

"Oh, hi, you must be the priest," the youth answers.

"Close, we call ourselves pastors," the host responds.

"Oh, sweet, tell me, those perishing, is that a song about hurricane relief? Radical!"

"Actually, that's talking about people's spiritual condition.

"Oh," the visitor notes. "How about that foundation? I'm a tradesman when I'm not in school."

"Oh, no, that's talking about Jesus. He is the one in whom we trust."

"All others pay cash, eh?" the visitor jokes. The pastor smiles. Another question follows.

"The last one?" he asks, not venturing to be more specific this time.

"Oh, that's about our faith being a battle." Nodding, the visitor thanks the pastor for his time.

"Tell me," the pastor inquires, "what do you study?"

"Constitutional Controversies, Website Development, and Another Look at History."

"Sounds interesting," the pastor replies. "Sunday, we have Methodist History if you..."

"Oh thanks, but I join a forum, *The Arena of Ideas*, on various topics, with a Q and A after."

"Great, I hope to see you again. Next month, maybe you can make our Baroque Cello concert."

"Thanks, pastor, this has been, um, educational." He turns to go but first flashes a gesture the pastor's way of which the cleric is not familiar, and so, responds: "Bye. God...bless."

Grace Lover: Let your light so shine before men, that they may see your good works, and glorify your Father which is in heaven (Matt. 5:16).

Curmudgeon: The woman saith unto him, Sir, I perceive that thou art a prophet (John 14:19).

122. ONE LEFT

Southern Ca, '79.

It would be blasphemy to call UCLA, USC, and visa-versa. But that's what happens when I and sports mix. I like sports, but sports don't like me. I always dislocate something or pull something else. As for sports by proxy, why watch somebody excel in what I perform dismally? Anyway, these two campuses are sports rivals in California.

At Christians in Action, we had three days of witnessing a week. We did a jaunt to the Jewish section of L.A. each month, hit a campus now and again, and once during our training went on Faith Trek to visit politicians. I guess the latter took an extra measure of faith. One day, Freddie Roberson and I teamed up; he had a car. We didn't want to bunch up, so we hit opposite sides of the campus. He was gone a long time, and I was running out of tracts. We had an important appointment at CinA—we were the dish-washing stewards. Finally, I saw Freddie approaching. I had one tract remaining. Some folks were leaving the tennis court.

"Hi, ...," I said. "I don't want to bother you, but I'd like to give you this. It's about knowing our final destination." I had one hand on his shoulder. He didn't speak, but took it, and I thanked him. It was Jimmy Connors and his girlfriend. He wasn't much taller than me and had a pimple on his nose. They got in his sports car, and Freddie pulled up—end of mission. Break out the dish towels! Freddie and I finished our tasks that day. It's sobering that some people in Hebrews 11, the Hall of Heroes, did not finish well, e.g., Barak, Gideon, Samson, and Jephthah. Let's keep our eyes on the real goal—Jesus.

Grace Lover: I press toward the mark for the prize of the high calling of God in Christ Jesus (Phil. 3:14).

Curmudgeon: For I am now ready to be offered, and the time of my departure is at hand. [7] I have fought a good fight, I have finished my course, I have kept the faith (II Tim. 4:6-7).

123. WINESKINS II: APOLLYON

A Millennial Man walks into a church. He knows the majors of Christianity; Nostradamus wrote Revelation, and Jesus promises believers a Mercedes—cool! Inside, he catches a UFO—an earlier generation called a Frisbee. Coming his way, a forty-something fellow in shorts, vies with teeming tots of the childcare group, and makes it to the doors before there are any escapees.

"Sorry about the sortie—be with you in 3 jumps of a toad, "he says. Thinking the guest is a Millennial Male, he affixes him, mentally, an M&M emoji, and loads kids on the aquarium bus.

"No prob," the M&M replies. He noticed that the man in shorts seemed well practiced at the task.

"Hi, I'm Peter," the shepherd says, returning unscathed, but a little winded, from his mission.

"Friends call me Apollyon," M&M offers.

Peter pauses a moment but comes back with: "Isn't that taken already?"

M&M had received this response before, and didn't pause: "Yeah, but so is Jesus."

"Point taken," Peter says. "Hey, we've got a new drink machine—let's check it out!

Cuppa in hand, Apollyon pans the office. There's a photo of an old church sanctuary. It reads: "Attendance: 37, Offering: $119.13, Songs: Rescue the Perishing, Evangelism Committee: Bowling Wednesday." A flat screen posts church activities: Head, Heart, and Hand, Let's Right a Letter—Literacy Lite, Colossal Childcare, Internet Prayer Net, etc. A rug hugs the corner.

"It's a Muslim prayer rug. An Imam friend I debated gave it to me in Constantinople."

Apollyon shook his head slightly. "You mean Istanbul, don't you?"

"I guess I'm nostalgic."

"The name changed six-hundred years ago."

They banter a little, then Peter asks: "Apollyon, what part do I play in your journey today?"

"Actually, I came to help you today," he answers.

"Ok, fill me in," Peter says.

"Well, I want to crush your myth. It hurts folks." The pastor poses a rhetorical question.

"Do myths have prophecies regarding time, place, or family? That's a few of over fifty?"

"People can tamper with prophecies," Apollyon asserts.

"To say the scriptures are adjusted, one has to be ignorant of culture, history, and Judaism. There has been no altering of the Word. The Judeo-Christian scriptures are the best-preserved texts of any time and place. Most extant manuscripts come on the scene eight hundred years after the original. Scholars dated the P 52 fragment of John's Gospel between 110-150 A.D.

"Whoa, that was a mouthful. Ok, but what about scientific realities?" Apollyon asks.

"Great question. We are starting an apologetics class next week— you are welcome to attend."

"Can I bring up opposing views?"

"Go for it," Peter says. "I love the arena of ideas!"

They discuss the Big Bang, Irreducible Complexity, evolution, flexible tissue in dinosaur fossils, and then flipping from Pastor's Office to Man Cave, the future of the Kansas City Royals.

"I'm curious," Apollyon says. "what's the story of that picture with the statistics?"

"My father met a pastor and took that picture. It was a collision of worldviews. I hope to be a bridge. One apologist said a worldview has to have logical consistency, empirical adequacy (is verifiable), and has to be experientially relevant. Do we want to make watermelons levitate, or discover the deep things of God?" Eyeing the clock, he adds: "To avoid injury, you must leave!"

"Wha…" Apollyon begins.

"Earlier you encountered the Lord's Lambs' bus. This group is the Lions of the Lair. Beware."

"Point taken," Apollyon agrees.

"Thanks for coming—hope to see you next week," Peter adds.

"I'll be there." He exits as a million kids race in their quest to be the first to hug Pastor Peter.

Grace Lover and Curmudgeon: Where wast thou when I laid the foundations of the earth? declare, if thou hast understanding (Job 38:4).

> Ye are the light of the world. A city that is set on an hill cannot be hid (Matt. 5:14).

> Wherefore, my beloved brethren, let every man be swift to hear, slow to speak, slow to wrath (James 1:19).

124. PADDLE CONFESSIONS

Stanford, Connecticut, 1897.

In 1982, I recorded some Grandma Clark's stories. She had some interesting tales. Her father was the first electric trolley driver on Staten Island. I think she said it was the #4 Trolley, in 1904—the story had a 4 somewhere. Traveling from Staten Island to her former residence in Stanford, she saw her first horseless carriage at the pier.

"Back then," Grandma said, "you went to the dock at night to meet folks coming home on the ferry from work. You recognized neighbors by their mount, a dappled, a chestnut. and so forth."

Movie buffs will like this next one. Grandma's family wasn't well-to-do, but they had a plot on the beach. When the last *Perils of Pauline* movie was filmed, the ship was blown up! Grandma's family found some flotsam, a door from one cabin, which they put on their cottage—sorry, no pictures survive.

She had a sad story of her Irish grandmother, who came over in the 1880's. Grandma saw her walk behind the house. She never saw her again; the new high-speed train struck her. The deceased had sewn beautiful Irish lace. Grandma liked her. There was a long line of carriages in her funeral. After this story, Grandma related her first two memories.

"Well, Christopher, I was standing on the front porch of our house in Stanford, with my brother, Andrew. A ship went by and he said: 'Look at the soapsuds!'" It's a riddle. Can you figure it out? The ship was a paddle-wheeler. Her second one was no less intriguing. She said: "I received an invitation to our neighbor's house. While I was there, the lady served toast. I didn't like it and threw it on the floor. 'You shouldn't do that,' the lady said. 'God will see it.' I put my shoe on top of it, and said, 'Oh, no He won't.'"

Paddling kids is out of style. It's beastly, so we progressed to spatulas. When the Dark-Side sued for sovereignty, a spatula on Caleb's bottom chased away the Hobgoblins of Rebellion. One day, we picked up a small spatula for our cooking collection. Caleb's eyes widened. "Is that for Corey?" he asked. We were smiling too broadly to fool him. It was for the bottom of pans, not cans. Paddle-wheelers and paddles may change, but we'll always need confession and forgiveness. If the former is there, the latter is also there. He has promised!

Grace Lover: Like as a father pitieth his children, so the Lord pitieth them that fear him (Ps. 103:13).

125. THE EMEROD CITY

Raiders of the Lost Ark was cool. A retake of old Swashbucklers, it had Nazis, desert, intrigue, and melting faces. Yet, for all its positives, it was predictable. The Nazis died when they opened the Ark. In real life, Uzzah, with good motives, died for touching it (II Sam. 6:6). As the feet of the priests who bore the Ark touched the Jordan, the river parted (Josh 3). Thinking they were invincible if the Ark was with them, the Israelites took it into battle against the Philistines, but lost it and the conflict (1 Sam. 5). The victors placed the Ark in Dagon's temple as a trophy, but Dagon bowed to it. Something was fishy! The Philistines set the idol on its tail—it was half man, half fish. Again, it did obeisance, and lost body parts. There was more fun. The people got hemorrhoids. Each of the five Philistine cities sent the Ark to its neighbor, hoping to find hemorrhoidal relief. If there were Preparation H., it wouldn't have worked. One can't escape the hand of God. This was a chance for the Philistines to embrace the true God. They didn't.

What does this half-fish story reel in? Have you settled things with the One whose presence filled the Ark? Dorothy and Toto went to the Emerald City to meet the Wizard. They discover the wizard is a sham. Contrariwise, the God of the Universe is holy. His only design is your welfare. Realize it is God's right to break into your fantasy and remind you He is Boss. He is without flaw, or any negative your imagination places on Him. Your gods will crumble at His feet. Your strength and excuses will falter before his righteousness. Don't try to lift Dagon. Leave him in pieces. Don't follow the Yellow Brick Road to find a con man. Jesus is the way! John 14:6.

Grace Lover and Curmudgeon: Then said they, What shall be the trespass offering which we shall return to him? They answered, Five golden emerods, and five golden mice, according to the number of the lords of the Philistines: for one plague was on you all, and on your lords (I Sam. 6:4).

126. GRANDMA'S TEAPOT MYSTERY

Clearwater, Fl., '75.

Mom died of Lupus when I was 17. Dad remarried, a woman with 5 kids. Dad liked punishment. Don't get me wrong, I loved my step-family. My step-brother and I evaded the Law together, but we missed this adventure. Move center stage, Grandma Clark. In her eighties and spry, she was slightly hobbled of knee. The step-kids loved her and so the car was loaded up. Two adults and three contraries endeavored to make the 1300-mile trip. Disney World was an incentive to suffer the ignominy of travel with siblings, but Mickey's Magic couldn't rival the Celtic Conjurer. When the Wilkins invaded 1312 Prospect Towers, that Daughter of Hibernia's first course was to put on the kettle. She then poured the tea into cups with amazing results. No wand had been waved, no incantation offered, but the tea in each cup was a different color!

"I love lemon tea," Tom remarked.

"Can't be; mine is orange," Karen insisted.

"I know what lemon is, stupid," Tom countered.

"That's strange, mine is cherry! Grandma how…" Joanne asked.

Grandma candidly confided, "I had no sugar, so I put Life Savers in your cups!" It was magic-of-old only in the sense that the augur was aged, or those candies had been around a few years!

At a wedding in Cana, Jesus performed His first recorded *sign*, as John calls them, turning water into wine. He didn't wipe out the Romans or reveal a new latke's recipe. His calling card sign was wine, the symbol of fruitfulness and life. If that is how He started, let's keep posted.

Grace Lover: And many other signs truly did Jesus in the presence of his disciples, which are not written in this book (John 20:30):

> And to know the love of Christ, which passeth knowledge, that ye might be filled with all the fulness of God. 21 Unto him be glory in the church by Christ Jesus throughout all ages, world without end. Amen (Eph. 3:19, 21).

127. JOE

"Here's your mic. When Doctor Verdades finishes, he will address you. Do you have a question?"

"Any prizes?" Joe asked. As the question went unanswered, he said: "It was a joke. I'm good."

"Thank you, Sir." In the next minute, Joe rolled his eyes twice, as if enduring eternities.

'Thank you for your story, Jill," the Doctor responded. "I'll think about what you said."

"Thank you for listening," Jill said. After an appropriate pause, Verdades turned to Joe.

"Hi Joe, did the Lord turn your water into wine?" he asked, but Joe had his own cask.

"What's up, Doc?" Joe answered, his smile joined by those familiar with the Cartoon Channel. I've got two words for you, Doc, Crusades and *Inquisition*?"

"Any takers out there, audience?" the Doctor asked, but no one wanted his turn. Joe tripled his previous eye-rolling as Verdades spoke of Sola Scriptura, transformed lives, and more.

"You took me down to one word," Joe said. Dr. Verdades waited. "Hypocrites," Joe concluded.

"The Church isn't perfect, Joe, the Savior is," Doc offered. "Thanks for coming today. Let's chat over a hamburger later." Joe, nearing the exit, waved to the crowd without facing the speaker.

- Ten Minutes Later

"Hey, Joe, what gives?" Jerry asked as Joe enters the butcher's shop.

"Talkin' heads, Jerry. I just came from the Center."

"I avoid that place. What can I get ya, t'day?"

"Gimme some sirloin. Don't mix it. I dropped your competition 'cause he pulled a fast one."

"Hey, you're *In the Know*, Joe. I couldn't fool you."

"You got that right. You're ok., Jer. Besides a guy can't stop eating because of one rotten apple."

"You want that gift wrapped?"

"Just stick it in a bag, dopey."

Curmudgeon: And why beholdest thou the mote that is in thy brother's eye, but considerest not the beam that is in thine own eye (Matt. 7:3).

128. SHAKESPEARE

W. Babylon, N.Y., '65.

Sir John Gielgud's *The Ages of Man*, and Sir Ian McClellan's Scottish *Macbeth* inspired me to stand under a tree on Roberts Wesleyan campus, and give a performance for the birds. Take that as you will, but the Elizabethans were not favorites in 9th grade. "Yon Cassius hath a lean and hungry look" (Act I, Scene II), is the only line I can quote from *Julius Caesar*. It speaks to where my adolescent sentiments lay—snack time. I did enjoy the ending—because it was over.

After it was explained, I understood the *end justifying the means*. How do you feel about it? One place we see this is in the Media. Mark Levin noted that newspapers in Jeffersonian times were biased, but it was known they were a Party extension. Does the Media sway us with half-truths? Nice people can do this because they see the result as positive. The emergency responder tells a victim they'll be ok because it helps the person cope. Take the "Me too," movement. A person's word could ruin a career prior to a trial by one's peers. *Due Process* was ignored for a good end, to root out perceived evil. Whether we hope to evoke change, or maintain what is, if we recognize scripture's moral absolutes, we won't be swayed by the flavor of the month. I want the truth, not spin. Shakespeare would agree. Hear his drunken sailor, Stephano: "Prithee, do not turn me about, my stomach is not constant," *The Tempest*: Act 2 Scene 2. Fortunately, our Guide leads us into all truth, Jn.16:13. Contrariwise, see how the end justifying the means unfolds:

Curmudgeon: And he said, When ye do the office of a midwife to the Hebrew women, and see them upon the stools; if it be a son, then ye shall kill him: but if it be a daughter, then she shall live (Ex. 1:16).

> Then Herod when he saw that he was mocked of the wise men, was exceeding wroth, and sent forth and slew all the children that were in Bethlehem, and in all the coasts thereof, from two years old and under, according to the time which he had diligently inquired of the wise men (Matt. 2:16).

129. FACING YOUR DONKEYS

Keauhou, Hi., '72.

It was kick-ass time! No, you misunderstand me. He turned abruptly to put his hindquarters in front of me, and I became a man of prayer. I'd gone to that section of the jungle to get bananas. I was walking home, only to stumble upon a donkey, *The Donkey of Honaunau*. Doubtless, you've heard of it in song. I talked to it, and the beast approached. That's what a mellifluous voice will get you. It licked my outstretched hand, then my arm and neck. My movement sparked his rearguard action. I spoke gently, put some distance between us, and sang all the way home. I'd faced my Donkey and lived! Actually, it was a mule—rather large. I didn't realize the connection, but we were in a drought. Later, I heard the Mule had died. No, it wasn't because he licked me.

In Hilo, the bay was behind our house. Afraid to go in the water at night, I did just that with a waterproof flashlight. I turned it on. Eyes surrounded me! The Bonefish' translucent bodies left nothing but eyes to reflect the light. Again, confronting my fear left me unscathed. Granma Clark used to say: "Christopher, the good Lord watches over drunks and fools." I praise Him for it. Nevertheless, kids, leave this to the professionals. Later I learned other visitors frequent the bay—sharks!

Contrariwise, let's not leave challenges of the spirit to professionals. Let's face our Donkeys, or Boneless fish, or Giants to be more biblical (I Sam. 17). And then there are the regular sized Philistines. Jonathan said to his armour bearer: "Hey, there's the Philistine outpost. If they invite us up, let's go, for the Lord will deliver them into our hand!" The Lord did, against outrageous odds. Outrageous only if you take God out of the situation. The Philistines didn't have a chance! So, whaddya say; where's that Donkey? You better beat it, Bonefish! Git Giant, I'm comin' your way! Make that: *We're comin' your way!*

Grace Lover: The horse is prepared for the day of battle, but victory belongs to the LORD (Prov. 21:31).

130. 1389 A.D.

"Felicity, Felicity, hold forth, I pray thee," young Willem beckoned.

Hearing her name the second time, the young maiden turned. Being less than rich but never near poverty, she was used to turning slowly, lest there be a ready request for a benefice.

"Yes, disturber of the noon's peace?" she asked.

"Ad Deum qui laetificat juventutem meam," Willem answered proudly.

"You have been studying your grammar, I see."

"Father Gilroy says I'm almost ready. He wouldn't be surprised if I be an acolyte next year."

"Is that the way the Lord leads you, then?" his quarry queried.

"What?" Willem said, thinking her a puzzlement. Felicity looked on lovingly.

"Fret not thyself, He will show you in His time." This explication, however, lent nothing to furthering his understanding. Felicity had another question. "So, upon what did you call me?"

"Oh yes," Willem, as if stirred from slumber, recalled, "Father Gil seeks you in the Chancel."

"I go forthwith," Felicity stated.

"Would you be in any trouble?" Willem asked hesitantly. "I could help, perchance..."

"No," Felicity answered directly.

"So sure you always are," Willem noted.

"'Trouble only persists when there is sin, or faith is lacking,' Grandfather Ross told me."

"You leave my thoughts unsorted, but I look forward to our next talk."

"The Lord willing, we shall have that opportunity," she said. They parted, and she entered the chancel. Father Gilroy was busy, but she was used to waiting upon the convenience of others.

"The list of pilgrims going to Augustine's bishopric lacked your mark. I suspected illness."

"No, we are all well," Felicity reassured him.

"Is there some impediment that keeps you from this holy opportunity?"

"None but faith," she responded.

The Priest, much like bellows, seemed to enlarge, as no small amount of air could satisfy his surprise. The condition left him unable to speak. Felicity, respectfully, lowered her gaze.

"But what of indulgences? Have you no need of merit?"

"I have great need of that, but not of my own," she answered. Father Gilroy was often of a position contrary to that of his student, Willem, but regarding Felicity, he and Willem shared the same perplexity.

"Can you explain more deeply?"

"*The Book of Lesions* says we are saved by grace through faith, not of works, lest any boast."

"I believe that's *Ephesians*," Father Gilroy corrected, smiling momentarily. "I know Ross procured a Bible. Be careful, the Lollards aren't condemned, but aren't far apace of disapproval."

"From Men?" Felicity inquired, "or from God?"

"I see you're baptized deeply into such beliefs. I will pray for you as I walk to Canterbury."

"Thank you," Felicity said. "I will be in prayer for your travels. God be with ye."

"And with you," Father Gilroy responded in kind.

Grace Lover: All scripture is given by inspiration of God, and is profitable for doctrine, for reproof, for correction, for instruction in righteousness (II Tim. 3:16).

> But Jesus called them unto him, and said, Suffer little children to come unto me, and forbid them not: for of such is the kingdom of God. [17] Verily I say unto you, Whosoever shall not receive the kingdom of God as a little child shall in no wise enter therein (Luke 18:16-17).

Curmudgeon: For laying aside the commandment of God, ye hold the tradition of men, as the washing of pots and cups: and many other such like things ye do (Mark 7:8).

Mom,1937

131. GRANDMA'S GODFORSAKEN CHAIR

Clearwater, Fl., 1964.

"Tinker's damn," and "godforsaken," were as salty as expletives got in my house, both upon the lips of Mother. I never heard anything untoward from Dad. The title for this devotion, however, was the creation of the family patriarch. In 1963, Grandma moved out of her boiler room in New York City. She had lived near to the Armory, a weapons cache dating to Revolutionary War days. It was torn down to put up the Verrazano Narrows Bridge. It was gone, and Grandma was going. Grandma, unlike the landmark, did resettle. 801 Chestnut St. Clearwater, the land of citrus and fewer knee pads, became her new haven of hope. In Autumns to come, I would send a colorful collage, wave offerings from her favorite trees, in case happiness was boring, and she longed for melancholy. Autumn's reds and yellows, for me, seemed best when mixed with a touch of the blues.

One item, not emancipated on moving day, was Grandma's favorite chair. One must realize Grandma had the *pilgrim and sojourner in search of an eternal city* principle, down pat. The proof was in the chair. The thin wood and cardboard seat was removable in that it was not, and had never been, affixed. It was a later addition; the original having been left on the Ark. What remained was a frail wood frame with chiseled carvings. Dad maintained, regardless of the chair's decorative markings, that it was Grandma who'd been chiseled. Be that as it may, we were requested, upon our drive to Florida, to make a stop on Staten Island, pick up the chair, and transport it to the Land of the Orange Blossom. Such requests were always accompanied by: "If it isn't too troublesome, my dear." Now, who isn't going to move Heaven and Earth for such a request? What was lost in time was gained in grousing. Dad found great satisfaction in a new nomenclature for the item of inconvenience: *Grandma's Godforsaken Chair*. There is more to the chair than I have so craftily spun so far. Albeit, all that has been said is true, there is one more thing of interest. In Eighth Grade I had read Robinson Crusoe. I loved it. I lived it. For a short dispensation, I was allowed to read at my dad's desk, the desk that harbored the aforementioned chair of providential abandonment. It had two finials, one on each side of the main uprights. One of them, however, over the centuries, had worked its way loose. I took Crusoe's example and wrote an entry for the day on a piece of paper, for posterity, the Salvation

Army, or the incinerator, whichever took the chair. I was not aware it was a forsaken chair or that it would be going on tour. Completing the missive, I stuck it in the upright, replaced the finial, and wondered when I would revisit my memory.

Well, I had my Defoe, but there is an even more remarkable time capsule story in the Bible. This one involves King Josiah. He was the last righteous king of Judah. He revered the Lord, and wanting to have the Temple renovated, ordered the High Priest, Hilkiah, to count the treasury and start the work (II Chronicles 34 and 35). During this endeavor, Hilkiah rediscovered the Law of the Lord. They'd not had the Torah for years! The first thing the King did was repent. Then he ordered the reinstitution of the Passover Feast. Wow, this makes godforsaken chairs look like just so much furniture! Can you imagine the news in Jerusalem? The celebration?

Has it been a while since you discovered the treasure of His Word? Ironic isn't it, the Word is always available to us yet remains hidden for many. It can change our lives! Let's dust if off, repent, and rejoice at its being re-found. Find a chair, even a forsaken one, and enjoy the Feast!

Excerpts from John for **Grace Lovers:** When therefore he was risen from the dead, his disciples remembered that he had said this unto them; and they believed the scripture, and the word which Jesus had said — 2:22.

> It is the spirit that quickeneth; the flesh profiteth nothing: the words that I speak unto you, they are spirit, and they are life. [68]Then Simon Peter answered him, Lord, to whom shall we go? thou hast the words of eternal life—6:63,68. Others said, These are not the words of him that hath a devil. Can a devil open the eyes of the blind (John 2:22. 6:63,68, 10:21).

Curmudgeon: And if any man hear my words, and believe not, I judge him not: for I came not to judge the world, but to save the world. He that rejecteth me, and receiveth not my words, hath one that judgeth him: the word that I have spoken, the same shall judge him in the last day (John 12:47-48).

132. LAVISH

Agra, India, 1634.

He stood by the long, magnificent pool, his reflection visible until a tear disturbed the image. Near him stood the lovely edifice erected for the object of his affection, but his beautiful bride was already dead. The Mogul Shah, Jahan, built the Taj Mahal in memory of Empress Mumtaz Mahal. Though unrequited, he lavished his love on her. The world, however, has witnessed an even greater love and gift. It also remains widely unaccepted. The Emperor of India, and the King of Kings, demonstrated their love in differing ways. The Rajah, while living, expressed his love for the dead. The King of Kings, by dying, expressed his love for the living and dead. Jesus gave himself for us while we were yet sinners (Ro. 5:8). It's nice to help those who love you, but those who despise you, and ultimately murder you? That's some intense dedication. How different it is from my usual late gift of chocolates for my Valentine.

Second, besides the recipients' unworthiness, there is the quality and scope of the gift. God became sin to take our punishment. The Taj Mahal is a work of art and a grand expression of love. Add an exponent of googles to it and you still aren't close to the Crucifixion. The Cross provides an eternity of forgiveness and joy in the Lord. It's indescribable! John says: "Behold what manner of love the Lord has bestowed upon us, that we should be called the sons of God…" (I John 3:1). Another translation says: *lavished* for *bestowed*. We're loved. Jesus, who, being God, let us pour out His blood. He could have left the Universe in ruins. WOW! *Lavished*, what a word. The King James version uses the words *abounded toward* and *manifested*. We don't cry at a memorial; we go to the fountain of His love. How about you? I feel a cannonball coming on! I'm going in…yahooo! I love you, Lord!

Grace Lover: Blessed be the God and Father of our Lord Jesus Christ, who hath blessed us with all spiritual blessings in heavenly places in Christ (Eph. 1:3).

Curmudgeon: They lavish gold out of the bag, and weigh silver in the balance, and hire a goldsmith; and he maketh it a god: they fall down, yea, they worship (Isa. 46:6).

133. BACON

London, England, Late 16th Century,

"How many evolutionists does it take to change a lightbulb?" See the answer of H. Kindell PhD., below.

"Just the facts, Mam," Officer Friday of *Dragnet* used to say. Presumed was the idea there are facts, and they're discoverable. Preceding the Detective by centuries was Sir Francis Bacon. He developed the scientific method: observation, thesis, experiment, control, and analysis. An age of discovery followed. Evidence replaced conjecture. Baconian Science and some disciplines today are quite different. They don't share a common ancestor, the former being concrete, the latter, theoretical. Experiments need theories, but often, no experiment can be performed, and the theory is unverified. *World-view.* and *expert testimony* replace evidence. World view determines how we interpret evidence. A naturalist will maintain a fossil is 70,000,000 years old, even if it has connective tissue, bone marrow, and a dozen compounds thought to remain intact for only 40,000 years. As for the latter, we'll believe a paleontologist, who states the supposedly vestigial tailbones of a whale (used in reproduction) are proof Cetaceans evolved from four footed mammals. Both conclusions are faith statements whose ledge is poised so distant from reality that for many it's a chasm too forbidding. Richard Lewontin illustrates the power of worldview:

> "*...we are forced by our a priori adherence to material cause to create an apparatus of investigation and set of concepts that produce material explanations, no matter how counter-intuitive, no matter how mystifying to the uninitiated. Moreover, that materialism is an absolute, for we cannot allow a Divine Foot in the door.*" The New York Review, January 9,1997, p. 31

Here are more examples:

> "*Evolution is not a fact. Evolution doesn't even qualify as a theory or as a hypothesis. It is a metaphysical research program, and it is not really testable science*" (Popper, 1976, p. 168).

Here's another:

> *"Evolution is promoted by its practitioners as more than mere science. Evolution is promulgated as an ideology, as secular religion-a full-fledged alternative to Christianity, with meaning and morality. I am an ardent evolutionist and an ex-Christian, but I must admit that in this one complaint-and Mr. Gish is but one of many to make it-the literalists are absolutely right. Evolution is a religion. This was true of evolution in the beginning, and it is true of evolution still today."* (Rusehttp://www.omniology.com/HowEvolutionBecameReligion.).

We've replaced the Baconian Method with the Cotton Candy Theorem. If a proposition fills enough space, no matter how ethereal, and is philosophically tasty, it is the new truth—for a while. It's said Creationism is religion, and Naturalism is science. Watch a debate and it will surprise you which position relies more on assumptions and theory. Scientists once thought matter was eternal. The Bible's position stood alone. Carl Hubbell's observance of planetary red-shift wavelengths proved a beginning. Does Naturalism answer the question of *First Cause*? Check out Creationism. Hundreds of scientists, many not Christians, have signed a paper refuting the Big Bang Theory.

> *"A hypothesis is empirical or scientific only if it can be tested by experience. A hypothesis or theory which cannot be, at least in principle, falsified by empirical observation and experiments does not belong to the realm of science. F.J. Ayala, "Biological Evolution: Natural Selection or Random Walk?"* American Scientist, 1974, Vol. 62, p. 700

Speculation has has taken over science. The scientific method has been suborned by theory and fancy. Let's get back to concrete science. Let's bring home the Bacon, Sir Francis, that is.

Joke Answer: "ecnahc yb neppah lliw ti dna hguone gnol tiaw tsuJ .enoN"

Grace Lover: In the beginning God created the heaven and the earth (Gen. 1:1).

> It is he that sitteth upon the circle of the earth… that stretcheth out the heavens as a curtain, and spreadeth them out as a tent to dwell in (Isa. 40:22).

Curmudgeon: The fool hath said in his heart, There is no God (Ps. 14:1)

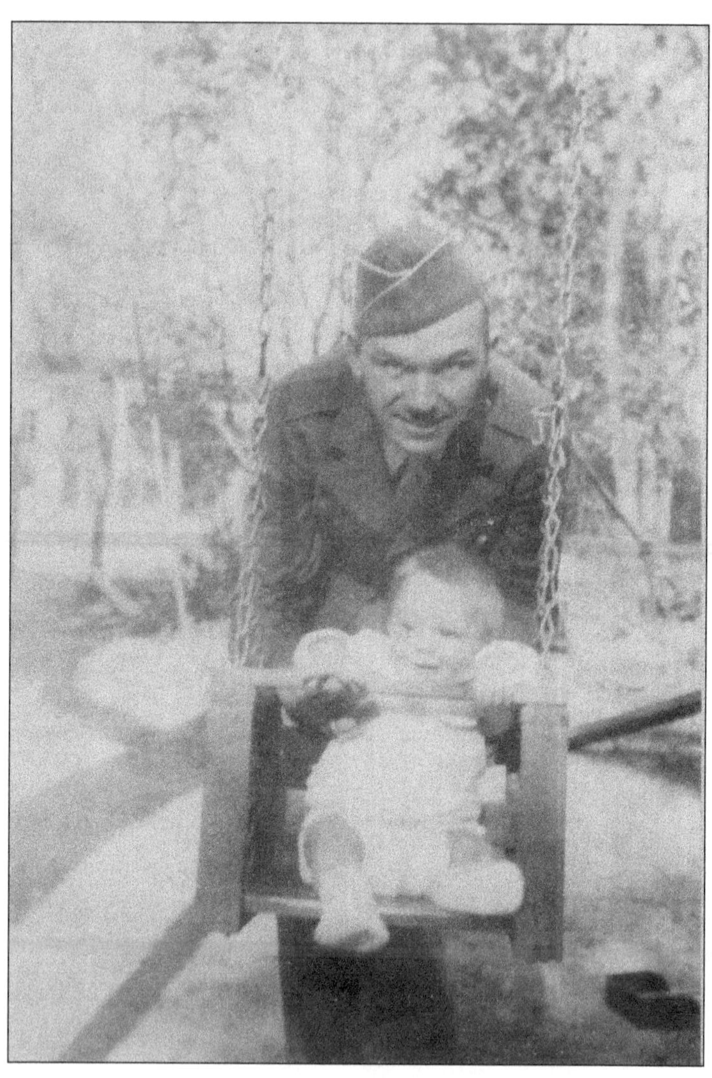

Dad and Robin, possibly at Matthew's Courthouse, Va., circa 1944.

134. EXIT STRATEGY

Whiting, N.J., 2001.

Dad jumped in the football's path for a surprise interception. He was just passing by and wanted to join the play. When Dad was a boy, and got those must have roller skates, he hit the road, then he hit a truck, dislocating both shoulders. One remained a problem. At our football game, interception equaled dislocation. Later, at seventy, he went para-sailing. In 2001, Yuko and I called Dad before Christmas. I told him I'd make her the happiest of women. He congratulated us. He was out of breath, but on the way to decorate the church tree. Five days later, a call from afar was a transfer. He'd said he wanted to pass this earthly veil in the alleys surrounded by friends. Well, that day, he went bowling, threw a strike, and collapsed. His wife, Evelyn, cradled his head as his spirit went to his Lord. What an exit!

Most Bible folks didn't end with a strike. Moses missed the Promised Land (Numbers 20:12). Aaron, the 70 elders, and the people could not enter for unbelief (Numbers 14), Gideon returned to idolatry (Judges 8:24-27). Joash, Asa, and others can be added. You're going to die! How will you end? Gutter ball? Split? I want to end like Dad, on a STRIKE! The Lord greets new arrivals with: "Well done, good and faithful servant (Matthew 25:21)," but I think Dad got a preface: "Wow, way to go, Bobby!"

Curmudgeon: And Jacob said unto Pharaoh, The days of the years of my pilgrimage are an hundred and thirty years: few and evil have the days of the years of my life been, and have not attained unto the days of the years of the life of my fathers in the days of their pilgrimage (Gen. 47:9).

> Hebron therefore became the inheritance of Caleb the son of Jephunneh the Kenezite unto this day, because that he wholly followed the LORD God of Israel (Joshua 14:14).

135. BEANS

Hitch-hiking in California, 1972.

"I'm gonna fly," he said, then added: "I mean it." I was not into high-speed chases, so I took the back seat. A mile later, he pulled into an airport. Twenty minutes later we were in the air over Sacramento, looking down at a recent flood and rooftop islands in a sea of green. He took us to Bakersfield, ending the most unique ride my brother, John, and I, ever hitched. After our flight, we went south and stopped at a freeway, hoping for a ride. Someone else had the same plan. He came our way.

"You guys got any beans?" Baked beans were cheap, but he had a different bean in mind.

"Whaddya mean, beans?" John asked.

"Beans, beans, yunno, beans," he said speedily and with no little perturbation. As he was revving a few rpm's ahead of us, he threw in:

"Uppers, yunno, uppers, ya got any?"

"No, sorry," we said. Expletives followed, and he was off in search of other bearers of beans. But our business wasn't finished. A patrol car pulled up. The officer politely instructed us as to the law regarding freeway on-ramps, gave us a ticket, and left. It was our first run-in with the law in 3,000 miles. We'd deserved more attention, but we didn't feel neglected. We were new believers. My thoughts changed from the first time I hitch-hiked. Then, the Law was a nuisance or worse. A Beaner was a liberated brother striving to throw off the shackles of the Man. Now, however, I felt sorry for the one in bean bondage and appreciated the officer who'd get me fined 50 dollars. Go figure! It's amazing what God can do.

Grace Lover: Let every soul be subject unto the higher powers. For there is no power but of God: the powers that be are ordained of God. [2] Whosoever therefore resisteth the power, resisteth the ordinance of God: and they that resist shall receive to themselves damnation (Ro. 13:1-2).

> Submit yourselves to every ordinance of man for the Lord's sake: whether it be to the king, as supreme; [14] Or unto governors, as unto them that are sent by him for the punishment of evildoers, and for the praise of them that do well. [17] Honour all men. Love the brotherhood. Fear God. Honour the king (I Pet. 2:13,14,17).

136. SAMSON

Kealakekua, Hi., '73.

I wanted to be a 99-lb. weakling! It beat being an 87-lb. weakling! With my low tonnage, men didn't respect me, and woman, even worse, hated me! It's been comforting to know "we are complete in Him who is the head of all principality and power" (Colossians 2:10). Lately, there's been an explosion of superhero movies. Except the first *Spider Man* movie, I haven't seen them; my boys were too little, and it scared me to see them alone. I'm a fossil, a D.C. guy. Stan Lee's artistry was Baroque; I like classics. In *Riverworld*, warring factions of historical figures, like Hermann Göring and Mozart, team against King John and Samuel Clemens. Well, the Bible has its own super heroes. Moses had the Urim and the Thummim to consult God. David had a Giant-slaying sling. Elijah got intelligence of his enemy's position, from God. Joshua's circular reasoning brought the house down. Jehoshaphat's choir sang its enemies into madness. The theme isn't the exaltation of individuals, but God, who exalts the humble, and helps His people despite themselves.

What do you think of Samson? He starts life consecrated to God as a Nazarite—no booze, no haircuts. Ok, most of us get that right. What about his physique? Muscles like a Stan Lee comic cover, right? Maybe not. To give credit where due, I heard this from a YWAM minister in Hawaii. Why would the Philistines wonder about the secret of Samson's strength if his abs were ripped and his bi-ceps bulging? Enter the 87-pound weakling. I'm not lifting myself up. The fact is, I'm not wild about Samson as Bible heroes go. And Super Heroes? The glory of their abilities returns to them. Contrariwise, biblical heroes are flawed people, used by the grace of God, to the glory of God. Fantasy is fun, but let's get real. Ever hear of Obadiah? Phoebe? Erastus? Take a Bible adventure. You'll discover flawed heroes—like you. Enjoy the discovery.

Grace Lover: With him is an arm of flesh; but with us is the Lord our God to help us (II Chron. 32:8).

Curmudgeon: A foolish son is a grief to his father, and bitterness to her that bare him (Prov. 17:25).

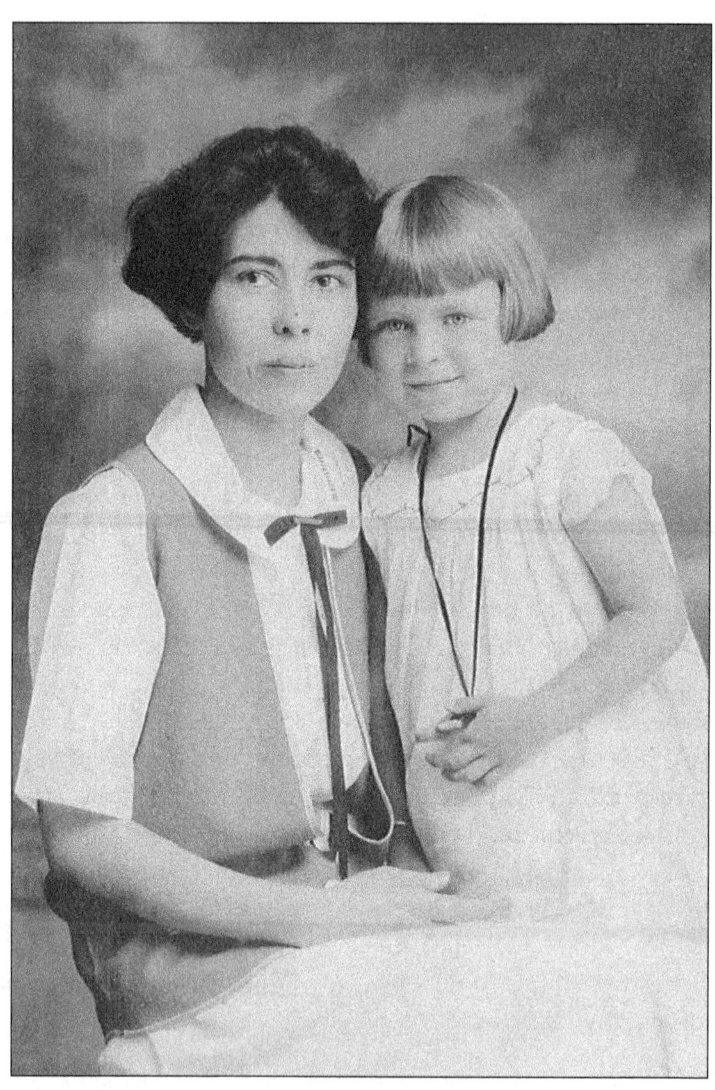

Grandma and Mom, 1928.

137. THE SEAMAN AND THE COMMODORE

NYC, '17.

Amphitrite was the Queen of the Sea, the wife of Poseidon, and the name of a destroyer escort during WWI. Penny Seaman Stuart L. Clark, not yet of age to serve, was an assignee of her crew. The ship docked in New York. Mary Elizabeth Blackham worked in Manhattan. Back then, reputations were not based on spin, but on character. One outcome was hotels with floor matrons. Their commission was to keep ledgers of guests. Mary Elizabeth's employer was the Commodore Hotel.

Stuart and Mary married near the end of the Great War. Clare Elizabeth Clark was born in 1919. They were my grandparents; she was my mom. The Clarks divorced in 1921. Grandma also worked as a phone operator and a teller. Mom lived with Catholic Sisters at The Star of the Sea Convent. On weekends, she stayed with her mom. They had a modest lifestyle and faith. It wasn't a pastime to content the deluded. They knew the truth about God's plan and received strength from that knowledge and relationship. Scripture tells us to give honor to whom honor is due. Lately, some individuals in the Roman Catholic Church have behaved heinously, but I have been a second and-first-hand beneficiary of blessing from the Roman Church. It helped raise my mom, and I came to know and love Jesus at parochial school. I owe much in my pilgrimage to that imperfect steward of faith. Many scriptures relate His care for the fatherless and widows. Grandma was divorced, her life burdened by the wantonness of others. God did not abandon her. Her reward came at 92. "Christopher, all this and heaven, too," she'd say. She was a Commodore of faith and thankfulness. I was glad to sail with her.

Grace Lover: A father of the fatherless, and a judge of the widows, is God in his holy habitation (Ps. 68:5).

Curmudgeon: He saith unto them, Moses because of the hardness of your hearts suffered you to put away your wives: but from the beginning it was not so (Matt. 19:3).

138. FEMINISM, THREE MISSIVES

1510-1575.

Renee of Ferrara was born in France, the child of King Louis the XII. Orphaned at five, King Francis I. raised her. More important than these two custodians, however, were Madame de Soubise her tutor and possessor of a Wyclif Bible, and John Calvin, her secretary during Duke Ercole and Renee's reign at Ferrara, Italy. From these contacts, a king's daughter became The King's daughter. Catholic France was her home, but the Kingdom of God had her fealty. She helped the persecuted Huguenots. Her Catholic husband opposed her. He, and most of Italy's dukes, were Catholic. In 1550, the duke burned Reformist preacher Fanino Fanini at the stake. Thereafter, the couple's marriage was annulled, and Renee, arrested. Informed she'd never see her daughters again, she signed a recantation that was sent all over France. Later, she fled Ferrara, returning to France, and her own fortress, the Castle Montargis. At great risk, she made it a safe-haven for Huguenots, who called it *The Lord's Hotel.* Finding her castle threatened by a Catholic army, she wrote to its commander: "Consider well what you are planning to do. There is no one in this Kingdom who commands me except the king himself. If you come, I will throw myself into the breach to see whether you have the audacity to kill the daughter of a king." There was no attack. Later, she was denied burial with the French nobility at St Denis Church. Though her children rejected her, she wrote them:

> "I pray that my children will read and listen to the Word of God in which they will find comfort and the true guide to eternal life."

Grace Lover: Then Esther bade them return Mordecai this answer, [16] Go, gather together all the Jews that are present in Shushan, and fast ye for me, and neither eat nor drink three days, night or day: I also and my maidens will fast likewise; and so will I go in unto the king, which is not according to the law: and if I perish, I perish (Esther 4:15-16).

139. SIMCHAT TORAH

"I'll scratch out your eyes!" she said. It was scary, but she was 70 years old. It was a Friday, 1979, in a Jewish neighborhood of L.A. We went twice a month to share about Messiah. Jewish homes had a Mezuzah on the doorpost (Deut. 6). Russian Jews were very hospitable. This day was *Simchat Torah, the Celebration of Receiving the Law*. The Jews received the Law on Pentecost to usher in the Old Covenant of the Law. The Holy Spirit was poured out on Pentecost about 1500 years later to begin the New Covenant of Grace. We took a pile of tracts to the parade area. I was warned the Jewish Defense League would find us. Their motto was: "Never Again!" a reference to the Holocaust. I was with Freddie Roberson, a Black brother, and Alan Chester, a Messianic Jew. Freddie had the tracts. When the Hassidim came, one shouted: "Get his literature." Freddie took no chances and raced across the road. A car just missed him. Alan, somewhere else, didn't fare as well, he got socked in the face. I only had to survive a series of questions. I mentioned Isaiah 53. One Hassidim said: "The Messiah's seed was to be blessed; your Jesus died without kids?" I said Isaiah spoke of spiritual seed. The Lord blessed though the questions were flying fast. Another surprise was the lady who threatened me, said:

"Look at his face. Look. It's like the face of an angel!"

I always left L.A. in tears; that day, it wasn't due to pollution.

Grace Lover: And I will bless them that bless thee, and curse him that curseth thee: and in thee shall all families of earth be blessed (Gen. 12:3).

Curmudgeon: For I would not, brethren, that ye should be ignorant of this mystery, lest ye should be wise in your own conceits; that blindness in part is happened to Israel, until the fulness of the Gentiles be come in (Ro. 11:25).

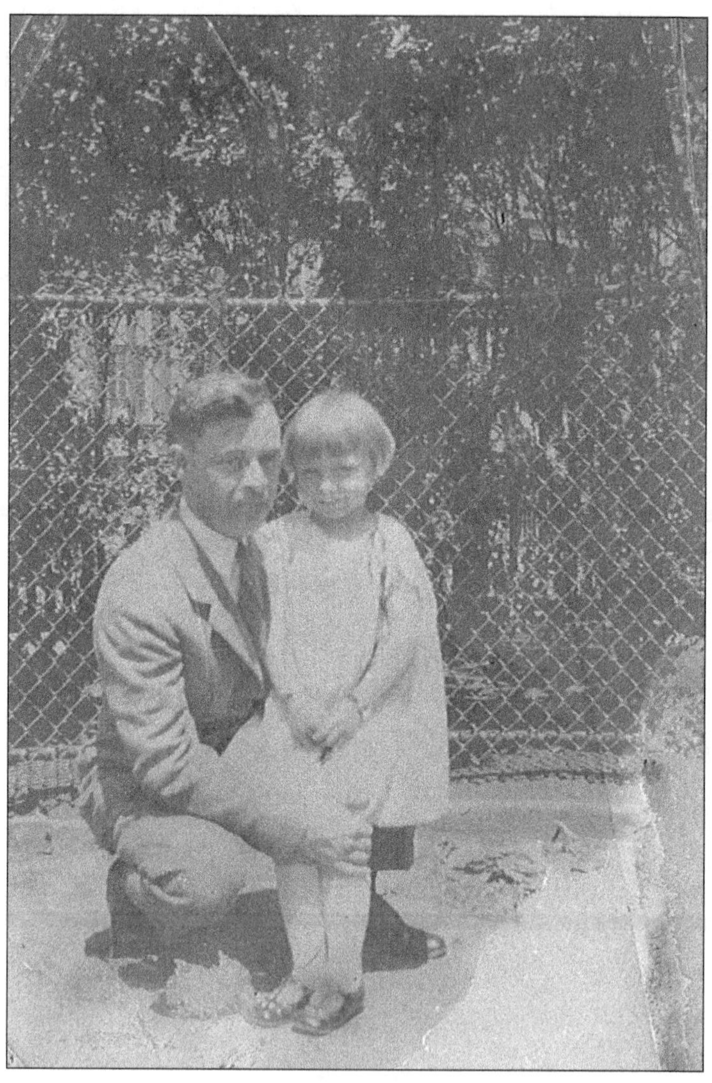

The Scalawag, Grandpa, and my Mom, circa 1925.

140. GRANDPA

W. Babylon, N.Y., 1950-1964.

Images are interesting. I recall a record album entitled *Salty Dog*, an image that evokes thoughts of Grandpa Clark. Born in nineteen-hundred, and sold to a ship captain at four, he served in the U.S. Navy in WWI. He divorced Grandma in 1921; mom was two. Grandma was eight years Grandpa's senior. He married a boarder at their home, later confessing the change may not have been the boon for which he was looking. To Grandma's family, he was *The Scalawag*. He became my grandpa. In my eyes, he could do wrong. I loved his bedtime stories, *The Adventures of Christopher*—that's me. One day I switched the tables and told him a story. He got a kick out of me taking an overnight hike in an afternoon! Another custom was hiding his tabacci. He'd survived lung cancer and rolled his cigarettes to cut down his intake. My mission was to hide his Prince Albert in a Can. Salty Dog that he was, Mom had concerns about what influence her dad would have on us boys. Her apprehension gained strength when we acted inappropriately. The first instance that comes to mind is a sea-ditty:

> Oh, there was an old sailor and he had a wooden leg,
> No tabacci could he borrow, no tabacci could he beg.

There are more verses which, while not setting a frigate aflame, get close to kindling a fire. Another eyebrow-raiser was pitchin' pennies on the side of a building. The closest coin to the wall won the chest of doubloons or the eight cents Grandpa and I mustered. I was exonerated of gambling, being the age of four.

In those days, if you owned a car, you had a second house. Those were cars! Grandpa had a '53 Buick, a tank with a deluxe interior. I could get lost inside. And the chrome! Wow, bumpers like deacon's benches. Deacons are a serious bunch, whereas the Buick wore a giant smile that blinked at you if it were parked in the sun. When I saw that car, my pulse would go from sixty to ninety in 3.5 seconds. You could hear my cry: "Grandpa!" from Tenth to Seventeenth Street.

I learned faith from Grandpa. He was a Yankee fan in the days of Kubek, the Moose (Skowron), McDougall, and Mantle. I sided with Grandpa, though the rest of the family liked the Dodgers. Grandpa only lent emotional support a few weeks of the year. Once he returned to Florida, the persecution was difficult to bear. Visions of him sitting by the T.V., however, sustained me, and helped my religious pilgrimage in years to come. Of course, the Yanks had a good winning percentage, whereas the Kingdom of God really seemed to take it on the chin in the '60's.

Grandpa retired from this Dockyard the summer of nineteen-sixty-four. Smoking caught up to him. Prince Albert was royalty, but the guy in the can was a cruel despot. Grandpa continued smoking despite warnings. Things catch up with us, now or later. He'd received some religious training from Methodists, but didn't attend church. Mom was on his case about faith, however, when his cancer operation approached. It may be the illness was his opportunity to get things ship-shape with the Captain of Salvation. That is my hope, and the hope of the fourteen-year-old inside me. To take an over-night hike with Grandpa on that far shore, why, that would beat pitchin' pennies any day. For now, I don't know if he booked passage. I can't do anything about that, but I can make sure everyone I meet on this side of that shore knows how to get a ticket. Other fourteen years old kids, too, want to see their grandpa there!

Grace Lover: Be not deceived; God is not mocked: for whatsoever a man soweth, that shall he also reap. 8 For he that soweth to his flesh shall of the flesh reap corruption; but he that soweth to the Spirit shall of the Spirit reap life everlasting (Gal. 6:7-8).

Curmudgeon: What shall we do unto thee, that the sea may be calm unto us? for the sea wrought, and was tempestuous.[12]And he said unto them, Take me up, and cast me forth into the sea; so shall the sea be calm unto you: for I know that for my sake this great tempest is upon you (Jonah 1:11-12).

141. ACTION NIGHT

"El Cheapo," is what my sister, Ellen, used to call me in '69. My weekly pilgrimage was the *No Cover Charge Tuesdays* at Vinnie's Disco, in Bayshore, N.Y. I was very devout. I only got thrown out once, and punched once, both of my doing or undoing. There were bands, and I pursued the various cultural aspects there, especially those five feet tall with bell bottoms. Ten years later, I was on staff at Christians in Action. Tuesday night was Action Night. Folks gathered at the church for prayer before going into the neighborhood with the Good News. Later, we'd have a live radio broadcast. Those with reports had an interview in the booth. I only remember one broadcast. That night our director, Lee Shelley, came in with thirty-seconds remaining. Lee was a master of the testimony:

"Chris, can you guess what happened to me tonight?"

"No, Brother Lee, fill us in."

"I got three holes in one at the golf course. I met three young people. We talked about God's love. Now, each one is following Jesus!"

"That's great, Brother Lee. And Friends, that just goes to show you that His fairways are not our fairways. This is Chris Wilkins for Christians in Action, reminding you that if you're a Christian, you're meant to be in Action." With that, the studio played our theme, *Go Tell the World That You're a Christian*. Action Nights began in trepidation and ended with exhilaration in the Spirit. And so, this is Chris Wilkins reminding you that if you're a Christian, you're meant to be in action. Hope to see you out there!

Grace Lover: For my thoughts are not your thoughts, neither are your ways my ways, saith the Lord (Isa. 55:8).

> Now while Paul waited for them at Athens, his spirit was stirred in him, when he saw the city wholly given to idolatry. [17]Therefore disputed he in the synagogue with the Jews, and with the devout persons, and in the market daily with them that met with him (Acts 17:16,17).

Curmudgeon: And with many other words did he testify and exhort, saying, Save yourselves from this untoward generation (Acts 2:40).

142. JUNE 1535

It was a plain door, but Patience didn't notice. It opened, as if instructed to do so, by the one who occupied the chamber. Supposedly a guard, to him, it was an open door. Patience, like a niece, was a distraction most pleasant. On this day, however, there was a reason she didn't frolic in the gardens.

"What's this *Faerie Princess of the Dew*?" he asked.

"Oh, Uncle Tomas," she erupted, gushing a fount of fear.

"Oh, my little wonder, what brings this on?"

"If you don't accept the King's edict, they'll take you to the Tower and darkness and then the pangs of Hell."

"Let's sort that conundrum a piece at a time. Is that amenable?"

"Yes," she agreed, hoping his assurance would banish her nightmare.

"First, your fortitude in talking to disingenuous souls encourages me. Second, my Princess, though a King sends a person to a tower, no one knows another's eternal destiny. Last, we'll all kneel before the Lord one day. Our conscience shall condemn or excuse us. Our Reformer friends make much of doctrine and discounting the Holy Church's traditions, but in matters of the State, conscience has as much place as a harem in Christendom. I can't bend my will to the King's statute, and still bend my knee to Heaven's King." Herein, the staunched flow of tears surged past its gate. "My dear, we'll not be tempted above that we can withstand (I Cor. 10:13). Hold on to thy namesake. Hold on to Christ."

"Yes, Uncle," she said. Such words from him, who'd be shortly dead and more alive, turned tears to fire. The plain door was left open. His gaolers came but found hospitality. Following that, a dark corridor awaited, and a Door, a wondrous Door, the Door of the sheepfold.

Grace Lover: In your patience possess ye your souls (Luke 21:19).

> Blessed are they which are persecuted for righteousness' sake: for theirs is the kingdom of heaven (Matt. 5:10).

143. COMEDY CENTRAL

Jerusalem, 31 A.D.

I'm from NYC's suburbs. John 9 sounds like a street corner chat. New Yorkers are like crullers, crusty outside, soft inside, i.e., in your face. It's an integrity indicator. If you can't talk back, you probably have nothing to say. We start in an Indian neighborhood. How do we know? The disciples ask: "This guy born blind, who sinned, he or his folks?" That's primo Hindu Karma. Jesus sets them straight; neither sinned. The situation exists for the glory of God. Jesus heals him, but his neighbors weren't sure it's him. It's sad they had so little to do with him. News gets to the Pharisees. Now the fun begins. The parents are afraid, so the young man speaks for himself—probably a first. He tells the truth, something you'd think would please men of God. However, they don't like the answer, and ask for another rendition. The young man won't accommodate them. Truth, failing to satisfy, name-calling takes its place.

27 He answered them, I have told you already, and ye did not hear:
wherefore would ye hear it again? will ye also be his disciples? 28 Then they
reviled him, and said, Thou art his disciple; but we are Moses' disciples. 29
We know that God spake unto Moses: as for this fellow, we know not from
whence he is. 30 The man answered and said unto them, Why herein is a
marvellous thing, that ye know not from whence he is, and yet he hath
opened mine eyes. 31 Now we know that God heareth not sinners: but if any
man be a worshipper of God, and doeth his will, him he heareth. 32 Since
the world began was it not heard that any man opened the eyes of one that
was born blind. 33 If this man were not of God, he could do nothing. 34 They
answered and said unto him, Thou wast altogether born in sins, and dost
thou teach us? And they cast him out.

See the local rags that day: "*Self-important religious types get owned by unschooled local boy!*" Here's a headline: "*Cult Members Tout Hindu Karma as Reason Man Born Blind!*" A tabloid asks: "*Are Pharisees Secret Disciples of Jesus?*"

Curmudgeon: At that time Jesus answered and said, I thank thee, O Father, Lord of heaven and earth, because thou hast hid these things from the wise and prudent, and hast revealed them unto babes (Matt. 11:25).

144. REUNION

West Babylon, N.Y., 1954

I remembered having my last nap with them, and then they were gone! To my shame, I eventually forgot about them. All that changed one day on *The Great Shoe Expedition*. Mom suggested some closet spelunking to help the rainy-day blues, and keep me busy for a few lifetimes. Hansel and Gretel used crumbs to find their way out of the woods, a strategy that came up wanting. Fancying the story of Theseus and the Minotaur twine would be a better plan. In the end, however, I decided to fear no beast, and enter—no strings attached.

I found no Minotaur, but confronted two other creatures. They were not met with fright. These were old friends—long-lost, furry friends. It was Lavender Bunny and Brown Bear, exiled since my last nap, absconded by… how can I speak it, by my own MOTHER. I wondered if I'd find the Sword of Damocles, the gold of Croesus, or the Howdy Doody Boatplanecarmobile in those depths of Closet Cave. Nothing else mattered, though; I had them back. My old friends, gone for years, at least two, were back. My Bear and Bunny were lost but now were found.

Reunions are nice, aren't they? My graduating class recently had its fiftieth. I couldn't make it, but 50 classmates did. I loved their comments on fb. There is a reunion, however, that will overshadow anything mentioned. On the Last Day, Justin Martyr, the Inklings, Grandma Clark, and a myriad of others will be there. The Savior, the Lord Jesus, will be there. It's gonna be a party—actually, a banquet. Y'all come!

Grace Lover: For the Lord himself shall descend from heaven with a shout, with the voice of the archangel, and with the trump of God: and the dead in Christ shall rise first: [17] Then we which are alive and remain shall be caught up together with them in the clouds, to meet the Lord in the air: and so shall we ever be with the Lord. [18] Wherefore comfort one another with these words (I Thess. 4:15-18).

> And he saith unto me, Write, Blessed are they which are called unto the marriage supper of the Lamb. And he saith unto me, These are the true sayings of God (Rev. 19:9).

Berean: Luke 14

145 SURE A LITTLE BIT OF HEAVEN

"Hello, Clark's residence," Grandma answered, as she always did.

"Hi Grandma, it's Christopher," I chimed, as I always did.

"Oh, bless your heart, dear. Where are you?"

"I'm calling long-distance from California,"

"Oh, bless you. Isn't it amazing the things we can do today?"

"I just sang *Sure a Little Bit O' Heaven* at the retirement party for our CinA Director, Lee Shelley," I said. She immediately began singing, and I joined her on our California-Clearwater, Fl., Irish connection. We prayed the *Our Father*, and she put her nephew, Bob Blackham, on the line: "Hey, don't think you're going to get me to pray!" he kidded. Bob was great. I asked Grandma if she'd like to go to Ireland, but she declined. Her knees knew better. Now I understand, as I sit with a pulled a muscle, losing at tennis to my wife. Doesn't a pulled muscle merit a consolation prize? Anyway, Grandma's knees had as much wrapping as Tony the shoemaker's olive tree in winter.

Not all our discussions of faith went as nicely. I wrote Grandma about an over-emphasis of Mary in the High Church. She closed her next letter using the names of the Holy Family; Mary was underlined. Grandma's letters were the things of legend, partly because we either didn't receive them or because they'd gone to another place first. In those days, schools taught cursive, but Grandma was not one to compromise uniqueness. We lived on Twelfth Street, though one wouldn't know it from the addresses Grandma assigned our modest dwelling place. I think she knew the Cyrillic alphabet and other syllabaries. That we ever received a letter confirms my theory the postman was a CIA decoder. We changed ethnicity at the caprice of Grandma's penmanship. Also unforgettable was her upbeat closing: "Cheerio, Grandma."

I called Grandma at her final earthly abode, the Corazon de Jesu Nursing Home. She was happy and attended Mass every day. Calling was difficult, however, as she had to travel far to a hallway phone. Bob Blackham called us on Thanksgiving Day, 1984, to tell us Grandma had made her final trip. Where? Sure, a little bit o' Heaven!

Cheerio Grandma, *Christopher*

Grace Lover: And Mary said, Behold the handmaid of the Lord; be it unto me according to thy word. And the angel departed from her (Luke 1:38).

146. JURKEN JORG (SQUIRE GEORGE)

"Tante Antje, you need rest, but could tell us your story?"

"I'm old but not dead, my young sprig."

"Oh, of course, I didn't mean to …" Hans began.

"There's the story of riding the flume," Antje said, grinning.

"Oh, no, not that one, though it is very good, I'm sure."

"Hans, you must embrace a tougher spirit. I know you have no interest in flumes."

"Oh, Tante Antje, you are a tease," Hans said, assuming a deeper tone.

"That almost got my blood warm," she replied, waving off further interruptions. "It was 1521, and I was in Wartburg with Grandmother. She was a firebrand, that one was."

"Oh, my goodness," Hans emitted, then held his mouth to deflect any blows. Antje had no intention of striking, she critiqued to encourage, and was zealous on that behalf.

"Yes, Grandma Hedda joined the movement. She had no time for priests, especially, well…"

"Did she say why?" Armando asked, his accent unmistakable.

"Yes," Antje said, pausing politely. Armando waited, but no further revelation was given.

"I was about 7 when I first met him," Antje proceeded with the tale. "I was coming home from market when I espied a new girl my age, in our neighborhood. She was dancing and not watching where she was going. She knocked into me, ripping my sack and spilling vegetables. My apple took to the cobblestones like a sow running from a butcher. I sighed, but just then a sword was quickly, though not deftly, drawn from its scabbard. Upon losing the apple, I'd sighed. This time I stopped breathing! The sword was laid, not for villainy, but to block the trespass of my miscreant fruit. The fellow then picked it up, returned his sword to its sheath, and bellowed like a merchant: 'What do I hear for this sumptuous treasure of the tree, Malus Pumila?' As I was young, I didn't catch the half of what he said. I thought him a daft fellow and piped up,

"Excuse me, but that apple belongs in this bag with its family!"

The fellow, not over-portly, but no wisp, either, lumbered over to look inside my burden:

'Hmmm, I didn't realize apples were related to cabbages."

"Well," I returned, "this family would like to learn if its relative will be returned or not."

'By all means,' he said, dropping the prodigal to its patch. I tried to lift the bag, but without a strap, it was as unwieldy as a goat.

'May I be of service, Fraulein?' he asked.

'Mother forbids me to talk to strangers,' I informed him.

'I be Squire George,' he said, 'though I've been called a Wild Boar. Now we are not strangers.' In the same breath, he asked my name. I hesitated, but relented. He was quite taken by it. He and Auntie Hedda got along as if they were old friends. It surprised me to meet a Squire so versed in the Bible. Once, when he came to see Grandmother, he told me a story. He'd been called to a meeting to give an answer for some things he'd said. In that regard, he was like Grandma! After giving his defense, he went outside and motioned to the crowd that had gathered. Suddenly, a horse-drawn wagon of hooded men pulled up, grabbed him, and drove off. At the end of the inquiry, he'd thought he only had a couple of months to live, but when the hooded men arrived, he revised his estimate to a few hours. As the wagon jostled him about, he noticed something peculiar. His books and papers were also captive. He then realized circumstances were not what they appeared."

"When did you learn your apple retriever, Squire George, was Professor Luther?" Hans asked.

"Those were violent times; my family didn't share the entire story with me until years later."

"I think the times have grown worse yet," Armando inserted.

"Yes," Antje agreed. "Let's pray for His peace amid the storm?"

"Yes," they all assented, leaving Saxony for the moment to visit the Throne-room of Heaven, and talk to God, a bulwark never failing."

Grace Lover: And ye shall be hated of all men for my name's sake: but he that endureth to the end shall be saved (Matt. 10:22).

Curmudgeon: So then because thou art lukewarm, and neither cold nor hot, I will spue thee out of my mouth (Rev. 3:16).

Turkish soldiers who guard Christian ruins, Anatolia, March, 1999.

147. GOEREME

Turkey, 1999.

As for academia, linguistics is not as totally useless as one may suppose. In Turkey, a conference gave me an opportunity to see Byzantium. Goereme is on the Anatolian Plateau. It was formed by volcanic ash. It's a cave-digging Heaven. One fully expects to run into a Hobbit! I, however, met Cenker Yurkudul. He was in a military detachment protecting Christian ruins. He took me to see a cave-church. Byzantium, the Eastern Roman Empire, fell in 1453, so the paintings in the cave were over five hundred years old. Across a chasm was an aviary (pigeon coop). It towered four stories up—talk about piled higher and deeper. Centuries ago, the egg yolks were used in paint for the Church's depictions. Though communication was labored, Cenker and I had fun. I saw my first DVD, *Gladiator,* in a tavern with him. The steep path to the church doubled as an ice slide. Cenker slipped first, upended me, and we went down in tandem. On that occasion, I was happy not to stray from the path. I was wearing a leather jacket; I offered as much resistance as copper gives an electron or a flue gives a bobsled. We were moving! On another day, I visited an underground Byzantine town, four levels deep. With only one door, a few defenders could hold off a larger force. Cenker also took me to visit the home of a nearby family. He and I kept in touch for a while, but e-mail addresses change. Do you ever wonder about encounters that go on for a few days? You feel you've known the person for a long time. Jesus healed many folks He'd not meet again on Earth. Were those encounters wasted? Did Bartimaeus follow Christ (Mark 10)? The Syrophoenecian woman (Mark 7)? The Paralytic lowered through Jesus' roof (Mark 2)? If we lose contact, we can pray, e.g. Abraham' intercession for Sodom.

Grace Lover: Wherefore I also, after I heard of your faith in the Lord Jesus, and love unto all the saints, [16] Cease not to give thanks for you, making mention of you in my prayers; [17] That the God of our Lord Jesus Christ, the Father of glory, may give unto you the spirit of wisdom and revelation in the knowledge of him (Eph. 1:15-17).

> And Abraham drew near, and said, Wilt thou also destroy the righteous with the wicked (Gen. 18:23)?

148. 89 A.D.: GRANITE AND SANDSTONE

I delivered grain to a widow and refreshed myself at the aqueduct. Sitting there, I realized the base-relief of the gods was soft stone, easily chiseled. It lost my favor, however, when I no longer served the gods. I was to meet Gaius but was of two opinions. I espied a comely maid and preferred to watch. She was no aristocrat, but had a look of the eye that bade one dream. Gaius led me to a mausoleum. Behind some trees, he descended a staircase with a torch. Meeting places often changed for safety. We heard voices in worship, and stories of deliverance either from persecution or this world. A slave gave a message he'd heard from an elderly saint. We prayed such prayers. We then rose to part with holy kisses, but all ended in an uproar. Except for Gaius, we ran. He guaranteed our escape. We never saw him again. I followed the light fleeing before me and made it home. The next day, Uncle Valerius took me to the Colosseum. The recent round-up of atheists, Christians, would meet the beasts. I prayed with eyes open to avoid suspicion. Then I saw her, the girl with the deep eyes. "Oh my God," I cried, and for no short passing of time, gave up hope of happiness in this life.

Another time, another place:

"So, Paula, when did you start coming to God's Place?"

"Two months ago. Jan wasn't happy at the Bible Church. This group helps her career goals. And you Leti?"

"Last year. The Way didn't fit. They wanted Jake's help. He's committed to our pool. Look, these dramas beat Netflix.

"My theatre season tickets may be a thing of the past!"

Everyone: [5]Remember therefore from whence thou art fallen, and repent, and do the first works; or else I will come unto thee quickly, and will remove thy candlestick out of his place, except thou repent. [10]Fear none of those things which thou shalt suffer: behold, the devil shall cast some of you into prison, that ye may be tried; and ye shall have tribulation ten days: be thou faithful unto death, and I will give thee a crown of life (Rev. 2:5,10).

149. THE NUTCRACKER

Brockport, N.Y., '88.

Ok, don't get shrink-wrapped because of the B-word, Ballet. I love the *Nutcracker*—no apology! One Christmas, the State University of N.Y. at Brockport, did a production. A collegian's ego can't suffer such a role, so the *Dance of the Sugar Plum Fairies* was left to borrowed children. The show included a plastic snow machine, which got stuck, causing the white stuff to accumulate. When gears sorted, six-year-old Faeries were pelted with a half foot of snow. Some feet were toppled, but fortitude slugged it out with Old Man Winter and the Plastic Phantom. Now, it's the only part I recall. Comedies and tragedies sometimes change roles.

I enjoyed sharing the Word in Cambodia, but at some churches the message was swallowed up by a latecomer's greetings or fish prices. As folks had no background in scripture, most things I said were new. They wondered, "Why did that guy walk on the water?" or, "Are there no monkeys in these stories?" Today, Cambodians lead that group. God turns things around. The wedding host with no wine ended up serving the best wine last. The man who couldn't walk ended up walking and forgiven of sin. Though Judah went without the Book of the Law for years, the Torah was found in the Temple, the Passover reinstated, and the high places destroyed by King Josiah. Though the Jews went 400 years without a prophet, the Messiah came, as promised, and the work of salvation was accomplished. Years ago, I was turned down for mission service, having completed a Master's degree in Missiology. Later, they accepted me and invited me to lead a team. Someone close to me said I wasn't suited to the job. I said, "Ouch," tightened my belt, and trusted the Lord. Remember the Faeries! Should a snowdrift attack, laugh, and kick your feet.

Grace Lover: To appoint unto them that mourn in Zion, to give unto them beauty for ashes, the oil of joy for mourning, the garment of praise for the spirit of heaviness; that they might be called trees of righteousness, the planting of the Lord, that he might be glorified (Isa. 61:3).

Curmudgeon: Do ye thus requite the LORD, O foolish people and unwise? is not he thy father that hath bought thee? hath he not made thee, and established thee (Deut. 32:6).

150. LETTERS TO GOD

"Oh God, what shall I do?" Ever pray like this? When things get difficult and I've sublimated the answer to my desires, things get confusing. It's usually because I didn't heed the warning signals on the way to the mess I'd created. That's when I resort to letters to God. I never send them, for obvious reasons. They follow a similar pattern: boy meets girl, God's limits unheeded, guilt, commitment to significant other unsure, misery, painful choice to have restoration with God. The limits I speak of don't land one in jail, but grieve the Holy Spirit. That's where trouble begins, regardless of semantics or excuses. Have a big problem? You may try a letter to God for clarity. Don't fudge with God. First, you can't, and second, it works against you. I know people who've walked away from God a step at a time, until the mist between them became a cloud, then a mountain. By the way, I fudged a little in the previous paragraph with a disclaimer. Don't you do it. Let it stink. Remember, you may offend a friend, but you've sinned against God. He's the one you need to worry about, or better yet, hope in.

A letter won't solve anything. Once you see the truth, you can ignore, deny, or recognize it. The first two options make things worse. The last leaves another step—acting upon the truth. If you're committed to doing the right thing, there's hope. Even God can't help if you choose against what is right: "God is not a man, that he should lie; neither the son of man, that he should repent: hath he said, and shall he not do it? or hath he spoken, and shall he not make it good?" Num. 23:19. He doesn't change for our convenience. The thing that is wrong will please you temporarily. The right will ultimately bless you.

Grace Lover: And Hezekiah received the letter of the hand of the messengers, and read it: and Hezekiah went up into the house of the Lord, and spread it before the Lord. [20] Then Isaiah the son of Amoz sent to Hezekiah, saying, Thus saith the Lord God of Israel, That which thou hast prayed to me against Sennacherib king of Assyria I have heard (II Kings 19:1, 20).

> And ye shall know the truth, and the truth shall make you free (John 8:32).

151. KING GEORGE

Kampong Cham, Cambodia, 2003.

"No Taxation Without Representation!" Truth be told, Parliament levied taxes, not King George III. Today, however, let's travel to a different kingdom, the land of the Khmers, and a province populated by the Cham.

Yuko and I, recently married, moved from Phnom Penh to Kampong Cham. Early on we discovered a Gokka, a lizard, of eighteen inches. They're formidable, stocky—and kill rats! Yuko wasn't delighted to let accommodations to primeval types; I suggested we befriend him. Not knowing his given or surname, I suggested *George*. Yuko piped up: *King George*, thinking of size, not lineage. Have you heard of the *Cry of the Banshee*? Gokka have a droll laugh of ascending and descending syllables. It's no cheerful laugh, more like mockery. Legend says, if done seven times, it's propitious for the host. Yuko, not keen on myths, wanted the King, trousseau, and Court set up elsewhere. This was indisputably apparent after Caleb was born. George, to use his common name, moved his boudoir to a section of wall which had a hole that opened into our bedroom where Caleb would be asleep by 7:00. Well, the Royal preference was to have a howling at 7:15, precisely linked to Greenwich time. One day, however, the King erred, leaving the Royal Chambers in the daytime. A coup ensued. Brooms ushered the usurper into exile. He tried to double back, but the Residence Royale's double doors closed, ending his reign. Thereafter, plaintive calls from beyond the castle's pale could be heard. Secure at last, Caleb enjoyed dreams in the absence of lugubrious lizards.

Grace Lover: Lift up your heads, O ye gates; and be ye lift up, ye everlasting doors; and the King of glory shall come in (Ps. 24: 7).

Curmudgeon: Then he saith, I will return into my house from whence I came out; and when he is come, he findeth it empty, swept, and garnished. 45 Then goeth he, and taketh with himself seven other spirits more wicked than himself, and they enter in and dwell there: and the last state of that man is worse than the first. Even so shall it be also unto this wicked generation (Matt. 12:44-45).

152. THE TIME OF DISTRESS

> II Chronicles 28:2—And in the time of his distress did he trespass yet more against the LORD: this is that king Ahaz.

"Did you take a copy of the exam?" Mrs. P. asked me.

"No," I said. That was enough for Mrs. P. It was a relief, but I would have felt less agitated had it not been a lie. To ingratiate myself to some cool guys, I bragged about my sleight of hand. Seeing an opportunity to ruin me and curry favor with the teacher, they snitched. Ironically, had I not taken the exam, I'd have scored high. With my character suspect, I had to perform below my ability.

Today's story is a character test. Ahaz scored low. He was a pragmatist of no principles. He did what he hoped would get the results he wanted. There was no ultimate right or wrong, only what works. People like this are bound to circumstances and trends and their vicissitudes. Without principles that recognize absolutes, we do the convenient, self-aggrandizing thing that leaves God out. A framework without Him will be lifeless, because He is life and the giver of life. This includes purpose and reality. Ahaz's mistakes paint a gloomy picture. He tried to stop the worship of the true God. He closed the Temple. In his time of distress, he worshipped the Syrian gods. Had he known God's Word, and the prophets, he'd have known the blessing of God was with those who obey.

Our reaction in a time of distress shows who we are. Will we do what is right or what's convenient? The latter won't endure; it isn't based on reality. Principle trumps pragmatism. Ahaz bet on what he could see; his vision was nearsighted. Contrariwise, King David looked to the hills, above circumstances, to God (Ps. 121:1-2). We're taking an exam, the real test—life. Sleight of hand won't help, character will.

Grace Lover: Lord, who shall abide in thy tabernacle? Who shall dwell in thy holy hill? [2] He that walketh uprightly, and worketh righteousness, and speaketh the truth in his heart. [3] He that backbiteth not with his tongue, nor doeth evil to his neighbour, nor taketh up a reproach against his neighbour. [4] In whose eyes a vile person is contemned; but he honoureth them that fear the Lord. He that sweareth to his own hurt, and changeth not (Ps. 15:1-4).

The tall and small, Great and redeemed. Thousands died for it, One, died for us.

153. PEOPLE

Do you remember the joke: "What's the difference between a giraffe and a bar of soap?" There's no relationship; the obvious answer is "I don't know." The Joker's retort is: "Well, I won't send you out for soap!" I guess out in the bush one could say "I won't send you out for a giraffe." It's *samui*, a cold joke, as they say in Japan. Please forget it. But I have a question for you. What have singing in French on the Trans-Siberian railroad, winning at Chinese Chess on the train to Urumqi, and celebrating Johann Strauss' death in Vienna, have in common? No, it's not a bar of soap, though one was badly needed. What's their link?

First there is Akiko san. I was in Vienna, Austria, during the one-hundredth anniversary of Strauss' death. I bought two raspberry filled cookies and went to a Waltz Concert. Hearing Japanese, I turned and saw Akiko. I explained her ticket was for a different theatre. We sat together, danced, and later, I visited her family in Japan. When Caleb was born, she sent a gift. Recently, we received a New Year's postcard.

In 1975, I met a man from the Philippines when I lived on the island of Hawaii. He was an Ilokano. He'd come to Hawaii prior to WWI with other single men to plant the coffee plantations. You've heard of Kona Coffee? He was still single, in his seventies, and lonely.

I met a young Chinese lad traveling by train, with his family, in 1991. They were going to Urumqi in the far west. We struck up a conversation, and he taught me Chinese Chess. The King has few spaces in which to move—he can't leave Court. Also, there's an elephant and a cannon. The latter only shoots when there is another piece between it and its target. Though he was probably being polite, I beat him. To soften the blow, I gave him a Bible.

To attend seminary in Kentucky, I traveled on the same Trans-Siberian train as the Mongolian Wrestling Team. I was sick but they invited me to drink their arkhi (vodka). I took some, hoping to wipe out a few billion bacteria, but didn't feel better. They also bought my lunch.

The first Moslems I met were Iranians, in Chicago. President Carter's term was not a good time to be Iranian in the USA. One fellow was somewhat faithful to Islam, though he did drink, The other, an apostate pointed out that though his fellow prayed five times a day, he didn't speak Arabic, and couldn't understand his prayers. I was disappointed I couldn't send them a Persi Bible, but they were, understandably, a little shy about giving away information.

I met a man in Beijing, at Tiananmen Square. He called himself Coffee. He was selling paintings he'd made on scraps of paper. He had a gift. I believe I still have a couple of his mini-renderings. I enjoyed our chat and his spirit, though I regret I didn't make him much richer.

Finally, I met a Catholic fellow in Chicago in the 80's. He was a flamenco dancer wannabe. He wore tremendous boots. He had no profession, only a dream, and he was getting old for a career in dance. A warrior, he had a passion, and battled daily the forces of despair and age.

Before I was a believer, I lived in a condemned building, built in 1906, in Jersey City. It had filigree and scalloped ceilings—the best! One day, I went to the bar at the corner, sat next to a blue-collar worker, and asked him: "So what have you done?" He realized I was a Pilgrim seeking the Holy City or was a flaming zonko in need of remediation. I learned about him and got a free beer. I'm not suggesting this strategy, but will say, people like to talk about themselves. Showing interest, or asking if they have a prayer request, can open doors. Yuko did this with one of our moms at English class, and discovered she went to Sunday School as a little girl, her mom is a Christian, and her brother has cancer. The question opened a door.

So, in answer to my question, the link for these folks was my traipsing hither and thither and meeting strangers. In a Douglas Adam's detective story, Dirk Gently used the principle of randomness. He'd look for clues by following a random passer-by. It sounds strange, but I like the concept. I propose we invite the Lord to go, too. That makes it more fun and fruitful. The Golden Rule talks about loving our neighbor as ourself. I'm glad someone shared the Good News with me. I sometimes make it complicated. I need to remind myself everything is about God and people. LIFE=Loving God+Loving People.

Grace Lover: And he said unto him, If thy presence go not with me, carry us not up hence (Ex. 33:15).

> When he saw the crowds, he had compassion on them because they were confused and helpless, like sheep without a shepherd (Matt. 9:36).

154. THE WINDSHIELD

W. Babylon, N.Y., '69.

This is the most mundane story of this collection. During my freshman year, baby-face Wilkie had to show ID at bars. I hadn't wanted to graduate. The WORLD was out there; why leave Camelot? Though not ready, it was time to leave. Ten minutes out, I was glad I'd left. After my first solo trip, I put the car in gear, and hit the gas—nothing. Ignorant of exorcisms, I revved the engine, but with no result. After calming down, I disengaged the parking brake.

In the tale, *The Windshield*, the window is the victim, the perpetrator, the wiper. I did nothing! The blade's rubber wore away, exposing a knifelike edge that etched a semi-circle every rainfall. My cultural heritage includes masterful etching—ever hear of Wexford? So, imagine my surprise at Dad's disappointment I'd not noticed the defacement that would further de-value the car. I felt embarrassed and angered. I never asked for a world with wipers! There he was, thinking I was immature and spoiled. The windshield episode was inconsequential. The window wound was not fatal, the maple tree was. It was a short bout, the '67 Chevy du Belair vs, the Magnificent Maple on a snowy outdoor canvas, on New Year's Eve. Television reception was blocked for the one round conflict, which had the Maple standing when the bell rang, or more accurately, the punctured radiator spilled its bowels.

This prosaic tale was a lead-in to an apology to my sons. I realized I expressed dismay, even anger, when they didn't perform, as I thought they should. *Underwhelmed* sums up the result. I asked: "You hear me?" One sat in the protected wilderness of the back seat whence were heard the blasts of Mario launching Bowser into oblivion, for the 10^{41} time. The other lad, quiet regarding heartfelt things, added nothing. Well, thanks for letting me dump this. I hope it helps someone.

Grace Lover: And, ye fathers, provoke not your children to wrath: but bring them up in the nurture and admonition of the Lord (Eph. 6:4).

Curmudgeon: Doth a fountain send forth at the same place sweet water and bitter (James 3:11).

155. HAND PAPER

Shenzhen, China, '91.

I met Katherine at a watermelon stand. She said: "Excuse me, is that a Bible?" I confessed it was. She looked harmless, but I was wary, having a bag of religious contraband. She, her friend, and Masahiro, whom I met on the ship, Ganjingo, traveled with me for a while. I liked her and visited her twice in Shenzhen. In between was a letter-writing campaign. Living in Japan, I knew some Chinese ideographs. In Oriental custom, I first thanked her for reading my *tegami* (Japanese pronunciation), which is *hand-paper* (in Japanese writing). In English it is *letter*. Her reply informed me the Chinese for *hand-paper* is not a *letter*, but toilet tissue. OOPS! To make amends, my next missive was on *toilet tissue*!

Communication is tricky. I once told my girlfriend I'd give her a ring. "Really?" she cooed. "No, not that," I backpedaled. "I'll phone you." I was noncommittal. Katherine and I shared many letters but were cautious about showing our feelings. We wanted the other to make the first move. Neither of us did.

Let me tell you about another set of love letters. They're one-way, and there's no reticence about commitment. That love is aggressive. It searches out its recipient. It gives even when rejected; it loves before the object of its love exists! I'm alluding to God's love. In both Testaments, God affirms his love for us. Hear Jeremiah 31:3:

> The Lord hath appeared of old unto me, saying, Yea, I have loved thee with an everlasting love: therefore with lovingkindness have I drawn thee.

John 3:16 sums up Genesis Chapter 1 to Revelation Chapter 22, our reconciliation! As John Wayne said, "No brag, just fact!" Jesus made it possible for us to be saved, changed, and eternally blessed. That's a love letter worth reading, be it on parchment, vellum, paper or toilet tissue.

Grace Lover: For I delivered unto you first of all that which I also received,
how that Christ died for our sins according to the scriptures; [4] And that he
was buried, and that he rose again the third day according to the scriptures:
[5] And that he was seen of Cephas, then of the twelve: [6] After that, he was
seen of above five hundred brethren at once; of whom the greater part
remain unto this present, but some are fallen asleep (I Cor. 15:3-6).

156. 715 B.C.: BREAK THE CYCLE

"He in the first year of his reign, in the first month, opened the doors of the house of the Lord, and reopened them" (II Chron. 29:3).

God used many individuals in the Bible. II Kings, II Chronicles, and Isaiah recount Hezekiah's story. We see the historical setting in which he reigns, and how he reacted to his circumstances. Hezekiah's life can show something to all of us. He became king when he was 25 years old. His father, King Ahaz, had not only stepped in the horse-pucky, he trampled it all over the place. In the previous chapter, we heard the account of how he followed foreign deities and closed the doors of the Temple to keep others from worshipping God. Hezekiah wasted no time to head in the opposite direction. There was no learning curve, no taking of polls. He gathered leaders, priests, and Levites to get ready for service to God. Then, he informed the larger community of the re-institution of Passover. The prophets gave guidance. He invited the Ten Tribes that embraced idolatry back to their roots. It was revival time, and it started with one person's tenacity. It was time to break the cycle of rebellion and judgment and return to the cycle of obedience and blessing.

Hezekiah turned a nation around. He had off moments, but God used him. His example wasn't followed. His son introduced the worst apostasy Judah ever experienced. Regardless of others' choices, we strive to break the cycle. Results are not the measure of our labors. Obedience is the key. Fling open those Temple doors, and obey.

Grace Lover: And the Lord hearkened to Hezekiah, and healed the people. [22] And Hezekiah spake comfortably unto all the Levites that taught the good knowledge of the Lord: and they did eat throughout the feast seven days, offering peace offerings, and making confession to the Lord God of their fathers (II Chron. 30:20, 22).

Curmudgeon: Beware lest Hezekiah persuade you, saying, the Lord will deliver us. Hath any of the gods of the nations delivered his land out of the hand of the king of Assyria (Isa. 36:18).

157. SAVED ALONE

"You took my money!" I told him. It was China, '92. I went to Shenzhen to see Katherine. We ordered watermelon juice at a restaurant. The waiter robbed its sweetness somewhat by keeping the change from the bill, what amounted to a day's wage there. Later, Katherine and I went to the P.O. to mail a package 30 minutes before closing. It was still 90 in the shade. The clerk said: "Meo," which translated means: *impossible, difficult, I don't feel like it, or get lost, foreigner*. I didn't care for any of them and was ready, with my 130 pounds and a ton of disdain, to pull the comrade over the counter. Unfortunately, I'd just given Katherine a Bible commentary. Manslaughter might take the shine off the Good News, so we left without incident, but with the package and heatstroke. Our stroll at the Cultural Center was a sauna. A horse keeled over, dead. Not only that was dead. Despite hopes, we knew we'd not be significant others. We continued, with a good face, if not to totally enjoy our visit, to finish it.

In 1873, the Spafford family wanted a rest. They'd lost their home and son to the Great Chicago Fire. The insurance company refused to pay. Mr. Spafford sent his wife and four daughters to Europe by the Ville du Havre, intending to catch up later, but the ship was lost at sea. Mrs. Spafford survived. Her telegram read: SAVED ALONE. Spafford then penned *It Is Well with My Soul*. He had a choice: go off the deep end, or go to God. Jesus asked the disciples: "Will you also leave me?" Peter answered: "Lord, you have the words to eternal life, where else could we go?" (John 6:67). Friend, if it's looking bad, go to Jesus. He not only has the words of eternal life, He is Life! Go to Him.

Grace Lover: It is of the Lord's mercies that we are not consumed, because his compassions fail not. [23] They are new every morning: great is thy faithfulness (Lam. 3:22-23).

> Blessed be God, even the Father of our Lord Jesus Christ, the Father of mercies, and the God of all comfort;[4] Who comforteth us in all our tribulation, that we may be able to comfort them which are in any trouble, by the comfort wherewith we ourselves are comforted of God (II Cor. 1:3-4).

158. BLOCK

The room was gray with blotches, the floor uneven and wet. There it was, in the center. We'd heard so many things. After all, it was a Block. Non-parallel striations creased it on one side. The other side was not squared and had an angular slice removed. The top appeared somewhat sunken, an imperfect concavity. It had no other discernible features. Then it happened. We'd been waiting for what seemed to be forever. An indirect light was discernable from behind a curtain. We'd been aware of that veil, but, at times, forgot it. We conjectured as to its meaning and accessibility, but no one had a viable conclusion. The light intensified. The curtain moved as if borne on a breeze. The Curator's presence became recognizable, though His features remained indistinguishable. Our attention turned from the greyness as He approached the Block. We expected the Block would move toward him, but it didn't. He held up a measuring square to the one side of the Block. He then replaced it with a protractor. This, in turn, was supplanted by a plumb line.

"What do you see?" He asked. Various among us plied interpretations for his pleasure. None won it. Notwithstanding, He was not disapproving.

"How can you explain, or judge, that which is not complete?" He touched the Block. With this catalyst, it exuded an inner light, like that at the Curator's appearance. It began to shimmer, pulsate, and change colors, then to vibrate, rotate, and change shape. It took on appearances, nuances of its character. Alas, it took on wings, multi-colored, glimmering extensions of itself that caressed the air. It left its clay foundation to fly magnificently, still changing form and essence. With no breakage of the structure or itself, it flew through the ceiling. The Curator had also disappeared. The only evidence He'd been with us was a fading breeze, similar with what had been the harbinger of his arrival. Again, we were in a room of grayness with a wet floor. One by one, we left.

Grace Lover: I praise you because I am fearfully and wonderfully made; your works are wonderful…I know that full well (Ps. 139:14).

> Not as though I had already attained, either were already perfect: but I follow after, if that I may apprehend that for which also I am apprehended of Christ Jesus (Phil. 3:12).

159. THE BURDEN OF PROOF

"Your Bible has been corrupted!" Nabeel declared.

"Go on," his roommate, David, replied.

Centuries ago, a hallmark development occurred in what is now Great Britain, i.e., one is innocent until proven guilty. There'd be no more trial by combat—a big deal for little guys like me! In his book, *Tactics*, Greg Koukl says it's the same in apologetics. If someone lays an accusation, it's not our job to defend the Lord. The burden of proof is on the accuser. Try cross-examination. David Wood did. Nabeel didn't know the *where's* or *how's* of his claim. Asked to prove their case, accusers are often two sheets to the wind or three if they're a Barkentine. People often speak from emotion, not thought-out positions with proofs and examples. A soundbite is considered a defense. We, however, direct a conversation by asking probing questions. It allows the other person to reach a correct conclusion by themselves. Questions expose logical fallacies. Questions like: Why? Are you sure? How did you reach that conclusion? Jesus knew the art of the question.

1. Matt. 5:46— For if ye love them which love you, what reward have ye? do not even the publicans the same?
2. Matt. 6:28— And why take ye thought for raiment? Consider the lilies of the field, how they grow; they toil not, neither do they spin:
3. Matt. 7:3—And why beholdest thou the mote that is in thy brother's eye, but considerest not the beam that is in thine own eye?
4. Matt. 8:26— And he saith unto them, Why are ye fearful, O ye of little faith?
5. Matt. 16:15—He saith unto them, But whom say ye that I am?
6. Matt 16:26—For what is a man profited, if he shall gain the whole world, and lose his own soul? or what shall a man give in exchange for his soul?
7. Mark 10:51—And Jesus answered and said unto him, What wilt thou that I should do unto thee?

Have questions for God? How about CROSS-examination?

Jiji, Grandpa Shiraishi, with Corey and Caleb.

160. JIJI

Kyushyu, Japan, 2001—2019.

"I'll think about it," he said

I'd spent a day, money, and a pound of humility to ask permission for Yuko's hand. Her Father put me off to show who was in charge. Other things he did would've landed him in jail in the U.S., but here, it was a father protecting the culture and tradition. Later, he tried to negotiate:

"We conceded Yuko could marry a foreigner, a Christian, a man her senior. Now you want to go abroad. We gave you three, give us one. Do your mission here." The request was reasonable.

"I'm sorry," I said, "we believe the Lord is leading this."

Differing positions usually met ridicule, at least annoyance. Caleb saved the day. After he was born, Jiji softened. Corey made it a double blessing. Jiji returned to church, trusted in Christ, and scheduled his baptism so we could be there. A year before his induction to the Cloud of Witnesses (Hebrews 12:1), he learned of his cancer. We visited several times. The boys helped in the garden. He requested Yuko and I perform his Christian funeral. It was a small affair, but we expected fewer people—relationships had gone awry.

Let me clue you in. A Christian doesn't abstractly surrender to the outrageous idea there is a God, and, driven by guilt, do nice things to get on His good side. We have a new birth in Christ (II Cor. 5:17). It was our key verse at the funeral. We lose our sin nature, and good works flow out of a transformed heart. Are we perfect? Yes, and no. We're forgiven by Christ's sacrifice, yet we still struggle against the influence of the World and the Flesh. All that to say, Jiji saw action in several spiritual skirmishes. Yuko found a devotional book he'd underlined in places, witnesses of spiritual battle. Paul said it so well:

> [19] For the good that I would I do not: but the evil which I would
> not, that I do. **[20]** Now if I do that I would not, it is no more I that
> do it, but sin that dwelleth in me. [21] I find then a law, that, when I
> would do good, evil is present with me. [22] For I delight in the law of
> God after the inward man: [23] But I see another law in my members,
> warring against the law of my mind, and bringing me into captivity
> to the law of sin which is in my members. [24] O wretched man that

I am! who shall deliver me from the body of this death? [25] I thank God through Jesus Christ our Lord. So then with the mind I myself serve the law of God; but with the flesh the law of sin (Ro. 7:19-25).

Jiji is perfect in God's sight because he has Christ's righteousness. For some of the family, he was an irritation. For us, visits to Jiji's house always meant great dinners and multiple trips to Kijima, an amusement park responsible for filling our drop-box with photos! He shined with our kids. We did have an argument once. I think my position was justified, but as I shared it with too much volume, I apologized. Later, in what I think would surprise his family, he called us in Cambodia to apologize. I'm very glad to have had him in my life. I rejoice he finished the course.

[12] For the which cause I also suffer these things: nevertheless I am not ashamed: for I know whom I have believed, and am persuaded that he is able to keep that which I have committed unto him against that day (II Tim. 1:12).

Friend, do you have an unbelieving relative? Are you God's seed sower? I pray for fertile soil. I hope to meet you all later; I'll introduce you to Jiji. For curmudgeons trusting their eternity to relatives' prayers or a far-off day of repentance, good luck with that. I'd hit the floor, Jack, and apologize to the One you've offended. Remember, He's pure, and you're the dust He loves. It's that simple. Why not slice yourself a generous piece of humble pie and enjoy Him.

Grace Lover: Not by works of righteousness which we have done, but according to his mercy he saved us, by the washing of regeneration, and renewing of the Holy Ghost (Titus 3:5).

Curmudgeon: But what think ye? A certain man had two sons; and he came to the first, and said, Son, go work today in my vineyard.[29] He answered and said, I will not: but afterward he repented, and went.[30] And he came to the second, and said likewise. And he answered and said, I go, sir: and went not.[31] Whether of them twain did the will of his father? They say unto him, The first. Jesus saith unto them, Verily I say unto you, That the publicans and the harlots go into the kingdom of God before you (Matt. 21:28-31).

161. STOLEN GLORY

What do the Bronze Doors of the Basilica San Marco, the statue of St. Theodore, and the sculpture of the Tetrarchy, have in common? Pieces of art? Yes, but no cigar. The Venetians plundered Constantinople in 1204 and carried away what ancient treasures of Byzantium they didn't melt down for coinage.

In 1999, I sat in St. Mark's Square with an entourage of pigeons, and ate *pan fromage*. Venice has a heinous history, but its sandwiches can make you forget. It was enchanting. I had a room over the canal. I wasn't close enough to spit in the water, but I could spit on the head of the guy close enough to spit in it. I learned the glory of Venice wasn't theirs. They even stole the supposed bones of St. Mark from Alexandria and made him their patron saint. Apparently, Mark had more pull than the former guy, St. Theodore of Amasea. The story is intriguing. The bones were smuggled out of Alexandria. Relics were expensive, deemed powerful, and well-guarded. So, the Venetians put the bones into casks of pork to hide them from Muslim inspectors who gave pigs a wide berth.

I can't be upset with the Venetians. I've done similarly. Why do we take His glory? We view our worth as meager compared to others? After seminary, I was 33K in debt, single, property-less, and beginning my first professional job. Men my age were at their peak career salary, their kids married, and their house paid off. I was zip. The Lord gave me a verse: "We are complete in Him who is the head of all principality and power" (Col. 2:10). The World isn't our touchstone. God is the final arbiter. We always have Him. In Him, we have all. Centuries after Venice's success, A Genovese Italian discovered America, and Venice was left in the dust. Stolen glory fades.

Grace Lover: For the earth shall be filled with the knowledge of the glory of the Lord, as the waters cover the sea (Hab. 2:14).

Curmudgeon: I *am* the LORD, that *is* My name; and My glory will I not give to another, neither my praise to graven images (Isa. 42:8),

162. SMELL THE COFFEE

California, '98.

It was my first coffee purchase. I was gathering a support team for a mission with Christians in Action. Trailways Bus was my conveyance, hotel, and community center. One day, we stopped at a tree, a rock, and a coffee machine. I was hungry, but drinks were cheap. As usual, I faced tea discrimination. I ordered coffee, double cream and sugar. It tasted good once I disguised it. Years ago, if you ordered tea, you'd sometimes get water from the coffee machine. Coffee drinkers may scoff, but I once went to a Chinese Restaurant with a pastor. We had oolong tea. Despite my advice, he added milk and sugar. Three Chinese fainted at the sight!

You've heard: "Wake up and smell the coffee," i.e., get real, stop dreaming. When riding a high-speed train in France, I went to the dining car for a cup of TEA! I sat at a lamp, and enjoyed Poirot, guessing sleuths, and nurtured cup of Ceylon tea thinking we had one more stop. Back in my car, some young men made it their purview to rifle my belongings. It's been said my feet seldom touch the ground. A good fling with fantasy is a prerequisite for sanity, but prolonged flights on gliders can turn reality into a harsher reality. Eli, a Judge of Israel, knew his sons were messing-up but did nothing. It was a sad ending for all of them (I Sam. 4). David thought he could have another man's wife and it would play out ok in the end—nope (II Sam. 11). Balaam thought he could play games with God—the ass he rode was smarter than he was (Num. 22). Today's theme and verses are not just for the occasional dreamer, but especially the ostriches amongst us. The Truth hurts; delusion can kill. Wake up my Friend, and smell the coffee—better yet, tea!

Grace Lover: When I was a child, I spake as a child, I understood as a child, I thought as a child: but when I became a man, I put away childish things (I Cor. 13:11).

Curmudgeon: Wherefore he saith, Awake thou that sleepest, and arise from the dead, and Christ shall give thee light (Eph. 5:14).

163. CHALOT

Phnom Penh, Cambodia, 2003.

An army of ants preceded us into a room on the top floor. There lay Chalot, the cat of our team leader, Pol Guazon. He'd been the victim of one of the many motorcycles in the capital. His back legs were cut and unusable. The ants came to answer the summons of the protein rich blood. Pol was away, so we took Chalot home. We dressed his wounds every night, and he healed slowly. His legs, however, remained useless attachments. I think he began to like us. At least, he bit Yuko on the nose.

Every day, we let him out in the morning to sit in front of the apartment. One day we couldn't find him. Later, we heard his mewing in the kitchen. He had climbed off the staircase and descended into the washing machine. That was not the only surprise. Days later, he crossed the street, enticed by another cat. I say enticed, but this was no romantic rendezvous. It was a cat fight. During the skirmish, something interesting happened. We didn't discover it until Chalot returned—walking normally. It became apparent that he had not lost the function of his legs; he had only dislocated them. His tussle with our feline neighbor set him straight, so to speak. I learned something from that feisty cat. One, sometimes we need a battle to get us on our feet again, and two, I might get away with biting my wife's nose. BTW, *Chalot* means brave.

Grace Lover: For a just man falleth seven times, and riseth up again: but the wicked shall fall into mischief (Prov. 24:16).

> These things I have spoken unto you, that in me ye might have peace. In the world ye shall have tribulation: but be of good cheer; I have overcome the world (John 16:33).

Curmudgeon: And Caleb stilled the people before Moses, and said, Let us go up at once, and possess it; for we are well able to overcome it. [31] But the men that went up with him said, We be not able to go up against the people; for they are stronger than we (Num. 13:30-31).

164. THE CHAMBER OF THE WIND

His name was *Athraithe*, (Gaelic *Transformed*). It sounds like *Ahara hay*, and as with all things Gaelic, makes one want to dance. His father was a pre-Armada seafarer, who when a tempest left him on Eire's shore, he wed. Hard times sent the son to Andalusia where his falchion found his sovereign's favor and no rivals. The duke whom he served summoned him to say:

"I need a conquering hero!"

Confirmed as a prince, Aharahay would cross the sea, to the land of the Moors. This surprised all, for the land on every side was already under the Omayyads. In a fortnight his contingent stood on shifting sand, its aggress to be the *Tudhar al Wassoul Iliha* oasis (Arabic *Unreached*). Berbers trained their sons the stars' way and desert water paths. Aharahay knew neither, nor that victory is not always a matter of a skillful sword. They soon lost their way and found great thirst. Then a camel descended a dune.

"Show us Tudhar al Wassoul Iliha, or this sand will be as red as the evening sun," Aharahay threatened.

"Is that the way you greet a brother?" the rider asked.

"How are you, my brother?" Aharahay demanded.

"I am well, by your grace," the visitor answered.

"I care not if you're covered with boils; why do you call me brother?"

Neheme (blessing), pronounced *Nyam*, produced a cross.

"Why not keep the Cross in a prominent place?" Aharahay asked.

"To keep a Cross on one's neck, one must keep their head intact."

"I'm a conquering hero. Take me to the oasis or die?"

"Discover the Chamber of Wind, and I lead you. If not, you go, killing none."

"How about I kill you now?" Aharahay suggested.

"You'll die drinking sand, for your folly." Nyam said, and began preparing a sand platform and tunnel. The contest was on. "These two spheres," he said, "are our instruments. To assure fairness, you may exchange them at any time." Nyam then grabbed some sand. It took shape in his hand. "These figures are Fire Sand. To start the game, we place two at the platform's middle. These act independently of us. We throw spheres at the Fire Sand on the platform, to advance our own, or dislodge our neighbor's. The winner makes it to the end first or dislodges his opponent. Offer a comment as you throw. It affects the outcome."

Shouting "Victory!" Aharahay hurled a sphere to dislodge Nyam's Fire Sand. The target took a diminished human form and jumped out of the way. The contestants' Fire Sand moved neck and neck on the platform, struggling to make the goal. Aharahay's words were bellicose, Nyam's, gentle. In the end, Aharahay's figure kicked his opponent off the platform, taking the victory. Some present noted Nyam's fellow, willingly tumbled from its place.

"Now," the prince said, "we go to make history, and win glory.

"And the secret of the Chamber of the Wind? Nyam asked. "You've seen, but have you discovered?" The prince, scowling, neared the tunnel-like chamber and crawled in, lost to sight. He soon returned.

"Captains, form ranks," he ordered, and then surprised them. "We go to the oasis to drink, and return home." Later, his fellows noted other transformations. He listened to the wind or caught a breeze in his hand. The duke, though vexed at the expedition's failure, admitted the prince's new demeanor was the catalyst to factions of his duchy finding reconciliation. The sovereign was also sad to see him return to the Unreached. Aharahay, bringing Blessing with him, would become known as *Transformed of the Wind*, and crucial in the transformation of the Fire Sand of Tudhar al Wassoul Iliha.

Grace Lover: Not by might, nor by power, but by my spirit, saith the Lord of hosts (Zech 4:6).

> The wind bloweth where it listeth, and thou hearest the sound thereof, but canst not tell whence it cometh, and whither it goeth: so is every one that is born of the Spirit (John 3:8).

> And I will pray the Father, and he shall give you another Comforter, that he may abide with you for ever; [17] Even the Spirit of truth; whom the world cannot receive, because it seeth him not, neither knoweth him: but ye know him; for he dwelleth with you, and shall be in you (John 14:16-:17).

165. TASTE-TEST

In the 80s, Pepsi had a taste-test. People preferred Pepsi to Coke. So, Coke added a New Formula. One article spun it: *Coke Blinks*.

Without transition fossils between species, and so much life appearing in a short time in the so-called Cambrian Era, evolutionists blinked. Some dumped the *Classic* explanation for the *Jump Theory*, claiming many genetic jumps took place in ten-million years. Everyone agrees mutations happen in genes. The changes, however, do not make one Kind into a superior Kind. Inbreeding in Shepherds, for example, gave them weak hips. Mutations are negative. No new genetic information is created, only changes caused by a loss of genetic information. Some bacteria developed an immunity to antibiotics, but only by losing a positive trait. The Jump Theorists should have kept Classic Evolution, rather than invent a New Formula. Like Coke, I suspect they'll retreat to past modest failures, without fanfare. Hear evolutionist Dr. Patterson, Senior Paleontologist, British Museum of Natural History, to L. Sunderland: "I fully agree with your comment on the lack of direct illustrations of evolutionary transitions in my book. If I knew of any, fossil or living, I would certainly have included them…Yet Gould and the American Museum people are hard to contradict when they say there are no transitional fossils…I will lay it on the line-there is not one such fossil for which one could make a watertight argument."

Besides disclaimers, there are doubters. Calling evolution "a theory in crisis," over two dozen scientists have come to the defense of the Cobb County, Ga. Board of Education. The scientists, all Ph.D.'s, portray evolution as "a live and growing controversy." Multiple authors, September 3rd, 2004, Discovery Institute.

Evolution is speculation, not science! Did you blink?

Grace Lover: For by him were all things created, that are in heaven, and that are in earth, visible and invisible, whether they be thrones, or dominions, or principalities, or powers: all things were created by him, and for him (Col. 1:16).

Curmudgeon: Where wast thou when I laid the foundations of the earth? declare, if thou hast understanding (Job 38:4).

166. THE SHINTO PRIEST

Tokyo. Japan, '17.

Wednesdays meant English and Bible classes, hours of train rides to Ibaraki, and people. One day I saw a man wearing vestments.

"Are you a Shinto Priest?" I asked.

"No," he said, offering no explanation. Another question revealed he was a Buddhist monk. There are a couple of plausible reasons for his reticence. Buddhists are not evangelistic. Buddhism is a personal thing, all about you. Another reason may have been he was emptying himself of illusions–like my shallow nature filling the place with noise.

"What kind of Buddhist?" I asked. He didn't answer at first. I asked again, changing my words.

"I'm a Nichiren Buddhist," he said.

"Nichiren was in the 7th century?" I was off, but what's six centuries between friends? He declined the offer of a Bible. Obon week was near, when priests invite ancestral spirits for a siesta from the Netherworld.

"Maybe the spirits won't come back if you take it," I said. He didn't laugh. I thanked him for the chat, but in that regard, the pleasure was all mine. People receive powers from spirits. See the Witch of Endor (I Samuel 28), the Gadara demoniac (Mark 5), the sons of Sceva (Acts 19), the books of Dark Arts and a girl with a spirit of divination (Acts 16). The ultimate end of the powers listed in Deuteronomy 18 is to draw us away from God.

While waiting for a bus in California, a fellow started talking to himself, gradually getting less intelligible. He said: "I'm going to kill the President," and turned towards me. My stomach knotted. I was tempted to be afraid. That's a weird way to explain it, but I was aware the fear was not of me. I pointed at him and said: "In the Name…" Like a shot, he ran off. If you're considering Jesus, know that faith is not books and traditions. It's a step into the Spirit, so gird yourself for battle, Friend.

Grace Lover: And Jesus rebuked the devil; and he departed out of him: and the child was cured from that very hour (Matt. 17:18).

Curmudgeon: For we wrestle not against flesh and blood, but against principalities, against powers, against the rulers of the darkness of this world, against spiritual wickedness in high places (Eph. 6:12).

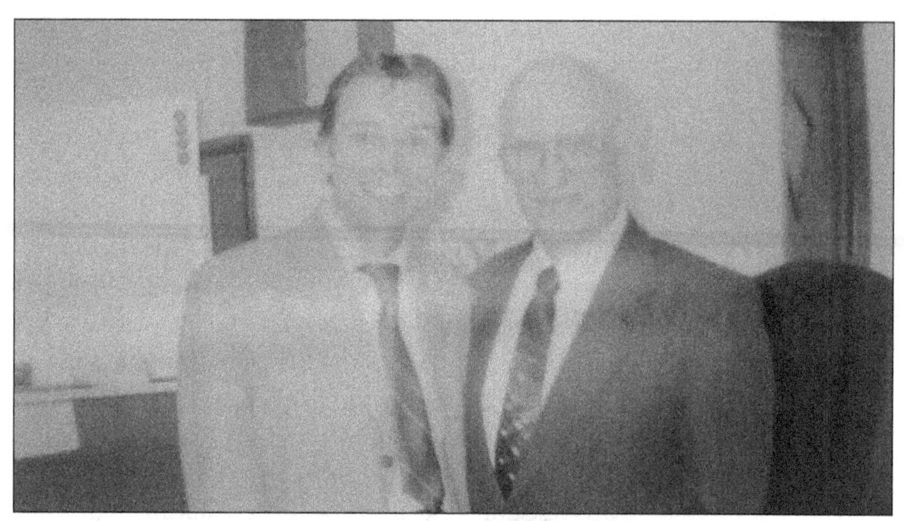

Jake DeShazer, circa 1997.

167. 4,000 CHEERIOS

Katsuta, Japan, '16.

About fifty years ago, in the town of *Katsuta*, which means *Victory Field*, Jake and Florence DeShazer started a church. In 1942, Jake had been on the Doolittle air raid on Japan in WWII. They had set off from the aircraft carrier Hornet. After bombing their targets, the crews had to dump their planes over China. The Japanese captured Jake. He was in prison until the war ended. Only two of a crew of five survived. Jake knew about endurance. He became a Christian in prison. After the war, he became a missionary to Japan.

So, what about the Cheerios? Well, the number of members at the Katsuta (Victory Field) Church has declined in recent years. I thought a good way to help would be to start English Bible classes. In April 2016, Ikeda san and I handed out 5,000 flyers for the proposed project. I handed out a thousand Christian tracts. No one was interested. I remember one lady on a balcony witnessed my tearful prayer at some mailboxes. For months, only a few people came, but the folks at the Church kept praying. Then, about Nine months later, people began coming. We grew to more than fifteen people, of all ages, coming to hear about God and speak English.

Some things in our life don't turn out like we had hoped. God answers our prayers with a *Yes*, a *No*, or a *Yes, but wait a while*. That's the usual list. How about adding *it depends on you!* Perhaps the blessing is contingent upon obedience. While we wait, He helps us build endurance and a stronger faith. Have a great day in your Victory Field, whatever the battle may bring!

Grace Lover: Except the Lord build the house, they labour in vain that build it: except the Lord keep the city, the watchman waketh but in vain (Ps. 127:1).

Curmudgeon: And there came thither certain Jews from Antioch and Iconium, who persuaded the people, and having stoned Paul, drew him out of the city, supposing he had been dead. [20] Howbeit, as the disciples stood round about him, he rose up, and came into the city: and the next day he departed with Barnabas to Derbe (Acts 14:19-20).

168. THE GOSPEL ACCORDING TO WU

Kumamoto, Japan, 9/11/2001.

"Did you hear the news?" Craig asked me.

"No, what's up?"

"The Trade Towers, they're gone! A terrorist attack by jets took them out!"

I had no T.V., so on 9/12. I went to the house of my Muslim friend, Ayad, to see re-runs. Murshed, from Bangladesh, and a Pakistani Communist also came. Ayad said: "Bin Laden is crazy; Bush is also crazy!" Ayad and I talked about our beliefs. I bought him a prayer rug in Turkey. He and Murshed came to my wedding. Though Ayad sympathized about 9/11, I suspect he felt God judged the USA for helping Israel. He's a friend, a soul for whom Christ died. I pray our chats lead to salvation, as others water, and God gives the increase (I Cor. 3:7). Friendship can keep differences from making enemies. Prayer can be the catalyst of a miracle. These weapons shouldn't be dismissed for sounding lackluster when compared to scatter bombs and drones. All this brings us to resolving our dilemma. I'm speaking, of course, of *Ninjago*. Cole has the power of Earth, Jay, of Lightning, Kai, of Fire, Zane, of Ice, and Lloyd, of Green. At practice their mentor, Sensei Wu, challenged them to discover the best way to defeat an enemy. At day's end, no one was successful.

"It's impossible," was their concerted opinion.

"To defeat an enemy," said Wu, "make him a friend!"

Let's give it up for Sensei: Oooooooh, Wuuuuuu!

Grace Lover: But I say unto you**,** Love your enemies, bless them that curse you, do good to them that hate you, and pray for them which despitefully use you, and persecute you (Matt. 5:44).

> Therefore if thine enemy hunger, feed him; if he thirst, give him drink: for in so doing thou shalt heap coals of fire on his head (Ro. 12:20).

169. MARK S.

W. Babylon, N.Y., '67.

Mark was unique; he had a Volvo. Nobody had a Volvo, only Mark. Where does one find a Volvo? Nobody knew! If it were spelled Volov it could be a palindrome. Nobody knew that either, or cared, but it adds to the mystique of Mark. Everyone listened to the Beatles, but Mark liked Cream. Only Mark would know of a band of three. His friends were unique, too. Bub, known to his parents as Tom, had a room of home-made martial arts gizmos and all the paraphernalia of a roadside market in New Mexico. Another friend, a Puerta Rican named Frank, had an Afro. It made his head about eighteen inches wide. Like his hair, Frank was fuzzy, *mellow*. I was white bread, middle class, so this influenced my worldview. Apart from Mark passing out from drinking in a cemetery, we never got into any trouble in the two years we hung together—not bad for high schoolers in the Sixties.

I flunked out of college, being in jail during finals. Mark disapproved of my enlightenment. He and his dad had talked; he'd seen the light about responsibility, community, blah, blah. I'd moved out of the house, and Dad came down to the disco I frequented to invite me home. I thanked him, but I enjoyed my freedom. I wasn't angry; it was just time to go. Mark and his dad got closer, I and mine moved apart.

As for Frank, he taught college math, going from mellow dude to professor. Folks change. People pass in and out of our lives, but past friendships are a part of us. I'm thankful for the part they played in my life. They remind me of who I was. They helped forge what I am. If friends have a change that is unsettling, we recall our more familiar times. But, when it comes to Jesus, He needs no retouching.

Grace Lover: Oh that I were as in months past, as in the days when God preserved me; [4] As I was in the days of my youth, when the secret of God was upon my tabernacle (Job 29:2,4).

Curmudgeon: Be not deceived: evil communications corrupt good manners (I Cor. 15:33).

170. DOG BISCUITS

The summer of '70, Tony's Pizza van, sporting a happy Italian on the side panel, launched from Bayshore, N.Y., for the West. I got the van for $500.00. I made a potty, and my fellow pilgrim, R. Smith, supplied the curtains, apart from the American flag, which we hung upside down as a sign of national distress. So, the three of us departed, myself, Richie, and the Plaster of Paris Buddha, that sat serenely atop of the aforementioned throne. We stopped by an Arkansas field to grab a puppy we named for the place. Crossing into Oklahoma, I missed a stop sign, but not the local preacher kid's car. Fittingly, Gore was the name of the town. We sustained minor cuts, but Buddha lost his throne and his head. The locals, finding long-haired hippies at the bar, wanted to show us a warm welcome, heated actually, but the sheriff came. I sold the van, and we hitch-hiked to California. We got a lot of rides because the dog was cute. One restaurant cook gave the dog a hamburger. The little guy looked like a basketball with legs. Contrariwise, we had nothing to eat but dog biscuits. The weather was getting cold, so we sent the dog by train from Flagstaff, Arizona, to Needles, California. After many dog biscuits, a check arrived, and we ate Chinese fare. Arkansas became a member of the Smiths of New York.

We aren't told how long it took the Prodigal Son to come to his senses. For me, it was four years from the time I abandoned faith until I was back in Father's arms. I needed to fall down and stay down before I had the sense to look up. If you've not enjoyed His embrace, let me ask how long must you stay down? You like pig scraps? Dog biscuits? But this isn't about the other side of the tracks. You may eat sirloin, but in the company of a guilty conscience. The Lord can fix it. The Father is watching the road for your return. Come on in, won't you? If you are in His embrace, try resting there. Reunions are great; no one hugs like Dad.

Grace Lover: I will arise and go to my father, and will say unto him, Father, I have sinned against heaven, and before thee (Luke 15:18).

Curmudgeon: And the Philistine said unto David, Am I a dog, that thou comest to me with staves? And the Philistine cursed David by his gods. [44] And the Philistine said to David, Come to me, and I will give thy flesh unto the fowls of the air, and to the beasts of the field.[45] Then said David to the Philistine, Thou comest to me with a sword, and with a spear, and with a shield: but I come to thee in the name of the Lord of hosts, the God of the armies of Israel, whom thou hast defied (I Sam.17:43-45).

171. NEHUSHTAN

Ootama, '19.

Ever been to Nehushtan? It's next to Tajikistan? I'm teasing. It's not in Central Asia. It's a pre-figure of the cross. The New Testament refers to it as a pole. If I may digress, polarity makes magnets attract, but sometimes they attract in other ways. In Tokyo, a truck hosted a pattern on its panel. It wasn't a manufacturer's emblem, or an advertisement. It wasn't for financial gain, though it was profitable. Give up? It was a magnet collection, shaped like a Cross, a great witness if one minds the speed limit. The Early Church had another symbol, a fish. It was a clue to others of *the Way* that there'd be a meeting. The Greek word *ichthus* is *fish*. It's also an anagram in Greek: *Jesus Christ, Son of God, Savior.* It's appropriate in another regard, we're *Fishers of Men*. That symbol had a resurgence in the '70's. It was the only fish for me!

Let's talk about symbols. While singing at the Kumamoto Arcade, I saw a youth.

"I like your Cross," I said. As he added nothing, I continued,

""My Cross is bigger than your Cross," I joked. His was metal, mine wood. My brazenness got a smile. "Do you know the Cross' meaning?" I asked. It was no Ethiopian Eunuch conversion scenario, but seeds were planted.

Back to Nehushtan, it was a brass snake on a pole. The Israelites challenged Moses, and the Lord sent snakes as judgment (Num. 21:4-9). The Lord told Moses if the people looked at Nehushtan, i.e., recognized sin's symbol, they would be saved. Fifteen centuries later, the sin-bearer of Isaiah 53 came to take away sin. Generations worshipped Nehushtan until Hezekiah destroyed it (II Kings 18:4). Likewise, we turn the Cross into a piece of jewelry. Jesus said: "And as Moses lifted up the serpent in the wilderness, even so must the Son of Man be lifted up: That whosoever believeth in him should not perish, but have eternal life" (John 3:14,15). Brass is symbolic of purging, or trials. The Brass Serpent prefigured the Crucified Christ. Both took away the judgment of God for others. The Serpent, on one occasion, the Son, for all time. Let's dust off our symbols and restore them to our hearts, our necks, or our truck panels.

172. THE PARCHEZZI PROTOCOL

W. Babylon, '57.

"We don't want to play with you," we said. There were reasons. Joe D. and I were soulmates; there were new rules. First, don't dilute the twosome. Also, there was the issue of dividing chocolates three ways. Limited distribution adhered to universal norms. But there was a deeper intent—humiliate Gary. Make him pay for his naïve niceness. He cried and left to tell his mom. We didn't care, we were two houses down. We were soulmates in a cause, and we had the stash. But and this is a significant *But*, we hadn't considered righteous indignation. The term wasn't as out of vogue as it is today. Now we would be hard pressed to find a quorum that could pronounce it without losing a syllable. Joe and I hadn't considered God's omnipresence or the dire consequences of playing foul with a concerned Mother's child.

Gary got on his girl's bike and rode off. I sniggered, though I couldn't ride anything until I was ten. Seconds later, Mrs. C showed up, riding in, as she did, on a lightning bolt. "Why was Gary left out?" she asked. The answer: "Oh, he didn't always share with us," she summarily rejected, claiming she always provided him with snacks. This was not an assertion to be gainsaid, being reinforced by fire of the eye. That fusillade being shot down, we didn't muster another arsenal except for a weak "Well-um..." that wasn't fully vocalized, the tail trailing off smothered by truth. We were encouraged to say sorry; Gary was encouraged to bestow forgiveness. Grace abounded, taking the contextually appropriate form of Parcheesi and pretzels. Mrs. C. sat with us under the Swamp Maple to insure the peace and forbid escape.

Twosomes rule, as a principle, lost lustre in the wake of hard-heartedness, tears, and twelve pieces on the Parcheesi Plain. Mrs. C was frightful, but right. I'm glad she confronted evil, even if it was mine. Gary and I are still in touch. I dare not malign him. Who can forget Firebolts?

Grace Lover: Wherefore I take you to record this day, that I am pure from the blood of all men. [27] For I have not shunned to declare unto you all the counsel of God (Acts 20:26-27).

173. INCENSE

How many of us have had sweaty palms before a fight, a race, or worse, a date? Imagine a bonfire with your name on it, or a lion whose visage makes Cassius' "lean and hungry look," (*The Tragedy of Julius Caesar*, Act 1 Scene II) something akin to the Happy Buddha. The Emperor Domitian, A.D. 81-96, imposed a prohibition of Christianity. It was the law until the 313 A.D. Milan Edict. Some people, preferring not to be a onetime only Colosseum appearance, offered incense to the emperor. Others chose an eternal weight of glory and death (II Corinthians 4:17). There were ten major persecutions.

> Fear none of those things which thou shalt suffer: behold, the devil shall cast some of you into prison, that ye may be tried; and ye shall have tribulation ten days: be thou faithful unto death, and I will give thee a crown of life (Rev. 2:10).

Stephen, the first martyr, was stoned. Ironically, Saul of Tarsus was the overseer. Later he wrote much of the New Testament.

> And he kneeled down, and cried with a loud voice, Lord, lay not this sin to their charge. And when he had said this, he fell asleep (Acts 7:60).

The Apostle John's brother, James, was killed by King Herod Agrippa (Acts 12:1-3). The emperor Trajan executed Ignatius of Antioch in 117 A.D. The weapon of choice was lions. The Apostle John discipled Polycarp. At the latter's execution, Polycarp said: "Eighty-six years I have served Him, and He has done me no wrong; how then can I blaspheme the King who saved me…? WHY DO YOU DELAY?"

Were these martyrs deluded? Does one embrace spears or flames casually? They had an inner witness (John 14). Nothing has changed. We are sacrificed in martyrdom, or we are a living sacrifice (Ro. 12:1). See: Tokugawa Shogunate, Armenian Genocide, and Yazidis.

Grace Lover: For we are unto God a sweet savour of Christ, in them that are saved, and in them that perish (II Cor. 2:15).

174. THE MAN IN THE ARENA

Sorbonne, France, 1910.

I had a Snapple, a book, and a porch (Pearce Mission House). What made this niche special was that I'd painted the porch with my sons. The book was about T. Roosevelt's adventures, who, like me, experienced challenges in foreign countries as an older gentleman. For many years, like the Athenians of Acts 17, I was eager to discuss some *new thing*, but not to undertake a real challenge. I forayed unchartered territory, but close to shore. In my twenties, I hitch-hiked, but that was not *doing* as much as *drifting*. I was critical of the Church. In the safety of a pew, it was easy to find fault. The President addressed my attitude in a speech at the Sorbonne. I found it in Dad's garage, on a poster entitled *Citizens in a Republic*.

"The poorest way to face life is to face it with a sneer. A cynical habit of thought and speech, a readiness to criticize work which the critic himself never tries to perform, an intellectual aloofness which will not accept contact with life's realities—all these are marks, not of superiority, but of weakness. It is not the critic who counts; not the man who points out how the strong man stumbles, or where the doer of deeds could have done them better. The credit belongs to the man who is actually in the arena, whose face is marred by dust and sweat and blood; who strives valiantly; who errs, who comes short again and again, because there is no effort without error and shortcoming; but who does actually strive to do the deeds; who knows great enthusiasms, the great devotions; who spends himself in a worthy cause; who at the best knows in the end the triumph of high achievement, and who at worst, if he fails, at least fails while daring greatly, so that his place shall never be with those cold and timid souls who neither know victory nor defeat."

In an age of spin and sofa sophists, this beats a Snapple anytime. Let's put up or shut up. Let's jump into the Arena! Ready...

Curmudgeon: Who art thou that judgest another man's servant? to his own master he standeth or falleth. Yea, he shall be holden up: for God is able to make him stand (Ro. 14:4).

175. THE COLOSSEUM

N.Y., '57

"Romans were fat slaveholders," my brother said.

"Were not," was my pithy defense, "look in the enkyloppedidia!"

At seven I loved Ancient Rome. I didn't know Pax Romana wasn't for everyone. For Star Trek fans, when Rome came to town, you'd encountered the Borg of the classical world. In Miss Paris' sixth grade class, I made rice art depicting the Pantheon and Parthenon, both lost to modern Visigoths—moving.

In 1999, with a Eu-Rail Pass, I saw Europe. Italy, I dissected! I spent days in Roma, Venetia, and Firenze. I drank deep draughts of ages past at the Forum. I stared, mesmerized by the Sistine Chapel, and regularly massaged my feet, the victims of new shoes. The Colosseum was shy despite her size. Scaling an incline, I sat at a café with an iced tea. My pulse appeased I scanned the scenery. There, in a break in the trees, it stood—The Colosseum. I knew of gladiatorial combat, trireme-battles, and the martyrdom of the brethren, but hey, this was the Colosseum, the Glory of Rome, the Republic, the Principate, and the Dominate. I drained my ice-cubes and scurried down the hill. Inside the walls I'd hallowed, my excitement changed to discomfort, sadness, and finally, loathing. "How long, O Lord?" is a question repeated by suffering saints (Ps. 13:1, Rev. 6:10) in a world that abuses them and Truth. Yet, we honor things anathema to God, e.g., a regime, a rock star, or a movement.

In Tolkien's Middle Earth, Bilbo and Gandalf say: "All that is gold does not glitter." They speak of Strider, a person of seemingly dubious pedigree, who later becomes King Aragorn. Shakespeare reverses the order, not the intent: "All that glisters is not gold," *Merchant of Venice* Act II Scene VII. It would seem in our best interest not to be overly impressed with earthly things, and rather, to "seek those things which are above, where Christ sitteth on the right hand of God" (Col. 3:1).

Redeemed: And I saw no temple therein: for the Lord God Almighty and the Lamb are the temple of it (Rev. 21:22).

176. THE RIGHT SIDE

"Listen up FISHING fans. The score, after hours of netting, stands at the Galileans, '0,' and the Divine, '153.' Peter, the Galileans' Captain, is suing for his team's forfeiture, being of the opinion he is unsuitable to play. Not typical by any stretch of a net, the Divine follows with the even more inexplicable appointment of Peter as Captain for His Team, The Providences! Don't miss our coverage of this bewildering development. We'll be back after a psalm from our sponsor, Heime's Gifilte Fish, where every fin is drawn from this very Sea of Galilee: Want your fish all pickly? Then buy the best from Hei-i-me!"

Ok, that was dreadful, but the story reminds me of jingles from boyhood. For the story, without commercials, see Luke 5 and John 21. In the former, Jesus is beginning His ministry. He tells Simon to lower his net in the deep. After an evening of zip, Peter and the Zebedee brothers catch two boats-full of fish. Peter, realizing with whom he is dealing, does a double knee-drop, recognizes his sin, and bids the Lord to leave him. Instead, he's commissioned a *Fisher of Men*. In John's account, Jesus meets Peter. Thomas, Nathanael, Zebedee's sons, and two others at the end of the Lord's ministry. Jesus tells them to lower their nets on the other side. They catch 153 fish! What stands out? The disciples worked fruitlessly all evening. In both stories, Jesus shows up. He asks them to do their work differently, in the daytime, in the deep, on the other side of the boat. Having obeyed, they have fruit, or as it was, fish. Other takeaways? The Lord asks us to do what hasn't worked but to do it with Him, to trust Him in a new way, in unfamiliar territory. Then our nets almost break,

In the second story, Peter went fishing. It was his old life, his strong suit. The Lord let him tire himself out, then showed him we find fruitfulness in trust and obedience. That's when we find ourselves on the right side! So how is our catch today? "0?" "153?"

Grace Lover: I am the true vine, and my Father is the husbandman. [4]Abide in me, and I in you. As the branch cannot bear fruit of itself, except it abide in the vine; no more can ye, except ye abide in me (John 15:1,4).

The Midorigaoka House wherein were the infamous Kumo Corners!

177. KUMO CORNERS

Sendai, Japan, 1989.

I loved Kumo Corners. *Kumo* has two definitions, *cloud* and *spider.* Usually, when a word has two meanings, the accent is on different syllables; a distinct combination of ascending and descending feet for each meaning. It is so with the word *kaki*, which means both *oyster* and *persimmon*. For *kumo* it's appropriate there's one pronunciation, because both cloud and spider join our story. Leaving grammar behind, the warm mist of the place championed higher temperatures in a building devoid of insulation. Wooden slats kept one's feet off cold ceramic tiles. Dark wooden panels enhanced the shower's ambience, magnifying it to the status of spa or sauna! There were drawbacks, however; the warmth was a breeding ground for mosquitoes. As Kumo Corners, or Spider Corners, wasn't a resort but a shower, my roommate, Ray, and I cleared the air by leaving the spiders unmolested. It was a Hail Mary pass to the line of scrimmage.

We've all had rooms in which we let something untoward remain, to keep other irritations at bay. We excuse our own sin by overlooking someone else's. Like Machiavelli, my enemy's enemy is my friend. The possibilities are endless and unpleasant. Instead of opening the window or draining the mosquito pond, we minimize, ignore, or legitimize a problem and its consequences. We enjoy the mist, or we're afraid to deal with the problem. Something is going to bite, a spider, a mosquito, or worse. Friend, pull the plug and open the window. Let the light in. At first, it may vex the eyes or raise goosebumps, but it will clear the air.

Grace Lover: Likewise, I say unto you, there is joy in the presence of the angels of God over one sinner that repenteth (Luke 15:10).

Curmudgeon: For there is nothing covered, that shall not be revealed; neither hid, that shall not be known. [3]Nay, but, except ye repent, ye shall all likewise perish (Luke 12:2, 13:3).

178. THE JOURNAL

Sendai, Japan, '89.

Missions take faith. Sometimes, a sense of adventure imitates the latter. I was somewhere in-between.

1. Hand out handkerchiefs to friends at airport. Nobody cries.

2. I cry on airplane, Canadian short-termers encourage me.

3. First sighting of Japan is Hokkaido Island.

4. International Dateline—pay guide for coming twice, extra $200.

5. At station, surprise Namekawa sensei, ask in Japanese if he's my contact.

6. 1st vocabulary entry in Japan is *ajisai*, in English, *hydrangea.*

7. Intros English class. A lady says she's a sexy receptionist. I ask again. She sticks to alibi. Her company was *Sekisui.*

8. Youth get hamburgers at *Bikkuri Donkey—Surprise Donkey*!

9. Drive 50 CC bike into drink machine—jarring experience. C.T. Studd: "Three things in successful missionary: A sense of humor, a sense of humor, and a sense of humor." Yay, I qualify!

10. An Australian, Louise, takes one-way street wrong way, police waiting. Spend hours at police station—I translate, ha ha! Apologize for minor infraction, officer yells: "Not minor!" Louise forgot license, home at 3 A.M. Hey C.T, what now? Give message at 6:30 A.M., "Be instant in season" (II Tim. 4:2).

11. 3 earthquakes 1 month. A sister crawls under pew for safety.

12. Busy! Urinate in hallway sink by accident—sooo sleepy.

13. Mystery-guest leaves fortune in gems. Roommate returns it.

14. Stop marking calendar days until return. Here 3 months.

15. Halloween NHK class, costumes—plastic bags, paper plates on chest and head=Kappa Japanese River monster. Enter water at own risk—You've been warned!

16. Bible study, lady asks me to explain circumcision.

17. Man passes me on left as I turn. Our motos get hitched.

18. Bring wedding envelope to funeral. Friend hides it in pocket.

19. Letters from girl at home, invitation to picnic from girl here.

20. P.O., I boxed gifts/coins for N.Y. teacher. I tell clerk—she says coins can't go. Re-wrap boxes. No more Mr. Chatty!

21. Fridays, Ray, I, franks, taters; watch 3 Stooges, and Combat. Re-roll'em in 3 months. Tradition, Tradition!

22. Asano san baptized. Sad to say she backslides, disappears.

23. I'm Santa at churches. Join play, *4th Wiseman*, still have book.

Please forgive my abbreviations and trivialities. Wherever we serve, His power is made perfect in weakness (II Cor. 12:9). Here's a gem even your roommate can't give away: "I am with you always, even until the end of the age" (Matt. 28:20).

Grace Lover: For who hath despised the day of small things? for they shall rejoice, and shall see the plummet in the hand of Zerubbabel with those seven; they are the eyes of the Lord, which run to and fro through the whole earth (Zech. 4:10).

179. GOHNGAIP AND SEMI

Abeno Ku, Japan, 1996.

When I was a boy, I heard of the Seven Year Locusts that would devastate farms and communities. Living in Long Island, the only farms I remember grew factories, or sod for factory lawns. Once, having discovered a locust exoskeleton, it became the most prized exhibit of my natural history collection. Years later in Japan, I found out more. Cicadas or Semis (Japanese), like the Book of Revelation, are legion and noisy. While living at Osaka Christian Girls College, I called my dad, in N. J. It started off well, but a minute into the call the semis were so loud we quit. Days later, at a pond, the semis plummeted from exhaustion into the water—it takes energy to be that annoying. Their nemesis, the Koi (Carp), were a patient and hospitable bunch, and pursued them relentlessly. I rooted for the fish!

To speak of Gohngaip, we travel to Cambodia. This land is like a bowl. In the rainy season, river flow reverses. The plain fills with water to the treetops, and creatures come out at night. Tie down your pets. The night belongs to Gohngaip! My wife detests them. Differing varieties have their own timbre, creating a chaotic chorus every evening. They are, of course, the Giant Bullfrogs of Cambodia. Whereas the Semi are a monotone oscillating sound, the Gohngaip possess a reverberating, ascending and descending scale that resembles anything between a cricket and bass drum. For me, they "...knit the raveled sleeve of care" with sleep. *Macbeth* Act 2 Scene 2. For Yuko, their cry was akin to: "Sleep no more! Macbeth does murder sleep." Ibid.

Recently my son bought a speaker, a cylinder that resembles a bomb. It has a bass beat that makes Gohngaip seem like coloraturas. It can be activated by an I-pod so he can share the blessing with many. It's enough to make one appreciate Semis. Anyone for a quiet walk in the desert? Do you need to flee to God's peace? Jesus often went to a mountain to pray.

Grace Lover: And when he had sent the multitudes away, he went up into a mountain apart to pray: and when the evening was come, he was there alone (Matt. 14:23).

Curmudgeon: What, could ye not watch with me one hour (Matt. 26:40).

180. THE BEST OF DREAMS

Phnom Penh, Cambodia, 2013.

What if God were evil? That's depressing. There is a better option, proven at the Cross, i.e., "God is Love" (I John 4:8). The Bible also says God is holy, but that's different. *Holy* is a characteristic, not an identity. It's an adjective, whereas *love* is a noun. The statement: "God is love" describes a state of being. WOW!!! Do 3 exclamation marks overdo it? What if God weren't love? What if He were, let's say, *patience*, instead? We'd have a universe with *waiting* as its foundation principle. For half of the married population, they think this is already the case, and the concept doesn't encourage the use of exclamation marks. Notwithstanding, Christ created the Universe, and sustains it:

> And he is before all things, and by him all things consist (Col. 1:17).

In addition, the future is disclosed. Those who want the good guys to win know everything comes out in the wash.

> And then shall that Wicked be revealed, whom the Lord shall consume with the spirit of his mouth, and shall destroy with the brightness of his coming (II Thess. 2:8).

What if God were evil? What kind of universe would we have? Would God keep destroying and re-creating? Would the world of an evil God be peopled? Would an evil God breath a part of Himself into someone else? Would an evil God be able to master himself? Questions make the picture darker. How about we enjoy the idea, the truth, that *God is love*?

Anselm offered the Ontological Argument for the existence of God, i.e., if we can imagine the greatest possible being, then that being must exist. Anselm suggests God is the personification of wonderful traits. That would make adjectives into nouns and my opening paragraph less than useful. Thanks, Anselm. Let's go back to dreams and love. The premise God is love is not only the best of dreams, it's reality. A table, molecularly, is mostly not there. Our idea of love, compared to His love, is full of holes. So, love, in the future, will be thicker—deeper! Isn't it great that of all the things God could be, He is love? I must say it again: "WOW " (Please add your own exclamation marks). Go ahead. Get exclamatory!!!

> Dreamless: He that loveth not knoweth not God; for God is love (I John 4:8).

181. THE THRONE AND THE DECEPTION

'Your Majesty, the assembly is on hand."

"The sun still sleeps, may not I?"

"You may, my King, but not if you want to reach Samaria before the sun sleeps thrice more.

"Never gain a counselor more persuasive than thyself, Abiezer.

"I will never have such a recourse to consider, my King."

"Well, these things are left to Heaven, but I pray your words hold the future."

As Jehoshaphat and his army depart a Jerusalem undisturbed, but for roosters, a lone individual can be seen on the road. He does not bow but waves his arms as one not well of mind.

"Is it the King? Does he go out unseen? No, God sees him, and sees his end."

"Shall I dispatch him, O King? It is the work of a moment," inquires the King's general.

"Surely not, he's said nothing untrue, though I know not his motives. Who is he?"

"Deservedly, his name is *Ben Nabal* (*Son of Fool*), my King."

"It may be the Lord humors or warns us." Turning to the intruder, Jehoshaphat speaks: "Draw near, my fellow. Have you a word for me?" At this point, the apparent churl prostrates himself within such breadth of the earth that no ant could part them.

"'You have not consulted my prophets,' says the Lord." That spoken, the Son of Fool rises, turns, and departs over a boulder strewn hillock to the dismay and disgust of most present.

At Samaria

The Court of Ahab is quite impressive; buildings, finery of décor and apparel surpass the glory of Jerusalem. The major, and all defining difference of Bethel being the Temple of the Living God is not there, and more importantly, neither is His Spirit.

"My Brother, is it not auspicious that brethren separated should finally unite in a common purpose? You are doubly welcome. You see, the Prophets have all portents of success.

The Southern King almost aligns his spirit with that of the place, but at the mention of the Prophets, remembered his early morning visitor days ago.

"Be there any prophets of the Lord (Yahweh), here? Shall we not hear them?"

"There be, but a contrary fellow," Ahab admits, summoning Micaiah, who does not disappoint as regards expectations.

"Israel will be scattered, and the people will have no master." Micaiah declares. God's Spirit then directs him to insult the Prophets of Baal with a story: "The Lord asked a question to the Heavenly Convocation: 'Who will draw Ahab into battle against Ramoth-Gilead to die there?' One spirit said: 'I will be a deceiving spirit in the mouths of his prophets.' Then the Lord said: 'Go and do it.'" The result of Micaiah's forthrightness is imprisonment. Before he is long in restraints, however, the Kings are on their way to meet the forces of Aram.

"My Brother, do don your kingly robes, but I shall dress as the others," Ahab suggests, hopeful of defying the prophecy laid against him. It will not be so, however. A *random arrow*, shot at no target, finds its mark between the sections of his armour. The armies of the two Kings retreat, and Ahab dies within the day.

This is a dramatized version of a biblical account (I Kings 22). Nabal, Abiezer, and attitudes are creations and speculations. Micaiah tells it straight; the other prophets, the majority, the yes men, get it wrong. Ahab was intent on booty, Jehoshaphat, on unity and reconciliation. He tries again later, with Joram, the son of Ahab, that time against Moab. Speaking of his death, I Kings Chapter 22 notes that he was at peace with the King of Israel, a rarity after the division of the tribes into Israel and Judah. Both outings saw him getting into trouble. The first time, he consulted Micaiah, the second time, Elisha. On both occasions, the prophet saved his neck or gave him a true perspective. Ahab thought he could alter the Lord's plan. A random arrow ended that. Friend, there is no such thing as a random arrow. See Job 1. So, what can we learn from all this? Some friends get us into trouble, others get us out. Let's be careful where we hang our hat. Also, numbers mean nothing. With God, you are the majority, so listen to the Prophets of God. Even the Son of a Fool knows that.

Grace Lover and Curmudgeon: Surely the Lord God will do nothing, but he revealeth his secret unto his servants the prophets (Amos 3:7).

182. ALWAYS

Everywhere, always.

Some things never change! Their constancy gives us a sense of security. Christmas is always on December 25th. The Nissan GTR always has circular taillights. The Ford Mustang always has six vertical taillights. The Ford Lincoln always has a hint of hub in the posterior, a reminder of the rear spare tire. We pin our trust and security on the constancy of our familiar things. In the USA, I relish a chance to sit on a porch with a Snapple (in a glass bottle), a book and, forgive me, some political commentary. What is it for you? We all have a comfort zone that is encircled with a different fence of certainty. In my early teens, I enjoyed watching the newly formed New York Mets. They had a .250 winning percentage their first year. We knew they would lose. The fun was guessing how they would throw the game away, or in which inning they would get slaughtered. The manager, Casey Stengel, when asked about the team's won-lost record, said: "Hey, we're improving; now we lose in extra-innings!" So, they were consistent with a minor variation. That was acceptable.

Like King Solomon said of our lives, "all this is chasing after the wind" (Eccles. 1:14). Our Christmas may be on December Twenty-Fifth, but we don't know the date of the first one. As for the Mustang, horizontal is the new vertical, the Lincoln is hub-less, and Snapple comes in plastic! Despair not. None of these familiarities mean more than the value we attribute to them. But that is okay, because none of these things have ultimate purpose. In fact, each of us will also disappear from the scene. We are as the grass that withers, Isaiah 40:6. Sound discouraging? The end of the verse declares that the Word of the Lord endures forever! In that Word, we learn our situation can be eternally secure by believing that Jesus is the Christ, the Son of God. We are promised His Word won't change, won't fail. As if this isn't enough, the Lord also states: "I am the Lord, I change not" (Mal. 3:6). Fords, and teams, and teas will change, even fail. We, however, can put our hope in that which will remain, not fail—in Him!

Grace Lover and Curmudgeon: Lay not up for yourselves treasures upon earth, where moth and rust doth corrupt, and where thieves break through and steal: [20] But lay up for yourselves treasures in heaven, where neither moth nor rust doth corrupt, and where thieves do not break through nor steal: [21] For where your treasure is, there will your heart be also (Matt. 6:19-21).

183. GENUFLECT: FOR CATHOLICS ONLY

Why *genuflect*? As a Catholic, I was no half-knee genuflector. I was a ful-downer. Today, I went to Father Mike for a Catholic view. He had 3 points. First, Jesus in the Eucharist is God, so we genuflect to say you are God, I'm not. Second, Father Mike refers to *Lord of the Rings*, in which Frodo, a Hobbit, volunteers to be the Ring-Bearer. Aragorn, the future King, bends the knee to him to say: "If by my life or death I can aid you in this quest, you have my sword." He committed himself to serve Frodo. When we genuflect, we present ourselves to God. Third, Father Mike compared bending the knee to a proposal of marriage, in which we declare our love to God, 3 great reasons to genuflect. Thank you, Father Mike, for an excellent devotion.

In Japan, folks bow a lot. I like forms of respect. So why this devotion today? In I Corinthians 12:31, Paul speaks of "a more excellent way." I'd like to use that idea. The Jerusalem Temple housed the presence of God, the Shekinah, until the idolatry of our Jewish friends was so offensive that He left. It seems the Roman Catholic Church tries to continue the Temple period. It considers the Eucharist, like the Shekinah in the Old Testament period, to be the presence of God. This, however, undermines a mystery of God, the Mystery of the Ages. Paul tells us in Colossians 1:27: that God has chosen to make known the mystery among the Gentiles, that is, Christ in you the hope of glory. Christ is in us, not only after partaking of the Eucharist. Again, His word instructs: If any man is in Christ, he is a new creature, old things have passed away, behold all things are become new (II Cor. 5:17).

Catholicism has pilgrimages to holy sites for indulgences, but we're the Temple of the Holy Spirit (I Cor. 3:16, 6:19). The Temple needs no holy site; we are the holy site. Chuck Smith of Calvary Chapel told this story of a brother: "Pastor, the youth are chewing gum in the church!" Chuck said: "No, the Church is chewing gum in the chapel." I like genuflecting or bowing to the Cross. Let's remember, as we are humble before Him, that He is in us? We are the Tabernacle. This is our hope of glory. Impossible? That's why it's a mystery.

184. THE MUCH MORES

Long Beach, Ca., '78.

Years ago, 7-Up had a great commercial. A deep Caribbean voice touted 7-Up as the Un-Cola. Fizzing, colorless carbonation accented the claim—it was a great comparison.

"Comparisons are odious," the adage says. Scripture agrees and disagrees. "Comparing ourselves with others is not wise" (II Cor. 10:12). But Hebrews 1-3 compare Jesus to angels, and Moses. Shirley E., at CinA, taught the *Much Mores* of Romans 5, in which Jesus is compared to Adam. Paul uses a comparative but suggests the superlative. I feel he'd love to say the *mostest* but grammar forbideth it. The Much Mores are the Un-Comparison and solution. Though Adam's Fall is bad, Christ's sacrifice is Much More better by degree than the other was bad. Let's see how much more worse I can do with a math metaphor. Here goes: Adam's sin put us at a negative five, Christ's sacrifice was a positive ten-squared! Happy? Ok, let's try it with astrophysics. Light years or magnitudes? Just kidding.

Let's compare the Fall and the Crucifixion. Adam's Fall killed us physically and passed sin to us. Christ, however, forgave our sin, and passed life eternal to us. The Much Mores throw out Ying and Yang. There's no balance. Christ holds everything together; His glory outshines evil's negatives. Let's smile as we say His magnificence, glory, and provision are Much More in abundance, effulgence, and efficacy than the evil they overturn. That felt good! I envision a candy bar entitled Much More, having nuts, caramel, bitter-chocolate, cranberry, and... I started saying *comparisons are odious* and now I'm comparing God to a chocolate bar. I've over-played the term, but it illustrates the character of God so well. No matter the circumstance, we can say: "Much more," and that's what He will do. That's who He is! So, have a much more day! Moreover, if you want the much more serious version, see Romans 5. More Much Mores are better than fewer Much Mores, more or less. Yours muchly, Chris.

Grace Lover: Much more then, being now justified by his blood, we shall be saved from wrath through him. (Ro. 5:9).

185. THE FORMICARY

Phnom Penh, Cambodia, 2014.

Hidden Darkness and Hidden Treasure are two stories evoked by today's setting. Both occurred, of all places, in a bathroom in Phnom Penh. It had white wall tiles, one in every twenty, bearing the image of a palm tree. The two memories mentioned have very different keys, ANTS and PEE! Which do you want first? Ok, ANTS in Hidden Darkness, it is. *Grout* is crucial to our tale. It holds tiles to a wall. Our tiles had pockets, excellent nests for ants that bite out of proportion to their mass. Flesh loses to mandibles on the Scale of Hardness. These apocalyptic hordes travel their grout expressways in search of play towels. Towels are for ants what theme parks are to adolescents—places to get ugly. A swath of bites in a land sporting average temperatures of 90 F. at midnight, is an invitation to irritation, like Dante's Circles 7-9. Drying yourself with such a towel is like eating a taco with Tabasco. The fire smolders a bit, but there's no mistaking it once it arrives. I once heard a conversation of these denizens of the Dark. Were they in my ear or did water magnify their transmissions?

"Excuse me, Sir Alate," the Worker communicated, fearing to touch a superior's antennae.

"How can I assist, honorable Hymenoptera?"

"I'm assigned to the West, but was separated in the Rain of 10326."

"You scarcely look 600 hours; how do you maintain vibrancy?"

"I was accidentally anointed with Royal Jelly. It altered me."

"I'll escort you. I'm dispatched to the Departure on Grout Rte. 16.

"Oh, you propagate the Formicary," the Worker communicated.

"And you reform a vein. Honor the Formicary, Anointed One."

"Honor the Formicary," the Anointed, signaled.

A blast from the shower ended their chat. No one flushes a toilet unless it's inconvenient. Despite their story, I still shake my towel!

Grace Lover: Go to the ant, thou sluggard; consider her ways, and be wise (Prov. 6:6).

186. THE OPAL'S APERTURE

This Hidden Treasure was a diamond in the rough, albeit smooth, oval, and its color like unto an opal. A hidden treasure in full view is an enigma. Our setting is the same house, with the 1 in 20 tiles graced with a palm tree. Today's memory is on the lighter side of the spectrum, the third wavelength from the top of the rainbow. Corey occasionally needed a pit stop in the wee (sorry) hours. Being 4 years old, the sensation tickled, and he'd laugh. I followed suit.

Setting isn't my artistic bent, but today, it's easy. We have a treasure of time and place, a humble place. Have you guessed? It had corrugated roofing and nail holes mid-span. As the room had a tile floor, it was ok. Rain swept ants down the drain—my apology to the Formicary. The toilet was situated beneath a nail hole. Suspense getting you? We could make an IQ test. Don't get irritable—you haven't found ants in your towel or danced with frogs. Anyway, one day, at noon, there it was. White, then blue and white, then blue and swirling. It was only a toilet seat, but rivaled a squid's color shifts. *But only* is an onus not to be ascribed to such a… a seat of wonder. I took off my shoes. No, it wasn't holy ground. I just didn't want to get the floor muddy. I recalled a word exiled for decades, i.e., *aperture*. A solitary hole of a missing nail was like a camera lens. On the toilet seat was a moving picture. Clouds in the sky, blocked from view by the roof, were moving. This is the first time I've…er, *come out of the bathroom*. It's difficult to tell family: "Mom, Dad, I, I have a Magic Toilet." Like toilet seats, people are profound. We don't recognize it until they stand under a nail hole at 1:17 P.M. Everyone you meet today is a wonder. The Lord places spiritual apertures hither and yon for us to discover Him, and our neighbors, more deeply. What treasure awaits?

Grace Lover: So God created man in his own image, in the image of God created he him; male and female created he them (Gen. 1:27).

Curmudgeon: And it repented the Lord that he had made man on the earth, and it grieved him at his heart.

187. UZBEKISTAN

Ueno Station, Tokyo, 2017.

"Could you tell me about Islam?" I asked. He was Indonesian. I hoped to hear his story and address any misconceptions he had regarding Christianity.

"Where does Jesus say: 'I am God,'" he asked me. I was ready. I knew Imam Dedat trained Muslims to ask this. Jesus never used those exact words but showed from prophecy, the seven *I am* statements in John, and by claiming the same attributes as the Father, to be Messiah. I gave my fellow a Bible with my e-mail address. On another day, three Uzbekistanis sat on a bench. I asked if they were Shia, produced a family picture, and enjoyed a chat like the cousins we are. On google maps, one showed me his home in Central Asia.

"Do you have a copy of the *Enjils* (Gospels)?" I asked.

"No," he said. I gave him a Bible, and he was reading as I left.

Josh Hemingway and I, visited the Tokorozawa Mosque to share a kind word. The Imam, Mr. Khan, was suspicious, so we didn't overstay our welcome. Another day, however, held an opportunity. Yuko and I, on a work-date at Starbucks, met Marcos and Keiko. He studies Japanese; I write and enjoy yuuzu tea. From Basra, Iraq, he's Muslim but doesn't attend a mosque. Saddam Hussein executed his father, an Iraqi official. We've shared our faiths, but there remain layers of worldview for us to work through. President Reagan said: "Democrats aren't stupid, they just know so much that isn't true!" We can say this for most of us. We invited them to Thanksgiving dinner, but they had plans. Maybe next year.

Nabeel Qureshi, of Pakistan, wrote *Seeking Allah, Finding Jesus*. His mother had a suitcase of gifts for Americans who invited her to dinner. Years later, she went home, her suitcase full. Has your home been graced by foreigners? They may or may not have a physical gift for you, but you will part with more than you started.

Grace Lover and Curmudgeon: But the stranger that dwelleth with you shall be unto you as one born among you, and thou shalt love him as thyself; for ye were strangers in the land of Egypt: I am the LORD your God (Lev. 19:34).

188. CEBU SIGHTING

Kampong Cham, 2004.

Cambodia's rainy season has unanticipated results. Sunday mornings I traveled to the village of *Suong* (Garden), close to Vietnam, to a home-church. I knew what month it was by how close to the road the cattle came to forage. As water spread over the plain, they had to search for higher ground. Rain was not the only seasonal change we had. Kilometers away, we had classes in a village. After the children began singing *Jesus Loves Me This I Know*, the village leader (*Mei Poum*) closed the door.

Though they are not cited specifically, the scriptures present some examples of seasons. "My Spirit will not always strive with Man" (Gen. 6:3). An example of a more limited scope is: "The iniquity of the Amorites is not yet full" (Gen. 15:14-16). God would not give the Promised Land to the Jews until the Amorites' sin merited judgment. A prolonged season of millennia is in Acts 17:30: "the time of this ignorance God winked at, but now commands all men, everywhere, to repent." Of the Jews, Jesus said that they could tell the face of the sky but not discern the time (Luke 12:56). Our Lord uses *time* as both an event and a period: "you knew not the time of your visitation" (Luke 19:44). After rejecting the Messiah, Jerusalem would be destroyed. We're almost finished, which is timely. For the short term, or present moment, we hear the phrase, "In that day..." and also "Today..." They warn about consequences. It behooves us to do the right thing and be aware of the times in which we live. Have you ever met an Amorite?

We could describe Ephesians 1:9-10 as your last opponent going down in three pitches, or waiting on standby to discover you not only have a seat but have received an upgrade to first class! [9] Having made known unto us the mystery of his will, according to his good pleasure which he hath purposed in himself: [10] That in the dispensation of the fulness of times he might gather together in one all things in Christ, both which are in heaven and which are on earth; even in him.

Anything you've been putting off? A time of reflection? A rest? Repentance? Don't waste time. Maybe you have today, or a season, or maybe this night thy life will be required of thee (Luke 12:20). Have a nice time! Better yet, have a glorious *fulness of time*!!!

Yuko baptizing folks, 2003. The next year, we moved; the problem—crocodiles!

189. THE RECYCLE CONNECTION

Phnom Penh, 2008.

People with recycle carts pass your home several times a day here. Many rent the cart. Some blow a duck whistle to let you know they're coming. I've seen five-year-old boys, and a leg amputee, pushing carts. I understand the motive behind child labor laws, but if you stop these kids from recycling, you take away their dinner, or their half dinner.

I have a recycling story from West Babylon in the late 50s. I had a Brontosaurus, sixty cents, and Hershey's chocolates in my pocket. It was a Saturday, and my friend and I went down to Rte. 109 and 18th Street, the Bowen Gang territory, in search of soda bottles. My family, however, had plans. It was a cold reception when the car search ended. I wasn't forthright about my breakfast menu, and my parents were suspicious. I felt guilty—besides having an upset stomach.

A boy who sniffs glue is easy to spot. He's a bit dazed and carries a bag of glue. When you are hungry, a little glue goes a long way. My heart went out to them. I remember my conversation with two of them on different occasions. I asked if they had heard about Jesus. One of them gave the Lord a thumbs-up. The Lord's name brought smiles and *aram laor* (lovely feeling); a glue fog ended further discussion. Ass the phone operator said: "Talk is cheap." The boys liked Jesus, but not enough to change. In Luke 13, Jesus talks about people who suffered ignominious deaths. He asks: "Were those people worse sinners than others in Jerusalem?" He says they will perish if they don't repent. Forgiveness is provided. We're foolish to smile, give a thumbs up, and not act upon it. We need a Recycle Connection. Worldly recycling turns old garbage into future garbage. Godly recycling turns a fallen creature into a new creation (II Cor. 5:17). Jesus came to make us new, not to condemn (John 3:17). The Lord may not use a duck whistle, but He does call. The question is, are we glued to inaction?

Grace Lover and Curmudgeon: For the Son of man is come to seek and to save that which was lost (Luke 19:10).

The Cambodian team and friends, Prek Thei, the mother church, 2015.

190. GOAT'S BLOOD

Suong (Garden), Cambodia, 2003.

If we're talking about goat's blood, we should start with the Death Angel. In Exodus, the Death Angel passed over homes that had their lintels and doorposts sprinkled with lamb's blood. The Israelites availed themselves of the blood; the Egyptians didn't. The firstborn of Egypt died. It sounds harsh, but the Egyptians killed the Hebrew baby boys.

One day at Suong, I noticed plastic bottles in the bushes of homes. They were filled with red liquid. It was artificial goat's blood to drive away evil spirits. I thought it interesting that evil spirits, in the villagers' theology, were stupid, unable to discern between goat's blood and red dye #40. I'd not have the audacity to fool a demon. The bottles were a perfect biblical analogy of the blood on the lintel.

Peace Child is also an example. Don Richardson went to Irian Jaya in the '60s. He learned their language, but frustrated with his Sawi hosts resistance to the Gospel, he decided to leave. The Sawi's hero was Judas. For them, treachery was virtuous. While Don prepared to leave, he heard what sounded like a war party, and prepared himself to depart this life. Fortunately, villagers from across the water came to assemble with his clans. A man from a neighboring village presented his son to the chief of Don's hosts. The infant would receive the title Peace Child, as the offering insured peace between the tribes. Don, seeing a biblical analogy, shared that Jesus is the Father's Peace Child. The Sawi then saw Judas as a wicked man, one who broke peace by betraying the Peace Child of God.

Jesus is the best Biblical analogy, being the Word made flesh. What He does, and who He is, relates in some way or ways to every culture—even to you. Draw your own analogy.

Grace Lover and Curmudgeon: For the Lord will pass through to smite the Egyptians; and when he seeth the blood upon the lintel, and on the two side posts, the Lord will pass over the door, and will not suffer the destroyer to come in unto your houses to smite you (Ex. 12:23).

191. ACTS 29

Waikiki, Hi., 1974

The sidewalks at Kalakaua Boulevard were meters wide. Tourists came from everywhere. I met the Reichlings, neighbors from Long Island, there. I also met hookers, G.I.s, Japanese—all kinds of folks. I bought a *Japanese-English Gospel Handbook* for evangelism and memorized Acts 4:12 in Japanese, or something close: "Neither is there salvation in any other: for there is none other name under heaven given among men, whereby we must be saved."

The night of my debut as evangelist to the Japanese, I recited it haltingly to some men exiting a bar. One fellow didn't quite catch it the first time, so I repeated it. He became very animated, threw his arms up in the air several times, with each repetition shouting: "*Bukkyou!*" (Buddhism). When I wasn't engaged in Oriental Studies, several of us would hand out our publication, Acts 29. It had some Bible lessons, and testimonies of folks in our fellowship. The title comes from the Book of Acts, which has twenty-eight chapters, the idea being each generation carries on the mission. Over the centuries, the Church has not gotten that point sharpened. Instead of honing a lance to go on the offense, it has, at times, whittled fenceposts to improve defense.

What were the Elders of Antioch, Syria, thinking? Was it a Brave New World, or a frightening one? Simeon (called *the Black Man*), Lucius (from Cyrene), and Manaen (the foster-brother of King Herod), sent Barnabas and Paul to evangelize the world. In the years to come, however, many, including Barnabas' nephew, Mark, would leave the work due to the hardships. Some would leave the Faith entirely, but the faithful left a legacy. Paul and Barnabas took the Gospel to Seleucia and beyond. They didn't know the future, but had confidence in God.

Now it's our turn—Chapter 29. Our actions, like the stylus of old, write future history. You've heard of ghost writers; we have the Holy Ghost writer! What will you compose together? What is your part in the chapter? How will you get started? What will you do? When?

Grace Lover: As they ministered to the Lord, and fasted, the Holy Ghost said, Separate me Barnabas and Saul for the work whereunto I have called them. [3] And when they had fasted and prayed, and laid their hands on them, they sent them away. (Acts 13:2-3).

192. MENNONITE MISSIVE

Secret messages grab our imagination! Remember Sidney Carlton, the barrister's assistant in Dicken's *Tale of Two Cities*? During a trial, he secretly passes a memo to Stryker, his bombastic boss, played by Sir Reginald Owen. Jowls flailing, the note is read revealing the Judge to be of the highest order of nincompoops! Some secret messages need careful handling. This is more evident in the story of Bellerophon, who delivers a letter containing his own execution order. And then there is the probable favorite, the message in a bottle. I found one in Hawaii that had a note from an Australian. Some secret messages are so secret they reside in our imagination and never cross the threshold from fiction. With so much water having passed since the bottle arrived, I can't tell if said bottle ever met a glassblower, an ocean, or an Australian. I think it did.

Have you ever met a Mennonite? I make them sound like some rare breed, but they keep the Faith similar to the Early Church. I find their approach compelling, objective, and frightening. This latter add on is only because I'm not brave enough to be a pacifist. I found the Mennonites I've met to be conservative Dutch or liberal hippies, a very interesting recipe for a faith community.

Our story today happens as a result of receiving an invitation to stay at a Mennonite church during furlough, while visiting my brother. I sat in the study on a cozy couch and popped open a Bible. Tucked away between its pages, waiting for me, was a slip of paper. It read: Luke 19:29-32. In that passage, Jesus tells two disciples to unloose a colt in a neighboring village, and if anyone asks why they do so, tell them it is for the Lord. It concludes:

> 32 And they that were sent went their way, and found even as he had said unto them.

Institutions and individuals may dissemble, but the Lord's promises come to be, even as He said. Let's not keep them a secret!

Bereans: Isa. 40:8, Mal. 3:6, II Cor. 1:20.

193. JASON

Ganjingo (a Chinese ship), 1993.

Hercules had his Labors, Jason had Charybdis, and I had the Commonwealthers, full of life, sarcasm, above average acumen, and ego. One thing was lacking, and that was everything. We had a two-day journey to Shanghai from Shimonoseki, Japan. We had rough seas and introductions on the first day. There was chatter about university testing and hopes for the future. Jason, a Brit, seemed to hold center stage. I met Shi san again; he'd been on a voyage with me a year earlier. During the day, I mingled with Europeans and Asians. We had a Frenchman and a Spaniard in our room. On deck, I talked with Guan and Mabin about the Lord, 8/4, and Ookawa san the next day, 8/5. Mabin took a tract. Also, among us were Ari and Shamri, Iranians who studied in China. Mr. Shu, a Han Chinese from Mongolia, had a Christian mother and sister. Oscar hailed from Holland, Chelsea from Australia, and Laura from Denmark. Mr. Yuan had a sister in Los Angeles. Mariam was a Moslem acupuncturist going to Saudi Arabia for the Hajj. Brian and Rachel, and Manuel had questions about faith. We had a colorful community. What followed was the great blessing and this bloated tale's theme. Passing through some doors, Jason, the life of the party, let the Commonwealthers slip in first, to catch a moment with me. He said:

"Chris, I'm a backslidden Christian. You are a credit to evangelicals." He patted me on the back and passed through the door. The hollow gaiety paused while the windows of the soul opened, and brothers communed. I saw the real Jason, or the Jason who could be. I saw him without the affectations. I saw him in the Spirit. I read *Jason and the Argonauts* in Latin. It was great, but Jason and the Commonwealthers were full of life. Pray they know the giver of life (Ps. 36:9).

Grace Lover: Rejoice, O young man, in thy youth; and let thy heart cheer thee in the days of thy youth, and walk in the ways of thine heart, and in the sight of thine eyes: but know thou, that for all these things God will bring thee into judgment (Eccles. 11:9).

> Let no man despise thy youth; but be thou an example of the believers, in word, in conversation, in charity, in spirit, in faith, in purity (I Tim. 4:12).

Curmudgeon: In the multitude of words there wanteth not sin: but he that refraineth his lips is wise (Prov. 10:19).

194. OBIDIENCE

In one of the top three quotes of the 20th Century, Obi Wan Kenobi faces his apprentice, Luke Skywalker, to say: "The Force be with you." The world was a flutter with *Star Wars* in the late '70s. At the time Luke was shooting *Womp Rats from his Land Speeder on Tatooine,* I was commissioned to a vehicle of less sophistication but superior aesthetics, a light turquoise, stretch limo! It guzzled gas and was bad on turns, but nobody could see it without smiling. Every Sunday, in 1977, I drove to Sunbury, Pa., to pick up Teen Challenge folks for the Lewisburg AOG church-plant. It was a difficult time for the Rebellion (Star Wars), but a wondrous time for the Kingdom. Ladies were wearing rolled kerchiefs, the Steelers won four Super Bowls, and I was thinking mission. The group changed as folks graduated or quit. They came from the inner-cities of N.Y. and Pa. I remember one Puerto Rican family. God was working in their lives. One week the husband sang: *Peace Be Still.* I teared up. Sadly, they later left the program. And then there was Obi.

Paul Peck was the pastor and a carpenter. The Pecks were so hospitable. I spent Sundays at their home watching the Steelers trounce other people's hopes. I didn't know a scrimmage from a tourniquet, but enjoyed being with them. Paul always asked if there were any song requests. Obi always requested *Trust and Obey*. He was a heroin addict who got saved at sixty. He had a powerful testimony. Obi has crossed the Great Divide, and is in the Cloud of Witnesses (Heb. 12:1). He did better than submit to an impersonal *Force*; he was filled with the Spirit of the Living God. What fills us?

P.S. Years later, at Heart and Hand Thrift in W.V, I told this story. The cashier asked, "Was it turquoise?" Her church had bought it!

Grace Lover: But God be thanked, that ye were the servants of sin, but ye have obeyed from the heart that form of doctrine which was delivered you (Ro. 6:17).

195. 43 KAPILI ST.

"Klang, thud, klang, thud. Dumph, phap, dumph, phap." It was August, '74, in Waikiki. It was morning. I was just getting off work. It was hot and noisy. Giant cranes did intrusive surgery on the Earth's crust, acupuncture with pylons for high tower resorts. It was the same the day before, and the day before. Ministry in Hawaii is tough, but somebody has to do it! I did, 1972-75, on two islands, Oahu and Hawaii. On Oahu, I lived upstairs in a two-story house. Our apartment was an afterthought. We had no insulation. On each side of us, high-rises were being constructed, which meant POUNDING. We glued cardboard egg casings to the wall for quiet, but they became cockroach tenements. Our neighbor, Toby, always had a beer. His friend, Ringo, was Portuguese and proud of it. He loved to remind us he "wasn't afraid of nobody." Toby was stocky and had been in seminary. They both loved to ridicule faith in between criticizing the government, or some athlete who was a bum. We tried to be a good witness for the Lord. We did this for a year, then tried something new. I'd not been to seminary, but unknowingly experimented with a Mission buzz word—*incarnation.* It proposes that, like Christ, we enter our host culture. Though well intentioned, we didn't follow the true spirit of the term. One day, I went down to Toby's porch with a beer. Toby rejoiced. It seemed his lifestyle was justified. This was not the type of justification to which I'd hoped to introduce him. Thereafter, I was transferred and heard no more of my neighbors. Some chapters in our life have a grand conclusion, others… When in the States, I go to Jake's Bar. I don't try to enhance the results; I leave those to God. I let the others imbibe spirits; I stick to being filled with the Spirit, iced tea, and Mama Brown's Baked Beans!

Grace Lover: And unto the Jews I became as a Jew, that I might gain the Jews; to them that are under the law, as under the law, that I might gain them that are under the law; [21] To them that are without law, as without law, (being not without law to God, but under the law to Christ,) that I might gain them that are without law. [22] To the weak became I as weak, that I might gain the weak: I am made all things to all men, that I might by all means save some (I Cor. 9:20-22).

196. BUS RIDE TO HELL

Roberts Wesleyan College, '86.

"Oh bother," is a phrase popularized by what personality? Yes, Pooh. Ok, let's try another: "Good grief!" Did you answer Charlie Brown? I see these characters, respectively, as the Everyman archetype of twentieth century British and American literature. Years ago, I came across *The Pooh Perplex.* The title was the thing to evoke, "Aren't you clever," from Grandma. I stand elbow to shin with the citizenry of The Hundred Acre Wood. My Pooh Books, with the rough-cut pages, were my solace as a boy, but the *Perplex* was alarming. Between its *Perplex*-ing covers, Pooh was dissected, delineated, and deconstructed by various philosophical approaches, e.g., Marxist, Feminist, and Freudian. I never realized searching for the North Pole was a trip to exploit the foreign masses, an escape from domestic responsibilities, or an attempt to bolster a sagging ego. The yellow book alters my imagination still. Pooh was no longer Pooh. He was a consortium, a conundrum, a complexity, and I don't know what. Pooh, who are you?

You're wondering about the bus, aren't you? Well, in C.S. Lewis' book, *The Great Divorce*, there is a chance to receive a *get out of Hell free* card. Departing Hell, a dozen folks take a Heaven-bound bus trip. One, mostly unsuccessful individual, encouraged everyone to stay. Only one, a hen-pecked husband, chooses Heaven. One character was a theologian. How could a theologian go to Hell? He loved to talk about theories, concepts, and truth; he just didn't love truth. So, what bus are you on? What do you love? Whom do you love? These three questions will determine where you end up. It's good to know where one is going, don't you agree? Tickets, please! For ticket stipulations, see: John 20:30,31.

Grace Lover: And they took him, and brought him unto Areopagus, saying, May we know what this new doctrine, whereof thou speakest, is? [20] For thou bringest certain strange things to our ears: we would know therefore what these things mean. [21] (For all the Athenians and strangers which were there spent their time in nothing else, but either to tell, or to hear some new thing) Acts 17:19-21.

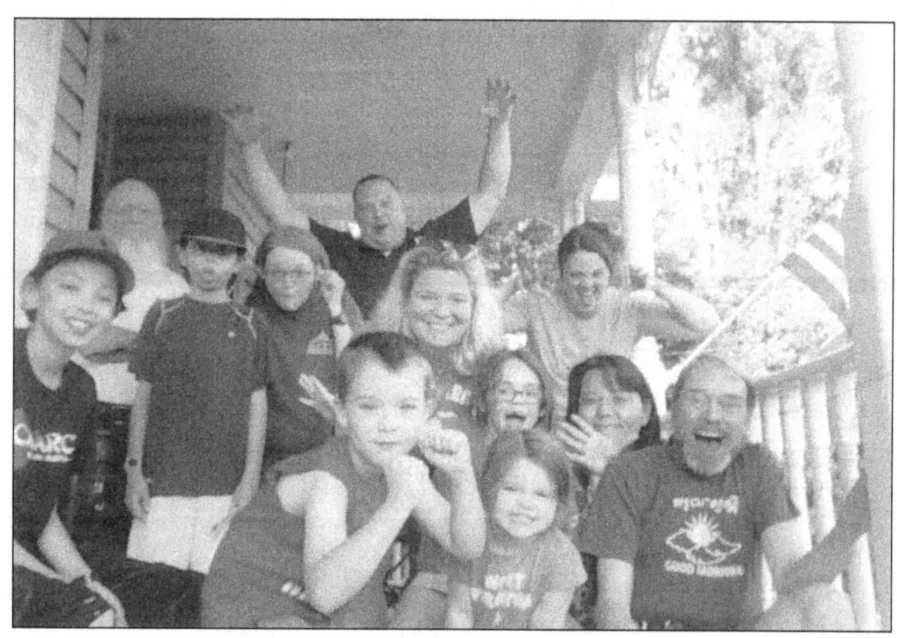

The Wilkins Clan. The joie de vivre continues!

197. THOSE WILKINS BOYS

Queens, N.Y., late 1920s.

A photograph has Grandma standing under Christopher's Willow Tree. The nomenclature is rooted in my love for the tree. Grandpa Wilkins planted it. He put fish heads in the hole. He said the Native Americans did that. I believed him, figuring he'd heard it first-hand. On the back of the picture, not to lessen Grandma's magnificence, was special. She'd written: "Christopher is a fun-loving, energetic, intelligent, clever… rascal!" I credit my genes. Dad was the youngest of four brothers, Lester, George, Harry and Robert Francis. Lester, died in the Powell St. Hotel, in San Francisco, my residence for months. Uncle George was tall and quiet. He liked pinochle, a game of knuckle torture. He married Aunt Betty, who had polio. I think he met her at a hospital, because Uncle Harry also had polio. Harry had a newspaper stand under a staircase of the Elevated Train in Brooklyn. He ran book there. No, it wasn't a lending library, it was gambling. He came to my house once; I was ten. He was fun. He made a home movie. One stunt was eating fertilizer. I cried buckets when he left.

As the car era got on the road, people needed licenses. Police stations received the task. In Forest Hills, Queens, N.Y., it was atop a hill. People parked there. Cars in those days had handbrakes. My Dad, and siblings would jump in the lead car, loosen the handbrake, and ride down the hill. Those were the days! Another thing those Wilkins Boys did was open the window of their cousin's bathroom—not a major scandal, but they followed this with filling the bathtub and pouring in magic powder—in Winter! An hour later, after fleeing the scene, *Voila*, JELL-O! Keep your young ones at home, Friends. Beware the Phantom Jelloists!

Later, Dad became a bank V.P., Kiwanis Club member, Homewood Farms Civic Association President, and leader of the Whiting Retirement Community. He helped neighbors, and was a faithful Mass-goer. He was an of example of devotion and love. It' just that if Dad was around, you'd better lock up your car and Jell-O.

Grace Lover: Be ye followers of me, even as I also am of Christ (I Cor. 11:1).

Curmudgeon: A merry heart doeth good like a medicine: but a broken spirit drieth the bones.

198. LEWISBURG PENITENTIARY

"You want to join the softball league?" Dean asked.

"I'm not burdened with much talent," I said.

Baker's Body Shop was our sponsor, and my uniform size, "P"—Puny. I was now a high-arc pitcher. Dean was a great player-manager. Before the game, we prayed. It seemed unfair. I said nothing because I knelt on the mound to pray. The Ump's "Play ball," got us going. My first pitch sailed upward, ending squarely in the catcher's mitt, its arc a thing of beauty, its rotation, spindeferous. The Ump called it: "Ball one!" I shook my head and threw a duplicate wonder; it received the same verdict: "Ball two!!" I almost forgot we'd prayed. I made a "T" with my hands. The Ump said my arc was too high. Though I say my gift is presumption, no one has ever thought I aimed too high in life. Spring training just went out the bullpen, or window. I gave my best; the team did the rest and I went 9-6 for the season. It was thrills and challenges for this 128-pounder. I stopped kneeling to pray—didn't want to be too presumptuous and resorted to doffing my cap to pray. Once I caught a hot liner, only because I couldn't get out of the way. As there'd been two outs, I tossed the ball in the air, Pete Rose, *in your face,* style. I considered smashing it into the ground, but feared the Ump would say I hadn't had possession. Another day I dislocated my ankle, but the fun didn't end there. I won a doubleheader at the Lewisburg Penitentiary. Eating garbage plates in Cole's Hardware basement, with Phil, #7, and Dean, #9, was great for a talker like me and eaters like them. They loved those numbers. We'd chat about Mantle and Maris. I was #13. I threw the high arc, so they dubbed me: NOAH. It made a great chant: "Hummany, hummany, Noah!" After my dislocation, it was GIMP! What great memories. *Winning Pitcher, Chris Wilkins*, such an oxymoron. We came in second place. Not bad for clerks, farmers, and a wimp. Mick, Maris, and Noah! '77, what a season!

How's your game? Slumping? The Holy Spirit, the *Paraclete* (Gr.), is - *one who stands with you* (Coach). He'll get you in the swing.

Grace Lover: Nay, much more those members of the body, which seem to be more feeble, are necessary (I Cor. 12:22).

199. NASTY NESTLE

W. Babylon, N.Y., 1957.

In the '80s some big companies took it on the chin from activist movements. They criticized Nestle for selling baby formula in Africa. Mothers diluted formula to stretch it a few days, but babies died of malnourishment. Proctor and Gamble was accused of having a demonic logo. Coors Beer was under fire for discrimination. I don't know if these cases went to court, but there was chatter in public circles about real or supposed abuses. Accusations can be accurate, misdirected, or malicious. I also had a beef with Nestle, but not about formula, it was about chocolate. It was just too good for a seven-year-old to resist. Joey Dunkley agreed to buy a bar of Crunch from my class fund-raiser at Our Lady of Perpetual Help. I received his money, then the bar, then the corner of the bar found its way into my mouth. I think he over-reacted. I offered a few cents for what was missing, not a bad deal. The entire bar cost ten cents, but he wanted to milk the situation for a refund. He felt betrayed. He was; I'd hurt him.

In *A Man for All Seasons*, Sir Thomas More, a Roman Catholic, is accused of treason by an ambitious lord who is to receive a demesne in Scotland. When More is accused, he says: "What doth it profit a man if he gain the whole world and lose his soul (Matthew 16:26), but for Scotland?" The lord lost his integrity for wealth and prestige. It was a bad deal, but mine was a cut from the same cloth. I lost my integrity, and a friend's trust over a nibble of chocolate. Are you nibbling on someone else's chocolate? Don't throw away treasure for a truffle, er, trifle.

Grace Lover: A good name is rather to be chosen than great riches, and loving favour rather than silver and gold (Prov. 22:1).

Curmudgeon: Thou shalt not steal. [17] Thou shalt not covet thy neighbour's house, thou shalt not covet thy neighbour's wife, nor his manservant, nor his maidservant, nor his ox, nor his ass, nor any thing that is thy neighbour's (Ex. 20:15,17).

200. DR. CARL PAGAN MEETS GOD:

The Father knows the where and when (Matt. 24:36). This devotion begins with apologies. It's unfair to assign to individuals that which they didn't say. This tale is inspired by a professor, whose name resembles that given. I mean him no ill; I use him only as a foil for the Western ethos. I know his son loved him. Last, I offer my apology to the Divine for speculating on what I know in part, and most likely misrepresent. That established, let's go to the Throne on the Last Day. Professor Pagan approaches the bench. His title remains, albeit on That Day, no title will survive the heat of the moment. I don't mean to make light of dignities, but Dignity Personified will exude a light to which no human beacon can hold a candle.

There's a variety of angelic beings present with the Redeemed. The former is evident because of their magnificent forms, the latter by garments washed in the Blood of the Lamb. These surround four-and-twenty Elders, recognized by crowns they cast before the Throne. Then, there are Four Living Beings surrounding the Throne, recognizable by their cries: "Holy, Holy, Holy, is the Lord." On the Throne is The Father and the Son, the latter being the Son of God and Son of Man. The glory of God pours out from the Throne. It's wondrous or horrendous, depending on the beholder.

Enter the Subject: He kneels and declares: "Jesus Christ is Lord" (Philippians 2:10). This is not a declaration of fealty or love, but akin to crying: "Oh my God!" when losing control of an Aston Martin at 100 mph. He continues: "I'm Dr. Carl Pagan, a great mind of the 20th Century."

"I am aware of you, Professor, though you are not known by us," the Lord responds, mixing singular and plural pronouns regarding Himself. The Professor either did not notice or care to discuss any of the enigmas expressed.

"You are about to judge me. I'd prefer a geological formation with the mass of the Rockies to bury me (Rev. 6:16), better yet, to be swallowed by a black hole, than live in your awful light. But I protest. You talk about an unjust weight (Prov. 11:1); what do you call your Divine scenario? You keep us in the dark, hide yourself, then roll back the curtain to tell us we got it wrong. (Rev. 6:14). We made progress. In time, we could have the right conclusions."

"You had my Word. All you needed was there."

"It was not conclusive. Even your own people disagreed."

"How is it that some got it right, and some didn't?"

"Deception!" Dr. Pagan declared.

"Could you be more specific?"

"You talk about 'looking through a glass darkly (I Cor. 13:12), You should know what I mean," the Professor remanded. "Listen, given the time, we could have devised the experiments to discover you (Acts 17:27). We could have even created life. You had thirteen billion years."

"Did I? With that amount of time, you could create life?"

"Being shrouded in light and glory doesn't mean you are right or real (Job 37:22). I choose Naturalism. Time equals possibility."

"On what do you base your assumptions? Math? Philosophy?"

"Probability," the Professor said confidently, at least by appearances.

"Well, I can be accommodating, Professor. How much time would you like?" God inquired.

"The Earth's age is 10^9 years. 10^{10} should do it."

"Dr. Thomas Kindell said you wouldn't have enough time in thirteen billion, or a trillion years, to make a simple protein, that needing10^{180}years, and if you did succeed, you'd only have a protein in isolation... well, you know this already, right? I will give you 10^{180}," the Lord decreed.

"And what happens when I win?"

"If you win, Professor, that is, if you prove evolution, it would mean this day never happened."

"You're on God, or whatever..." the Professor began. His gesticulation suggested his Interviewer's position was absurd in the neighborhood of 10^{180}. His action stopped midway. That sort of thing would never again be tolerated except in a place prepared for it.

"Michael, please transport the Professor to the Majesty in Motion Star of the sixth dimension." The Professor knelt again, and was whisked away. Though the time would only be 10^{180} it would seem an eternity. Without the presence of God, it would be Hell.

Curmudgeon: The fool hath said in his heart, There is no God. Corrupt are they, and have done abominable iniquity: there is none that doeth good (Ps. 53:1).

201. GARY C.

W. Babylon, N.Y., 1955-77.

Elf shoes got the most attention at the Megumi Chalet in Karuizawa. Our garb was part of a skit. I with Elf shoes and a polka-dotted bowtie, Joel Cowin with finery I provided. Leaning over, he remarked: "You get me into the strangest situations." We've all had acquaintances that have helped, cajoled, or black-mailed us into doing the unusual. Gary C. was that guy for me. He got us a lawn care business, hired and fired at a catering firm, time to fix HIS boat, to have dates in said vessel, and go to a dance. He always had a girlfriend, I never did. He was 145-lbs. of muscle, I was 111-lbs. of bones. The Storyboard: Gary and Chris in hallway. Gary spots girl for whom Chris pines. Gary says: "He likes you!" Chris, glowing red, pops the question: "Would you like to go to the dance?" She responds in the affirmative. Kudos to Gary, a *Fait accompli*. Chris envisions Gary's homicide and beatification with rpm's rivaling a muscle car.

Paul describes the gifts in the Church (I Cor. 12). The passage extols uniqueness. Polonius advises Hamlet: "To thine own self be true," *Hamlet* Act 1 Scene 3. It's not a bad idea; a better one is: I am what I am by the grace of God (I Cor. 15:10). Paul wasn't accommodating a character flaw. He proposed contentment in Christ. Some folks are movers and shakers, others are soothers and smoothers. Let's not beat ourselves for not being what the Lord didn't design.

Dance Scene: I wear dorky jacket. Meet dream girl. Ask her to dance. Oops—a slow dance. Two leave room to talk. Hallway lined with coats, no chairs. Return to gym, hand in sweaty hand. Friends surround her to prevent further embarrassment. End first and last school dance. Final Hallway Scene: Days later. Friends mock protagonist. Girl: "Leave him alone." Chris smiles, sheepishly. Four-minute bell. Enter classes. Life continues. New maiden of surpassing winsomeness casts former fiascos into sea of forgetfulness. To be continued.

Grace Lover: For do I now persuade men, or God? or do I seek to please men? for if I yet pleased men, I should not be the servant of Christ (Gal. 1:10).

202. TRASH

A Moving Works Ministry video shows a Japanese woman who, feeling worthless, went to a train station to commit suicide. Arriving, she decided to give life one last chance. At a church, the counsel of the pastor's wife was: "Say aloud: *God loves me*, and *I am a valuable person*." The woman did so, burst into tears, and found transformation in Christ.

God enjoys recycling; it's His chief occupation. *Toy Story IV*, illustrates this so well. Sheriff Woody watches over Molly's toys. He feels it's his duty to insure Molly's happiness. She's afraid to go to school, so Woody hides in her bookbag to monitor the class. On her first day, she makes a toy of recyclables. She has a broken spork, which she fits with feet of wooden ice cream spoons, unwieldy arms of pipe cleaners, and eyes of different sizes. This conglomeration of junk, whom she names Forky, believes he is trash. A poor self-image is unhealthy, but Forky thinks he should remain trash. At every chance, he returns to the-garbage. Woody spends days rescuing him. At first, he wants to save Forky to please Molly. Gradually, the two become friends as Woody shares his life's lessons. It's a story of destructive tendencies, loyalty, and reclamation. Be careful whom you call trash. And yourself? God spared no expense to rescue you. Come out of the garbage. Join the family. Nobody is trash! You are of inestimable value—like Forky!

Grace Lover: O lord, thou hast searched me, and known me. [2] Thou knowest my downsitting and mine uprising, thou understandest my thought afar off. [3] Thou compassest my path and my lying down, and art acquainted with all my ways. [5] Thou hast beset me behind and before, and laid thine hand upon me. [14] I will praise thee; for I am fearfully and wonderfully made: marvellous are thy works; and that my soul knoweth right well (Ps. 139:1-3,5,14).

> Therefore if any man be in Christ, he is a new creature: old things are passed away; behold, all things are become new (II Cor. 5:17).

> In whom we have redemption through his blood, even the forgiveness of sins (Col. 1:14).

Sully at Shimizu Station with a bevy of Marios and Luigis.

203. HALLOWEEN II

Shibuya, Japan, 2016.

Banshees, Goblins, and Ppffssigz were everywhere. This under thirty crowd moved by inches. The website read: "Join us for Halloween witness!" We had prayer and evangelism teams and a band. I preached at a bus stop, without a mike, and was soon hoarse.

"Do you have a BBBible?" I asked of the Werewolf heading straight for me!

"No," he said. His name was Ryuu, a Chinese exchange student. He took a Bible, gave his heart to Jesus, slept at the church with us, and got baptized weeks later. The next Halloween; he joined the prayer team. I like Halloween more now than I did as a kid. Once, a policeman, trying to keep order, told me to leave. An inebriated fellow had decided to be my accompaniment, so leaving was ok. I'd played for a couple of hours, so words were getting twisted and chords twangy. Halloween, it's a chance to offer an encouraging word to youth when they're incognito. Let's go invite those Banshees and Goblins to the Lord's Feast! Oh yes, and don't forget the Ppffssigz!

Grace Lover: Then said he unto him, A certain man made a great supper, and bade many: [17] And sent his servant at supper time to say to them that were bidden, Come; for all things are now ready. [18] And they all with one consent began to make excuse. The first said unto him, I have bought a piece of ground, and I must needs go and see it: I pray thee have me excused. [20] And another said, I have married a wife, and therefore I cannot come. [21] So that servant came, and shewed his lord these things. Then the master of the house being angry said to his servant, Go out quickly into the streets and lanes of the city, and bring in hither the poor, and the maimed, and the halt, and the blind. [22] And the servant said, Lord, it is done as thou hast commanded, and yet there is room. [23] And the lord said unto the servant, Go out into the highways and hedges, and compel them to come in, that my house may be filled (Luke 14:16-18,20-23).

https://www.youtube.com/shorts/kfWISA9gPBw

204. AGENON: CREATURE OF THE DARK

Anderson's Cottage, Lighthouse Camp, 2021, 3 A.M.

I slid the door open. With eyes adjusted, I reached the kitchen, then the den. The skylight's muted rays revealed a form on the couch. Pace unchanged, I moved on. The flooring squealed. I grabbed my quarry—a pen. Ok, that was a letdown, but the inspiration for this intro was seeing a strange shape hours before dawn. I realized it was harmless, a thing of tissue boxes, towels, and air. My need for a pen was to capture the event before my short-term memory came up a loser. What I thought I saw was not there. Had a light been on, we'd have nothing to talk about. In the darkness, however, I believed what was not true, "a tale told by an idiot," as Macbeth would say (Act V, Scene V).

Fear, fantasy, or perception are ways we can describe Agenon, the name by which I addressed my numinous visitor. It wasn't a horrific experience; I was too tired to be terrified. Frazzles take energy. But sometimes, instead of ignoring Agenon, we seek him. We prefer Darkness to Light. If you like Darkness, this tale will avail you naught. For those tired of Agenon, what should we do? You could remove the tissue boxes and towels, but then you couldn't sneeze or take a shower. That would make YOU a monster. For low-level Agenons, a 60-watt bulb will do. A tisane or a Swiss Miss adds fire-power. For formidable foes of a spiritual nature, the real Darkness, one needs the True Light. Spectres in your closet? Did you hear that?

You: "Agegegenon, is, is that yoouu?"

Agenon: "BUMP, BUMP!

You: "What to d,do? Let me, er, tell you about Jesus."

Agenon: "Bump, Bump.

You: "Yes, He is a, HE is the LIGHT of the WORLD!"

Agenon: "Rrmmmfh."

You: "Oh, you have to go? Do listen… For God so loved…"

Agenon Defeaters: In him was life; and the life was the light of men (John 1:4).

Photo stickers, Girls of the Night, 1996

205. YAKUZA

Osaka, Japan, 1996.

I saw him enter the phone booth. He didn't pull out a phone card. He checked the photos of girls on the booth's side panels. He seemed ready to make his choice. I had no paper, so I wrote in my textbook: "*Baishunfu ha tsumi desu* (Adultery is sin)!" I don't remember if he called, but he didn't punch me. Months later, I had another adventure. Two of them were tall and well proportioned. They stood in front of the phone booth, facing each other, but looking down the road in opposite directions. In front of the phone booth was a fellow my size, a comparison that would suggest some commonality between badgers and poodles. It was early morning, and nobody, except us four, was out. As was my custom, I tore down the display of girl's photos advertising the girls' availability. The Yakuza put them up by the tens of thousands; I tore them down by the thousands. Well, these folks, on that morning, did not appreciate my labors.

"Just a moment," I said, finishing up. I then opened the door and wished them a good morning.

"What are you doing?" the short guy, the one my size, asked. I was polite, but not apologetic.

"I'm pulling down these photos," I said, "because adultery is a sin."

"You are an American?"

"Yes," I answered, "I am also a Christian." He informed me I was in Japan. I said there is one God in the universe. He conveyed what I was doing was not a good idea. I thanked him for the suggestion. He laughed when I said "suggestion." The sun came up, the neighborhood stirred, our opportunity ended, the Lord delivered—again. I parted with: "God loves you."

Curmudgeon: And, behold, there met him a woman with the attire of an harlot, and subtil of heart. [12] Now is she without, now in the streets, and lieth in wait at every corner. [27] Her house is the way to hell, going down to the chambers of death (Prov. 7:10,12,27).

206. THE SECRET WORD

Do you know the SECRET WORD? It has been handed down in many cultures, religions, and myths over the years. In the second century, Irenaeus wrote *Against Heresies* to counter the spread of Gnosticism. This religion had many heads, variations of a theme. The Greek word *Gnosis* means knowledge, and to many groups, it was hidden knowledge, which could be revealed for a benefice of sufficient sincerity. In C.S. Lewis' *The Magician's Nephew*, Queen Jadis used a version of the Secret Word, the Deplorable Word. She topped King Pyrrhus, gaining a victory over her world, but killing everyone else in it.

In the 90's, at a linguistics conference, *dead verbs* and *Valley Girl* were our conversation topics. Beware Academicians! I met a Mormon professor there. Though our theology was kingdoms apart, he shared something poignant. He'd done linguistic work with a tribe in decline. As the last member of the tribe lie dying, the man spoke the tribe's secret word to him. What a tribute.

The Secret Word, do you know it? There is the revealed secret Word, and the hidden secret word. The first would be Jesus. He is not a secret; His name is spoken in many places, but many do not know His real nature and character. They are tantamount to a secret. The second, the unrevealed word, is in Revelation 2. Jesus promises *overcomers* a white stone on which a new name is written. Only God and the receiver know that secret name. It suggests an intimacy beyond our human love. Wanna know a secret? If God is your Father, he has one—just for you. What do you think your name is? Dances of praise? Causes his Father to smile? Warrior of Truth? My sweet handmaiden? And then there is… See John 3:16 or Revelation 3:20 for the invitation—it's no secret!

P.S. Not to boast, but I get two white stones! Yuko's maiden name is *Shiraishi*—white stone.

Curmudgeon: But if our gospel be hid, it is hid to them that are lost: [4] In whom the god of this world hath blinded the minds of them which believe not, lest the light of the glorious gospel of Christ, who is the image of God, should shine unto them (II Cor. 4:3-4).

207. LAST CALL

"You are going to die!" This is the opening line of one of my sermons. It may, or may not, be an outstanding work, but once I get started, people either walk out or wake up! When I was younger, the division between the living and the dead seemed so definite, unyielding, and not a little scary. In my early days, photos were still in black and white, so people looked partially dead already. As I've gotten older, and pictures are in color, I've gone the other direction. Death seems so flexible, rather undaunting. I even forget some people are dead. My attitude is quite upsetting to my elder son when, in the middle of a movie, I note offhandedly: "He's dead you know!" Part of this approach is age, and another would be theology. Paul says: "I know in whom I have believed, and am persuaded that He is able to keep that which I have committed unto him, unto that Day" (Gal. 2:20), "that Day," being when the Lord, sets everything right. Also, I know "all things work together for good to those who love God, to those who are the called according to his purpose" (Ro. 8:28), so, as Bob Marley sang, why not "Be happy."

I'm not a fan of Jacob. He was self-centered, like me, but I like how he dies. He is one of the few O.T. saints that finishes well. He has become a humbler man than he was in his youth. He chooses to be buried with Leah, his first wife, and not Rachel, his favorite. He also aligns himself with his forbears and the God they served. What I really like is he gathers his sons to pronounce unbiased blessings and admonitions, goes to bed, pulls up his feet, and dies, (Gen. 49:33). I'd like to have last words with family, commission them, fall asleep, and wake up in Heaven.

How about you? Are you ready? Friend, get ready—you are going to die!

Grace Lover: And he said unto Abram, Know of a surety that thy seed shall be a stranger in a land that is not theirs, and shall serve them; and they shall afflict them four hundred years; 15 And thou shalt go to thy fathers in peace; thou shalt be buried in a good old age (Gen. 15:13,15).

Curmudgeon: And also all that generation were gathered unto their fathers: and there arose another generation after them, which knew not the LORD, nor yet the works which he had done for Israel (Judges 2:10).

208. DIRECTION-FINDER

"Have fun and be careful," Mom said.

"We will," we promised gleefully, the screen door slamming behind us. You can tell by this opening, or in the door's case, the closing, that something will go wrong. You're spot on. I grabbed a towel and jumped into the car with my brother, Robin. He was 6 years my senior. We didn't do a lot together, but it was nice to have him with me for the opening of Phelps Lane pool. I was 7 years old and wiry as they come. My friend and I got to having too much fun running in the pool area. Then I jumped off the pool into the sand. It was not a tremendous height, 4 feet, but when you're 3 feet tall, it's exciting. There is a *however* to this story. The sand hid clumps of un-discarded concrete. One of these found itself under my knee. Rumors of tears are unfounded. I staunched the blood with my towel. Rob noted that since the towel had touched my skin, I would have a scar my entire life! I didn't see what the towel had to do with it, but being only 7 may explain that.

I didn't die, and I have no other memory of the towel. I did get a scar, but it was useful. Which brings me to my question, how did you learn to tell right from left? For me, it was easy—if I was wearing short pants. The scar was on my right knee! Though I haven't needed it so much lately, it's still there. Second question, how'd you learn right from wrong?

The phrase Moral Compass describes the ability to navigate life in the right direction. It's a great phrase; it's even greater to possess such a compass. My third question is, do you know where to find this moral compass? Let's look at a few hints.

Grace Lover: Blessed are the undefiled in the way, who walk in the law of the Lord. [2] Blessed are they that keep his testimonies, and that seek him with the whole heart. [9] Wherewithal shall a young man cleanse his way? by taking heed thereto according to thy word (Ps. 119:1,2,9).

> Jesus saith unto him, I am the way, the truth, and the life: no man cometh unto the Father, but by me (John 14:6).

Curmudgeon: Because that which may be known of God is manifest in them; for God hath shewed it unto them.[20] For the invisible things of him from the creation of the world are clearly seen, being understood by the things that are made, even his eternal power and Godhead; so that they are without excuse (Ro. 1:19-20).

209. THE PREACHER

W. Babylon, N.Y., '63.

Have you ever dueled? Two individuals put their lives in jeopardy for honor. Alexander Hamilton, America's first Secretary of the Treasury, author of most of the Federalist Papers, died in 1804, in a duel. Was it an age that should've passed?

Kirby, Little John, Billy, Doc, Gage, and Sergeant Saunders are names that mean a lot to a few people. They were King Company; their radio code was White Rook. They were the cast of *Combat*, a '60s WWII, T.V. show. Every week, they had a mission. The title today was one episode. The Preacher joined the squad the day they took a German prisoner. Kirby wanted to kill the German. The theme of the story, not only spoke of forgiveness, it portrayed a message somewhat forgotten. In Japan, there's a sense *duty is all. Tanshin funin* has no exact English translation. It describes a family with an absentee husband. He lives in a company dorm. On weekends, he returns home. He's a Salaryman, a *Work-Warrior*. It's his role. There's no philosophical position to navigate. The wife has her role, to support the man, so he functions well. My friend Tami-san once said: "A Japanese family is a mother, two children, and a father's money." The West pays less attention to roles. Sometimes they view duty as an infringement of personal freedom. Mom used to say: "Christopher, work doesn't have to be fun!"

In *Combat*, the Preacher died to save the German. Kirby asked why? Saunders simply said: "He was a preacher." The man had character. He did what was incumbent on his role. We see this dedication in emergency responders, military, and police. For many, this episode is outdated. The Son took on the roles of a man and sacrifice, Paul, the roles of apostle and slave, and Timothy, a son in the faith. What's your role?

Role Seeker: Look not every man on his own things, but every man also on the things of others.[5] Let this mind be in you, which was also in Christ Jesus: [6] Who, being in the form of God, thought it not robbery to be equal with God: [7] But made himself of no reputation, and took upon him the form of a servant, and was made in the likeness of men: [8] And being found in fashion as a man, he humbled himself, and became obedient unto death, even the death of the cross (Phil. 2:4-8).

210. A MIRROR REFLECTION

"I am over one-hundred years old," my Cambodian friend said. "We have Khmer, Chinese, and the calendar New Year, all in one year." I was glad for his longevity as long as he didn't expect extra gifts.

The year we arrived in Cambodia, a drunk driver killed two of our childcare youth. More have died since then. Cambodia had the highest per capita motorcycle deaths in Asia. Now they have helmet and mirror laws, but there was a learning curve. One person, instead of displaying a rear-view, installed the mirrors in front of the driver, and used them as a make-up mirror. We laughed, but I'm humbled as I sit before a smart phone and wonder what to do next! Driving without mirrors is dangerous, as is admiring one's looks inappropriately. Vanity can kill.

What do you think of these lyrics: "If you want to be happy for the rest of your life, get an ugly girl to be your wife!" A girl twice my weight once told me she could love me with God's love and make me fulfilled. I appreciated her good taste, but I aspired to marry beauty. Since then, I've wondered. Had I to do it over, would I, like Professor Higgins, say: "Throw the baggage out!" or reevaluate the beauty-queen dream? Do we want honest companionship or fleeting physical beauty? For guys, we'd do better to make a Queen of our Maiden than search for a Queen among Maids. And ladies, maybe the Frog is your Prince. This echoes God's heart. He exalts the humble and humbles the proud.

Grace Lover: Whose adorning let it not be that outward adorning of plaiting the hair, and of wearing of gold, or of putting on of apparel; [4] But let it be the hidden man of the heart, in that which is not corruptible, even the ornament of a meek and quiet spirit, which is in the sight of God of great price (I Pet. 3:3-4).

Curmudgeon: For all that is in the world, the lust of the flesh, and the lust of the eyes, and the pride of life, is not of the Father, but is of the world (I John 2:16).

211. FOOTPRINTS

Keene Camp, Pennsylvania, 2003.

Don't you love camps? I joined the Free Methodist Church because of camps. You could probably find better reasons, e.g., doctrine, leadership, cool vibes. Well, maybe not, but you get the idea. I'd been in the Shepherding movement on a Christian commune in Hawaii, 1972-75, and a non-denominational mission society, 1978-85. I loved them. Both had great outreach, but were weak in nurture. I didn't realize most of the Church had it the other way. As a result, in '86 I joined the FMC. In '89, I became a volunteer in Japan, and in 2002, I joined the FMC Mission, married Yuko, and went to Cambodia.

On one furlough, we were the guest missionaries at a camp. One day I told a story about Buzz Light Year (*Toy Story I*). He was feeling at home since he'd landed, or thought he'd landed, from another quadrant of Space. He told the toys that Ande, the child to whom they belonged, had written his name on the bottom of Buzz's boot. Not only that, it was in indelible ink. Buzz had the Master's seal. Indelible ink was an affirmation for Calvinists (there are no expulsions from God's family)! He that had been lost in Space was found. "Wouldn't it be grand," I said "if we had Jesus' name written on our feet—in indelible ink." The next day, while I spoke, a woman draped her feet over the bench. The bottoms of her sneakers had written: Jesus! I tried not to laugh. So, how about you? To whom do you belong? A foot print (print on the foot) makes all the difference where, and with whom, you go.

Grace Lover: I am the vine, ye are the branches: He that abideth in me, and I in him, the same bringeth forth much fruit: for without me ye can do nothing. [15] Henceforth I call you not servants; for the servant knoweth not what his lord doeth: but I have called you friends; for all things that I have heard of my Father I have made known unto you (John 15:5,15).

> Who hath also sealed us, and given the earnest of the Spirit in our hearts (II Cor. 1:22).

212. THE BLACK HAND

If you're from New York, you know about the *Black Hand, The Family*, or *Organized Crime*. Those organized folks will come into play later. When I was a boy, Dad bent his knee for 2 reasons. One was bowling, the other to genuflect. Dad was a good bowler, a 165 average, but I liked the latter more. Humbling himself before God always made him bigger in my eyes. Scripture says we are saved by grace through faith, not of works, lest any man should boast (Ep. 2:8,9). Some folk's faith is defined by *don'ts*, others by *do's*. I can't remember Dad cursing—not once. I never saw him drunk, and seldom angry, and I never saw him look at a woman in the wrong way. He was good with the *thou shalt nots*. The positive side brings a smile. He worked a lot, but when *The Flintstones* first aired, he'd try to watch it with me. Then, when I was 17, Dad got a new habit.

"Christopher," he shouted down the stairs: "the Bible says we are to tithe." My thought was: "What's a tithe?" but I stayed mum until he finished. "I'm going to start tithing," he said.

"Good," I said, but thought, "so this is a new to the text?"

After Mom died, Dad found a Catholic singles group. He asked my permission to marry—nice thought. He had two silver wedding anniversaries. Dad was a social animal. He was a member, and a president, I believe, of the Bensonhurst Kiwanis Club. Our neighbor, Bill Marvin, asked: "Kiwanis, what kind of bird is that?" Dad, the token Irishman of this Italian group, called himself Roberto Francesco Wilkini, and beat them at bocce, but missed the target in other ways. One day he stated: "A Family Boss (Mafia) came to our meeting. He seemed to be a regular businessman." Not given to perspicacity, I thought, "In what universe?" Later the guy was machine-gunned and dead several times over! Only God knows all. Dad was also a president of the Homewood Farms Civic Association. We used stencils and an ink drum to print monthly newsletters, which I handed out—my version of the Black Hand. I always had stained hands afterwards. My brother, Rob, played Taps on Memorial Day at the renovated Homewood Farms Hall. I learned about community service from Dad, though my first impression was working with old people in a rundown building that smelled of the 19th century.

Dad was strict, but had a soft spot, too. When I left home, I wasn't twenty-one or a college graduate, two rites of passage Dad thought merited independence. Tuesday was El Cheapo night at Vinnie's Disco, so he came one night to offer me a chance to come home. Hey, I had his old car, a minimum wage job, and freedom—all the cards, I thought. I thanked him, but passed. I just wanted to be free. Was I in for a ride!

I can't forget Dad's doctrinal statements. He was a banker. That industry, for me, summoned *Revelation* and the *Mark of the Beast*. I tried to get the inside skinny on tech-developments, but when I mentioned Revelation, he remarked: "Oh, that's prophecy." For Dad, prophecy and the far side of the moon were co-conspirators of the Realm Inscrutable to keep Humans in the dark. His other position was more painful. As part of my mission obligation, I called 50 pastors a week to raise funds. While visiting Dad, I talked to a Hispanic fellow. He booked me for a service. I was stoked! On the day appointed, I took my projector, donned my best and only suit, and Dad drove. The gentleman and I agreed on service, but when I arrived, he wanted to tune-up my car. We went home, and I did some witnessing door to door. Later, Dad, to my chagrin, asked: "Are you like the J.W.s?" Speaking of witnesses, it's time for someone else share about Dad. "This is the third time I am coming to you. In the mouth of two or three witnesses shall every word be established" (II Corinthians 13:1). We sometimes had priests to the house for Sunday dinner. When I was ten, Father Rampmeier came. Dad had to run through the rain to get the car. Father R. said: "He's such a brave man." I didn't see the bravery, but I saw the goodness. That was Dad.

Grace Lover: A good name is rather to be chosen than great riches, and loving favour rather than silver and gold (Prov. 22:1).

> Bring ye all the tithes into the storehouse, that there may be meat in mine house, and prove me now herewith, saith the LORD of hosts, if I will not open you the windows of heaven, and pour you out a blessing, that there shall not be room enough to receive it (Mal. 3:10).

> Finally, brethren, whatsoever things are true, whatsoever things are honest, whatsoever things are just, whatsoever things are pure, whatsoever things are lovely, whatsoever things are of good report; if there be any virtue, and if there be any praise, think on these things (Phil. 4:8).

213. WAYS TO PEACE

So, which is better, Marvel or D.C. comics? This question decides affiliations, and who sits where at lunchtime. Alphabetical order takes on a whole new meaning—D.C. first, then Marvel! My kids don't answer. Living in Japan, they can't buy the comics, and second, they've not seen the movies which are $15—before snacks. Finances cast a ballot, but the major obstacle has been *innocence.* I'm not a big fan of truncated bodies, and my boys, the younger especially, are averse to violence. Corey has often called me bedside for prayer, "Daddy, can you pray? I have bad thoughts." He'd word it the same, I'd respond the same:

> "Lord, you promised to keep them in perfect peace whose mind is stayed on thee" (Is. 26:3).

After many recitations, I suggested ways to stay our mind on the Lord: giving thanks, intercessory prayer, worship, and recalling His wondrous works. Those are good ways to find peace. I still worry about my children, but Proverbs 3:25 is part of my shield: "you shall not fear for the sudden calamity." Is safety part of the Covenant? I can't say "Yes" 100% of the time, but I choose to trust Him. I've brought my children to Asia for us to serve the Lord. It's a crazy place occasionally. Someone asked a missionary if she was not afraid of missionary life. Her answer was: "There is no safer place than the center of God's will." This is a good way, too.

Grace Lover: When a man's ways please the Lord, he maketh even his enemies to be at peace with him (Prov. 16:7).

> [4] (For the weapons of our warfare are not carnal, but mighty through God to the pulling down of strong holds;) [5] Casting down imaginations, and every high thing that exalteth itself against the knowledge of God, and bringing into captivity every thought to the obedience of Christ (II Cor. 10:4-5).

214. WHAT'S THE MATTER?

August 29, 2017, Chili, N.Y.

Is *Thou shalt be friendly* in scripture? No! Years ago, I had a depiction of Jesus with Cleopas and another disciple on the Emmaus Road. Jesus, just risen from the dead, asked: "What are you talking about?" The men left Jerusalem not believing a report of the Resurrection. That morning, they didn't recognize Him. Aware of their mood, Jesus didn't withdraw, but entered their world again. That evening, they commented: "Didn't our hearts burn when He spoke to us from the scriptures?"

Jesus talked to Nicodemus (John 3), the woman at the well (John 4), the lame man (John 5), the man born blind (John 9), Lazarus' family (John 11,12), Simon the Pharisee (Luke 7), the Centurion (Luke 8), the Rich Young ruler (Luke 18), and Zacchaeus (Luke 19). There was *kibitzing*, Yiddish for *shootin' the breeze*, but there was also truth.

When our friend's plane was delayed, Yuko and Caleb went shopping. I stayed in the car and finished reading a book. A Black gentleman's music was on, so I closed the window. When Yuko and Caleb returned, I got out of the van.

"Excuse me, Sir," I said. "What's the matter?" he asked.

"Nothing," I said. "I want to wish you a nice day." He smiled. "I'm Chris. Can I ask you your name?"

"Frank," he said. I extended my arm and we shook hands. "I'll pray for you today, Frank, and you pray for me, ok?"

"Ok," he said. I patted his shoulder, saying: "Have a great day."

Grace Lover and Curmudgeon: A man that hath friends must shew himself friendly: and there is a friend that sticketh closer than a brother (Prov. 18:24).

> And when she hath found it, she calleth her friends and her neighbours together, saying, Rejoice with me; for I have found the piece which I had lost. [10] Likewise, I say unto you, there is joy in the presence of the angels of God over one sinner that repenteth (Luke 15:9-10).

215. STEPS TO THE GALLOWS

A hangin' was free entertainment! Frontier Justice had no *appeals.* The climb from obscurity to infamy took days, and 12-steps to the noose. Such things enthralled my generation for 20 years before being replaced by muscle cars, bikinis, and modern sleuths, like lawyers and doctors. Today we return to a civilized time when Law had such precedence, even the King couldn't rescind it. We're in the Book of Esther, a blockbuster movie in waiting. Our antagonist is Haman, an Agagite. They were ancient enemies of the Jews. When Haman comes on stage, you hiss *a fortissimo*! Jews stomp their feet at the mention of Haman's name in Purim's reading. How did his fortunes plummet, and his feet ascend the gallows' steps?

Haman's star is rising, but… enter tragic flaw. Hear a Greek chorus wailing? The Greeks had flawed heroes, whereas he was a flawed villain. Nevertheless, Haman had his chorus. His wife, Zeresh, assuaged his pride with songs of revenge. When success became lackluster, superiority took on a new sheen. When Mordecai the Jew refused to grovel, the only recourse was to wipe Jewry off the planet—Near East logic 500 B.C. to the present. He built a set of gallows 70 feet high for Mordecai—quite the neck-stretcher. Its dimensions discouraged thoughts he was a man of half-measures. It seemed so alpha-male until you see through the pheromones. When the Jewish Queen apprised the King of her upcoming execution, Haman begged for his life. He was hoisted on his own petard, or rope. It wasn't Frontier Justice; it was Divine Justice. Haman worked hard for those steps to the gallows. He stopped his ears and hardened his heart. There are two ways to get on the ascending staircase of downfall. One is to hate the Jew, the apple of God's eye. The other is to be prideful. Haman decked himself. How many steps have you left? Is there a noose or a reprieve in your future? For the noose, don't change a thing. For the reprieve, see John 3:16, or I John 1.

Curmudgeon: Whoso diggeth a pit shall fall therein: and he that rolleth a stone, it will return upon him (Prov. 26:27).

216. CLOUD

Chiba, Japan, 2019.

When I was a boy, Dick Tracy was the only one who thought of a camera when he heard a phone: "Dick Tracy, this is Jo Jitsu. Come in Dick Tracy!" Words evolve. If we talked about a *net* when I was a boy, it was the one missing on the basketball hoop. If *windows* were mentioned, we hid the Windex. When we talked about a *cloud*, it was about cirrus, stratus, or cumulonimbus. I knew my clouds. Now, what got a *B* on the science quiz, refers not to airborne vapor, but to a storage place of encoded ideas. I have a password somewhere to take me to this magical place of whirling-swirling electrons. Clouds are amazing. Like a wood fire, or waves, clouds evoke an air of melancholy, of contemplation. What is the mystery of clouds that attracts us? I'm not clever, but I've aspired to be so. I suspect you are clever or you aren't. It's not an app you can upload. Hey, there's another one —*application*. I once asked a friend: "What's the meaning of a flower?" He asked if I was referring to Aristotle's cave? I wasn't up on it, so I nodded. My moment of cleverness was lost underground with an ancient spelunker,

I could say clouds are Jungian in an archetypal sense, but that would get me in more trouble than Big A's Cave. But what can we say without getting in over our heads, we're talking about clouds? They move, change, disappear, reappear, obscure, and indirectly reveal things. They're a metaphor of a reality beyond us. God gave us a reminder *what you see is not what you get!* I've mentioned Charlie Brown and Linus before, but theirs is an illustration of many themes. They're gazing at clouds. Linus sees the contour of a country. and the profile of a famous personage. Charlie Brown confesses to have seen a ducky and a horsy, but in retrospect may have been mistaken. Parables, like clouds, reveal things (Unto you it is given to know the mysteries of the kingdom), and obscure things (that seeing they might not see) to others, Luke 8:10. Parables are matters of the heart. Have a nice, clear, cloudy day!

Curmudgeon: While we look not at the things which are seen, but at the things which are not seen: for the things which are seen are temporal; but the things which are not seen are eternal (II Cor. 4:18).

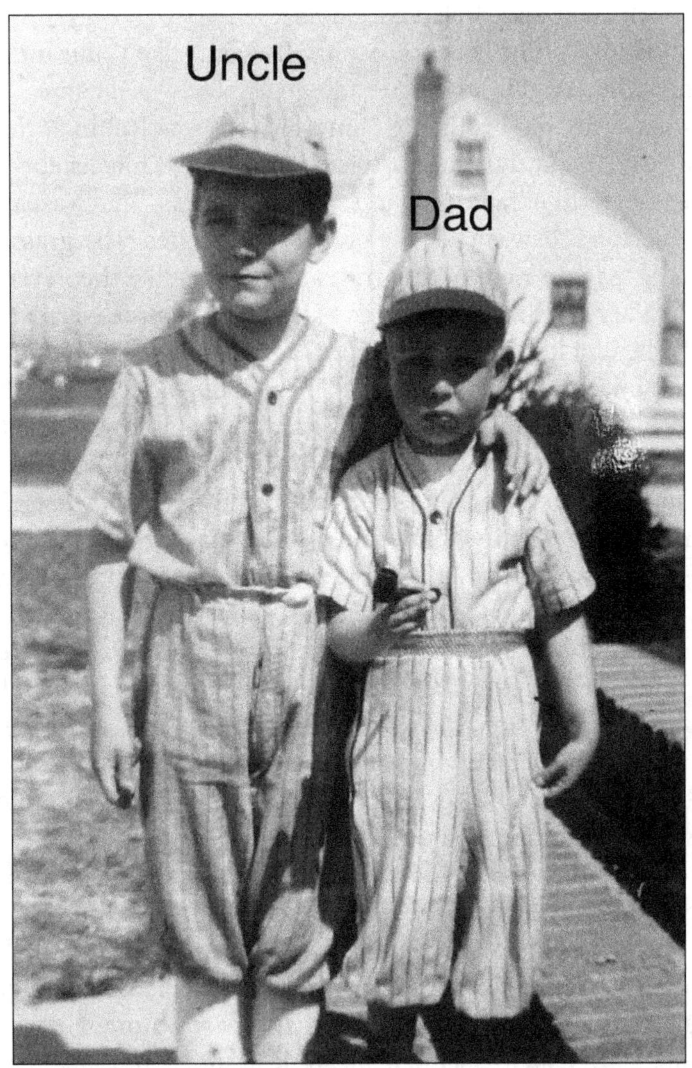

Robin and I, ready to romp, West Babylon, N.Y., 1955.

217. T-13

W. Babylon, N. Y., '57.

I tiptoed to the tent and peeled back a flap.

"Hey, no kids," Willie Pellegrino said. His name, like Willie himself, was full of life. It danced off the tongue and gesticulated as it came.

"He's okay," my big brother, Robin, said. He was Robin at that point; later, he'd be Clark, and then Bob, to everyone except me. I stepped inside. It felt like the world of fantasy that permeates canvas. That wasn't the only sensory overload. It wasn't socks or old sandwiches. The grass had the fragrance of loam, a rich, hearty fragrance. It was like the Pevensie kids arriving in Narnia—they got taller and stronger the more Narnian air they breathed. The tent had an eerie, mystical aura of orange as the sun worked its magic upon it. Later, I went again to hear all the big scouts talking. That contented me—that and my brother's kindness. Robin was like that. He was deep—of course, he had six years on me. Thoughtfulness was coupled to other superpowers. One Christmas, we received cowboy hats. He drew a star on the front of mine. That summer, he made me a jewel bedecked wooden sword. True, the weight of it made me a two-handed warrior, and the gem was only a four-cent marble, but what are trifling realities to a boy of 7 whose cohort is imagination? Spiritual battles, also, were part of Rob's training for me. One Christmas I received a Catholic Missal! I don't remember the inscription, but its multi-syllables reeked of reverence. He was like the T.V. infomercial that declared: "and that's not all, there's more besides…" He was fun; he'd even have rubber band fights with me. Those were the days, living in the shadow of RCW.

He added to the legend, though, sometimes strangely, e.g., he favored the Rebel cause of the Civil War. Dad served at Fort Dix for a time during WWII, so Rob was born in Virginia. And then there was the Election of '64! He voted for Barry Goldwater. I think he had a placard, though it may have been my nightmare. But that's not all, there's more. He went off to college and charted an ice island in an arctic ice floe. The plane sent to pick up the team on T-13 got stuck in slush and had to be propped up with snow to take off. He then tended Timberwolves in Barrow, the northernmost town of North America. One tried to have his arm for dinner. A logging group was next until a log roll awarded him with a pin. It remained in his leg for forty years. He graduated from Alaska University, which was great, but lost all his worldly possessions in the Earthquake of '64, which rerouted the Chena River through his basement apartment. That was not all that Alaska had in store. Its parting gift was a hospital airlift after a car accident in the middle of nowhere, which in Alaska, is everywhere.

After Mom died, Rob gave up adventure to return to New York. It took courage to move in with little brother and Dad. He added something new to his super powers—Cool! He bought a Chevelle. At this point I was 17, and thinking more of me than others. My Big Brother has done nothing to tarnish this sterling account I've awarded him, but what has this testimonial of sibling admiration to do with you? Well, I had a bead on my brother. I was clueless about my future. Teaching was out. Standing in front of people? No, thank you! I'd lived in the same house for 18 years. I'd have been happy to die in our Cape Cod house, but Mom died, Dad re-married, and Rob married. The times they were a changin' as Bob Dylan's song prophesied. Robin, Clark, and Bob planted the seeds of adventure. Transition wasn't so bad. That which I'd feared became that for which I yearned. The road I traveled was rocky, even making it to the FBI list—though not the Top 10. I may as well confess, there are witnesses. But that's not all, there's more. I not only had my Big Brother's example, I had the Hound of Heaven's leading.

Grace Lover: Now the Lord had said unto Abram, Get thee out of thy country, and from thy kindred, and from thy father's house, unto a land that I will shew thee: [3] And I will bless them that bless thee, and curse him that curseth thee: and in thee shall all families of the earth be blessed. [4]So Abram departed, as the Lord had spoken unto him; and Lot went with him: and Abram was seventy and five years old when he departed out of Haran (Gen. 12:1, 3-4).

> Behold, I will do a new thing; now it shall spring forth; shall ye not know it? I will even make a way in the wilderness, and rivers in the desert (Is. 43:19).

> Be kindly affectioned one to another with brotherly love; in honour preferring one another (Ro. 10:12).

Curmudgeon: For I am the Lord, I change not; therefore ye sons of Jacob are not consumed (Mal. 3:6).

218. THE LANGUAGE OF GOD

Language is wild!

The African Khoisan tribes use the click. Robin Williams mimicked it in *Night at the Museum I.* A fellow seminarian at Asbury, Cowboy Bob, had a *click* trained horse. One click was for slow, two for a gallop, etc. I rode it once. Too many clicks had me planing atop the horse. Since then, a glottal stop is as close to a click that I get. The Inuit have 20 ways to say, *snow*, i.e., crunchy, glompy, etc. In Japan, it's the same with mushrooms. We have thin stick-like mushrooms, *Enoki*, gooey mushrooms, *Nameko*, and more. Two unique words I like are *Shimobashira*, frozen steam in the soil that creates sculptures, and *Hanabie*, a reverse Indian Summer, cold weather prolonging cherry blossom time.

Language is limited by, or expressive of, our concepts. So, what kind of language would an omniscient God use? The verse *we shall see Him as He is, for we shall be like Him*, I John 3:2, suggests an automatic vocabulary enhancer. Throw away your Rosetta Stone! What kind of language does a God, who is love, speak? The quality, the depth of such speech is boggling. Here's a question: can language have color, taste, fragrance, emotion?

In Acts 2, the disciples spoke in other tongues, a language they didn't know. Is Heaven's language like that? Will we need language? A famous commercial in the USA was, "When E.F. Hutton speaks, people listen!" If someone mentioned E.F. Hutton, everyone grew quiet. Does God's language get attention like that? If there is such a language, it will be the person of God who speaks glory into it. Whatever mode it is, I'm waiting to hear: "Well done, my good and faithful servant" (Matt. 25:23). What are you waiting for?

Grace Lover: The Lord thy God in the midst of thee is mighty; he will save, he will rejoice over thee with joy; he will rest in his love, he will joy over thee with singing (Zeph. 3:17).

Curmudgeon: A naughty person, a wicked man, walketh with a froward mouth (Prov. 6:12).

219. THE TAPE

Did Haldeman's plea bargain sabotage the Nixon White House? Some blame the President for having tapes. Had he been honest, we would've forgiven Mr. Nixon. But that was Washington D.C. Have you heard of the New York tape? I almost ruined my brother's marriage—before he even pledged his troth! I was entrusted with audio-taping the wedding. Tape recorders were dreadful in the '60s. I put in a used tape, pushed *pause*, and walked to the sacristy. As the priest shared the order of service, Connie Francis sang in the sanctuary. I hurried out, hid my laughter, and turned off this incriminating lament:

The tears I cried for you could fill an ocean; But you don't care how many tears I cry

And though you only lead me on and hurt me; I couldn't bring myself to say goodbye.

'Cause everybody's somebody's fool; Everybody's somebody's baby

Yes, everybody's somebody's fool; (Lyrics Keller and Greenfield).

My erratum went unnoticed compared to the cameraman—he left the lens cap on while filming. As for love, the song's themes are powerlessness and selfishness. We all stand on a tipping scale, and there's Hell to pay. Your life is on tape. Jesus, and only Jesus, can erase your mis-takes—just ask Him.

Grace Lover: For the wages of sin is death; but the gift of God is eternal life through Jesus Christ our Lord (Ro. 3:23).

> For godly sorrow worketh repentance to salvation not to be repented of: but the sorrow of the world worketh death (I Cor. 7:10).

Curmudgeon: herefore whatsoever ye have spoken in darkness shall be heard in the light; and that which ye have spoken in the ear in closets shall be proclaimed upon the housetops (Luke 12:3).

220. LITERARY TYPES

Rochester, N.Y, 80's.

"Gotta make the do-nuts," was a commercial in the '80's when the Heeks opened the Donut Express. It had a long counter and enormous windows. Jim was a talented dough sculptor and a trainer with Stephen Ministries. I was going to Japan. One day, we were to meet at the shop. I came early and wandered into a bar. The door was open—maybe. Then, Jim arrived.

"Did you just come out of that bar?"

"Oh, that bar? Yes," I confessed, "I had a friendly chat—C.S. Lewis and the denouement of evil in white-collar communities." Jim wasn't wearing boots, and so, deferred further questioning. In my Master's thesis, I delved into Lewis' *Narnia Chronicles*, and Tolkien's *Lord of the Rings*. I enjoyed the Christ-figure, Aslan, in the Chronicles. In Tolkien, Gandalf, figuratively, rose from the dead. Arathorn, the returning king, came to rule the reclaimed realm, and Frodo bore the Ring, to bring deliverance to Middle Earth. In class, my fellows used the term, Christ-figure, dispassionately. Discussions were academic exercises, modern illustrations of "hearing they shall not hear" (Isa. 6:9-10).

In Brecht's play, *Waiting for Godot*, the protagonists wait for one whose name sounds like God. "Blathering and void," describes their meaningless life and talk. It's a view of a secular religion of nothingness. Stuck in blathering and void? Don't discuss Christ, meet Him. John 3 fills the void, and exchanges blathering for meaning.

Jim worked a lot. His commitment gained a group of coffee drinkers. Now he leads a food ministry that blesses hundreds. What's our part? Literature and the Bible have their lessons, but their value is in application. Christ is more than a concept in a book. He is the Word made flesh so each of us can be a King or Queen of Narnia, a Gandalf, an Arathorn, a Frodo!

Grace Lover: Not as though I had already attained, either were already perfect: but I follow after, if that I may apprehend that for which also I am apprehended of Christ Jesus. [14] I press toward the mark for the prize of the high calling of God in Christ Jesus (Phil. 3:12,14).

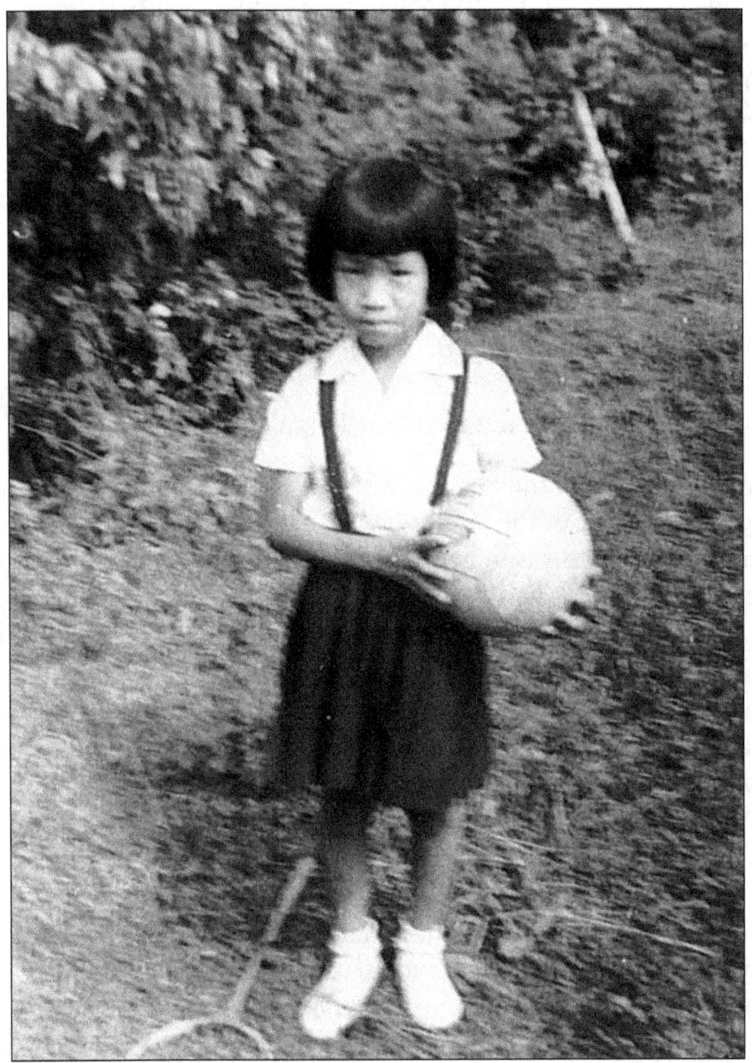

Sau Fan, Taiwan, circa 1976.

221. THE LAST DAYS MUSEUM:

RAISER OF THE LOST ARK

"I'd like to see the Ark of the Covenant!" Wilson said.
"Did any of you see the movie?" Eliakim asked.
"Oh yeah, melting faces..." Thy Venn exclaimed.
"It was really the Shekinah glory," Blong clarified.
"Turn here," Hiro said. They paused for respect to the Ark. The Curator came out, and music filled the place.
"Thank you for coming," the Curator said. "My name is Uzzah."
"No kidding?" Wilson asked.
"Wilson's surprise is... an Uzzah died..." Sau Fan said,
"Yes, friends, I trifled with the Holy One."
"Is this the real Ark?" Fung Chil asked.
"Did the Levites hide it from the Babylonians?" Wilson asked.

No one living knows the answer, but let's think about what Uzzah did. Manipulate is a mix of the Latin, *manus*, hand, and *plere* to fill. It means to control. God, not us is in control. Acts 17, declares He does not live in houses made by men's hands as if He needeth anything (vs 25). He is the I Am that I Am, (Ex. 3:14). Human manipulation is ineffective. He holds the world together by His power (Col. 1;17).

"You wouldn't be happy if Jesus were here," I said in anger. I realized what I'd done as the can I held cut into my finger. I'd used the Lord for my purpose—my Uzzah experience. The New Covenant is one of grace, so I lived to tell the story. The Law came by Moses, grace and truth from Jesus (John 1:17). Sin can't abide in His presence, yet, and this is the biggest *YET* you'll encounter. He extends grace. The Chinese proverb, *Pushing is not pushing*, suggests actions have unexpected reactions. Trying to manipulate God would top the list. It's better to serve Him than to push Him. Besides, He wants to bless—there's no reason to be pushy!

God revealed the Ark of His Testament in His temple, accompanied by lightnings, voices, thunderings, an earthquake, and great hail (Rev. 11:19).

222. THE GOLD ALBUM

This is not about a million-seller CD. As a Cub Scout, I licked triangle corner fasteners to affix postcards to an album—yuk! Nevertheless, I'd love to have that scrapbook today. Later, I made scrapbooks at Christians in Action. I hold on to friends and memorabilia. I have, by stealth, boxes of heirlooms. When Yuko throws out an item, I retrieve it. My friend, Jim, has a business, *Keepers of the Past*. That sums up me to the P. Capturing a memory beats a bug in the eye any day.

Does God have an album? He has a ledger—the Book of Life. Yes, memories are important to the Lord. At Passover, children ask questions to remind everyone of the Lord's works (Exodus 12:26). Ancient markers were not to be removed (Prov. 22:28). Stephen and Paul recount God's works in their defenses before the Jews (Acts 7 and 22). Remembrance is a cultural trait of the Jewish family. Who doesn't gyrate when Tevye sings "Tradition," in *Fiddler on the Roof*?

The Lord has memories of you. That time you failed miserably and hoped you'd die. Or, like Nathaniel under the fig tree (John 1:45-51), a solitary time you poured out your heart to Him. After a debacle with one son, I told him I'd always, whether he failed or succeeded, love him. Our Lord does better. He does all things well (Mark 7:37). He has more to be nostalgic about, forgetting nothing, and knowing us before the creation (Eph. 1:4).

Grace Lover: And Aaron shall bear the names of the children of Israel in the breastplate of judgment upon his heart, when he goeth in unto the holy place, for a memorial before the Lord continually (Ex. 28:29).

> Then they that feared the LORD spake often one to another: and the LORD hearkened, and heard it, and a book of remembrance was written before him for them that feared the LORD, and that thought upon his name (Mal. 3:16).

Curmudgeon: And if anyone's name was not found written in the book of life, he was thrown into the lake of fire (Rev. 20:15).

223. THE RECITAL

Though not a discerner of the intents of the heart, the Bell could divine. The Door was possessed of yet another feature—the Spring. The latter possessed old magic, its commission being to protect the premises. It was not disadvantaged by its antiquity, being able to catapult unwary minors from the threshold. One day the Door swung full measure, circumscribing an arc hitherto unreached, the possible exception being when a John Deere slipped past an employee at closing. It sought sanctuary in the appliance section, but the toaster-ovens wouldn't have it. The Door, on this day, was not alone exceeding margins. The Bell rang until it lost consciousness. Light dimmed until the Bell-ringer stepped in, allowing the sun access again. The Giant's arrival had personnel scurrying.

"How was the weekend?" Alan inquired of the red-haired Colossus.

"My son fell," he said, "a guy in his hot car thought it was funny."

"So, what did you do?" Phil asked.

"I pulled the sucker out of his window!" The crew chortled, sharing expletives. To be fair, the Gargantua's son was a hemophiliac.

This brings us to pianos. At a recital, Corey, 4, and Caleb, 7, did a number together. Caleb played piano, Corey, a handmade marimba. A mother noticed Corey's nervousness and sniggered. I didn't pull her out of her chair, but I did stand, camera in hand, my other hand giving my son a thumbs-up. I kept the thumb in the air. Corey never missed a beat. I've messed up, but that day I stood for my boys. Many references have Jesus sitting at Father's right hand. In one, He is not. You may want a tissue.

Grace Lover: But he, being full of the Holy Ghost, looked up stedfastly into heaven, and saw the glory of God, and Jesus standing on the right hand of God, [59] And they stoned Stephen, calling upon God, and saying, Lord Jesus, receive my spirit And he kneeled down, and cried with a loud voice, Lord, lay not this sin to their charge. And when he had said this, he fell asleep (Acts 6:55,59,60).

Jesus stands for you! For whom do you stand?

224. WHERE'S WALDO

12th Century, France.

At the turn of the century, there were two interesting fads in books. One was hidden dimension pictures. To see them properly, eyeballs had to be coaxed out of synch; 3 dimensions were hidden in 2. I'm a 6th Level Master. The second phenomenon was *Where's Waldo?* the goal being to find Waldo, accoutered in a shirt of red and white stripes, in various settings. Like Origen, an Early Church apologist, liked allegory. I find these fads analogous to spiritual truth. II Cor. 4:18 states: "while we look not at the things which are seen, but at the things which are not seen. For the things which are seen are temporal, but the things which are not seen are eternal." Searching for Waldo is like Matthew 13:44: "Again, the Kingdom of Heaven is like unto treasure hid in a field, which, when a man hath found, he hideth; and for the joy thereof goeth and selleth all that he hath, and buyeth that field." The analogy becomes clear after spending hours on a couch on a sunny day, looking for a striped shirt, i.e., losing all to gain the prize.

Peter Waldo was a rich, cloth merchant, in 12th Century Lyon. While at a gathering, a friend died suddenly. Talk about a dead party! Later, a philosopher at the square, told the story of St Alexis. a rich, 4th Century man who had embraced poverty. These events changed Waldo. He translated the Bible into Provencal, to read it himself. He preached against Transubstantiation and Purgatory, as being doctrines of manipulation, and warned against the love of riches (Mk. 4:19). The 4th Lateran Council made Transubstantiation a Church doctrine, in 1215. Some Dissenters lost their heads. This put them in a difficult position—two, actually. Many Waldenses were killed, but the group continued for centuries, ordinary people loving an unordinary God. I want the spirit of the old, new Waldo.

Grace Lover: These were more noble than those in Thessalonica, in that they received the word with all readiness of mind, and searched the scriptures daily, whether those things were so (Acts17:11).

Curmudgeon: So then because thou art lukewarm, and neither cold nor hot, I will spue thee out of my mouth (Revelation 3:16).

225. BOLT COLA

Lewisburg, Pa., '77.

The inventors of Bolt Cola at Cole's Hardware, were my colleagues, Dean, Phil, and Alan. They knew I sampled leftovers and decided to spice things up. One day, I discovered abandoned donuts. I was new to the Commonwealth, and surprised Pensylknavians ate salted doughnuts. I also sampled a discarded cola. Understand, I wasn't Scroogish; I was squirreling away walnuts to help support World Vision's Childcare. Putting the can down, I heard a rattle. An inspection uncovered a bolt with its finish somewhat corroded. That which was missing now lined my stomach. "Hey maybe now I can eat chili peppers!" I'd begun to laugh at my mischievous colleagues, but then just hoped to live out the month. The Gang of Three displayed affection often. My first month there, Dean put Christian tracts on everyone's time card. The staff thought it was my doing. This scenario backfired; he spared me the prayer time to get emboldened to do it. Those were fun times. Phil hissed when he laughed, and Al, you hoped he was laughing. If not, he'd look at you sideways, and chew his soup strainer.

These stories came to mind when my son's classmate, Isaac, skyped him to introduce their new cat. Caleb is nobody's fool; he perceived the prank. The cat was borrowed for the deception. Caleb upped the ante, taking a picture of me sitting in a nice car, our alleged new vehicle. Isaac, being possessed of less guile than my progeny, accepted the story.

We've all created and been subject to falsehoods. The latter is part of the sowing and reaping deal. What I laid out so far were fun stunts. Most of us don't prank a stranger, fearing reprisal. Sadly, some folks do plan harm to others. These verses are more for placating than prosecuting. If you're at risk, call in some prayer! A final thought, sample discarded donuts at your peril.

Grace Lover: But I say unto you, Love your enemies, bless them that curse you, do good to them to them that hate you, and pray for them that despitefully use you, and persecute you (Matt. 5:44).

> Confess your faults one to another, and pray one for another, that ye may be healed. The effectual prayer of a righteous man availeth much (James 5:16).

226. 1959

She was beautiful, her dress was green. My uniform was blue. She presented a lofty view; people put her on a pedestal. I viewed life from a height of 3". She was not quite 100 years old; I was 9. She never moved, I never stayed still. She is Lady Liberty; I was a Cub Scout. We saw her and the Museum of Natural History. The latter had two of my favorites, T. Rex and Dung Beetles. I forfeited a hot dog and snacks to buy a decorator box entitled: Shells from the World. It was 1959, the greatest year ever. Sister St. Ludger, my teacher, thought I was smart, I joined the altar boy class, Cadillacs had wings, and I went on 2 awesome adventures.

The altar boys went to Rye Beach. Two things are etched in my mind. One was a low-tech water ride. The highlight was the waterfall. Between the passage of boats, the ceiling unleashed a deafening deluge. Joseph B. was my neighbor. He did a baseball play-by-play to rival Mel Barber. On that day, I discovered Joe's other talent—mischief. He tried to slow his boat so people in the next one would get soaked. That would be–me! He failed. He couldn't slow the plan in progress. The creator of Boat-World had seen the contingencies. Nevertheless, Joe tried, and everyone was screaming and scrambling. That also would be–me! Joe put on a show; my fear was genuine!

Then the serpent spewed forth water from his mouth to overtake the woman (Revelation 12:15). The other aspect also had to do with water. I forgot the W.C. Our two-hour trip with a full cistern was the same as an eight-hour trip without snacks! I was water-logged and prayerful every second, but I made it! Which brings us to the spiritual life. Not to understate the plight of suffering saints today, the Church has difficult days ahead. God not only has a plan, He will take us through the waters, or help His people endure.

Grace Lover: A thousand shall fall at thy side, and ten thousand at thy right hand; but it shall not come nigh thee (Ps. 91:7).

Curmudgeon: Are they not all ministering spirits, sent forth to minister for them who shall be heirs of salvation (Heb. 1:14).

227. THE BUTCHER, THE BAKER, AND THE CANDLESTICK MAKER

Ding, Ding…

"Hi, Sully, how's it goin'?"

"Hey, Christian, win some, lose some, ya know. What can I get ya today?"

"This looks good. What is it?"

"That is no blend; it's unadulterated 100% beef, no colors, no hormones, no fat—just taste."

"Sounds like our conversation about the character of God—no sin, just holiness."

"Oh Christian, you say the funniest things. So, what do you think, see anything that grabs you?"

"Yes, I'll take this. A full pound."

"There you are. See you next week."

"God bless you."

"Oh yeah, they're all fine. Marti is going to graduate next week. See you.

…

Jingle, Jingle…

"Nemaste, Mr. Singh. Nice to see you again."

"Nemaste. Is it a propitious day for everyone, or am I the only one?" Mr. Singh joked.

"This is the day that the Lord hath made… I guess it is good in that respect for everyone."

"I hope so. What is your delight today, the usual?" Mr. Singh asked.

"I'd like a dozen laddu, and half a dozen of the gajar ka halwa and gajar ki barfi, please."

"Amazing, you are my only customer who can get that to roll off their tongue like rose syrup."

"You're an excellent teacher," Christian lauded. "If you want the real thing, get it from Singh."

"May the gods see to it the nan and chai are never lacking in your home!"

"Thanks, but Jesus is Jehovah Jireh, my provider. He's the Bread of Life sent from Heaven."

"Hey, if one god is good, three hundred million have to be better."

"Jesus said I am the way, the truth, and the life; no man comes to the Father but by me."

"The weather is getting warmer. Next week try the boondi, it's good with a cool tea."

"Thanks Mr. Singh," Christian offered, leaving behind him a trove of truth.

Zwooosh

"Hello, Naomi," Christian greeted, a sweet-smelling savor entering the shop with him.

"Ah, Christian, nice to see you again. I hope the Birthday candles were a hit."

"Oh, they were perfect."

"Let me guess, you want the balsam eight-inch candle for Christmas. It is a great scent."

"You are a prophetess?" Christian said, smiling.

"Who needs a prophet? You buy one every year."

"Oh, I love the prophets, especially Micah and Isaiah's Christmas prophecies.

"Blah, blah, blah...would there be anything else?" Naomi remarked.

"Yes, the Advent candles. Each one represents..." he explained, but "blah blah blah" is what she heard. "Have a glorious Christmas, Naomi."

"Have a prosperous New Year," Naomi said, turning to inventory stock. It took a moment, as her heel got stuck in a grate. Christian paused outside to thank the Lord for everything.

"Joy to the World..." he sang, his feet barely touching the ground.

Grace Lover: But thou, Bethlehem Ephratah, though thou be little among the thousands of Judah, yet out of thee shall he come forth unto me that is to be ruler in Israel; whose goings forth have been from of old, from everlasting (Mic. 5:2).

> But blessed are your eyes, for they see: and your ears, for they hear (Matt. 13:16).

Curmudgeon: Our fathers worshipped in this mountain; and ye say, that in Jerusalem is the place where men ought to worship (John 4:20).

228. THE AWARD

Hitachi, Japan, 2019.

Six days of antibiotic failed to extirpate the beasties in my lungs. I'd have a 3-hour trip on 4 trains. Should I carry a guitar and briefcase on the buttresses of a fortress under siege? In the end, we'd be traveling companions. Arriving at Hitachi, I had 25-minutes until my meeting. In 3-minutes I had my guitar out, finger pinching music stand ready, Ethiopian Cross displayed, and voice crooning. In the next 12 minutes, I sang to 7 people. One of them clapped in passing. After I packed up, I thought I'd give my enthused audience a Gospel *manga*, but she returned with a hot tea for me. She received the Gospel graciously. "Let's meet in Heaven," I said in parting. That got a big smile.

At the pastors' meeting, I had a moment's silence to recall the life of missionary Paul Overland. As I closed, I presented my tea gift to Baba Sensei, the chairperson, entitling it: The Train Station Evangelism Award. The Japanese, not usually a crowd to grasp my humor, applauded without provocation or bribe. That night, the family was to reconnoiter at another station. While waiting, I set up and sang. Three high schoolers stopped for a song and a Gospel manga. I got a "thank you." My parting shot, our eyes meeting, was: "God is love." Again, I was awarded smiles. I carried a guitar to sing to 10 people! Good thing I didn't rent an auditorium. Could I have better spent my time? I'll take the tea and smiles, and trust God for results. That was my best tea, ever, and I didn't even drink it!

Grace Lover: Ask of me, and I shall give thee the heathen for thine inheritance, and the uttermost parts of the earth for thy possession (Ps. 2:8).

> And Jesus took the loaves; and when he had given thanks, he distributed to the disciples, and the disciples to them that were set down; and likewise of the fishes as much as they would (John 6:11).

Curmudgeon: And whosoever was not found written in the book of life was cast into the lake of fire (Rev. 20:15).

229. MURPHY'S LAW

What's your favorite law of the fabled Murphy? Mine is: "The probability a falling dish of butter will hit the carpet face down rises proportionally to the price of the carpet." I had no carpets or butter, but researched its claims on other's floor coverings. One experiment was in Cambodia. It was raining. In Cambodia, it is raining or so hot as to rival sunspots. A donor country had just completed a bridge across the Mekong. What had been a single road was now 4 lanes of merging mayhem. Have you seen cattle herds? They do it better. There were no streetlights, but bumps and pot-holes were generously represented. Every decent driver blocked line-jumpers. A student of culture, I closed in on the car in front. "Don't hit the Lexus," I said aloud to 3 witnesses, all of whom, for once, were awake and listening. Not one to tarry, I hit it within 5-minutes. Why wasn't it a Toyota, an old Toyota? The other driver and I got out to inspect my handiwork.

One day in Tokyo, I braked suddenly. Yuko said: "Don't hit the Porsche." It took us down a bumpy Memory Lane.

Back to the Lexus, our office manager, Kaleum, said a foreigner hit his cousin's car. Being a civil servant, the government paid half of the car's cost. As a result, Phnom Penh has the highest per capita Lexus numbers in the world. Fortunately, the car had no damage. I confessed I was the culprit, and our chat moved on. I forgot about it until braking for a Porsche. Besides monsoons or blistering heat, what do we get from this tale? Any titles? How about *A Crash Course, Discovered, or Lexus Revisited.*

Grace Lover: Verily I say unto you, Inasmuch as ye have done it unto one of the least of these my brethren, ye have done it unto me (Matt. 25:40).

Curmudgeon: But if ye will not do so, behold, ye have sinned against the LORD: and be sure your sin will find you out (Num. 32:23).

> Therefore whatsoever ye have spoken in darkness shall be heard in the light; and that which ye have spoken in the ear in closets shall be proclaimed upon the housetops (Luke 12:3).

230. WIZARDS N' STUFF

Dowling College, N.Y., '68.

"Existentialism is beating the scabs off your dog!" my friend offered, illustrating the themes of Sartre and Camus. He was a Jewish nihilist. I hadn't a clue, but it sounded disrespectful, so I liked it. Ignorance is bliss, and I was riding high on a 1. 5 GPA. Herman, our Irish sage, regaled us with ribald tales of the sensual disciplines. He had a Firebird, a thing of beauty and expense. His humour was also expensive—ask Dr. Chang, whom he parodied. I couldn't laugh at her pronunciation. *Deoxyribonucleic* didn't slide off my tongue without a fumble for the first few plays. Anthropology had its enigmas, too, though I embraced my professor's disdain for missionaries covering up indigenous women's nakedness. My first paper was about Navaho shamanism. The topic seemed unscientific and superstitious. but those aspects didn't disqualify it from the status of *real* (Deut. 18, and I Sam. 28). It was nasty, predominantly curses and the manipulation of spirits. Sprites and Muses found a happy haven in my Romanticism, but a spiritual realm of negativity was unappealing, and therefore untrue. Yes, the ivory tower of Academia loomed many floors over my head.

I've researched wizards and deities in folk tales. Spirits or gods can be entreated or manipulated, but benefices cost. In modern literature we have the *Reluctant Hero*, in classic tales—the Reluctant gods. The overriding theme is *there is no free lunch*. The Ogre of the Bridge demands a riddle or a pound of flesh. The mountaintop seer gives wisdom in a conundrum. Those with the stuff are Scrooges. What a contrast to God in Psalm 40, a savior and advocate. I've naively entrusted my intellect and soul to people who taught destructive, joyless, unsupportable theories. We have a planned Creation, the Word confirmed by people of character, and fulfilled prophecy. The tender-hearted One paid your entrance fee with His own blood. Don't destroy yourself trying to pay the Ogre of the Bridge of Man's Wisdom. The grade is too steep, the span too wide. Jesus is the way!

Grace Lover: The Lord appeared to us in the past, saying: "I have loved you with an everlasting love; I have drawn you with unfailing kindness" (Jer. 31:3).

The Machida Church Family, 2020.

231. JACOB KARANJA

Tamagawa Gakuen Mae, Tokyo, 1992.

He looked at me as he passed, backed up, and looked again.

"Are you a Christian?" he asked.

"Yes, I am," I told him.

We exchanged names and histories. He was of the Kikuyu Tribe, from Kigoro, Kenya, was single, passionate about God, and new in Japan. He wanted to sing, but knew no Japanese. I suggested he pray, and I sing. Later, we went out to eat. In the days to come, he wanted to take Machida for God. I recommended a team, fund-raising, and an information campaign. He said let's fast and pray. He easily trusted God, but I was educated and had a bank account. One Sunday, Jacob preached at a large house-church. I translated. English was Jacob's fourth language; Japanese was my third. It was a recipe for incoherence a la Japfrica. Folks knew we talked about the Lord. Other than that, I make no claims. The last adventure was at the airport. He had an economy ticket with At Your Own Risk Airlines, and four suitcases of clothes for his village. As he needed hundreds of dollars for them, alas, their end was the dumpster. Since then, he has planted several churches in Kenya. Before I met him, I thought I was in high gear spiritually, then Jacob showed me a seventh gear!

Grace Lover: Then he answered and spake unto me, saying, This is the word of the Lord unto Zerubbabel, saying, Not by might, nor by power, but by my spirit, saith the Lord of hosts (Zech. 4:5).

> And let us consider one another to provoke unto love and to good works (Heb. 10:24).

> Hearken, my beloved brethren, Hath not God chosen the poor of this world rich in faith, and heirs of the kingdom which he hath promised to them that love him (Jas. 2:5).

232. DREAM KISS

Phnom Penh, 1/16/2023.

Darien was 14. She was the first girl I kissed, really kissed. I walked in a dream for weeks, but a personal postcard sacked future kisses. The game scorecard read: one completed pass, Wilkins, game ending interception, Mom!

Today held another dream kiss. Yuko and I are in Cambodia. We just had covid. We've been in 4 hotels in as many days, with 3 rendezvous a day. The regimen has left me a little flattened. Before rising today, my thoughts raced, and my stomach felt like I'd drunk a half-dozen demitasse. The Lord suggested I think on Him. I often nap when I pray; today followed the norm. Before reaching Nod, I meditated on the Lord's Prayer. turning it over in my mind. *Father* and phrases like *hallowed be Thy name,* took on depth. The Four Beings at the throne proclaimed praises. *Thy Kingdom come* pictured Jehovah *Tsidkenu*, the Lord Jesus, returning on a white horse with ten-thousands of His saints. To conclude, I saw myself in the Lord's presence. I knelt and placed my cheek on His hand. Embracing His calves, I kissed His feet. I claim no vision, but enjoyed a lovely moment with the Lord.

Days later, in Thailand, I went parasailing. Takeoff was easy, but I was nervous about re-entry. "I've got your feet, Lord," I prayed. That said, I felt feet on my shoulders. WOW! "Lord, is that You?" I thought, turning to look behind me. Sadly, it wasn't a spiritual experience. Unbeknownst to me, one of the crew jumped on the parachute to insure a safe landing. Regardless, it was a reminder He is there when I hold on to Him!

Grace Lover: For thou hast delivered my soul from death: wilt not thou deliver my feet from falling, that I may walk before God in the light of the living (Ps. 56:13)?

Curmudgeon: Kiss the Son, lest he be angry, and ye perish from the way, when his wrath is kindled but a little. Blessed are all they that put their trust in him (Ps. 2:12).

> But Jesus said unto him, Judas, betrayest thou the Son of man with a kiss (Luke 22:48)?

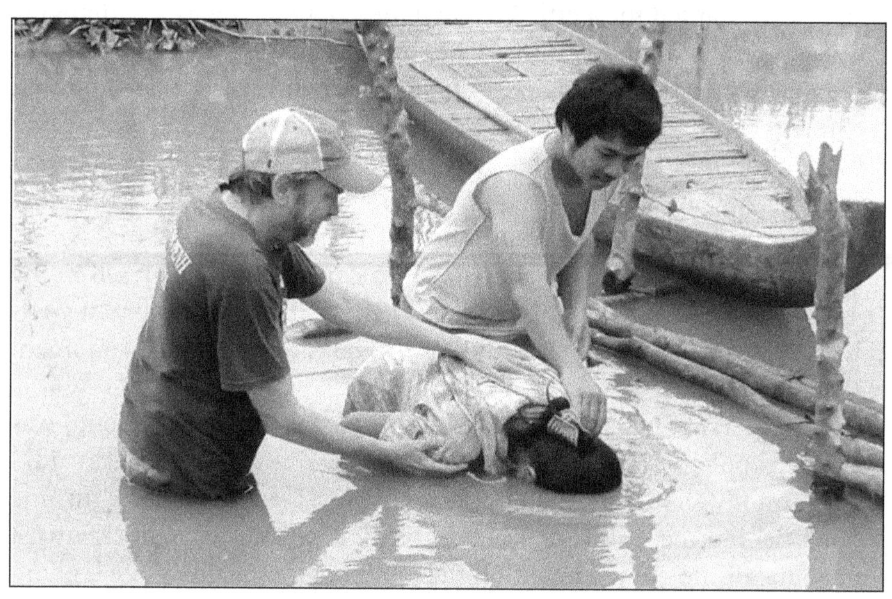

Baptizing saints with Pastor Thy Venn, Village 95, Cambodia, 2014.

233. LDM: THE CHARIOT ROOM

"Wow! Dah awchah!" Thy Venn said, marveling.

"Sugoi!" Hiro said. "We didn't have those in my country."

"We had elephants," Thy Venn shared.

"Cool," Eliakim exuded, "so did we, in Ethiopia!"

"Hello," an elderly arriver, said, "I'm your Host."

"Bible characters for $500.00," Wilson joked.

"King Solomon had 1,000 chariots, are you he?" Blong asked.

"It was 1400 but sorry, no," the Elder answered.

"Are you King Ahab?" Eliakim asked reluctantly.

"I was called: The Troubler of Israel,"

"Elijah. You're Elijah," Fung Chil erupted.

"Right you are, Fung Chil," the prophet said.

"Hey, how did you know my name?" Fung Chil asked.

"I won't say who is coming," Elijah said. "Sau Fan likes surprises."

"How did he know that?" Sau Fan asked herself.

"I'm Sunburn," the guest said. He had a steely demeanor and a burn.

"Will you show us your chariot, Sir?" Thy Venn asked.

"Sunburn has shown you already," Elijah said.

"What? I didn't see it anywhere," Thy Venn replied.

"Well, this is he," Elijah concluded.

"Top prize surprise," Sau Fan said. They then took a ride, Sunburn sporting flames that would make Hot-Wheels jealous.

"Who'd have thought Elijah's chariot was…" Thy Venn began.

"…better than an elephant?" Hiro concluded.

Grace Lover: Are they not all ministering spirits, sent forth to minister for them who shall be heirs of salvation (Heb. 1:14).

Curmudgeon: Now the serpent was more subtil than any beast of the field which the LORD God had made. And he said unto the woman, Yea, hath God said, Ye shall not eat of every tree of the garden (Gen. 3:1)?

234. CANNED: THE SUMMER OF '69

August, '69.

Black and big, Eugene had hands like plates, and a smile that circumnavigated his face. He was the sweetest man I'd ever met. Usually, I read *Lord of the Rings* during break, but when Sol was 90-degrees to terra firma, we sought libations to make terra less firm. Eugene would ask: "Mr. Chris, you gonna get Bali Hai, t'day?" He always got the affirmative. We were the Pinelawn National Cemetery Groundskeeping Team. Many interred were Black, posthumous receivers of the Purple Heart. We had a diverse crew. John, a Vietnam vet who'd lost a lung, was on a mission to out-drink us. Bob, also a vet, married a girl I'd wanted to date. He wasn't faithful. Paul and Tracy were fellow alumni of the W.B. Class of '68, diminutive in stature but gifted in the tall tale. Then there was Carmine, with prostate trouble, who needed 2 stops a day at the lavatory. Thereafter, I considered getting old quickly. Our field leader, John, was a Polish workhorse. Our senior citizen was a lanky Italian, Angelo. He was tanned on the outside, gold on the inside. He once stopped on the road to give his spare tire to someone. Bill, our boss, was normal and lacklustre. We were an interesting bag of mixed nuts.

I got educated that summer. A "No thanks," when invited to Happy Hour, will leave you happier and with fewer headaches. Also, recollections are often linked to hyperbole. Another observation is, sadly, infidelity pops up anywhere. There were positives, too. My bosses were diligent men with an unruly crew. I got close to those guys; we were all lost together. It was my first experience of life. I had the strength, presumption, and ignorance of youth. When our season finished, I gave up the drink for a day, and tied some cans to our van's bumper. I didn't get to hear those cans sing. I was canned instead. I didn't know it, but the Lord was working behind the scenes, contrasting the World and His Kingdom. That difference became more apparent as I strayed further from faith. A final lesson was: don't pull a stunt in front of the superintendent's window. Even more important: Neither is there any creature that is not manifest in his sight: but all things are naked and opened unto the eyes of him with whom we have to do (Heb. 4:13).

Curmudgeon: Then Peter said unto her, How is it that ye have agreed together to tempt the Spirit of the Lord? behold, the feet of them which have buried thy husband are at the door, and shall carry thee out (Acts 5:9).

235. TRANSGENDER FRIENDS

They were brothers, Black, and Transgender people. They were more popular at work than drug dealers. One, Herman, was my boss. He was always positive, and didn't criticize my long hair, patched bell bottoms, or lack of musculature. I liked him.

Transgender Friend, in my early twenties, my buddy and I would toast our deaths: "Twenty-three!" I was destructive and had all the answers. It wasn't a good time to make life affecting decisions. You are in a similar situation. We're being manipulated. The codewords used to be *Wall Street, or The Establishment*. Now they are *The Media*. As for your issue, the verdict is out on everything except our use of technology before society catches up. People are making judgments and legislation without a clue. They tell half a story. What do puberty blockers do to one's health? Some girls can't bear children. What are other physical and psychological effects of using hormones in the long term? What percentage of those who have had surgery would reverse it—if they could? Should children be able to decide? Most studies point to negative results, though to say so is to risk being labeled transphobic. You may not care about any of this. Maybe you're tipping your glass and saying "Twenty-three." I didn't destroy myself. I discovered at twenty-two I was loved, really loved. It was difficult to choose Christ. I liked living on the edge, and in my estimation, being morally superior. But the truth kept haunting me. God's love changed me. Please think about that. He says you are wonderfully made (Ps. 139:14), made in His image (Gen. 1:27), and He has loved you with an everlasting love (Jer. 31:3). What do your champions want? Politicians vie for your vote, and recognition. Medical Associations profit from your surgeries and counseling sessions. Drug companies profit from your medications, and the Media sell copy with controversial headlines. Choose Jesus, Friend. He allowed Himself to be manipulated for your sake. Others will manipulate you for their sake. Please see: sexchangeregret.com for Walt Heyer's story.

> And ye are complete in him, which is the head of all principality and power (Col. 2:10).

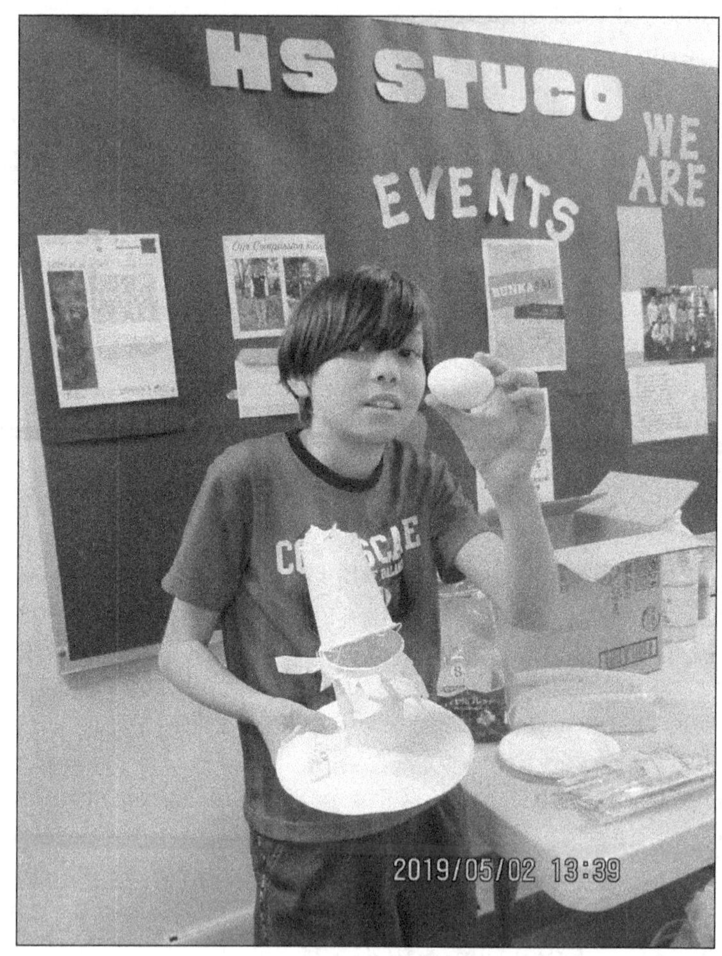

Corey versus gravity.

236. THE DROP

Christian Academy Japan, 2019.

I could see a youth lingering in the shadows. His gaze was upward; I followed it. A man on the third floor was leaning over the balcony. Suspended from his extendable arm was a parcel. A thud signaled the drop was made. The lad ran to the packet. My heart went with him. What appeared illegal was not. The protagonist was my eleven-year-old, Corey. First, he pulled off the ring used to suspend the package. He then tore the tape. It gave way to his persuasion; the tube opened. He extracted the shredded paper liner. At last, he had it, the prize! His experiment had been a success. !!!DEVIVRUS GGE EHT Corey had gathered materials, researched previous attempts, consulted others, ignored his dad, designed his egg case, did a test experiment, and was successful. His prize was an egg sandwich!

Missions have become intentional in recent years, having goals, specific prayer, strategies, and accountability—real discipleship. In war, you need a cause and strategy. What's your next plan? Rear echelon sniping? Jousting windmills? No, none of that for you. The Lord called Gideon, a complete novice to warfare, a "great man of valor" (Judges 6:11-12). How will He lead you—a surveillance mission? Infiltration? Full-on attack? Get your strategy in prayer. Next, grab your ordnance (a heart of love), your sword (sword of the Spirit), and then, CHARGE!

Grace Lover: I made haste, and delayed not to keep thy commandments (Ps. 119:60).

Curmudgeon: And whosoever doth not bear his cross, and come after me, cannot be my disciple. [31] Or what king, going to make war against another king, sitteth not down first, and consulteth whether he be able with ten thousand to meet him that cometh against him with twenty thousand? [33] So likewise, whosoever he be of you that forsaketh not all that he hath, he cannot be my disciple. (Luke 14:27,31,33).

P.S. Speaking of great men of valor, Corey is a counselor this summer for two sessions of summer camp!

237. SIDEWALK CRESCENTS

Higashi Murayama, Japan, 2023.

Emiko and Hisao are very generous folks. Emiko was on the receiving end when Lindsay, one of our evangelism team, gave her a Christmas tract. She met us again when we were boarding a train. It turned out we all disembarked at the same stop, and from there, a deepening relationship, including English lessons, Bible studies, and complimentary, all you can eat dinners, unfolded. More interesting than all this build-up, however, is that Emiko has stated on two occasions she is seeking for purpose in her life.

Can I mix two stories? You may as well assent because it is going to happen. Say what you will about New York, its state tree is the maple. Not too shabby. I have always enjoyed spring leaves because, in their thin newness, they allow light to play with them more than their older selves. We had an eclipse during springtime when I was in seminary, in Kentucky. Those new, thin leaves provided lenses for a phenomenon playing out in the heavens. The result was countless sidewalk crescents. It was mystical, surreal, okay; it was astronomy, but very cool. New, ethereal, powerless entities were reflecting an event of players far distant and transcendent by comparison. Are you catching a ray of theme from above? God has a purpose for Emiko, Hisao, me and YOU! We can be His reflectors. Forgiveness is fantastic. Beyond that, He aspires to form us in the image of His son, just as the son reflects the glory of the Father.

Grace Lover: For whom he did foreknow, he also did predestinate to be conformed to the image of his Son, that he might be the firstborn among many brethren (Ro. 8:29).

> And as we have borne the image of the earthy, we shall also bear the image of the heavenly, (I Cor. 15:49).

> But we all, with open face beholding as in a glass the glory of the Lord, are changed into the same image from glory to glory, even as by the Spirit of the Lord. II Cor. 3:18).

238. STATUARY CLAWS

"Should have done it years ago," Pastor Henry said. Growing up Black in the South, he was glad a Confederate statue was gone. This report is prompted by two men I admire, Pastor Henry and our 25th President, "Trust Buster" T. Roosevelt. Henry had no problems as a youth, but says he "knew his place." I'm glad he feels freer. Mom said: "there's two sides to a story," so, I asked Blacks of various backgrounds about the issue and got a variety of answers. The removal of Pres. Roosevelt's statue in NYC prompted this tale. My purpose isn't to ridicule, it's pointing out what C.S. Lewis called, "Chronological Snobbery," i.e., my generation is the end-all of knowledge and wisdom. The same could be done for the Religious Right or Green Peace. So, buckle up, you're entering the 22nd Century.

Headline: Toppled, 2121. The end of the Rainbow had no pot of gold, but a crash. Cow suits stormed the statue of ATOZ hero, Alexia Zach Janus, plaintiff in the Janus vs. Aliteia Case that secured rights for the ATOZ community in 2029. The statue, sporting gender symbols, required the Bovine Brigade, milch kine of the real kind, to tear it down. The road rancor began with uncovered dirt. A time capsule revealed Janus met friends at McDonalds, a Mammal Murderer a century ago. Mooers hit the streets. People's Cooperative Politicians jumped on the oxcart to Woo the Moo. Placement of security forces in M.L.K. D.C. (Martin Luther King D.C.) ended years ago, so the People had no resistance. A reporter was moo-ed, pelted with soy shakes, and told generational norms were no excuse for a lack of liberation. A stucco calf abducted from a dairy's roof, went from flying over the Moon to being painted and placed on the previous Altar of Alternative Activism. The end of the matter was the replacement of the Rainbow by a Golden Calf, an idol, to remain forever—i.e., until the next generation knows better.

Grace Lover: Thou shalt not follow a multitude to do evil; neither shalt thou speak in a cause to decline after many to wrest judgment (Ex. 23:2).

Curmudgeon: There is a way which seemeth right unto a man, but the end thereof are the ways of death (Prov. 14:12).

239. TAMPOPO

Higashi Murayama, Japan 2018.

A spot of yellow sends Yuko scrambling with the swiftness fighter pilots strive to attain. The enemy—*Tampopo!* Dandelions! She has strategically stashed trowels in combat readiness for just such a scenario. She is the Minute Man of the Manse. She loves to join the fray. Her battle cry: "Tampopo dayou! There are dandelions!" is oft repeated whilst she wildly wields her weaponry. Happily, to their good fortune, Forsythia and Daffodils, though bearing a similar hue, have ne'er been deemed trespassers. I'm inclined to feel sorry for the wayward weed, who, though its root goes deep, is not the root of evil, its only transgression being it is a flower that, with a few exceptions, no one seems to need. Okay, it displaces the lawn—not a capital offense. It's reminiscent of Falstaff's defense to young Hal: "… if to be fat is to be hated, then Pharaoh's lean kine are to be loved…" *Henry IV*, Part I, Act II, Scene 4. There is a similarity there somewhere, if you search for it. Poor thing, the dandelion; as a metaphor, it's rich, having a deep root and prolific production of seed that is propagated by no effort of itself, that being entrusted to its co-conspirator, the wind and its wiles. No wonder it's the bane of lawn care. Alas, even telling Yuko her nemesis is good in salads won't assuage her wrath or temper her vigilance.

Contrariwise, there is no doubt what kind of seed we are. We've got a bad root that displaces the *imago Dei*. The best of us is still a weed. Get the root out before the flower goes to seed. Ask the Tender of the Garden to pull it out, otherwise that taproot is your Garden's doom! Not to worry, He'll replant you, and your root will be in Him.

Grace Lover: Truly, truly, I say to you, Except a corn of wheat fall into the ground and die, it abideth alone: but if it die, it bringeth forth much fruit (John 12:24).

Curmudgeon: Cast out the scorner, and contention shall go out; yea, strife and reproach shall **cease** (Prov. 22:10).

A little leaven leaveneth the whole lump (Gal. 5:9).

240. GETTING A HANDLE ON THINGS: THE FOUR MESSENGERS

Sendai, Japan, '91.

TOTALLY WRONG? I don't usually catalogue my failures, but that day the Young Willows (Wakaiyanagi) School secretary yelled at me. Going home on my 50cc excuse of a motorcycle left me frozen. At home, my hot tea was on the sink. I turned to my roommate, Ray, and said: "What else could go wrong today?" Grabbing the cup's handle, it accompanied me, whereas the cup, that naughty cup, remained on the sink. Ray and I stared in disbelief.

The Four Messengers were the sole survivors of different tragedies, i.e., marauding Sabeans and Chaldeans, the Fire of God, and a windstorm. Three apprise Job that he's lost his stuff. The fourth, that his children are dead! What would you do? Listen to Job: "the LORD gave, and the LORD hath taken away; blessed be the name of the LORD" (Job 1:21).

Contrast this to culture icons who complain about the least offense. They replace God with vitriol. Job's best friend was his boil-scraping potsherd, not the blame game. He lamented his birth, but he'd lost all and gained pain. Hear his wife: "Dost thou still retain thine integrity? curse God, and die" (Job 2:9). I hear her whining. She uses that sophisticated psychological principle—*Twisting the Knife*. Job's friends, convinced bad things only happen to bad people, lean on the blade. Then God has some rhetorical questions for Job. Skipping details, Job is exonerated, instructed to offer sacrifices for his friends, gets double his stuff and the same number of children as before, which suggests many relatives aren't a blessing. God puts limits on our trials. To get a handle on things, put the handle in His hand.

Grace Lover: Submit yourselves therefore to God. Resist the devil, and he will flee from you (Jas. 4:7).

Curmudgeon: And the LORD said unto Satan, Hast thou considered my servant Job, that there is none like him in the earth, a perfect and an upright man, one that feareth God, and escheweth evil. And the Lord said unto Satan, Behold, he is in thine hand; but save his life (Job 1:8, 2:6).

241. IMPACT

W. Babylon, N.Y., '55.

Hardheaded best describes Harvey Beckwith. That's not nasty, it's literal. As kids will, we all promoted ourselves as the fastest, strongest, and whatever. So Harvey and I raced in opposite directions around his house. Neither of us was the fastest (sorry, only superlatives for children of 4 years). We rendezvoused at the corner to butt heads. There was laughter, but all I knew was I had to get home. I was sick to my stomach, and it wasn't because of Mrs. Beckwith's home-permanent solution. I couldn't see straight. Mom wasn't concerned, but I lay down for some time. Years later, I made two discoveries. Doctor Greenberg saw my enlarged eye ridge eye and asked if I'd had an accident. I declared: "Harvey!" I'd sustained a concussion that day. On another day, I learned that I'd been at Harvey's house because Mom was recovering from a miscarriage. She needed her own rest.

Some wounds we have for years before we know their import, others we feel immediately. In our despair, don't we discover God more deeply? We know most Bible personalities for their trials. There is no triumph without a struggle. Songwriter Andraé Crouch said it well in *Through It All*: "For if I'd never had a problem, I wouldn't know that He could solve them…"

Grace Lover: Fear thou not; for I am with thee: be not dismayed; for I am thy God: I will strengthen thee; yea, I will help thee; yea, I will uphold thee with the right hand of my righteousness (Isa. 41:10).

> For when we were yet without strength, in due time Christ died for the ungodly. (Ro. 5:6).

> Blessed be God, even the Father of our Lord Jesus Christ, the Father of mercies, and the God of all comfort; [4] Who comforteth us in all our tribulation, that we may be able to comfort them which are in any trouble, by the comfort wherewith we ourselves are comforted of God (II Cor. 1:3-4).

242. STOP SIGNS

Losing control? Not able to stop the thing that is going to derail your life? Need a sign to help you stop? I've a solution I discovered in 1969, in N.Y., though I've not come forth publicly, until now. First, you need a car with a trunk. Second, a large adjustable wrench, a Phillips, and a regular screwdriver, and last, a catalyst for unlawful behavior. This can be a chemical, literary, or a Hell-bent nature that you may or may not recognize. As for strategy, have a lookout with a phone, and find a series of dead-end streets. Back into position in front of the dead-end stop sign. A little sewing machine oil helps lubricate unyielding bolts. In 15-minutes you can have possession of 3 to 5 stop signs. Shocking, isn't it!

If this option fits you, I should mention the day of this event I skidded into a car. I had a trunk of hot stop signs. Stealing from Joe Shmoe is naughty, but the Man gets irate when you steal from him. So, inconspicuously, I dumped the signs in an empty lot minutes before the Police arrived. The result of the day's adventure was higher car insurance payments and a bad reputation. So, I was half successful in my thinking. There are alternatives to irate neighbors, the long arm of the law, and divine retribution. It's obvious I didn't heed the message of the signs before me—STOP! Is it coincidental I had an accident after an afternoon of folly? Following the Lord may not immediately end our destructive behaviors, but it will turn us in the right direction. With Him, *stopping* loses its emphasis, to be replaced by *starting*; starting a new direction, setting a new goal. A riverside picnic beats a failed heist and dented bumpers, anytime. See details below:

Grace Lover: The LORD is my shepherd; I shall not want. [2] He maketh me to lie down in green pastures: he leadeth me beside the still waters. [3] He restoreth my soul: he leadeth me in the paths of righteousness for his name's sake. [4] Yea, though I walk through the valley of the shadow of death, I will fear no evil: for thou art with me; thy rod and thy staff they comfort me. [5] Thou preparest a table before me in the presence of mine enemies: thou anointest my head with oil; my cup runneth over. [6] Surely goodness and mercy shall follow me all the days of my life: and I will dwell in the house of the LORD for ever (Ps. 23:1-6).

Curmudgeon: Surely they shall not see the land which I sware unto their fathers, neither shall any of them that provoked me see it (Num. 14:23).

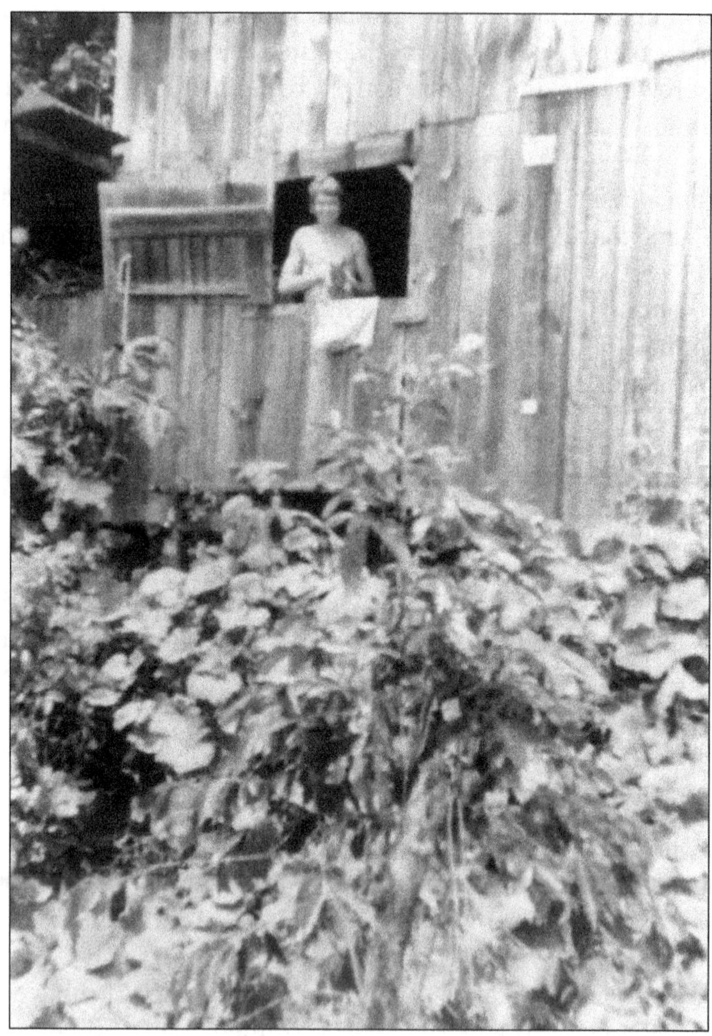

The Branch, Shechem and I, 1972.

243. SHIRLEY

Kealakekua, Hi., 1973.

The 50s and 60s had many love ballads with girls' names for titles. Another popular theme was dying young, usually in a car accident. This story involves both. Serafino, Richard, and I lived at a house called The Branch. It was a coffee house—not a café, but a house with a drying platform for coffee beans in the plantation area of Kona. We were part of the Pilgrim Fellowship, a Christian commune of assorted dropouts. We had cats, Zion, and Shechem which had a beautiful greyish blue coat. There also were the Hammonds. Bill was the steward of the house; Shirley was his wife. They had a boy, Shawn, who at four could beat me in an arm wrestle! Bill was gone occasionally and Shirley, the picture of Proverbs 31, would, while knitting, dispense wisdom to the three new converts, as simple tasks were challenges in the same league as Dancing with the Stars, or rolling Sisyphus' stone.

One day, two ladies arrived. One was pregnant, single, and angry. We shared God's love with her, but her resentment was directed at the Lord. When they left, her last words denounced Him. Days later, we heard she'd died in a car accident. Bad news did not end there. Months later, Bill and Shirley would be in an accident that would send Shirley into the arms of her Savior. We may try, but there are no words to be spoken that can make sense of such events. It's ironic that when Judah was going into captivity, Jeremiah said: "His compassions fail not, they are new every morning; great is thy faithfulness" (Lamentations 3:23). It seems God's love is the only thing that holds meaning in troubled times. It's an enigma like the Book of Job, a book of Human questions answered by Divine questions. Our questions can be answered by meditating on Him, our comfort.

Grace Lover: And the Lord, he it is that doth go before thee; he will be with thee, he will not fail thee, neither forsake thee: fear not, neither be dismayed (Deut. 31:8).

> My brethren, count it all joy when ye fall into divers temptations;[3] Knowing this, that the trying of your faith worketh patience (Jas. 1:2-3).

244. THE THIRD NAPKIN

Higashi Kurume, Japan, '18.

What a catchy title! No, this is not a murder mystery, though death is involved, and there is a mystery. Oh yes, a train also has a role—that's nostalgic! It could be a murder mystery in that someone has been killed, albeit is still walking, ignorant of the culprit's identity, or that they are a victim. Ok, enough build-up. Adam and Eve died spiritually the day they ate the forbidden fruit. In addition, they set in motion physical death. Also in scripture are the mysteries of Godliness, I Timothy 3:16, Iniquity, II Thessalonians 2:7, the Mystery of the Ages, Colossians 1:27, and others. The Mystery of Iniquity speaks of the coming of the Lawless One in the End Times, but it has an influence in every heart.

At *Misuta Donatsu* (Mister Donuts), the Lord showed His favor upon two napkins, their accompanying donuts, and the napkins' message I'd written. The beneficiaries were grateful. But… remember Judah's King Amaziah? He'd made Edom a vassal, and wanted to meet Israel's King Jehoash in battle. They did, and he got whooped! He should've quit while he was ahead. Leaving donuts behind, I grabbed a napkin—one for the rails (road). On the train, I sat by an elderly man, and offered him my donut-less napkin, with the ideographs: "*Kami ha ai de aru*" (God is love). I said it was a reminder of God's love. He took it, crumpled it, and threw it to the floor. Stop while we're ahead? That's ok for nations, but in the Kingdom, we stay in the fray. We go to battle with Him. Was my encounter a lost battle? No! The invitation was given. In the future, he may reconsider. Rejected or not, we need to bear the Good News, and the occasional donut.

Grace Lover and Curmudgeon: Because he hath appointed a day, in the which he will judge the world in righteousness by that man whom he hath ordained; whereof he hath given assurance unto all men, in that he hath raised him from the dead. [32] And when they heard of the resurrection of the dead, some mocked: and others said, We will hear thee again of this matter. [34] Howbeit certain men clave unto him, and believed: among the which was Dionysius the Areopagite, and a woman named Damaris, and others with them. (Acts 17:31-32, 34).

The Misdonians, 1997, after a successful mission!

245. MISDONIANS

Tennoji, Japan, 1996.

It started with pet bottles, nothing furry or cute, just polyethylene recyclables. Osaka had a lot of homeless. I prepared *miso* (soy bean paste) and *wakame* (seaweed) for them when winter came. Pets were the obvious choice of receptacle. Later, hard-boiled eggs joined the menu. The homeless were a solace, having fewer cultural stops in place. Thursday was the evening of choice. The crowd changed over the years, but I noticed folks bedded down in the same place every day. Otosan was part of the neighborhood in front of the bank at Tennoji Station. Once and I had to pull a razor knife out of his hand. During the War, he got hit in the neck with a round from an airplane. There was also an elderly couple that, like most folks, slept in a box. They cut a door and window into the box and pasted pictures on the inside. One fellow used to watch my bike when I went shopping. I purchased a cheap cart for him so he wouldn't have to carry everything. Another member of the community was an elderly lady with braided grey hair that reached the ground. Every day she ate hot noodles. I heard she was rich, but didn't want to live at home. One high tension event came from a family sitting under the power lines. They invited me to share their cooked veggies. Another memory is of Fujiwara-san. I used to sing on Sundays at what is now the site of the tallest building in western Japan. There were three homeless men who would get a free lunch if they met me there, and endured my crooning. Well, Fujiwara-san didn't show up for about eight months. One day he came back. He prayed for the meal and sang a couple of songs with me. That was great. Other folks, too, met the Homeless. We coordinated our distribution times, and afterwards met at Mister Donut, also called Misdo. Representatives from Canada, Japan, America, Missouri, and Sweden were there. I came up with our title: Misdonians! They were great days and folks. The '50s tunes and the angel crème donuts added to the sweetness.

Grace Lover: He that hath pity upon the poor lendeth unto the Lord; and that which he hath given will he pay him again. (Prov. 19:17).

246. MARBLED PEAS

Mark Morrison, sermon illustration, Thailand, 1/19/2023.

"Hi Willy, what are you doing today?"

"Just admiring those peas, Mr. Miller."

"How's your mom, Willy?"

"Oh, she's getting better, Mr. Miller."

"Is there something I can get you today, Willy?"

"No, Mr. Miller, I don't have any money today."

"Well, is there something you could trade?"

"All I have with me is this blue marble."

"Can I look at it."

"Sure thing, it's a beaut, my favorite!"

"Yes, indeed," Mr. Miller observed, turning it over in his palm. "Do you have a red marble at home?

"Yessir."

"I'll tell you what. Take a bag of peas and bring the red one next week.

As Willy left, Mrs. Miller explained to me that when Willy would return with a red marble in a few days, Mr. Miller would decide he didn't like it as much as a green one. So, it would get sent home with another bag of peas in anticipation of a green marble. I learned there were three poor boys that had such dealings with Mr. Miller. Years later, Mr. Miller died. At the funeral, three young men, one in a military uniform, and two in business suits, embraced Mrs. Miller, and then, one by one, passed the casket to drop something inside. They had each brought a marble.

Grace Lover: Let your light so shine before men, that they may see your good works, and glorify your Father which is in heaven (Matt. 5:16).

Curmudgeon: Wherefore then gavest not thou my money into the bank, that at my coming I might have required mine own with usury? [24] And he said unto them that stood by, Take from him the pound, and give it to him that hath ten pounds (Luke 19:23-24).

Men for Mission converging on Higashi Murayama, 2018.

247. MAKE MY DAY

Akitsu, Japan, 2019.

One-liners have long been a tool of the trade in movies. We may not have seen the movie, or even know the performer, but we know the line. I'm not an avid movie-goer, but saw enough of Clint Eastwood's *Dirty Harry* to witness the segment with "Make my day." Occasionally a phrase captures an event, a unique creation of our own experience and wit. Usually, preceding these declarations of courage or satire is a tragedy, a challenge, an altercation, or an adventure.

This adventure was at Akitsu train station. Our bags of tracts were full, as was the Valley of Decision. I sang, and the OMS Men for Mission passed out tracts—lots of tracts. It was March and still cool for my total mass of one hundred and thirty-two pounds. My co-conspirators were mighty men of valor and stature. The biggest guy, Corey, moved into the center of the street, where he could reach more people. He was on the plus side of six-foot, less than three-hundred pounds, and had a long, flaming red beard.

"These things burn in my hands," he said of the Gospel manga he held. "I've gotta hand 'em out."

I posted our picture on fb. Someone noted I was vertically challenged! How rude! When we'd been there an hour, my fingers and voice slowed. I told some junior high girls (chugakusei) God loves Chugokujin (Chinese), so the brain was slowing, too. Regardless of fumbles, the bakery gave us breadsticks! It was about this time Corey shouted out his famous one-liner:

"I've got lots of tracts left; KEEP PLAYIN' TIL THOSE FINGERS BLEED!"

It may not be in the league with "Remember the Alamo," but it inspired. We give birth to memorable sayings during memorable experiences. Faith treks are a good place to find one.

Grace Lover: Watch ye, stand fast in the faith, quit you like men, be strong (I Cor. 16:13).

248. THE CUP OF VICTORY

Grandpa only came to see us twice, once by himself, so it was great to have him. We went to a mall and did what the boys had hoped—toy shopping. Passing the supermarket, Grandpa (Jiji) stopped to get some sake. The most popular brand is called One Cup, and comes in a large, covered, drinking glass. Sake is called rice wine, but it's more like vodka. It doubles as paint remover. I have to say that my Father-in-law was respectful, and asked permission to bring sake into the house. Preferring conviction to compulsion, I allowed it, not knowing what would unfold. Corey, seven years old, saw what Jiji was doing, and came to inform me. I told him it was Jiji's choice. Upon our return home, Corey hid the sake in a closet—he always liked a game of Hide-and-Seek. Eventually, the absconded spirits were discovered, as was the reason for their going missing. Corey confessed: "Jiji acts funny when he drinks." The thirty-proof potion added *drain cleaner* to its job description. Jiji, as Baba (Grandma) attested to, never drank the stuff again, preferring his Father's new wine and his grandsons' respect. Jesus tells us the Spirit leads us in all truth (John 16:13), so we mustn't overlook the role of God in what transpired. Yuko and I thanked the Lord and were moved by the power of our child's concern. Even Yuko's Mom, an unbeliever, expressed delight how Corey's love for grandpa conquered the Cup.

Grace Lover: Behold, children are a heritage from the Lord, the fruit of the womb a reward (Ps. 127:3).

> Even a child makes himself known by his acts, by whether his conduct is pure and upright (Prov. 20:11).

Curmudgeon: But Jesus said, "Let the little children come to me and do not hinder them, for to such belongs the kingdom of heaven" (Matt. 19:14).

249. THE GREEN MONSTER

Tokyo. 2020.

If you are a baseball fan, you know about the GREEN MONSTER. It's the Boston Red Sox' Stadium's tall green wall. It's close to home plate, so it's high to lessen the advantage of its proximity. Well, I love catchy titles, but we're not going to talk about Boston. The Green Monster I have in mind is the Green Card. If you have foreign relatives seeking admission to the USA, you're painfully familiar with the Green Card. Though you may use its conventional name, you probably think of it as a monster. It isn't even green, it's white. Lately, I've been in one stage of application and approval—or disapproval, and feeling twisted out of shape by the ordeal. Today, I went to my office to get a folder for the reams of paper I've amassed to feed the Green Monster. I found one folder bearing a label secured with clear masking tape. Written on the label was a word—"HOPE." Above that were the words: "RETURN TO."

At first it was just a nostalgic reminder of the school our boys attended in Cambodia—Hope School, and a folder I'd inadvertently pilfered. But then, the folder became more than a memory; it became an encouragement—RETURN TO HOPE! It was a Providential tap on the shoulder to say: "Hey, remember me? Why worry?" I remembered Peter's letter. He talks about having a living hope. The title of this book, in part, is: "...Hope for the Heathen, the Laodicean, and other Losers." We're not talking about your everyday type of hope. Our hope is based on the Resurrection, an event immutably fixed in history, as planned by the Father. There is no undoing that kind of hope. The Resurrected Jesus is our hope. Our Hope is Jesus! Pretty wild, eh! Our hope isn't a thing, a thought, or a feeling—it's Him! That's a Hope to hold on to, Friend. Got a Green Monster in your way? RETURN TO HOPE! RETURN TO JESUS!

Grace Lover: I have set the Lord always before me: because he is at my right hand, I shall not be moved. 9 Therefore my heart is glad, and my glory rejoiceth: my flesh also shall rest in hope (Ps. 16:8-9).

> Blessed be the God and Father of our Lord Jesus Christ, which according to his abundant mercy hath begotten us again unto a lively hope by the resurrection of Jesus Christ from the dead (I Pet. 1:3).

Curmudgeon: And if Christ be not raised, your faith is vain; ye are yet in your sins. (I Cor. 15:17).

Visiting the Boat People, 2005.

250. WALK THE PLANK

Kampong Cham, Cambodia, 2006.

"My name is Sithan, not Satan!" he joked, his smile filling the room. He was my Khmer language teacher and friend, and the Bible League leader for Kampong Cham Province, going to fifteen villages in all weather, on an old motorcycle. We discussed sharing the Gospel with the Vietnamese Boat People. He got us free tracts, albeit some were worm fodder. He became ill, entrusting his family to me before entering the Lord's presence. I carried on solo. It was fortunate I was not an outstanding student. Knowing I was going to visit the Boat People, some young Cambodians made a rude remark I didn't completely understand. As I went, I was armed with Vietnamese and Khmer (Cambodian) tracts. Planks connected the boats to the shore. Algae covered the first one I stepped on. It was very slippery. Fortunately, a young girl helped me. So, I got to walk the plank and stay dry! Inside, she was hesitant to answer whether she was Vietnamese or Cambodian. I realized there were issues about ethnicity, so I gave her one tract of each, and I received a cup of Vietnamese coffee.

I had the chance that day to share, with her Vietnamese grandfather, the first chapter of Mark's Gospel in Khmer. I made more trips, sometimes mistaking whom I'd visited, as the water rose and the scenery changed. I also found a good cup of coffee. That narrow plank was a wide blessing.

Grace Lover: And if a stranger sojourn with thee in your land, ye shall not vex him (Lev. 19:33).

> Go ye therefore, and teach all nations, baptizing them in the name of the Father, and of the Son, and of the Holy Ghost: [20] Teaching them to observe all things whatsoever I have commanded you: and, lo, I am with you always, even unto the end of the world. Amen (Matt. 28:19-20).

Curmudgeon: And the LORD said, Behold, the people is one, and they have all one language; and this they begin to do: and now nothing will be restrained from them, which they have imagined to do (Gen 11:6).

251. HOMER SIMPSON

Kampong Cham, Cambodia, '05.

We had 3 DVD titles: *Barney the Dinosaur, The Pie Wars: Vegie Tales, and Homer Simpson: Season #109.* I once had ambitions of being a paleontologist, but thanks to Barney, I'm ready to assure the extinction of any dinosaur I encounter, regardless if it's purple, loves me, or wants to be family! As for *Pie Wars*, Caleb, then an infant, would erupt into staccato "ech, ech, ech," whenever he espied a tomato. Remember Bob the Tomato? "If…you…like…to…talk…to…tomatoes," I can sing it in three languages, backwards, or standing on my head. And then there is Homer. He was my therapy. Turning your neighborhood into a cobalt blue radiation belt that rids you of exacerbating neighbors, held more than subliminal attraction. One furlough, my friend Jim, also a Homerian, had a new gismo in his car. Push a button, and Homer complains about the old toad in front of him. Push it again, and he's complaining about the pain in the Aston Martin speeding behind him. It was primo Homer—egocentric. The preface to every complaint was a vacillating: "Oooooh, and then a "why…?" We laugh because it's the *other guy*.

One positive of old age pains is that at bedtime, if one finds a comfortable position, it's thanks time. Lately, upon getting the comforter aligned and pillow beaten to my desired thickness, I take a breath, and praise the Lord with a: "Ooh, that's nice." It's great to extend the practice to good times during the day. For the spiritual, I've heard of a sacrifice of praise (Heb. 13:15), e.g., your boss frowns when the colleague you offered to pick up made you late. I know it isn't curmudgeonly, but I hope our "Oooohs" and "Whys?" become "Ooh, that's nice."

Grace Lover: I will bless the Lord at all times: his praise shall continually be in my mouth. [2] My soul shall make her boast in the Lord: the humble shall hear thereof, and be glad. [3] O magnify the Lord with me, and let us exalt his name together. [4] I sought the Lord, and he heard me, and delivered me from all my fears (Ps. 34:1-4).

Curmudgeon: It is better to dwell in a corner of the housetop, than with a brawling woman in a wide house (Prov. 21:9).

252. THE TREE OF STRIFE

December 25th, '58, W. Babylon., N.Y.

I was in the Redwood Forest and thought, this tree was here when Jesus walked in Galilee! We have a link with trees. They provide homes, heat, and air. We'd be dead without trees, but at times they are to be avoided. Such a tree was in my home. It was 15' high, translucent, and visible 1-month a year. It had no leaves, but had abundant fruit in a variety of colors and flavors. Some folks call the fruit gumdrops. In my 8th year, on Christmas morn, I saw this tree. No one posted prohibitions, so I partook thereof—a purple one. As the household stirred, I mentioned my good fortune. To my surprise, I was ineligible for Communion for 3-hours. I went to late Mass with Grandpa. He left the house on Sundays, but it's probable he didn't go to church. He was not jubilant. The appeal of the exotic almost ruined Christmas, but my parents stayed true to principle, and Grandpa heard a sermon. My teeth are the better for it, and to this day I give a wide sweep to short trees and candy dishes.

No one remembers that day. Two trees tower over my 15-inch replica, The Tree of the Knowledge of Good and Evil, and The Tree of Life. The former we don't see after Man's debut goes afoul in Genesis 3. The Tree of Life is different. Its fruit is to be eaten in the future. An angel bearing a flaming sword prohibits this Tree suffering the same calamity as the other. It sounds harsh, but this measure kept the Human Family from eating it, and being locked into sin for eternity. It awaits the Redeemed and the appropriate time. It would've been nice if the Tree of Strife and purple gumdrops had been put out of view of eight-year-old eyes. I'm delighted, however, God, in His foresight, kept the Tree of Life at bay, so we could enjoy it on the Last Day.

Grace Lover: He that hath an ear, let him hear what the Spirit saith unto the churches; To him that overcometh will I give to eat of the tree of life, which is in the midst of the paradise of God (Rev. 2:7).

> In the midst of the street of it, and on either side of the river, was there the tree of life, which bare twelve manner of fruits, and yielded her fruit every month: and the leaves of the tree were for the healing of the nations (Rev. 22:2).

253. THE YELLOW SHARD

Higashi Murayama, Japan, 2019.

The old comic strip, Blondie, was a great illustration of the gender divide. In one adventure, she returns from yet another shopping spree, to enter the presence of her husband, Dagwood, with a trove of treasures. The very name Dagwood suggests that nothing in the artist's creation approximates reality, and so it is on this day. Blondie may be the protagonist, but Dagwood is at least the Reluctant, if not the Tragic Hero. At the sight of his further indebtedness, his jaw drops so wide as to approach his shoe size. Unaware of her husband's apoplexy, the heroine of the Bonanza Blitz heralds her own victory:

"Look how much money I saved! Everything was forty percent off!"

I recently recounted this to Yuko, when she disclosed her own version of Blondie Economics. Tohoku (Northern Japan) experienced a tsunami in March 2011. Thousands died, and the wave devastated a large area. After the tragedy, Sue Takamoto, a missionary from the USA, started a project for widows in the area. They rebuilt their lives by reclaiming pieces of broken pottery to make jewelry. The enterprise was quite successful, given in part to Yuko's singular efforts to purchase one item of every shape and color. The other day, she almost lost an earring because the post clasp had been derelict in its duty, and is AWOL to this day. Yuko wrote the folks at Nozomi (Hope) about procuring new post fasteners, and was told they were not an item for sale, but with another purchase, a few extra fasteners could be added. I doubt there was as much rejoicing over the discovery of the proverbial Lost Coin. Aren't we fortunate, a month earlier, she found another jewelry box to store these additions!

To close in on the actual story, we live in a row of homes at the OMS Mission Station. It has only one portal to the outside world, so there is no traffic. I have walked that short street for years, but until last year I'd never noticed the treasure of our title—the Yellow Shard. It reminds me of a couple of verses, "For now we see through a glass darkly" (I Cor. 13:12), and James 1:23-24: For if any be a hearer of the word, and not a doer, he is like unto a man beholding his natural face in a glass: 24 For he beholdeth himself, and goeth his way, and straightway forgetteth what manner of man he was.

For me, the Yellow Shard is like revelation. Revelation has two classes, Bike Revelation and Cloud Revelation. The first stays with you, like riding a bike. You don't fall off once you're in the know. The other, Cloud Revelation, provides an *AHA* moment, and then retreats or fades until, to your amazement, you re-discover it. I've seen the yellow remnant of some pottery piece embedded in the road, on only two occasions, even though I've had several expeditions to confirm its coordinates.

All of us, have these two operations in our life. Sometimes, He opens up something new in our routine. Other times, He puts us on a bookshelf for no apparent purpose. Corrie Ten Boom was forty-seven at the outbreak of WWII. She was a shy assistant to the clock meister, who never had been anywhere. After imprisonment in concentration camps, for hiding Jews, she traveled the world to share His reconciliation. Her sister, Bessie, died in Ravensbruck. The Lord put one piece of jewelry in a traveling art exhibition and stuck the other in His pocket.

Shards owe their character, their form, to difficulty. Shardness is preceded by something that stretches us, at least, and in extreme cases, breaks us. Contrary to the world, in the Kingdom, that condition increases their lustre as His plan and purpose fill their facets. At other times, we are the shard of His pleasure, of His Rejoicing, in the shadows for a season. Whether we are a revealed shard, or a hidden shard, it's all according to His direction. Either way, we testify of His glory, plan, and provision. Enjoy whatever new direction He reveals. Be His light on a hill. If you are sidelined, endure with hope and patience your anonymity. We sometimes shine our brightest in the shadows. Wherever you are, on a hilltop or in the shadows, Shine on Shard!

Grace Lover: It is the glory of God to conceal a thing: but the honour of kings is to search out a matter (Prov. 25:2).

> Behold, I will do a new thing; now it shall spring forth; shall ye not know it? I will even make a way in the wilderness, and rivers in the desert (Isa. 43:19).
>
> In your patience possess ye your souls (Luke 21;19).

Curmudgeon: And Jeremiah commanded Baruch, saying, I am shut up; I cannot go into the house of the Lord (Jer. 36:25).

254. BUBBLES

32 A.D., the Sheepgate, Jerusalem.

Bubbles are the things of fantasy, fun, and happy memories! The word for *Bubble* in Japanese is *shabon*. The English, for me, elicits thoughts of playtime with toddlers. The Japanese, not only sounds French, but evokes thoughts of a hot tub and frothing body soap! Theology rarely comes to mind when one thinks of Bubbles. For many, however, the Bubble Principle is their only doctrine. Jesus entered Jerusalem by the pool near Bethesda of the five porches. It sounds lovely, but the place was crowded with the poor and infirm. One fellow, lame for 38-years, lay there.

"Would you like to be healed?" Jesus asked.

"I have no man to put me in the waters when they are troubled," he said. There was a belief one could be healed when the waters were agitated. The man waited for the water to be stirred, but no man would help him. There are two messages here. One, no man is going to fix your deepest need, and second, the traditional or latest approaches are not the answer either.

The man didn't answer the question. We have reasons for our liabilities. God asks us a simple, closed question: "Would you be healed?" The answer is "Yes" or "No." Don't mucky up the waters. The man had excuses, but no thanks, praise, or prayer—only hope in bubbles. Toss out the Bubble Principle—making excuses for what isn't right in your life, and waiting for the wrong things to change your circumstances or heart. Jesus asks: "would you be healed?" What do you say to Him? Most folks ignore their true condition or Who can help them. The lame man knew he was in need, but when his cure came, he didn't recognize Him. Friend, don't chase bubbles—they are empty excuses and hopes. Follow Him!

Grace Lover: I am that bread of life—6:48, I am the light of the world: he that followeth me shall not walk in darkness, but shall have the light of life—8:12, Verily, verily, I say unto you, Before Abraham was I am—8:58, I am the good shepherd: the good shepherd giveth his life for the sheep—10:11, Jesus said unto her, I am the resurrection, and the life: he that believeth in me, though he were dead, yet shall he live—11:25, I am the way the truth and the life—14:6, I am the true vine, and my Father is the husbandman (John 6:48, 8:12, 58, 10:11, 11:25,14:6, 15:1).

255. THE MEANING OF MASUKO

1998, Fukushima, Japan.

I walked into the hospital with a full head of hair. When I came out, I was nearly bald. My girlfriend, Masuko, was losing hair to chemotherapy, and I hoped to raise her spirits by lowering my ears. I was teaching at a girls' college in Osaka. On Friday nights, I'd jump on the Yakkou Bus (overnight), watch a movie, and wake up about 5:30 A.M. at my destination. Sunday night I'd reverse the itinerary. At night in the hospital, I slept in a chair. In the evening, I'd read Romans Chapter 8—her favorite. Verse twenty-eight was her first pick.

"And we know that all things work together for good to them that love God, to them who are the called according to his purpose."

Romans 8 is popular, so I didn't marvel it was special to Masuko. I discovered the reason over twenty years later. Soon, my visits ended; Masuko moved to her Father's home. Before she left, she asked me to pray for her parents' salvation. Unfortunately, I misplaced their address, and couldn't keep in touch. Decades later, while walking our dog, Rosey, I asked the Lord to send them someone if I couldn't fulfill my promise. That week, I received a call from Masuko's mom. The next week I sent a letter and a Bible. Months later, we chatted again. I mentioned I'd read Romans 8, especially verse 28, to Masuko at night. It was then I learned why she loved the verse. An ideograph in Masuko's name is pronounced *eki* when used by itself, and *masu* when in a compound. The former means *good* and the latter, *increase*. So, the ideograph of her name was imbedded in that message in Romans 8:28. It was her personalized verse. I was so moved. The next day, at the doctor's office, I told another patient Masuko's story. She enjoyed the "Meaning of Masuko." I hope you did, too. We really find our meaning, our purpose, in His Word. Some of us even find our name.

Grace Lover: There is therefore now no condemnation to them which are in Christ Jesus, who walk not after the flesh, but after the Spirit. [37] Nay, in all these things we are more than conquerors through him that loved us (Ro. 8:1,37).

256. A LITANY OF GRIEVANCES

Athens, Greece, 410 B.C.

Where would we be without Boswell, Eusebius, and Herodotus? We'd know little of Samuel Johnson, Constantine, and the Trojan War. We're fortunate Plato's *The Republic* opens with Socrates returning from Athena's festival.

Cephalus: "Come more often. The more the pleasures of the body fade, the more I desire conversation."

Socrates: "You're at what poets call the *threshold*; further down the road we all travel. Is it a steep road or a gentle journey?"

Cephalus: "Old people recall sex and drink, and complain as if they've suffered great loss. I feel they're wrong to blame old age."

Socrates: "What do you mean?"

Cephalus: "Sophocles was asked if he could still make love to a woman. His response was, 'No, I'm released from that.' Character is important. For the content, old age is a slight burden. For those without character, old age and youth are difficult."

Socrates: "Some say finding old age a slight burden is because the rich have many consolations. I like what General Themistocles said. He told about a man from Seriphos who spoke disparagingly of the General's reputation, saying if he weren't born in Athens, he'd not be famous. Themistocles replied that were he, himself, born in Seriphos he'd not be famous, but likewise, were the man of Seriphos born in Athens, neither would he be famous. Old age is the same. The poor of good character may not find old age easy, but neither will the rich man of low character."

Bette Davis said: "Getting old ain't for sissies!" Another comment is: "He died well." Today's topic has inspired zillions of sayings. Hear the Word:

Grace Lover: These things have I written unto you that believe on the name of the Son of God; that ye may know that ye have eternal life, and that ye may believe on the name of the Son of God (I John 5:13).

257. KAMIKAZE

2013 Kyushu, Japan.

The Mongols attacked Japan in 1274 and 1281. Typhoons, called Kamikaze (Wind of God), decimated their force. During WWII, men came to Kyushu for Kamikaze training. Makihiro, a teenager, joined, but the conflict ended. His niece, my wife, Yuko, tells more:

Please keep pray for my Uncle. I tried to shear the Gospel but he stopped me and He said "It is good to have some faith for our life. but for me when I was young I grown up with worship The emperor. Many of my friends died for the emperor during World War II. After finished war The Emperor became human but when I(my uncle) remember my friend who died for the emperor.... to believe in Christianity is too difficult... I still have hope for him untill last minutes before he will die. Tonight I will stay at Hospital with my uncle. I want to try to share again when he has consciousness. Please pray for my uncle and me. I really hesitate. because he already stoped me once. Thank you.

A day later, it was Yuko's turn again. Takako, Makihiro's daughter, was also there. At one point, Yuko's uncle smacked his forehead.

"You have a headache?" Takako asked. He smacked his head again.

"Do you want to get baptized?" Yuko asked. He nodded, pointing behind them. They turned but saw nothing. The scenario was repeated.

"Jesus is behind you," he said faintly. Yuko baptized him. He went home to Jesus that night. Jude talks about *just made it* experiences: And others save with fear, pulling them out of the fire; hating even the garment spotted by the flesh (Jude 1:23). Luke and Yuko tell of last moment reprieves, but why wait?

Grace Lover: And he said unto Jesus, Lord, remember me when thou comest into thy kingdom. [43] And Jesus said unto him, Verily I say unto thee, Today shalt thou be with me in paradise (Luke 23:42-43).

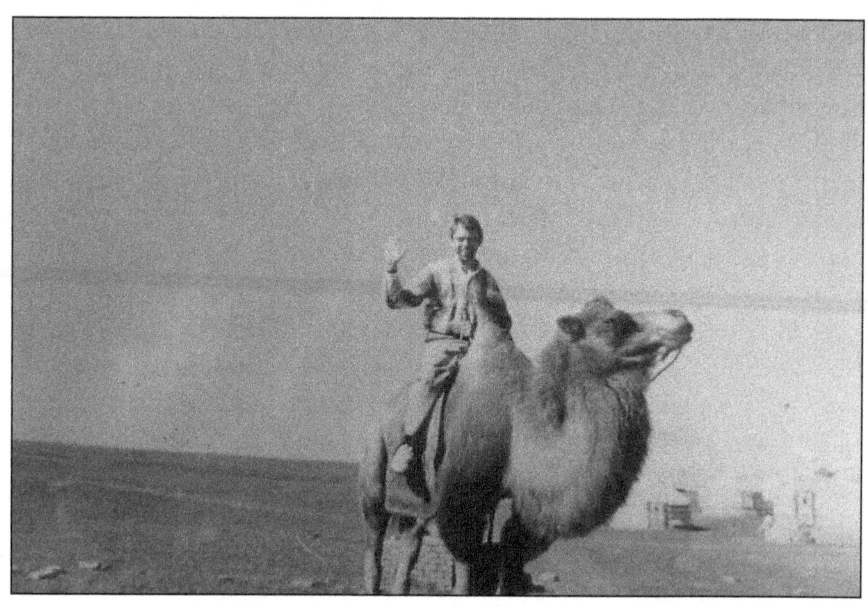

"How's the ride?" she asked. "Rakuda raku da (the camel is comfortable)," I said.

258. AN AUSTRALIAN MILLIONAIRE

Kumamoto, Japan, 2000.

$1,000,000.00—I was a millionaire in Australian dollars. Before class, I stopped at my office at Tokai University, Kumamoto, and checked my stocks. I'd have a short devotion, but that could wait. I was looking forward to my trip to the Asian mainland. I considered giving God a hospital—a small one, or a big one should profits continue to explode.

Mongolia was great. I took a train from Ulan Baatar to Erdenet, with a fellow working with Habitat for Humanity. He shared the challenges of the ministry as we traveled. I also put together a prospectus for my denomination's mission, checking out Christian ministries, their scope, goals, and methodologies. I had a great time in the land of the Kahns. Far from the high-flying world of finance, I focused on a *boots on the ground* future in Missions.

Upon return to Japan, three weeks later, I learned my stocks had dropped half their value. In addition, rules in the Japanese exchange differed from SEC requirements. I was required to supply shortfalls when stocks split. When the year ended, I had enough resources to purchase myself a postage stamp size plot of land with a large, deluxe toilet. I didn't buy God a hospital, large or small, but I got back to starting my day in the Word of God. So, as it turned out, I got a good deal!

Grace Lover: But lay up for yourselves treasures in heaven, where neither moth nor rust doth corrupt, and where thieves do not break through nor steal: For where your treasure is, there will your heart be also. (Matt. 6:20-21).

Curmudgeon: And the cares of this world, and the deceitfulness of riches, and the lusts of other things entering in, choke the word, and it becometh unfruitful (Mark 4:19).

259. THE RING OF SAURON

Middle Earth.

It was the Age of Aquarius, in a Brave New World. To say we had *the sight* suggests a para-normal gift. Actually, we had a blurred vision that came in a plastic bag, and cost fifteen bucks. So, why call them nickels? That much marijuana provided a weekend of buzz. Lysergic acid would take you beyond the buzz to the land of altered reality. It was a short-lived age that had its highs and lows, and pseudo-enlightenment. It wasn't a new age, just an old one dressed in paisley shirts and bellbottoms.

Frodo, of *The Lord of the Rings*, knew about altered reality. He slipped on Sauron's Ring of Power to escape the Nazguls, but it made him visible to them. The Ring had perks like invisibility or dominion over all other powers—not too shabby except for what it did to the soul. Frodo's uncle, Bilbo, wore it and stopped aging, but said he felt "thin, sort of stretched, like butter scraped over too much bread." Something new may make us more of what we think we are or deserve to be. It may be a nickel bag or a Ring. Every generation has its enticement. What has God designed? Peter says:

> Blessed be the God and Father of our Lord Jesus Christ, which according to his abundant mercy hath begotten us again unto a lively hope by the resurrection of Jesus Christ from the dead (I Pet. 1:3).

The Age of Aquarius had trappings: music, revolutionary icons, Carnaby Street fashion, lingo like *groovy* and *far out*, the butterflies of artist Peter Max, and drugs like Purple Haze. We accepted a bag of tricks instead of the sure mercies of the Lord. The First Couple took forbidden fruit instead of the Tree of Life. And you? Some shortcut being offered? Advancement if you'll blink on a character issue? Or something seemingly less sinister, like wasting life with frivolities when He would have you passionate for Him. There's no free lunch. Jesus offers to pay for your costly redemption. Or, you can attempt to pay for it by your own merit. Good luck with that. Don't get suckered into a fool's bargain.

Curmudgeon: For what shall it profit a man, if he shall gain the whole world, and lose his own soul (Mark 8:36).

260. SUPERLATIVE COMPARISONS

"Good enough!" Mom echoed sarcastically. It was 1958, in W. Babylon. She wasn't usually sarcastic, her kids being exceptional, but I remember this event of decades ago. I'd been commissioned to clean my room. I did so in record time, it not being in much disarray as one counts natural, or human induced, disasters. A critique of the bedspread's fit was leveled. As it had no effect on the Yankees' standing in the American League, Rin Tin Tin's safe, desert return, or the cost of a Schwinn bike with streamers and a generator light, I commented: "Good enough," not knowing the rancor it would create or the memory that it would cauterize in my being. Mom's obvious, yet not posited, question was: "Why not the best?" The exceptional was never my constant companion. I was third chair trumpet, came in third in one race in track, and finished high school with a B- average. Ho-hum. Now, however, I'm a prince, discovered of the grace of God in 1972, though it was known before the foundation of the world (Ephesians1:4).

Hebrews has at least one *much more*, and in addition uses *so much, rather*, and *moreover*, to exemplify Christ's superiority to angels, Moses, the Levitical priesthood, and animal sacrifices. The book offers a collection of comparisons, rendering the subject of its testimony by its volume, superlative status. Christ, our perfect example, has come; that which was good has passed away. We see this in Hebrews and II Corinthians Chapter 3. Paul uses *much more* regarding the Spirit and the righteousness in the New Covenant as exceeding the glory of the Law:

But if the ministration of death, written and engraven in stones, was glorious, so that the children of Israel could not stedfastly behold the face of Moses for the glory of his countenance; which glory was to be done away:[8] How shall not the ministration of the spirit be rather glorious?[9] For if the ministration of condemnation be glory, much more doth the ministration of righteousness exceed in glory.

God's plan for us isn't just *good enough*; neither, in serving Him, should ours be.

Grace Lover: For this man was counted worthy of more glory than Moses, inasmuch as he who hath builded the house hath more honour than the house—1:3. For if the blood of bulls and of goats, and the ashes of an heifer sprinkling the unclean, sanctifieth to the purifying of the flesh: [14]How much more shall the blood of Christ, who through the eternal Spirit offered himself without spot to God, purge your conscience from dead works to serve the living God? (Heb. 1:3, 9:13-14)

261. YOUR DEATH

“You are going to die today,” the Dark Angel informed him.

“I hoped it was. ‘Precious in the eyes of the Lord is the death of His saints’ Psalm 116;15, I just love that verse,” Julio declared.

“You’re cheery for such news,” the Angel noted. “You are Julio Diaz?

“Yo soy, I confess, but friends always call me Jubilio. In English I be a cock-eyed optomotrist.”

“Optimist,” the Angel said.

“Oh, you too! It means we don’t see darkly—we see brightness.

“You don’t see things as they are,” the Angel asserted.

“You’re sounding more of a cara triste than an optomotrist!”

“Optimist.”

“Oh, bueno, good to hear it.”

Sensing this assignment was more difficult than he’d been duped into believing, the Dark One took another direction.

“Have you never heard of *The Unknown?*”

“Yes, but I’ve also heard of assurance, ‘But these are written that ye may believe that Jesus is the Christ, the son of God, and that believing ye may have life in his name,’ John 20:31. Vida en el nombre de Cristo!”

The Dark one shuddered at such declarations, but held his airspace.

“You’ve heard of the *fear of death*? There must be a reason people are afraid of dying. Are you superior to others?”

“Maybe better informed. Jesus has delivered them who all their lives were in the fear of death. That’s Hebrews somewhere.”

“It’s 2:15, but you missed something important. Your friends, Joe, Koji, Ayad, and relatives. Have you considered them?”

“I’m not sure of your meaning,” Julio returned.

“You’re thinking of yourself. What about those who will miss you, who aren’t the chosen, as you call it? Do you abandon them?”

“This is funny. You encourage me to stay longer so I can tell the good news to those you want in your net?”

“As usual, you judge everything from your narrow world-view.”

“‘Narrow is the way…,’ but at the same time it is *all-inclusive*. I just learned that phrase in my English lesson last week—preety good, eh? ‘Whosoever will come let him come,’ Revelation 22. But backup, it’s not as if I could stay longer. When it’s time, it’s time.”

"As the Yankee, Yogi Berra said: 'It ain't over till it's over.' I'm instructed to offer concessions if you adjust your position."

"First, death is in His hands. Second, I'd rather have His, eh, what's the word, *commendation*, than your concessions. I'm waiting for Matthew 25:21, 'Well done, thou good and fateful servant.'"

"'Faithful,'" the Angel corrected.

"Gracias. You are one polite diablo."

"Yes, however…" the Angel began, but ceased, departing quickly when Julio, or Jubilio, added hymns to his jubilations. It was more than the Fallen Angel could bear. He left, failing his mission. And so, at the appointed time, Julio, amidst great fanfare, entered glory, escorted by a spirit of a more than equally positive nature,

Is this the pattern your death will take? It could be if you take the right steps. See John Chapter 3 for more details. Enjoy the peace, the love, the commendation and the jubilation. Say "Hola" to Julio. I can hear him now: Hallelujah mi hermana y hermano. Gloria Dios!

Grace Lover: Yea, though I walk through the valley of the shadow of death, I will fear no evil: for thou art with me; thy rod and thy staff they comfort me (Ps. 23:4).

Curmudgeon: And fear not them which kill the body, but are not able to kill the soul: but rather fear him which is able to destroy both soul and body in hell (Matt. 10:28).

The Actionaires in Michigan,1983.

262. NO ROOM AT THE INN

Southern California, Christmas, 1983.

One year in Cambodia we got a late start on Christmas. So, we left up the decorations until March. My boys say, late March. But that was not my most memorable Christmas. What is your most memorable Christmas? My story involves the Actionaires of CinA, missionaries Jim and Miriam Marquardt, Norma Hunt, Margaret Morgan, Tom Hodges, Gary Wood, and me. Six of us received an invitation to have Christmas with an engaged missionary couple in San Francisco. Jim drove. A couple of hours out he said: "With the headlights on, the battery power drops." Our location was an expressway that is infamous for its multiple car pile-ups in the fog. The idea of a battery lacking confidence did something to me. "Jim," I said, "don't turn on the lights again. Take this exit, or we'll die!" Sadly, my hubris was fear induced. Fortunately, there was a garage on the cloverleaf. As soon as Jim turned off the engine, the car died—better it than us. Oh, did I mention it was Christmas Eve? The mechanic said: "Sorry, I'm going home." We asked if we could stay at his garage. He gave the ok if we were happy to be locked in. We agreed. I remember singing Christmas carols and sleeping sitting up in the car. As we were a full contingent, we didn't freeze. What we lacked in numbers, we substituted with girth. It wasn't a manger, and we had no swaddling clothes, but that experience was the closest I've had to what the Holy Family experienced on the First Christmas. We didn't sing in the language of the Heavenly host, but we did sing *Es ist ein Ros Enstsprungen*. We didn't get refused at the inn; we were incarcerated at the garage. We didn't sleep with the horses and camels, we slept with the Mustangs and Mavericks. For all of that, He of whom the day is named, was just as much with us in that garage as He was present in the stable long ago. Sometimes blessings have an early exit, or late arrival, for us to receive them.

Grace Lover: Therefore the Lord himself shall give you a sign; Behold, a virgin shall conceive, and bear a son, and shall call his name Immanuel (Isa. 7:14).

> For unto you is born this day in the city of David a Saviour, which is Christ the Lord (Luke 2:11).

263. NEAR MISS

Phnom Penh, Cambodia, 2012.

What does a gecko, a stake, cement blocks, and a Cessna have in common—a NEAR MISS! In Kampong Cham, a man with a bicycle drawn cart transported items for market vendors. His green side panels read: Milo Malted Milk. I called him the Milo Man! He was a superhero who put on a lot of kilometers in the heat. We had a cannister of Milo. One day, I poured the powder into my cup. Like the Red Sea did when Moses raised his staff, it gathered in a heap. As it was hot, I had second thoughts about sucking from the cup. I was delighted I hadn't when I stirred the concoction to discover a limp gecko at my frothing place!

As for the stake, it pushed into my tear duct when I bent over to pick a hermit tomato hiding in the fronds. I was so thankful I didn't lose the eye; I thanked the Lord many times a day for days.

Phil Blankenship, of CinA Mission, was our Cessna pilot to LAX. When landing, a jet came down right over us. A humble brother, Phil, let the big fellow go first. I was going to end here but thought curiosity, perchance, would drive you mad, so I'll share one more. I had a 1970 Ford Maverick that needed some work done; when didn't it? Not having jacks or risers, I used cement blocks. Having finished, I crawled out from under the car, intent on a cold, iced tea. No sooner had I stepped away than there was a tremendous thud. The car pulverized every block to powder. Maybe using cement blocks wasn't concrete logic. Where does this leave us other than averse to gardens, frightened, and wary of chocolate beverages? Near misses for many folks are a chance to thank their lucky stars or the good Lord that they have survived an ordeal or missed one. Those who credit the cosmos are foolish; those who remember the Lord's mercy do well. Have you ever said: "Lord, if you get me out of this, I'll turn things around," only to forget when the dust settled? At the end of *Dr. Doolittle*, the Doctor's nemesis, Mr. Blair, seems to have an epiphany. He's grateful to escape death, but then sacrifices a grenadier to save himself. You'd never do that, would you. I left it a rhetorical question, but, if honesty moves you, you may put a question mark where I placed a period. Friend, the Lord gives us chances. Let's not squander them.

Grace Lover and Curmudgeon: It is of the Lord's mercies that we are not consumed, because his compassions fail not (Lam. 3:22).

264. THE MONK

Ulan Baatar, 1991.

The plain was strewn with bodies. A man drove a cart packed high with hides. The *Zudt* (cold spell) had preceded me and left behind thousands of dead animals in Mongolia. With the end of the USSR, herd limitations also ended. Everyone was free to over-graze, so, instead of a few fat kine there was an abundance of lean kine. Herders left carcasses to rot and took their hides to sell in the cities. The cattle were sacrifices on the altar of poor policy. Horses fared better. On a bridge one day, a riderless horse zipped past me without a centimeter to spare. She must have found some breakfast that morning!

The Russian occupation had just ended. Until recently, religion was persecuted. I met a man, however, who aspired to be a monk. He was 25, and dressed in a yellow saffron robe. I don't suspect he was practicing for long because he was happy. Sorry if that is too direct, but the Buddhist worldview is about seeing life as illusion, and emotions as vain. I ended up at his home for lunch. Fortunately, there was no Mongolian tea—it has salt instead of sugar! Mongolians, being nomadic, don't have a lot of furniture, but this family had beautiful rugs. How different from the Yurt in the countryside I visited. There, as I crossed the threshold, I kicked the head of a goat. It's noteworthy because it was unaccompanied by a body. As for the monk, he wanted to know about Buddhism abroad. I sent him a book, and my thanks. I told of another itinerant preacher, who came in the Monk's interest. He didn't sit under a bodhi tree and escape emotion; He embraced pain for us, hanging on a tree. I'm praying to see the Monk again, in white robes.

Grace Lover: I, even I, am the Lord; and beside me there is no saviour (Isa. 43:11).

> And I said unto him, Sir, thou knowest. And he said to me, These are they which came out of great tribulation, and have washed their robes, and made them white in the blood of the Lamb (Rev. 7:14).

Curmudgeon: Neither is there salvation in any other: for there is none other name under heaven given among men, whereby we must be saved (Acts 4:12).

265. THE PITCH THAT CHANGED THE GAME

January '85, N.Y.

"Whoooaaahhhh?!#^%! Looooord!" Chaos punctuated my first reaction to slipping on the roof. The second outburst, the Word itself, held all the emphasis necessary. Let me ask you: Can you wait while moving?

I was working with my brother, John, the one with the muscles, drive, and savvy. He was the operation; I was the dot of the "i." We were installing a sunlight window. Most roofs have pitch. This isn't a fish tale but that roof was really pitched. A standard accessory that week was a ton of snow. Being the *utility guy*, I got to sweep the roof. Ready to employ my talents, I was soon in trouble. To wrap a leg over the peak while sweeping suggests abject fear. I was middle of the road with my fears, that coinciding with my aforementioned talent—presumption. To answer the question posed: "Yes!" I waited on the Lord as I slid down the roof. He had my attention, not to say a bunch of requests, one actually, though repeated a gazillion times—"HEEELP!"

I took a day off and matriculated at Roberts Wesleyan College. It was sudden, but John found an employee with less need for workman's comp, and less likely to put him in the hospital. I once dropped a board that he happened to be under. The probability that a board with a nail will fall sharp point down increases proportionally with the employment of relatives and the untalented. I started classes, received a teaching degree, and went to Asia. The pitch of that roof threw a curveball. It had a lot of stuff on it, as they say in baseball. An unexpected slide may get an extra base; a fall can get us standing. I thank the Lord He stopped me before the gutter. Friend, wait on Him so you don't slide. If you slip, He will do what is best—catch you or… Seek Him daily and you don't have to worry about the pitch.

Grace Lover: I will call upon the Lord, who is worthy to be praised: so shall I be saved from mine enemies. [36] Thou hast enlarged my steps under me, that my feet did not slip (Ps. 18:3, 36).

266. MIKE SALTA PONTIAC

Honolulu, Hi, '74.

Rainbows are a promise from God, and a natural phenomenon, but haven't we seen enough replicas on mobiles, sun-catchers, and unicorn's flanks? We think of them as two-dimensional. Have you seen a double rainbow? Is there a dry space between layers? Is the angle of refraction playing tricks? I'm brainstorming, so drip with me. Experience only adds questions. One day, the pilot of my flight banked our plane to show us a rainbow dome—a giant half-bubble. In Honolulu, I could see Tripler Hospital from Mike Salta Pontiac. It was unique. It was pink, and there was often in its vicinity a rainbow or a double rainbow, and twice, a tripler. Enough of rainbows; they illustrate perceptions are only a part of the whole.

Salta Pontiac had its mysteries. Jim, Mike, and Don were in charge. Don was the General Manager, but it was to Jim that I confessed. Now you're listening. Used-cars had extras. Not power-windows, rather, shoes, car wax, even snorkels. They took up space, so I took them home. Later, I delivered a box of parts to the mechanics. Don knew of the *Snorkel Affair* and followed me. I apprised Jim of the third dimension I'd overlooked. He said: "Keep the junk."

There were other mysteries, too. Ed, newly married, invested in gold for retirement. A Filipina yearned to follow Christ, but struggled with passion. Tony, a Portuguese, warred with God. Last, a clerk ridiculed me to please the staff. Her accusation hurt, albeit I don't resemble a squirrel! There was more to the crew than was visible. Occasionally, I shared the mysteries of God with them. Some folks only see two dimensions. When being compared to a rodent, or finding a box of snorkels, it is good to look deeper. Remember the Rainbow! Add your example here:

Grace Lover: Behold, I send you forth as sheep in the midst of wolves: be ye therefore wise as serpents, and harmless as doves (Matt. 10:16).

Curmudgeon: Then said Jesus, Father, forgive them; for they know not what they do (Matt.23:34).

267. 159 A.D.: HOMO MENSURA

"So, you are the Jew I've been hearing about," observed the balding man in the expensive toga.

"It's possible," the newcomer responded. The inquirer waited, but nothing further was offered.

"I hear the Jews have a tight string on their purses. Is it the same with their lips?"

"Why spend one's words on that which has not proven profit will follow?" The Jew offered.

"Jew or not, I find you amusing. Welcome to the school."

"Our Holy Book tells us to welcome the foreigner. You have no book, yet offer me an open door. I pray the pestilence can't find your threshold."

"Moments ago, your words needed enticement; now we speak of Holy Books and pestilences. Have your feet traveled as far as your thoughts?"

"From Rome to Smyrna, I am come."

"I offer my part freely. I am Albinus. I employ logic as witnessed in the *Dialogues of Plato*. Greeks have no holy book; we draw truth by observation. We view ethics philosophically."

"I'm Asher. I find it good the Book says a neighbor will reimburse me if his bull destroys my field."

"We have civil law." Albinus answered.

"Does your civil law and your philosophy always match?"

"You'll fit in here. Consider Protagoras' conclusion: '*Homo mensura*' 'Man is the measure.'"

"Have your opinions authority? Are they arbitrary? Logic leads to a panoply of gods who lie… well, my words are many for our first meeting?"

"I live for such banter. Thinking is living; otherwise, I leave this eternal world not having lived."

"'Eternal world?' here too we stand on different shores. The Book tells us God created all."

"How did this come to pass?" Albinus asked.

"In six days, He spoke and it was so. The Earth is a circle that He hung on nothing (Job 26:7)."

"We hold the opposite to be true, Tellus being flat and eternal, and the gods coming later. Plato said things in motion must be put in motion. A self-moved mover would describe how this began. It seems you ascribe to myths, whereas we to logic and observation."

"I see no logic in gods that owe their creation to another. Are these observers reliable? Prophecies fulfilled and holy men who withstood evil at the cost of their lives attest the to the Book's veracity. It is beyond Man's surmising. Besides, it exhorts us, contrary to our nature, to live good lives. Who would not rather join the endless libations and service of one's own pleasures? We have turned from the Book and suffered each time. A myth holds no attraction to us."

"We have prophets. You have heard of the Oracle at Delphi?"

"Do they have a perfect ledger for accuracy?" Asher asked.

"Croesus was told a nation would be defeated if he warred. It was, but it was his."

"Our prophecies lead us closer to the will of God, not misdirection."

"Can you give me an example?"

"My people were taken to Babylon 700 years ago, as prophesied, for disobeying the Book. It happened. Jeremiah prophesied we'd return 70 years later. It also came to pass."

"Don't the prophecies preclude a miss by coming from both sides?"

"Have you ever heard of a dispossessed people being restored to their lands?"

"I can't, but I'm glad we didn't meet today at the Academy. My tenure would be reconsidered, and I dispossessed."

"It is written, 'His mercies endure forever (Psalm 136).'"

"I look forward to our next talk. Vale (*goodbye*, Latin)."

"As do I. Shalom."

Grace Lover: Thus saith Cyrus king of Persia, The Lord God of heaven hath given me all the kingdoms of the earth; and he hath charged me to build him an house at Jerusalem, which is in Judah (Ezra 1:2).

> For the prophecy came not in old time by the will of man: but holy men of God spake as they were moved by the Holy Ghost (II Pet. 1:21).

268. GOING POSTAL

"Ding Dong! Ding Dong!"

"Mom, John is here."

Mother wished I'd ignored the postman. Civil servants don't get gifts, but it was Christmas, and our bell would ring until we paid up! But who hasn't enjoyed meeting neighbors at the P.O., or perusing philately while Mom checks zip codes? And how about the tributes, i.e., the Marvellettes single, *Please Mr. Postman*, or Ray Heatherton's, *I Am the Merry Mailman*?

In 2014, we left Pleasantville Camp, and took a locomotive and last mobile U.S. P.O., to Oil City. Yuko and Corey slept, so Caleb and I mailed a postcard of a Locomotive, to them. Returning home, we were excited about them receiving the card. I reached into the mailbox, but there were two cards! One was addressed to Caleb and I. Corey and Yuko pulled the same sneaky trick we did. The cherry on top of this postal parfait—we all chose the Locomotive card!

So many hopes, dreams, and blessings have passed through the mail; the term *gone postal* seems inappropriate. Let's not view our positives as negatives. When things are going postal, God is sending a sleek locomotive of blessing your way, but it may take a few days for delivery. Faith is the substance of things hoped for, the evidence of things not seen (Heb. 11:1). Hey, what's that? Can you hear it? Is that a whistle in the wind?

Grace Lover: Let no corrupt communication proceed out of your mouth, but that which is good to the use of edifying, that it may minister grace unto the hearers (Eph. 4:29).

Curmudgeon: Come now therefore, and let us slay him, and cast him into some pit, and we will say, Some evil beast hath devoured him: and we shall see what will become of his dreams (Gen. 37:20).

> Thou shalt not raise a false report: put not thine hand with the wicked to be an unrighteous witness (Ex. 23:1).

Early Soulmates! 2016.

269. BOW TIE BOYS

Higashi Kurume, Japan, 2016.

The new kid on the block, in my neighborhood, meant this kid doesn't know anything, or needs to be initiated. Living in three countries has widened our boys' worldview but also made them, at times, outsiders. A Japanese dining with us once asked Caleb: "Are you a monkey?" In Japan, chicken is not "finger lickin' good."

We've all felt like an outsider. Our boys have done well, despite our moves. Corey is a *people person*, whereas Caleb is an *idea guy*. At camp, Corey will get ten kids and start a game or mutiny. Caleb will search for a soul-mate. As parents, we hope our children can grow up without criticism so their uniqueness can flower. Adults may be more judgmental than children. I once commented about a woman in disheveled clothes. A charitable friend explained: "Oh, that's dishabille!" Once I knew it was French, that made all the difference. So, my judgments can be selective. When Caleb was eight, he wore fedoras. *Pittari*, in Japanese, means, *it fits you or perfect.* That's what hats were for him. Then he added a bow tie…I mean, we're talkin' *the cat's meow!* When he began the fifth grade, I was delighted Isaac became a friend. One day at their classroom, I beheld them both accoutered in bow ties! I snapped a quick picture lest the scene disappear. They didn't always fit in, but they're still friends.

The search for approbation can be long and unfruitful. The man that hath friends must shew himself friendly: and there is a friend who sticketh closer than a brother (Prov. 18:24). I don't know if it's dishabille or not, but he has a garment for us, washed in His own blood (Rev. 7:13-14). As for the fit or style, we don't know that either, but it will be pittari. His name is Jesus. Talk about friendship, He's the ultimate blood-brother!

Grace Lover: For whosoever shall do the will of God, the same is my brother, and my sister, and mother (Mark 3:35).

Curmudgeon: And the LORD said unto Cain, Where is Abel thy brother? And he said, I know not: Am I my brother's keeper (Gen. 4:9).

270. SWITCH-HITTERS: MIKE AND THE MICK

N.Y., '61.

I was eleven. Unless you were under a rock, eating grubs, you'd heard of Mickey Mantle. He received 3 Most Valuable Player awards, a Golden Glove, and the Triple Crown. He hit 536 home runs, 372 of them left-handed, and 164 of them right-handed. He hit home runs from both sides in 10 games. Mick had another switch–fear. By 40, his dad and relatives died of Hodgkin's disease, so he partied. When his Yankee days ended, teammates came in bottles. Later, cancer put his body out of the game. Mickey called Bobby Richardson, an old teammate, for prayer. At the hospital, Mick greeted him quoting John 3:16. Mickey's best award is a Crown of Righteousness. His final switch wasn't left or right, but straight and narrow.

San Francisco, '77, Stage Door Deli. We had two Mikes, one a gay cook, the other a waiter. I visited the cook's house; the waiter and I were cordial to each other. One day, he told a waitress, Jane, he was a switch-hitter. Jane was straight, but twisted out of shape at Mike's disclosure.

Mick never ran the bases clockwise. Why lose a homer? Baseball and God have rules. His boundaries are good. When little Corrie Ten Boom asked her father about sex-sin. He put a suitcase by her. "Can you lift that?"

"No Papa," she said, "it is too heavy!"

"So is the knowledge of sex-sin. Later, you'll understand."

Adam and Eve didn't know why the fruit was prohibited. We may not grasp the why, but our Father's motives spring from love. Let's keep switch-hitting on the Field, and in love, make our way straight.

Grace Lover: For this cause shall a man leave his father and mother, and shall be joined unto his wife, and they two shall be one flesh. [32] This is a great mystery: but I speak concerning Christ and the church (Eph. 5:31-32).

Curmudgeon: So he drove out the man; and he placed at the east of the garden of Eden Cherubims, and a flaming sword which turned every way, to keep the way of the tree of life (Gen. 3:24).

271. "APRES MOI, LE DELUGE": THE OPEN PAINT CAN

1757.

What did King Louis XV mean by these words? A bath for April 1st. is a washout. The translation is: "After me the deluge!" But what does it mean? Did the King despair his defeat at Rossbach to a small force of Prussians? Was it a callous hope the day of reckoning was secure in the future tense? Regardless, retribution fell 36 years later with the execution of the last king, Louie's grandson, Louis XVI.

Hezekiah, the King of Judah, had the latter attitude. When emissaries of Babylon received a full tour of his treasury, Isaiah rebuked him for mixing Babylon and Bling. He foretold this Chaldean Connection would someday empty the King's coffers. Hezekiah's reply resembled Louie's (II Kings 20). He was a good king—God's commendation, not mine, but notice people with early success often get smug. Kings Asa and Solomon had great beginnings, but later ignored God. There are few touch-ups and no scarcity of warts in God's Word. Saul ignored David, Ahab ignored Elijah, Jehoash ignored the priest, Zechariah, and Jehoiakim ignored Jeremiah. Balaam ignored the donkey, the Angel of the Lord, and God—three strikes and you're out!

In Hezekiah's defense, he submitted to the will of the Lord. So, what can we learn? These folks didn't end well. They pooh-poohed the advice of subjects, priests, prophets, and God. "He who hesitates is lost," isn't written in scripture but you'd be unaware of the open paint can on your new carpet, to miss it. Put a lid on it, Friend. Close the deal. Make the commitment. Apologize. Repent. End well!

Grace Lover: Sow to yourselves in righteousness, reap in mercy; break up your fallow ground: for it is time to seek the Lord, till he come and rain righteousness upon you. Hosea 10:12

Curmudgeon: Therefore to him that knoweth to do good, and doeth it not, to him it is sin. Ja. 4:17

272. THE PAVEMENT OF SAPPHIRE: 1500 B.C.

Twelve pillars stood at the base of Mt. Sinai. Those chosen performed a sacrifice. Moses sprinkled the people with the blood of the Covenant. Joshua gathered the Elders for the ascent. Aaron and sons, Nadab and Abihu, joined them. The Mount seemed steep.

"Shall I help you, Father? Abihu asked, nearing the incline.

"No! I was a shepherd." Aaron said, "at the age you learned to count," Nadab enjoyed the drama, as it put him in a better position than his brother. Before rancor uttered a word, the Lord's presence stopped every mouth. Under His feet was a pavement of sapphire blue, like the sky. Later, Moses and Joshua ascended the Mount, with the younger, at last, left behind. At the peak, a cloud formed. Moses waited outside it for a week. Summoned by the Lord, he entered and received the Ten Commandments.

Exodus 24 shows us if you want to get close to God, you may have to wait on Him. What if you saw that Sapphire Pavement or the Cloud at the peak of the Mount wherein was God. Would you be moved? Only one human on Sinai that day entered the Promised Land—Joshua. Moses acted rashly, Aaron made an idol, and the Lord killed Nadab and Abihu, Levitical priests, for making light of their office. The doubting Elders died in the Wilderness. They'd seen the Plagues, the Red Sea parting, the Pillar of Cloud and Fire, but weren't moved beyond the moment. Are you still a Curmudgeon? You've heard of changed lives, prophecies fulfilled, apologetics, and God's promises. There comes a point the Spirit of God no longer strives with you. Billy Graham used 2 verses repeatedly. One was John 3:16. The other was Proverbs 29:1—He, that being often reproved hardeneth his neck, shall suddenly be destroyed, and that without remedy. Don't be stuck in the Wilderness, check out the Promised Land.

Grace Lover: But the fearful, and unbelieving, and the abominable, and murderers, and whoremongers, and sorcerers, and idolaters, and all liars, shall have their part in the lake which burneth with fire and brimstone: which is the second death (Revelation 21:8).

Curmudgeon: Then beware lest thou forget the LORD, which brought thee forth out of the land of Egypt, from the house of bondage (Deut. 6:12).

The Wilkins-DelaRionda Crowd, Christmas, 2000.

273. WHINGEY MARY

You've probably had someone in your life who was a homespun pundit, a compendium of common sense, and a master of maxims. Usually, the person imbued with this excess is Mom! My step-mother, Evelyn, is no exception. In the family interviews recently filmed with her, a similar pattern was seen in football terms. The first half would show an equal time of possession. Questions and reminiscences were fielded with equal agility, but once half-time was reached, there was no marching band, and the game was changed to a spin-off of *The Dr. Phil Show,* or *Dear Abby.* Evelyn, however, was not always the Master Mentor, she was trained by the best—Aunt Elvira! Class, back in the 50s, was in session when Evelyn heard from the other side of the house: "Sister-in-law: let's have coffee!"

On the bus to work, Mary, a neighbor, would bury Evelyn under a pile of woe. Evelyn didn't dump this garbage as easily as Mary gave it. Learning of the dump routine, Elvira called Evelyn: "Hey, sister-in-law. Ya know who I saw at Macy's today? Whingey Mary. She was trying on hats while you're feeling bad for her."

My friend, Gary, the one with the dreams, muscles, and the girl, said: "Christopher, you're complainiest kid." Complaints help ward off perceived threats to our comfort zone. They can come from bitterness or attempts to elevate sagging self-esteem. What makes you complain? As for lessons from today's tales, one, being a good neighbor doesn't mean being a garbage pail. Boundaries are ok. Second, if you go around dumping garbage, your reputation may begin to stink.

Grace Lover: Let your speech be always with grace, seasoned with salt, that ye may know how ye ought to answer every man (Col. 4:6).

Curmudgeon: But let every man prove his own work, and then shall he have rejoicing in himself alone, and not in another. [5] For every man shall bear his own burden (Gal. 6:4-5).

274. TWO OR THREE QUASI-QUESTIONS

Dearest Curmudgeon, is using *Dearest* a little indelicate? After all, if you don't believe in God, you've probably concluded you're just a collection of molecules. Would it be correct to infer affection, especially when poured on thick, would be out of place in your worldview—like a yellow leprechaun in a green forest? Who has ever met a molecule in search of intimacy? I apologize if I've been offensive. If you've endured thus far, you've answered Question #1, i.e., *How sporting are you?* Let's continue the harangue with Q#2.

Question #2 is only moderately offensive: "Do you believe in aliens?" The question comes with a prophecy. In twenty years, we'll witness a shift from Evolution, the unscientific excuse for not believing in God, to reports of UFO sightings, speculations of alien technologies, and the *seeding* of galaxies by Brother Squid. Why Squid? Cephalopods are hardy. Why would Squid create Humans? Maybe to harvest us. Professor Dawkins has already espoused seeding. Even discounting the Garden Galaxy idea, does he have evidence? The Professor has explained a Quantum Shift happened. What a Quantum is, and how they shift are not known. Everything comes from nothing is the new something. Even Winnie the Pooh may have weighed in on their side. When hearing "Nothing is impossible," he replied, "I do nothing every day," implying nothing is something. Am I missing anything? Making too much of nothing? He also confessed he's a Bear of very little brain. Are large brained arbiters of truth in league with brainless bears? I think King Lear had it right: "Nothing comes from nothing." Act I Scene I. Yes, I'm with the king, and the King of Kings who says He stretched out the Heavens. So, before I am accused of being Teuthiphobic, let me say I like Squid. I even refrain from eating them when the sushi platter comes by, but the Borg or Squidlings can't know salvation. God became Man, the Second Adam, to die as our Kinsman Redeemer. If we and aliens had a common DNA, and the hard-won redemption of Calvary was extendable to Life Forms in other galaxies, I would rejoice—If they were real. The fact is that God created the Universe and put us at the center of its purpose. Are you up for the last question? You're bold enough to disbelieve, what would you ask Him? It's your question time.

Grace Lover: I have made the earth, and created man upon it: I, even my hands, have stretched out the heavens, and all their host have I commanded (Isa. 45:12).

275. THE WOMAN OF KOMPOT

Cambodia, 2003.

We were new missionaries in Cambodia. We had fun with church plants in Kompot and Kampong Cham. They were hundreds of miles distant, so we rotated weekly visits. Trips to Kompot involved such adventures as reaching the church in time to view a parade of its chairs, its destination being as many directions as there were chairs. The perpetrators' defense for this pilfering parade didn't have a leg to stand on, and we almost didn't have a chair to sit on. Another day had us driving in the rain across a bridge of two parallel coconut trees with no crossbeams. What was I thinking? Today's story, however, is about a Bible study. Not as funny as the first or as dramatic as the second, this one is poignant. After time in the Word, we had a Q. and A. That God holds our tears in a bottle had one woman enchanted. She asked where it was in the Bible. I suspect her eyes were no strangers to tears, *terk p'nek*. I don't know what evoked the sorrow in her life, but Cambodian villages score high on tears per capita. Cambodian weddings can run for several days and incur indebtedness for the new couple. Some women in need say they are widows. Occasionally, this means their husband is a bigamist and has deserted her. More than an enchanting idea, God cares about our tears, your tears. He will not forget you. An unfeeling Earth does not swallow up your tears. He may seem unfeeling for what He allows in your life. Remember this, His own Son asked Him three times to take away the cross. He allowed the Crucifixion so Jesus could have a bride and we could have forgiveness. His plan may bring no comfort at first. It will, however, in the end. Tears have purpose. He won't waste them. Share the joy of the Woman of Kompot.

Grace Lover: Thou tellest my wanderings: put thou my tears into thy bottle: are they not in thy book? (Ps. 56:8).

> He will swallow up death in victory; and the Lord GOD will wipe away tears from off all faces; and the rebuke of his people shall he take away from off all the earth: for the LORD hath spoken it (Isa. 25:8).

276. MORNINGS WITH JOHN

Tuesdays with Morrie recounts a man's weekly visits with a terminally ill friend, Morrie. My friend read it; I'm not sure I did. I'm not well read, a point you have most likely discerned. The inspiration for today's title is a combination of that book, and a Presbyterian, Bruce Gore, who labors in the Pacific Northwest wasteland. Garrison Keillor, host of The Prairie Home Companion, observed that the place was populated by more dogs than Christians. His crowd applauded. Risking redundancy, I'm grateful for the stubborn Presbyterians entrenched there. Bruce shared what Elijah's coming would look like(Isa. 40:3-5). The passage has played a part in two stage-productions: Handel's Messiah, and Godspell, providing the latter's opening song. The Prophet's advent would herald four things. Every valley would be filled, every high place made low, the crooked made straight, and the glory of the Lord revealed.

Jesus tells us John the Baptist came in the spirit of Elijah. John was the Voice of one crying in the wilderness, "Prepare ye the way of the Lord" (Isa. 40:3, John 1:23). Bruce encourages us to start our day with John's list. Get our valleys filled. Where we lack confidence to do what the Lord has put before us, get our strength from Him. When we're presumptuous and go our way without His Spirit, let humility level us. The next one bites a little. Where we try to make a Gordian Knot out of His plumb line, let's do what is necessary to get straightened out—Repent. Last, get into the World and let His glory in us proclaim Him. Have a glorious morning with John and "Prepare ye the way of the Lord!"

Grace Lover: Comfort ye, comfort ye my people, saith your God (Isa. 40:1).

> Behold, I will do a new thing; now it shall spring forth; shall ye not know it? I will even make a way in the wilderness, and rivers in the desert (Isa. 43:19).

P.S. This is good for every day!

277. THE RED COUCH

Kotesashi, Japan, 2023.

The banana was an after-breakfast snack. I opened it so I could eat while driving to a café. Yuko and I were moving and my less than youthful body needed a day of rest. We decided to drop off one or two items that didn't require strength to lift. As we turned near our new home, a red couch exited an apartment. Carrying it was a young man. Yuko commented on the couch's comeliness. We went another hundred yards and turned down our lane. Yuko stayed at the house and shuffle items from here to there and back again, and I headed for the café. Turning onto the avenue, behold, what came into view but a bright red couch. The same young man was walking with it. No one was behind me, so I pulled up next to them and asked if the couch would like a ride. The young man offered me his gratitude, so I figured he spoke for them both. What ensued took eight minutes. The couch took up the van's back seats and the young man sat in the front with me. We arrived at their apartment in less than a kilometer, but during our time together the couch-bearer received a copy of the Good News of John, and heard how after being in jail twice, the friend who had introduced me to LSD also introduced me to the Savior. He thanked me profusely for the pamphlet and the ride. The couch was mute. The Good News sometimes educes such a response. For me, an eight-minute adventure was the perfect release from a schedule devoid of excitement and life, i.e., people.

We all carry burdens. For some, it is a red couch. If you have a van, that may be the vehicle (pardon the pun) to share His grace. But we all have another burden—sin. Let's help folks exchange their burden for the freeing yoke of Jesus. Some will thank you; some will be mute. It is so with couches and people.

Grace Lover: Come unto me, all ye that labour and are heavy laden, and I will give you rest. [29] Take my yoke upon you, and learn of me; for I am meek and lowly in heart: and ye shall find rest unto your souls (Matthew 11:28-29).

Dorothy, Anna, and Elgin, early 70's.

278. FIRE AND ICE

N. Ireland, '70s.

Its nickname was *The Mission on the Doorstep of Hell*, the given name was *The Olive Branch Mission*. Nearby was *The Maze*, a prison for the IRA. Women attending the Mission had husbands there. The positions of pastor, mother, and confidant of the Mission were placements for tough individuals. Anna Todd did it all. Tall among saints, she was only 4'9", her top 3 inches being a bun in her hair. It's already been mentioned that entering a bar, her target would be the biggest and ugliest biker she could find. I know, I went with her–once. In Long Beach, we once knocked on the door of a Brazilian:

"Good day, Sir. We'd like to talk to you about the Lord's love."

"I just moved," he said. "I have no furniture," he demurred.

"We don't need any, come Christopher" she said, and entered.

Just as Anna is the Fire of our account, Elgin Taylor is the Ice. He was cool under pressure. He came back from serving as the Director in Europe to steady the Christian in Action Mission in a time of transition. Doctrines, procedures, and gripes had to be addressed. It was like Paul meeting the Corinthians. On one occasion, Anna and Elgin, having visited a Field, returned to Great Britain. No sooner had their shoes hit the tarmac than Anna was in search of sinners. Elgin was a few paces behind—he did better than most folks. In no time, Anna espied a janitorial worker and asked,

"Sir, do ye know the Lord?"

"No," he replied, to which Anna turned to Elgin to declare:

"Elgin, come here, it's a Heathen! A big White Heathen."

I don't remember the ending. There are, however, two sayings these Giants of Faith used that I haven't misplaced. Elgin, being unable to enter Africa because of visa problems, went to Great Britain. Arriving, he saw a sign: "TAKE COURAGE!" It lifted his spirits, but later, made him laugh—it was an ale advertisement. Anna had her memorable line, too. She'd sign her letters: "Yours, on the side that won, Anna." Fire and Ice, courage and victory, two lives with God that made a difference.

Grace Lover: One man of you shall chase a thousand: for the Lord your God, he it is that fighteth for you, as he hath promised you (Joshua 23:10).

Curmudgeon: And he saith unto them, Why are ye fearful, O ye of little faith? (Matt. 8:26).

279. JUDAS QUISLING

W. Babylon, N.Y., '68.

BETRAYAL! Our title is a double nastiness, the antithesis of a double-blessing—the double indictment. Occasionally we like to take out the self-flagellation whip, and give ourselves a few good *what's for*. My senior year of high school I got slurpy with my best friend's girlfriend. It was tacky. I almost regretted it. It wasn't, however, a big problem; he was smaller than me. Years later, my dog's dinner bill was interfering with my larder of recreational drugs. I asked a friend to take him out and lose him. How would I know he'd use him for archery practice? I guess the *coup de grâce* to my sense of personal nobility was taking nuptial papers with me to visit my cancer-stricken girlfriend in Fukushima. A college salary had offered me the chance to speculate on more than poverty. If we were married, would I be responsible for funeral costs? Would I marry her knowing she would live? Love bogged down in rationality. Those papers never saw the light of day. I'd thought myself the Romantic—wrong again.

Is feeling guilty redemptive? Do we pay a debt by being miserable? Why send a mortgage payment for a house paid in full? If guilt clears us, Christ need not have come, suffered torment, or taken the punishment of our sin upon Himself. That's a bit presumptuous, ya think? Forgiveness is as near and clear as repentance. Don't beat yourself, beat the Devil.

Grace Lover and Curmudgeon: As far as the east is from the west, so far hath he removed our transgressions from us. [13]Like as a father pitieth his children, so the Lord pitieth them that fear him (Ps. 103:12-13).

> And saying, Repent ye: for the kingdom of heaven is at hand. [8]Bring forth therefore fruits meet for repentance (Matt. 3:2,8).

> Christ hath redeemed us from the curse of the law, being made a curse for us: for it is written, Cursed is every one that hangeth on a tree (Gal. 3:13).

280. TOWERING THOUGHTS

I have an 80-meter pilgrimage to the deli to quell my wanderlust. There, in 3 corners of the Take-In section, are pictures of London, Paris, and N.Y. I am then prevailed upon to choose my destination. It's great. There are no cheerless lines or clearances. It's gay, impromptu, and altogether delicious. My flight includes jasmine tea, and an apple custard pie. In Paris, I land at the Eiffel Tower, reminiscent of a marijuana smoke-filled hostel, where I didn't smoke, and a sidewalk bistro near the train station where I ate fish. The geometric shapes of girders burgeoning into patterns, mix with arrays of curved filigree. Pythagoras and da Vinci would find rapture in its angles and squiggles. But I find more at this portal of transformation. The Tower's arches frame a view of my friends, *cumulonimbi*. One can almost taste this pastry crème that fills the structure's heights. Above, tufts with higher ambitions depart the Tower for adventures as of now only dreams for all but the Divine who knows the end from the beginning (Isa. 46:10).

Last is the crowd. A singular verb misleads, as this is a torrent of laughter, let-downs, oaths, and prayers. They are unmoved since our last rendezvous, yet I see them differently at each meeting. They have not changed; I have. Heraclitus said we never enter the same river twice. Next, is enjoying the cuisine, and waxing contemplative. Soon, the world presses in again, and I return. Family and work are there; I love both. A dualism is at play. Towering thoughts enhance life this side of the ocean, and encourage my more prodigious trip, beyond clouds, in the future. Rudolf Otto addressed what lies beyond with the word *Numinous*. His response to, "Is anybody there?" would be a resounding "YES!" Had any Towering Thoughts of late? Is the Mundane in ascendancy? The Lord made the Heavens on Day 4 (Gen. 1:16). An aside states: "...He made the stars, also." Billions of galaxies, each with billions of stars, may give us perspective. Quiz Question: "We are surrounded by a cloud of..." Heb. 12:1. Below is a one ticket to the Tower whose builder and maker is God. Bon voyage!

Grace Lover: I will lift up mine eyes unto the hills, from whence cometh my help (Ps. 121:1).

281. EDWIN DROOD

N. Chili, N.Y., 2007.

Caleb was two and loved cars. He had a row in formation on the couch when bath time made its disruptive appearance. He was slow to rise, and I was quick to get impatient. He got off his knees only to turn his back on me, kneel again, put his face on a horizontal plane with the couch, and tweak the position of one car. We're talking millimeters. Some would say he had an eye for detail. Others would say he was fussy. His dad has no comment at this time, but we could say resolution has its place.

Did you know Dickens wrote a murder mystery? It took the same title as this devotion, but Providence interrupted his timetable. He died. I can't fault Charles for not giving two weeks' notice, but Mr. Drood was left unresolved, and in perpetual limbo. There's a message there, don't you think? Our daily endeavors seem relevant, even important, but our time ends on this terrestrial ball, and we are gone. In two generations we'll be forgotten. If we knew the time of our departure, there would be things we'd like to tidy up, to close out, to reconcile, to add to our bucket list, etc. So, here's a proposal. Why not sit down and take stock of things? What is important in the light of eternity? Hold fast that which is good (I Thes. 5:21). We have New Year's resolutions. Even if you seem to have a long future ahead of you, why not try a *Final Year's Resolution*, not a plan of action for this life, but making sure everything is in formation as your next life approaches. Lining up toy cars was practice.

I wonder what Dickens had in store for Mr. Drood. I suppose we will never find out because he didn't get to fin...

Grace Lover: And he said, Behold now, I am old, I know not the day of my **death**: (Gen. 27:2).

> Yea, though I walk through the valley of the shadow of **death**, I will fear no evil: for thou art with me; thy rod and thy staff they comfort me (Ps. 23:4).

> A time to be born, and a time to die; a time to plant, and a time to pluck up that which is planted; (Eccl. 3:2).

The Lord's Garden, fruit from all over the world!

282. NANKI POO AND THE ROGUE

Camp Baiting Hollow, N.Y., '64.

"Wilkins!" His shriek tore through every tent of the Tuocs campsite. Like a pit bull, Stein, the scoutmaster's enforcer, was on my heels. My offense? I'd loosened the taut-line hitches of their tent. Big deal! In their defense, it had rained. As the tent wall snuggled them, it resembled cytoplasm's permeable membrane—it leaked. They searched for days. Bill C., a fellow scout, delivered the scoutmaster's ultimatum: Come back or get sent home! B.C., however, and his initials are significant, didn't come to save me from expulsion. I'll just say he'd not allow me to leave the swamp until I'd not only uttered a list of expletives, but done so with passion. As he had a weight advantage and was nastier by degree, I acquiesced. I felt dreadful. It's a toss-up which of us I hated more. Earlier, I'd designed signs bearing the Jolly Roger to enhance the legend of Chris the Rogue. Teasing overseers was fun, but suddenly, life lost its color.

Ever disappoint yourself? Hate yourself? This morning's devotion took me to Mark 3. and the blasphemy of the Holy Spirit, the only unforgiveable sin. Commentaries suggest it means calling God's attributes evil leaves you no options for forgiveness, not that any sin is unforgiveable. So, if you are feeling out of God's reach, you are being bamboozled!

I once had the fun role of Lord High Executioner, Nanki Poo, in Mikado. One of my numbers was *"I've Got a Little List."* It had the names of expendable folks I could execute without remorse or recourse—a fun song and a dreadful idea. Peter had a list, too. He denied the Lord 3 times. In John 21 we see Jesus' list. After Peter's denial, the Lord tells him 3 times: "Feed my sheep." Unlike Nanki Poo, the Lord restores. The Bible repeats themes of significance. You can be forgiven. God so loved you He gave His Son to forgive you. Feelings to the contrary are wrong. Take Him at His Word, His repeated Word.

Grace Lover and Curmudgeon: He saith unto him the third time, Simon, son of Jonas, lovest thou me?.... Jesus saith unto him, Feed my sheep (John 21:17).

283. THE GARDENER

Antediluvia1800, Iraq.

He never forgot his first day. He felt something. It was his back. Something was pushing on it. No, he realized, he was on the ground, and he was pushing down on it. He put his hands to his face. It had ridges, fissures, and eyes. His eyes were interesting. They could open, so he decided to have them do so, slowly. "Light is beautiful," he thought. Moving in the light was a form. As he saw more clearly, it was a form like his own. All about him was green and splashes of color. This other, who was pruning a bush, turned to him.

"Hello Adam. I am so happy to meet you. I am God. I am your Maker.

"Hello, God," the first man said, his eyes opened wide, and every sense attentive to the voice.

"I made this Paradise for you. Would you like to see it?"

A.D. 33, Jerusalem, probably The Temple Area

I am Black Simon from Cyrenaica. We are Gentiles by birth. My Father converted to follow the God of Israel. I was not yet twelve, and not permitted to go beyond the Temple gate, but I can tell you, it's a majestic sight. I have come to Jerusalem often for the Feasts. One day I saw the One we called the Prophet of Galilee. At first, I said it disparagingly, but then I heard Him speak—fire and water. A Temple guard said: "Never man spake like this man" (John 7:46). We listened to His amazing words:

Abide in me, and I in you. As the branch cannot bear fruit of itself, except it abide in the vine; no more can ye, except ye abide in me. I am the vine, ye are the branches: These things have I spoken unto you, that my joy might remain in you, and that your joy might be full (John 15:4,11).

33 A.D. 16th Day of Nissan,

She'd been forgiven much, therefore she loved much. The Rabbi's friends were good people, but she was more comfortable alone, without the real or perceived glances of others. It was dawn with just the hint of new light as she approached. Her load of spices was bearable, the burden of her heart was not. Fortunately, she'd not have to wrestle with one of her several questions; the stone of the tomb had been rolled away. But how? Why? Seeing that the Lord's corpse was not there, she went to tell the disciples. Peter and John came to see, wondered, and left. Mary, however, lingered, weeping. Grief bid her look again. Two angels inquired why she was crying, but someone else was there. She supposed He was the gardener. Was the One who spoke the Worlds into existence, and breathed life into Man, trimming bushes in a cemetery? He speaks: "Don't cling to me, for I have not yet ascended to my Father" (John 20:17). Was He about to present Himself in the Heavenly Temple as the sacrifice for sin? Mary would have stopped Him. Peter, when the Lord spoke of going to Jerusalem to die according to scripture, would have stopped Him (Mark 8:32). The crowds traveling to Passover would have made Him king (Jn. 6:15). Thank God human plans fail. His is the better plan, but Mary wasn't mistaken. God is the Gardener. The meaning of the word *paradise* in Hebrew and Greek is *garden*. Go to Him and walk in the garden in the cool of the day (Gen. 3:8). You will find yourself amazingly refreshed in His presence and by His Word. He'll probably invite you to help Him in the garden. Enjoy!

Grace Lover: Many, O Lord my God, are thy wonderful works which thou hast done, and thy thoughts which are to us-ward: they cannot be reckoned up in order unto thee: if I would declare and speak of them, they are more than can be numbered (Ps. 40:5).

> The LORD will surely comfort Zion and will look with compassion on all her ruins; he will make her deserts like Eden, her wastelands like the garden of the LORD. Joy and gladness will be found in her, thanksgiving and the sound of singing. (Isa. 51:3).

> Those that be planted in the house of the LORD shall flourish in the courts of our God (Ps. 92:13).

Curmudgeon: There are many devices in a man's heart; nevertheless the counsel of the LORD, that shall stand (Prov. 19:21).

284. LOGIC?

And so, it is time. All good things come to an end. That's not entirely true-Heaven will be eternal, but presently, it is what it is. I will end our journey, drawing from my illustration treasure trove, my heart country, Narnia. We book our visit in Book 1, *The Lion, the Witch, and the Wardrobe.* Three Pevensie children are discussing with Professor Kirke, their youngest sibling's odd behavior. She has claimed to have been to a foreign country inside a wardrobe. The are afraid she has gone mad or is lying. The Professor dismisses the mad option, having observed her behavior. He then inquires if she has been given to lying in the past, to which they confess she has been the best of them. It is here the Professor expresses his dismay at the lack of logic taught in schools.

So, I have a Logic Survey for you. It's not to see how logical you are, but to demonstrate the claims of the Bible are logical. We're just looking at a series of questions. Accept the challenge or don't. First, how do Judaism and Christianity differ from other religions? They declare God is holy. If the biblical account is not true, if it is just make-believe accretions from one generation to another, do you think this would be a sticking point? Wouldn't the holiness thing be dropped for something more progressive? Why invent a god that takes away all your fun? Baal worship had temple prostitutes! Hey, that sounds a lot more appealing. And what about those prophets preaching about justice—come on, the rich and powerful aren't crazy about that one. Why not prophesy about total subservience to rulers? That kind of propheteering they could get behind. Well, you may say, those Jews and Christians they were nice or enlightened people. That's why their religion developed a higher ideal. If so, why would they make up miracles? Why lie? How does the idea of a holy God benefit anyone if the idea isn't true? The idea is contrary to human nature. Ask a teenage male what he feels about the opposite gender. I doubt *holiness* will come to the fore. Bring a handkerchief in case he salivates.

Why do the Jews even exist? How many deliverances have they experienced? They've been returned to their land three times! Ask a Native American or a Kurd if that has happened elsewhere. Also, would Jews claim their deliverance was from God if, by their own strength, they won the victory? Picture this scenario after the battle:

Wife: "My hero, you saved us, come here you hunk of man!"

Warrior: "Oh, no. God gets the credit. I'm the same wimp. Heck, I'm not even scratched. Wait, come back!"

The Jews embraced historicity. They didn't write about mythological figures. Their genealogical records were meticulous. Around 450 B.C., Levites lacking proof of lineage were put out of the priesthood. Their sense of history then was stronger than yours is now!

Peter reminds us of the sure Word of prophecy. Is it logical to think dozens of fulfilled prophecies could result from manipulation and then be squeezed into one comprehensive scenario? Is it logical the Apostles would die, knowing their tale to be a falsehood? I could go on. Even though the logic of the biblical account has been demonstrated, Logic is not the answer for which we're searching. I only have shown that faith is not illogical. We need to come to God in faith. Not sure what is real? God will not ignore a sincere plea for the knowledge of the truth. Such a request is the logical thing to do. Being curmudgeons by nature, it is possible you won't avail yourself of this option. He knows we're a contrary lot. We've seen this verse before; did you act on it? Fortunately, the invitation is still offered:

> "Come now, and let us reason together, saith the LORD: though your sins be as scarlet, they shall be as white as snow; though they be red like crimson, they shall be as wool." Isaiah 1:18

So, my last question, Friend, is: do you like a happy ending? I speak of your book. You get to write the ending. I'll be praying for you. Beyond that, I can't help. Reject His invitation, and write a tragedy; accept His invitation, and you'll have a happy ending. Which will it be?

Grace Lover: But the wisdom that is from above is first pure, then peaceable, gentle, and easy to be intreated, full of mercy and good fruits, without partiality, and without hypocrisy (James 3:17).

Curmudgeon: The fool hath said in his heart, There is no God. They are corrupt, they have done abominable works, there is none that doeth good (Ps. 14:1).

285. THE INVITATION

Dear You,

As Ambassador, Priest, and New Creation, by the express will of His Majesty, the Lord of Love and Truth, I hereby pass His Invitation to you, …, for the Royal Wedding Banquet of His Only Begotten Son, Jesus the Christ, and His Bride, the Church, to be held at New Jerusalem on a day of the Father's convenience. Transportation, and wedding attire, will be provided, the latter being a garment that removes all stains of guilt, and the very nature of the aforementioned. Entrance will not be permitted without the proscribed attire. It will be great effrontery to approach the Gates improperly clad, the vestments being of immense cost to the Son, necessitating the blood of His veins, and anguish of soul. The Banquet will continue *ad infinitum*. Upon admission, every tear will be wiped away. Consider yourself fervidly invited. The Spirit and the Bride say: "Come!"

RSVP by confession.

Grace Lover: And I saw a new heaven and a new earth: for the first heaven and the first earth were passed away; and there was no more sea. [4] And God shall wipe away all tears from their eyes; and there shall be no more death, neither sorrow, nor crying, neither shall there be any more pain: for the former things are passed away. [7] He that overcometh shall inherit all things; and I will be his God, and he shall be my son. [27] And there shall in no wise enter into it anything that defileth, neither whatsoever worketh abomination, or maketh a lie: but they which are written in the Lamb's book of life (Rev. 21:1,4,7,27).

Have you accepted His invitation? It's the celebration of the Ages! Job, the widow of the two mites, the washerwoman who came on Tuesdays, and former curmudgeons, will be there. He'd like YOU to come. There's room on the Registry for your name! Please think it over. You will never, Never, NEVER get a better offer. Hope to see you there!

CONSOLATION PRIZE

Hey Friends, Grace Lovers, and Curmudgeons,

I've got a hypothetical idea for you. Suppose, just suppose, you find this literary endeavor akin to a case of acne at fifty-two, or a flat tire in a desert at 11 A.M. I know we're talking slim possibilities, but should that be descriptive of your attitude, be encouraged. Yes, the Curmudgeon will lay claim to no portion of the offering you placed on the Altar of Wild Speculation. All profits, above original costs and fees, will find their way to foreign enterprises, for the furtherance of the Good News. That may include my family for a while. As of now, our sending group hasn't given us the boot. Our projected sales are between fifteen and twenty copies, predominantly impressed relatives. Thank you for your contribution. That God would think kindly of you is my heartfelt prayer, and the reason for this hodgepodge collection. So, that said, buy ten copies and hand them out to your curmudgeonly friends. Etymologically speaking, and here's my last chance to sound clever, *curmudgeon* is thought to have originated from the Gaelic, *muigean*, which means *disagreeable person*. You could gather curs (short for curmudgeons) and have convocations called Muigeans. You could read the book together, complain, and act irascibly in a group setting. The possibilities are endless. I have an address for shillelaghs should there be interest. If you're looking for a life-changing book, this isn't it. That Book, of one author, compiled by forty writers, is the world's bestseller. It should be your first choice. Being that you make a lot of poor choices, however, this book is for you. And so, like Polycarp, I would ask: "Why do you delay?"

P.S. If you like a joyful sound as opposed to a skillful one, check out my YouTube site:

thecurmudgeon5087.

Printed in the USA
CPSIA information can be obtained
at www.ICGtesting.com
JSHW011102040224
56529JS00002B/3